Ourselves Alone?

S.J. Connolly
Photograph by Martyn Boyd, Photographer, Queen's University Belfast.

Ourselves Alone?

*Religion, society and politics
in eighteenth- and nineteenth-century Ireland*

ESSAYS PRESENTED TO
S.J. CONNOLLY

D.W. Hayton and Andrew R. Holmes

EDITORS

FOUR COURTS PRESS

Set in 10.5 pt on 12.5 pt Ehrhardt by
Carrigboy Typesetting Services, for
FOUR COURTS PRESS LTD
7 Malpas Street, Dublin 8, Ireland
www.fourcourtspress.ie
and in North America for
FOUR COURTS PRESS
c/o ISBS, 920 NE 58th Avenue, Suite 300, Portland, OR 97213.

© the various authors and Four Courts Press 2016

ISBN 978–1–84682–592–7

All rights reserved. No part of this publication may be
reproduced, stored in or introduced into a retrieval system,
or transmitted, in any form or by any means (electronic, mechanical,
photocopying, recording or otherwise), without the prior
written permission of both the copyright owner and
publisher of this book.

SPECIAL ACKNOWLEDGMENT

This publication has been made possible by financial assistance from
Queen's University Belfast, St Patrick's College, Dublin City University,
and the Marc Fitch Fund for research and publication (established by
Marcus Felix Brudenell Fitch, CBE, DLitt, HonFBA, FSA in 1956).

MARC FITCH FUND

Printed in England
by CPI Ltd, Chippenham, Wiltshire.

Contents

LIST OF ABBREVIATIONS	7
LIST OF CONTRIBUTORS	8
PREFACE	11

1 Introduction: Contesting Irish exceptionalism: Sean Connolly's Irish history   13
  D.W. Hayton and Andrew R. Holmes

2 An image war: representations of monarchy in early eighteenth-century Ireland   20
  D.W. Hayton

3 Swift's *Modest proposal* (1729): historical context and political purpose   42
  L.M. Cullen

4 Novel spectacle? The birth of the Whiteboys, 1761–2   61
  David Dickson

5 'Ravaging houses of ill fame': popular riot and public sanction in eighteenth-century Ireland   84
  James Kelly

6 Educating eighteenth-century Ulster   104
  T.C. Barnard

7 'So many wheels within wheels': the 1793 Catholic Relief Act revisited   126
  Thomas Bartlett

8 Mary Leadbeater: modern woman and Irish Quaker   137
  Mary O'Dowd

9 Migration, mission and identity: Presbyterian fundraising and the evangelization of the Irish Catholic diaspora, *c.*1840–70   154
  Andrew R. Holmes

10 Love, loss and learning in late Georgian Belfast: the case of
    Eliza McCracken   169
        Jonathan Jeffrey Wright

11 Ireland's clumsy transformation from confessional state to
    nation state   192
        David W. Miller

12 What's in an Irish surname? Connollys and others a century ago 206
        Cormac Ó Gráda

Bibliography of the publications of S.J. Connolly to 2014   219

INDEX   227

Abbreviations

BL	British Library
CJI	*The journals of the House of Commons of the kingdom of Ireland*
DIB	James McGuire and James Quinn (eds), *The dictionary of Irish biography* (9 vols, Cambridge, 2009)
ECI	*Eighteenth-Century Ireland*
EHR	*English Historical Review*
HJ	*Historical Journal*
HMC	Historical Manuscripts Commission
HO	Home Office
IESH	*Irish Economic and Social History*
IHS	*Irish Historical Studies*
LJI	*The journals of the [Irish] House of Lords*
NAI	National Archives of Ireland
NLI	National Library of Ireland
ODNB	*The Oxford dictionary of national biography* (online edition: http://www.oxforddnb.com)
PRONI	Public Record Office of Northern Ireland
RCB	Representative Church Body
RHS	Royal Historical Society
RIA	Royal Irish Academy
RO	Record Office
TCD	Trinity College Dublin
TNA	The National Archives [of the UK]

Contributors

T.C. BARNARD, FBA, MRIA (hon.), is Emeritus Fellow of Hertford College, Oxford. Among his books are *A new anatomy of Ireland* (New Haven & London, 2003), *Making the grand figure* (New Haven & London, 2004) and *Improving Ireland? Projectors, prophets and profiteers, 1641–1786* (Dublin, 2004). He is completing a study of the cultures of print in Ireland between the 1680s and 1780s.

THOMAS BARTLETT, MRIA, is Professor Emeritus of Irish History at the University of Aberdeen. A graduate of Queen's University Belfast, he was previously Professor of Modern Irish History at University College Dublin, and has held visiting professorships at the University of Michigan, Ann Arbor, the University of Washington, Seattle, and the University of Notre Dame. In 2001–2 he was Parnell Fellow in Irish Studies at Magdalene College, Cambridge. His many publications include *The fall and rise of the Irish nation: the Catholic question, 1690–1830* (Dublin, 1992), *Ireland: a history* (Cambridge, 2010), and (with Keith Jeffery) *A military history of Ireland* (Cambridge, 1996).

L.M. CULLEN, MRIA, is Emeritus Professor of Modern Irish History, Trinity College Dublin. His main research interest was in foreign trade, especially of England and France. His French researches led to studies of the brandy trade, *The brandy trade under the* ancien régime*: regional specialisation in the Charente* (Cambridge, 1998; French translation, Paris, 2002) and *The Irish brandy houses of eighteenth-century France* (Dublin, 2000; French translation, Paris, 2006). His main field of research since the mid-1990s has been in Japanese history. He was a Visiting Scholar in the International Research Center for Japanese Studies in 2002–3, and is the author of *A history of Japan, 1582–1941: internal and external worlds* (Cambridge, 2003). A particular point of interest has been the analysis of archival sources and of the problems they pose for the interpretation of Japanese history: papers on some of these themes have appeared in *Japan Review* (nos 18, 21, 22 and 25).

DAVID DICKSON, MRIA, is a Professor in Modern History in the School of Histories and Humanities in Trinity College Dublin, and has published widely on Irish social history. His work includes *New foundations: Ireland, 1660–1800* (2nd ed., Dublin, 2000), *Old world colony: Cork and South Munster, 1630–1830* (Cork, 2005); and *Dublin: the making of a capital city* (London, 2014).

D.W. HAYTON, MRIA, is Visiting Professor in the School of English and History, Ulster University. He previously worked at Queen's University Belfast, where he is Emeritus Professor. From 1997 to 2007 he was joint editor of *Irish*

Historical Studies; he is now joint editor of *Parliamentary History*. He has published widely on British and Irish politics in the period *c.*1680–*c.*1740, including two volumes of collected essays, *Ruling Ireland, 1685–1742: politics, politicians and parties* (Woodbridge, 2004), and *The Anglo-Irish experience, 1680–1730; religion, identity and patriotism* (Woodbridge, 2012).

ANDREW R. HOLMES is a Lecturer in Modern Irish History at Queen's University Belfast. He has published extensively on the history of Presbyterianism in Ulster, including *The shaping of Ulster Presbyterian belief and practice, 1770–1840* (Oxford, 2006) and (with Frank Ferguson) *Revising Robert Burns and Ulster: literature, religion and politics, c.1770–1920* (Dublin, 2009). He is currently preparing a monograph on Irish Presbyterianism between 1830 and 1930.

JAMES KELLY, MRIA, is Cregan Professor of History, and Head of the History Department at St Patrick's College, Dublin City University. His many publications include *Poynings' Law and the making of law in Ireland, 1660–1800* (Dublin, 2007); *The proceedings of the House of Lords, 1771–1800* (3 vols, Dublin, 2008); *Sir Richard Musgrave, 1746–1818: ultra-Protestant ideologue* (Dublin, 2009); *Sport in Ireland, 1600–1840* (Dublin, 2014) and (edited with Martyn J. Powell), *Clubs and societies in eighteenth-century Ireland* (Dublin, 2010).

DAVID W. MILLER is a Professor Emeritus of History at Carnegie Mellon University. He is the author of *Church, state and nation in Ireland, 1898–1921* (Dublin, 1974) and *Queen's rebels: Ulster loyalism in historical perspective* (Dublin, 1978) which has been reissued by University College Dublin Press in its 'Classics of Irish History' series. He has also published a number of essays on aspects of religion in social and political Irish history, primarily in the eighteenth and nineteenth centuries.

MARY O'DOWD, MRIA, is Professor of Gender History at Queen's University Belfast. Her recent research has focused on the history of gender and women in Ireland. She is the author of *A history of women in Ireland, 1500–1800* (Harlow, 2005) and (with Gerardine Meaney and Bernadette Whelan) *Reading the Irish woman* (Liverpool, 2013). She is currently writing a book on the history of marriage in Ireland, 1660–1925, with Professor Maria Luddy.

CORMAC Ó GRÁDA, MRIA, is Professor Emeritus of Economics at University College Dublin. His most cited works are on the Great Irish Famine of the late 1840s, on famines generally, and on many topics relating to the history of the Irish economy. He is the author of several monographs, including *Ireland: a new economic history* (Oxford, 1994); *Jewish Ireland in the age of Joyce* (Princeton, 2006), and *Famine: a short history* (Princeton, 2009). Over one hundred of his academic papers are available online. He was a recipient in 2011 of the Royal

Irish Academy's gold medal, and past co-editor for the *European Review of Economic History*.

JONATHAN JEFFREY WRIGHT is Lecturer in British History at Maynooth University. Having completed his PhD under the supervision of Sean Connolly in 2010, he went on to hold an IRCHSS-funded postdoctoral fellowship at Trinity College Dublin (2010–13). His first book, *The 'natural leaders' and their world: politics, culture and society in Belfast, c.1801–1832*, was published by Liverpool University Press in 2012, and he is currently working on a second, provisionally entitled *Career-building, unionism and empire in mid-Victorian Britain: James Emerson Tennent's British life*.

Preface

This volume was conceived as a tribute to Sean Connolly, who is scheduled to retire as Professor of Irish History at Queen's University Belfast in 2017. As editors we would like to thank Sean's wife, Mavis Bracegirdle, for assistance with many vital matters, not least in keeping the project a secret from her unsuspecting husband. She has endured this domestic strain with great fortitude. Publication was made possible by grants secured from the Marc Fitch Fund, Queen's University Belfast, and St Patrick's College, Dublin City University, and we are very grateful to Professor Roy Foster, Professor Peter Gray, Professor Crawford Gribben, Professor James Kelly, Professor Marian Lyons and Ms Frances Mercer for their assistance in this process. We are grateful to Martyn Boyd, photographer for Queen's University Belfast, for providing the portrait of Sean, and to Michelle Ashmore, Picture Library Executive at National Museums Northern Ireland, for arranging the supply of the cover image. Martin Fanning and the staff of Four Courts Press have done all that could be hoped for from a publisher. We must also acknowledge our appreciation of the way in which the contributors have borne with summary requests, short deadlines and arbitrary editorial impositions, and must record that many other friends, colleagues, former colleagues and research students of Sean's would have liked very much to contribute to the book but for reasons of space and coherence of subject-matter within the volume had to be disappointed.

D.W.H.
A.R.H.
Belfast, August 2015

Introduction
Contesting Irish exceptionalism: Sean Connolly's Irish history

D.W. HAYTON AND ANDREW R. HOLMES

Sean Connolly's family origins lie in rural Ireland. As demonstrated in Cormac Ó Gráda's entertaining and illuminating essay in this volume, the Connollys came from south Kilkenny, on the border with Co. Waterford; while Sean's maternal ancestors hailed from Co. Clare. He was himself brought up in Dublin, on the northside of the city, and, at least for public benefit, will still occasionally give vent to the archetypal Dubliner's metropolitan prejudices. But he has not followed the advice supposedly given by Brendan Behan's mother to her sons, to avoid only two places on their travels, 'the north, and the country', for he has spent most of his career in Northern Ireland, and given over much of his research and writing to understanding the history of social, religious and political life in the Irish countryside. After an undergraduate degree in history and politics at University College Dublin, he undertook research in Coleraine, at what was then the New University of Ulster, under the late Tony Hepburn, completing his DPhil in 1977 on 'Catholicism and social discipline in pre-famine Ireland'. A spell as an archivist at the Public Record Office in Dublin (now the National Archives) was followed by a lectureship at St Patrick's College, Drumcondra, before he moved back to Coleraine in 1981 to a lectureship in history. In 1996 he was appointed to the professorship of Irish history at Queen's University Belfast, a post which had originally been created for J.C. Beckett, and at the time of writing remains the last established chair to be held in the university.

Those who know Sean Connolly only by his published work will have the material to form an accurate picture of some aspects of his character: the powerful analytical intelligence, the broad range of learning derived from voracious reading across many different historical fields, the determined pursuit of historical truth combined with a relish for controversy and an acerbic, and on occasion slashing, wit. They may also infer – correctly – that in teaching and administration, the other two elements in the trinity of what is now the academic historian's 'workload model', he has been conscientious to a fault. Mastery of his subject, both in outline and in detail, has resulted in courses, lectures and classes that are invariably well organized and structured, and delivered with exemplary clarity. And to the various senior administrative posts that he has occupied, within his department and beyond, including a term of confinement in the joyless cell of head of department, he has brought the same high levels of concentration and responsibility. What they will not know, is that this most formidable and combative of historians is also, despite what sometimes seems a conscious effort to cultivate an image as a hanging judge, a compassionate and caring teacher and a supportive colleague who has been exceptionally generous with his time, especially to younger members of staff. The fierce interrogator of lazy seminar papers, whose opening gambit is often 'Surely, the fundamental flaw in your argument is ...', will also expend much more than the required time and effort in helping weak or disadvantaged students to improve their level of performance. As a tutor and research supervisor at Queen's, Sean has been unrivalled. In the two decades in which he has held the chair of Irish history he has published six books, and a sheaf of articles, essays and conference papers, but he has done all this while discharging a full complement of academic and professional duties, as a teacher and administrator, and outside the university as a journal and book-series editor, a councillor of the Royal Historical Society, and an active member of the Royal Irish Academy.

It was as an historian of religion that Sean gained his reputation as one of Ireland's finest historians. *Priests and people in pre-Famine Ireland* (1982), the monograph based on his doctoral thesis, was a ground-breaking study, and *Religion and society in nineteenth-century Ireland* (1985) an unsurpassed work of synthesis. What was important and distinctive about both these books was the obvious desire to see Irish history, not as something *sui generis*, but as a distinctive local example of broader European developments. From the first, Sean's work has been informed not only by a strong familiarity with archival materials, as might be expected from someone who began his working life as an archivist, but also with the conceptual formulations of historians working outside Ireland. Where his predecessors had often worked within well-worn paradigms, he sought to interpret Irish religious experience, both Catholic and Protestant, within much broader contexts. *Priests and people*, now properly thought of as a modern classic of Irish historical writing, explored the interaction between official and popular Catholicism and in doing so moved well beyond the confines of traditional ecclesiastical history by employing the insights of historians influenced by social anthropology, most notably Keith Thomas and Peter Burke. This was the history of religion not written from a confessional perspective, but seen as a social, economic and cultural phenomenon.

Sean's interest in an alternative history of Ireland not dominated by traditional political history was signalled by his early involvement in the Irish Economic and Social History Society. He compiled jointly a bibliography of publications on the topic for the first volume of the journal in 1974 and subsequently served with great distinction as a committee member and sometime editor of the journal. He was also involved in academic collaboration with historians of Scotland in an attempt to compare and contrast Irish and Scottish economic and social developments from the early-modern period.

Sean has recently returned to these themes and has shown a willingness to modify the functionalist understanding of religion he displayed in the 1980s in favour of a more open attitude to the potency of religious motivations.[1] He has also reiterated the argument that the emergence by the 1880s in Ireland of two political traditions, each expressing their identity through religion, was a contingent and complex process. Building upon the comparative work of the English historian Hugh McLeod, most notably his *Religion and the people of Western Europe* (1981), Sean argued that the exceptional levels of religious observance in Catholic Ireland before 1990 were not the product of faith and fatherland, but that Catholicism found itself able to articulate a sectional identity in a context when churches throughout Europe were no longer able to express a broader national identity. These themes are discussed below in the essays by David W. Miller, himself a distinguished scholar of nineteenth-century Catholicism with a similarly broad conceptual approach, and by Andrew R. Holmes. Miller tackles the relationship headlong by charting the clumsy transition from an Irish confessional to nation state while Holmes looks at how a transatlantic Presbyterian identity was expressed through a shared desire to convert the Irish Catholic diaspora in the mid-Victorian period.

As its title indicates, religious, or rather ecclesiastical, history played an important part in Sean's next major book, *Religion, law and power: the making of Protestant Ireland, 1660–1760* (1992). Here, however, he was painting on a broader canvas. He was tackling a period that was still relatively unfashionable: with a few exceptions most historians still skipped quickly over the century between the Cromwellian reconquest and the emergence of movements for political reform and Catholic emancipation in the 1760s, and the standard account was that provided by a departed generation of scholars, notable among them J.G. Simms, J.C. Beckett, J.L. McCracken and R.B. McDowell, whose work is enshrined in the seventeenth- and eighteenth-century sections of the *New history of Ireland*. The publication of detailed studies of particular topics was beginning to open up cracks in the ice, but there was no new overarching narrative which could replace the old story of self-serving Protestant conquest, English constitutional oppression, and the suppression of the Catholic religion, and indeed the 'Catholic community' as a whole, by an iniquitous penal code, stigmatized once and apparently forever by Edmund Burke as unique in the European *ancien régime*.

The most controversial elements in Sean's reappraisal of this forgotten century were his overtly revisionist reinterpretation of the 'penal laws', and his depiction of eighteenth-century society as relatively peaceful and well-ordered: neither a powder keg, nor a pressure-cooker. In both cases, the key to his approach was his rejection of the notion that Ireland was somehow isolated from

[1] Contrast, for instance, 'Religion and history', *IESH*, 10 (1983), 66–80, with 'The moving statue and the turtle dove: approaches to the history of Irish religion' in ibid., 31 (2004), 1–22.

historical developments elsewhere: that Ireland had followed what in Germany would be called a *Sonderweg*. Thus the penal laws were not an especially malign contrivance of the English/British government and the Irish Protestant parliament; they were of a piece with arrangements being made in confessional states across Europe, from France to Habsburg Hungary. Nor were they a 'code', a term which implies a systematically constructed and enforced set of regulations. Rather, they were a 'rag-bag' of legislative measures put together over more than two decades, by different individuals and different political institutions, across two kingdoms. They did not represent an agreed and explicitly articulated strategy designed to turn Catholics into second-class citizens in their own land. While endorsing the findings of previous scholars like Maureen Wall, who had shown the inevitable patchiness of law enforcement in a country without the resources to police its population effectively, Sean modified the interpretation that Catholic and nationalist historians had placed on this pattern of governmental and legal action.[2] Whereas they had concluded (again following Burke) that the Protestant political establishment was only interested in the political and economic impact of the laws, and not in winning souls to the reformed religion, Sean led the movement towards a revisionist history of the eighteenth-century Church of Ireland, analogous to the work of revisionist historians of the Church of England, who had been rescuing the eighteenth-century clergy from contemporary caricature and the condescension of posterity.[3] Far from being complacent and ineffectual, the churchmen who peopled his pages were serious-minded and diligent, attempting to carry out their duties to the best of their abilities. And allowing for the limited resources at their disposal, they provided a respectable standard of pastoral care.

Religion, law and power, and Sean's other contributions to the debate over the 'penal laws' also contested Burke's argument that the particular perniciousness of the Irish confessional state lay in the fact that it discriminated against the majority of the population rather than a dissenting minority. After all, he argued, an essential element of the political culture of the eighteenth century was the belief that political rights should be dependent on the possession of landed property. Since the Protestant ascendancy class, the creation of the Cromwellian conquest, controlled the vast majority of Irish land, it was only natural that they should also monopolize political processes. This was part of a broader reinterpretation of the nature of Irish society, and of the Irish polity in the so-called 'penal era'. The Irish nationalist conception of the Protestant propertied elite as a 'colonial' class akin to the planters of north America and the Caribbean, and Ireland itself as a colony, remained pervasive.[4] It had even found expression

---

2 Maureen Wall, 'The penal laws', repr. in *Catholic Ireland in the eighteenth century: collected essays of Maureen Wall*, ed. Gerard O'Brien (Dublin, 1989), pp 1–60.   3 See, for example, the essays in John Walsh, Colin Haydon and Stephen Taylor (eds), *The Church of England, c.1689–c.1833: from toleration to Tractarianism* (Cambridge, 1993).   4 Although not unchallenged:

in the chapters of the *New history of Ireland*, with their characterization of the 'patriotism' of Swift, Molyneux, Grattan and Flood as 'colonial nationalism'. There were certainly elements of the colonial in Ireland's constitutional relationship with Britain, but Irish society as configured in *Religion, law and power* appeared not as a colony like Virginia but as a constituent element in a European composite state which was in many ways entirely typical of the *ancien régime*.

In pressing this case Sean was influenced by the work of the English historian J.C.D. Clark, whose writing had emphasized the features of social and political life in eighteenth-century England that most resembled continental states: reverence for monarchy, deference to aristocracy, and the overpowering importance of religion in intellectual and political life.[5] In fact, Clark's formulation turned out to work much better for Ireland than for England. Although Sean has had relatively little to say on the influence of monarchy (a gap which the essay by Hayton begins to address), he has demonstrated among other things the deferential nature of Irish rural society, and the enduring importance of religion alongside economic pragmatism in Irish political thinking. He has also paid particular attention to the question of whether Ireland was, or was not, a fundamentally disordered society in this period. His research student Neal Garnham (who has unfortunately been unable to contribute to the present volume) tackled the subject of crime and punishment, exploiting the insights of English historians of crime as Sean had done himself in a suggestive essay.[6] In a series of articles Sean has also disinterred a rare example of agrarian protest in the century before the Whiteboy disturbances of the 1760s – the so-called 'houghers', who were responsible for an outbreak of attacks on livestock in the Irish midlands and in Connacht in 1711–13. Where anxious contemporaries detected in these frightening events the first stirrings of a Jacobite insurgency, Sean was able to show that houghing was in fact a non-sectarian protest against the expansion of large-scale grazing at the expense of the small tenant and cottier, and thus akin to the economic protests described by E.P. Thompson and others in England,[7] and by Charles Tilly and others farther afield.[8] The nature of popular protest, in the eighteenth century and beyond, has been an enduring

see D.G. Boyce, *Nationalism in Ireland* (London, 1982), pp 106–8.   **5** J.C.D. Clark, *English society, 1688–1832: ideology, social structure and political practice during the* ancien régime (Cambridge, 1985).   **6** Neal Garnham, *The courts, crime and the criminal law in Ireland, 1692–1760* (Dublin, 1996); S.J. Connolly, 'Albion's fatal twigs: justice and law in the eighteenth century' in Rosalind Mitchison and Peter Roebuck (eds), *Economy and society in Scotland and Ireland, 1500–1939* (Edinburgh, 1988), pp 117–25.   **7** E.P. Thompson, *Customs in common* (London, 1991); Charles Tilly, *Popular contention in Great Britain, 1758–1834* (London, 1995); Adrian Randall and Andrew Charlesworth, *Markets, market culture and popular protest in eighteenth-century Britain and Ireland* (Liverpool, 1996); John Bohstedt, *The politics of provisions: food riots, moral economy, and market transition in England, c.1550–1850* (Farnham, 2010).   **8** Charles Tilly, *From mobilization to revolution* (London, 1978). Cf. S.J. Connolly, 'Tupac Amaru and Captain Right: a comparative perspective on eighteenth-century Ireland'

interest of Sean's history-writing, and this collection includes two fine essays on the theme, by David Dickson (on the Whiteboys) and James Kelly (on brothel riots), which show the same attention to the detail of the evidence, and the same awareness of the broader historical literature.

Of course, the new insights and new interpretations included in *Religion, law and power*, which were developed and extended in the second of his two great synoptic histories of early modern Ireland, *Divided kingdom: Ireland, 1630–1800* (2008), did not satisfy everyone, and there have been anti-revisionist restatements of the traditional interpretation of the penal laws, and of the colonial nature of eighteenth-century Irish society. The notion of a repressed Catholic nationalism simmering away until the pressure could no longer be contained has found an expression in a renewed interest in Irish Jacobitism, and in the Gaelic poetry in which Jacobite sentiments were most frequently expressed.[9] Sean has tackled these issues with typical verve, and a willingness to engage in single combat if necessary in the pages of learned journals in order to defend his own position.[10] But even if his redrawing of the contours of the Irish eighteenth century has not met with unqualified endorsement it has played an important part in revitalizing the study of the period. It has also led him into new fields of interest: significant contributions to the history of political thought in Ireland (both as an author and a research supervisor), repeated ruminations on the Irish writings of Jonathan Swift, and on the general problem of how to approach a creative writer as a chronicler of his times, and a venture into gender history through a sensitive investigation of the relationship between the amateur artist Letitia Bushe and her intimate friend, Lady Anne Bligh. These themes are also picked up in the essays which follow, as Louis Cullen turns the eye of an economic historian on Swift's most famous Irish political pamphlet, the *Modest proposal* (1729), and Mary O'Dowd scrutinizes the life and correspondence of the Quaker Mary Leadbeater.

After his prolonged sojourn in the early modern period, Sean eventually returned to the nineteenth century and to the history of the city that has been his home since 1996. In various works, most notably the edited volume *Belfast 400: people, place and history* (2012), he has sought to modify the traditional portrait of the city by noting 'that there is a great deal more to the history of Belfast than a zero-sum contest for possession between mutually hostile groups defined exclusively by their religious and political allegiance'.[11] His own contributions to

in David Dickson and Cormac Ó Gráda (eds), *Refiguring Ireland: essays in honour of L.M. Cullen* (Dublin, 2003), pp 94–111. **9** Breandán Ó Buachalla, *Aisling ghéar: na Stíobhartaigh agus an t-aos léinn* (Dublin, 1996); Éamonn Ó Ciardha, *Ireland and the Jacobite cause, 1685–1766, a fatal attachment* (Dublin, 2002); Vincent Morley, *Irish opinion and the American revolution, 1760–1783* (Cambridge, 2002). **10** Vincent Morley, '"Tá an cruatan ar Sheoirse"– – folklore or politics?', *ECI*, 13 (1998), 112–20; S.J. Connolly, 'Jacobites, Whiteboys and republicans: varieties of disaffection in eighteenth-century Ireland', *ECI*, 18 (2003), 63–79. **11** S.J. Connolly (ed.), *Belfast 400: people, place and history* (Liverpool, 2012), p. 7.

the Belfast story owe much to approaches he first adopted in his work on nineteenth-century religion – a careful comparison with other industrial towns in the Victorian period, a readiness to challenge traditional interpretations, and a willingness to engage with disciplines outside history. Indeed, his research on Belfast grew out of a shared interest with the anthropologist Dominic Bryan, a colleague at Queen's, in the use of urban space in Belfast during the past 200 years. It is fitting that a former research student of Sean's, Jonathan Wright, should offer for this volume a thought-provoking essay on the experience of Eliza McCracken in late Georgian Belfast that exemplifies his supervisor's imperative to explore hitherto-ignored themes within a comparative context.

Although Sean Connolly's career as a full-time academic and teacher is nearing its end, there is no need to suppose that in retirement he will stop researching and writing about Irish history. Indeed, he is already talking of new projects, which will doubtless challenge accepted wisdoms and supposed authorities. This book is intended to mark a stage in his scholarly life, and also to pay homage to the relentlessly innovative contributions he has made to Irish history over three centuries, which have demanded of his fellow labourers that they broaden their horizons and place their findings in international rather than merely national perspectives. This is not to say that the general has always to be preferred to the particular, and indeed much of Sean's own work illustrates the overriding importance of a proper understanding of specific context, in relation both to time and place, but what it has also shown, perhaps more than anything else, is the importance to historians of raising their eyes beyond their own patch of territory to appreciate the wider significance of what they have discovered.

An image war: representations of monarchy in early eighteenth-century Ireland

D.W. HAYTON

In recent years historians have scrutinized the ways in which monarchy was represented in early modern England. In a highly acclaimed trilogy, the late Professor Kevin Sharpe traced the story across the sixteenth and seventeenth centuries, culminating in a final (posthumously published) volume in which he considered at great length (over 800 pages) the 'rebranding' of kingship (and queenship) after the politically traumatic events of the Interregnum and Glorious Revolution.[1] Although the heaviest and most comprehensive contribution to the genre, Sharpe's work can by no means be said to stand alone; indeed, the reverse is true, since the subject has attracted many scholars interested in discussing royal representation in various forms: literature, the visual arts, and the ritual and spectacle of the court.[2] Sharpe himself suggested that it was the emphasis on 'spin' in contemporary British politics, associated most obviously with the public-relations witch-doctors of 'New Labour', which sparked his own interest in representations of Tudor and Stuart monarchy. But

1 Kevin Sharpe, *Selling the Tudor monarchy: authority and image in sixteenth-century England* (New Haven & London, 2009); idem, *Image wars: promoting kings and commonwealths in England, 1603–1660* (New Haven & London, 2010); idem, *Rebranding rule: the Restoration and Revolution monarchy, 1660–1714* (New Haven & London, 2013). 2 Limitations of space prevent a comprehensive bibliography, but for the period covered by this essay, see R.O. Bucholz, '"Nothing but ceremony": Queen Anne and the limitations of royal ritual', *Journal of British Studies*, 30 (1991), 288–323; idem, *The Augustan court: Queen Anne and the decline of court culture* (Stanford, CA, 1993); idem, 'The "stomach of a queen", or size matters: gender, body image, and the historical reputation of Queen Anne' in idem and Carole Levin (eds), *Queens and power in medieval and early modern England* (Lincoln, NE, 2009), pp 242–72; Tony Claydon, *William III and the godly revolution* (Cambridge, 1996); Julie Farguson, 'Art, ceremony and the British monarchy, 1689–1714' (DPhil, Oxford Univ., 2013); Paul Hoftijzer and C.C. Barfoot (eds), *Fabrics and fabrications: the myth and making of William and Mary* (Amsterdam, 1990); R.P. Maccubbin and Martha Hamilton-Phillips, *The age of William III and Mary II: power, politics, and patronage, 1688–1702* (Williamsburg, VA, 1989); Esther Mijers and David Onnekink (eds), *Redefining William III: the impact of the king-stadholder in international context* (Aldershot, 2007); L.G. Schwoerer, 'Propaganda in the Revolution of 1688–9', *American Historical Review*, 82 (1977), 843–74; eadem, 'The Glorious Revolution as spectacle: a new perspective' in S.B. Baxter (ed.), *England's rise to greatness, 1660–1763* (Berkeley, CA, 1983), pp 109–50; eadem, 'Images of Queen Mary II, 1688–95', *Renaissance Quarterly*, 42 (1989), 717–48; Hannah Smith, *Georgian monarchy: politics and culture, 1714–1760* (Cambridge, 2006); Claudine van Hensbergen, 'Carving a legacy: public sculpture of Queen Anne, c.1704–1712', *Journal for Eighteenth-Century Studies*, 37 (2014), 229–44; J.A. Winn, *Queen Anne: patroness of arts* (New York, 2014); M.S. Zook, 'History's Mary: the propagation of Queen Mary II, 1689–1694' in L.O.A. Fradenburg (ed.), *Women and*

his work reflects broader fashions in historical writing: a 'cultural turn' to political history, encouraged by the work of continental historians, who have long understood that early modern European monarchs, whether 'absolute' or 'limited', were obliged to cultivate the image of kingship to reinforce the loyalty of their subjects;[3] and a general upsurge in 'court studies', which over the past two decades has proved to be a remarkable growth area in scholarship on early modern Europe.[4]

Historians of Tudor and early Stuart Ireland have kept up with the general trend in exploring the cultural dimensions of political history. But this interest has tended to stop at the Glorious Revolution. In particular, there is no equivalent of the substantial body of work by English historians on the representation of monarchy in the late seventeenth and eighteenth centuries, aside from a limited discussion of the 'propaganda' campaigns of 1688–91, in which the rival kings, James II and William III, were publicly portrayed,[5] and several articles on the way in which the great events of the seventeenth-century conflicts were commemorated.[6] Otherwise the subject has been approached tangentially. Studies have been published on the public architecture of eighteenth-century Ireland,[7] and there is now an emerging literature on court music.[8] But no historian has attempted a systematic analysis of the Dublin court and its culture, considering its political context, and the ways in which cultural capital was used to influence and mobilize opinion.[9] Partly this is because Ireland

---

sovereignty (Edinburgh, 1992), pp 170–91.   **3** For a general account of cultural politics in the eighteenth century, applying the theories of the German sociologist Jürgen Habermas concerning the development of a 'public sphere', see T.C.W. Blanning, *The culture of power and the power of culture: old regime Europe, 1660–1789* (Oxford, 2002).   **4** As witnessed by the success of the Society for Court Studies (est. 1995), for which see www.courtstudies.org, and its journal *The Court Historian*, which has so far published 19 volumes since its inception in 1996.   **5** See, for example, the present author's 'The propaganda war' in W.A. Maguire (ed.), *Kings in conflict: the revolutionary war in Ireland and its aftermath, 1689–1750* (Belfast, 1990), pp 106–21. There has been, of course, a much more sustained examination of references to the exiled Jacobite dynasty in Irish-language poetry during the eighteenth century (including contributions by Sean Connolly).   **6** T.C. Barnard, 'The uses of 23 October 1641 and Irish Protestant celebration', *EHR*, 106 (1991), 889–920; James Kelly, '"The glorious and immortal memory": commemoration and Protestant identity in Ireland, 1660–1800', *RIA Proc.*, 94 (1994), sect. C, 25–52; idem, 'Introduction : the emergence of political parading, 1660–1800' in T.G. Fraser (ed.), *The Irish parading tradition: following the drum* (Basingstoke, 2000), pp 9–26.   **7** Maurice Craig, *Dublin, 1660–1860* (3rd ed., Dublin, 1992); Edward McParland, *Public architecture in Ireland, 1680–1760* (New Haven & London, 2001); Robin Usher, *Protestant Dublin, 1660–1760: architecture and iconography* (Basingstoke, 2012).   **8** H.E. Samuel, 'John Sigismund Cousser in London and Dublin', *Music and Letters*, 61 (1980), 158–71; Brian Boydell, *A Dublin musical calendar, 1700–1760* (Dublin, 1988); Samantha Owens, 'Johann Sigismund Cousser, William III and the serenata in early eighteenth-century Dublin', *Eighteenth-Century Music*, 6 (2009), 7–39; Estelle Murphy, '"Liveridge is in Ireland": Richard Leveridge and the earliest surviving Dublin birthday odes' (forthcoming). I am very grateful to Dr Murphy for allowing me to see this important article in advance of publication.   **9** The brief, pioneering study of Toby Barnard, 'The viceregal court in later seventeenth-century

lacks the kind of core documentation concerning the court and its activities that survives in England, where researchers can luxuriate in the records of the lord steward's and lord chamberlain's departments, as well as the archives of the College of Arms. In Ireland, accident of survival has given us little more than a list of the viceregal household and a diary of dinners held at Dublin Castle, together with occasional glimpses of court life in letters and diaries.[10] However, the rich print culture of early eighteenth-century Dublin offers some compensation: poems, pamphlets, texts of court music and entertainments, and above all press reports (in both the Dublin and the London newspapers) provide enough evidence to enable a preliminary survey of the way in which monarchy was represented (or as Sharpe would have it) 'rebranded' in post-Revolution Ireland.

II

The most obvious difference between Ireland and the rest of eighteenth-century Europe (apart from the Habsburg Netherlands and Bourbon Sicily) was that it was ruled by a viceroy (usually holding the rank of lord lieutenant). After William III left the country in 1690 no monarch visited Ireland until George IV in 1821. Royal absence meant that there was no opportunity for direct engagement between sovereign and subjects: no interaction with the social elite at court or on visits to country houses, no public appearances at state functions or royal progresses through the country, as occurred in England.[11] This was not a new problem: ever since Henry II had taken on the lordship of Ireland royal visitors to Ireland had been few and far between. The Irish viceroyalty was a long-established institution. By the seventeenth century it had come to be accepted that the holder of the office would preside over a court in Dublin which was organized on the same lines as the court in England. In this respect it was no different to viceregal courts elsewhere in Europe or in Spanish America, which

Dublin' in Eveline Cruickshanks (ed.), *The Stuart courts* (Stroud, 2000), pp 256–65, has only been followed up in J.H. Murphy, '"Mock court": the lord lieutenancy of Ireland, 1767–1922', *Court Historian*, 9 (2004), 129–45; Rachel Wilson, 'The vicereines of Ireland and the transformation of the Dublin court, c.1703–1737' in ibid., 19 (2014), 3–28; and in a popular history by Joseph Robins, *Champagne and silver buckles: the viceregal court at Dublin Castle, 1700–1922* (Dublin, 2001). The essays covering the late seventeenth and early eighteenth centuries in Peter Gray and Olwen Purdue (eds), *The Irish lord lieutenancy: c.1541–1922* (Dublin, 2012), deal with political and administrative aspects of the viceroyalty. 10 List of the viceregal household, 1713 (RIA, MS 24.H.22); 'Bills of fare for his grace James, duke of Ormonde, 1711' (formerly BL, Loan 37/8: this collection was withdrawn by the depositor in 1994 and subsequently offered for sale at auction; its present whereabouts are unknown (*ex inf.* Mr William Frame of the British Library)). 11 For William III on progress, see Henri and Barbara van der Zee, *William and Mary* (London, 1973), pp 398–400; for Anne, Edward Gregg, *Queen Anne* (London, 1980), pp 176, 196–7; Winn, *Queen Anne*, pp 251–5, 402–5; for George I, Ragnhild Hatton, *George I: elector and king* (London, 1978), p. 346; and for George II, Smith, *Georgian monarchy*, p. 117; A.C. Thompson, *George II* (New Haven & London,

all served the same function: the maintenance of the monarch's authority by proxy. In the medieval and early modern periods ritual and gesture were of the first importance, so it was normal for the viceroy, in representing the monarch, to replicate as far as possible the representational nature of the royal original. In Dublin the viceroy was enthroned on formal occasions in the state rooms at the castle and in the House of Lords. He also carried a sword of state (fashioned in 1660) as a sign that he was invested with royal power. There was, it is true, a more limited ceremonial calendar in Dublin than in London: no monarch was crowned in Ireland after William III; there were no public investitures before the 1780s (as in Britain for the order of the Garter, the Thistle, and later the Bath), no distribution of the royal Maundy, no touching for the King's Evil (a practice that Anne revived but her successors, for obvious reasons, discontinued). But on other occasions, such as the opening and closing of parliaments, the commemoration of royal birthdays, the celebration of peace, and the state sermons at Christ Church cathedral on major public anniversaries, the viceroy would proceed with appropriate pomp. There was, however, one significant difference between the Irish viceroyalty and its continental counterparts. By 1702 viceroys were not present in Dublin throughout their tenure of office. The custom had evolved whereby a lord lieutenant came to Ireland for the prime purpose of holding a parliamentary session, and returned to England as soon as the session ended. The day-to-day business of government would then be entrusted to a commission of local lords justices, reporting to the viceroy. But although scaled down, the court remained in existence during the viceroy's absence: the lords justices presided when royal birthdays and 'state days' were celebrated, even if the ceremonial aspect of these events was less elaborate.

The standing establishment of Dublin Castle comprised a constable, two heralds, two serjeants, three pursuivants, a keeper of the council chamber and a separate housekeeper for the castle apartments, gatekeepers, a water-pumper, twelve state musicians, a kettledrum, and two trumpets.[12] When the viceroy was in residence, the complement might increase considerably, depending on the ability and willingness of an individual viceroy to spend in excess of the equipage money formally allowed: the duke of Shrewsbury in 1713 employed over a hundred in his household, including a steward, comptroller, gentlemen ushers, gentlemen of the bedchamber, secretaries, and chaplains, as well as the menials: messengers, footmen, cooks, servants, and ostlers.[13] Other viceroys with a taste for extravagance were the 2nd duke of Ormond (lord lieutenant 1703–7 and 1710–13), who inherited from his grandfather not only a belief that it was his duty to spend money to maintain the family's prestige, but also a pathological inability to live within his means;[14] and the 1st duke of Dorset (lord lieutenant

2011), pp 66–7.   12 *Hiberniæ notitia: or, A list of the present officers in church and state, and of all payments to be made for civil and military affairs for the kingdom of Ireland ...* (London, 1723), pp 47–8.   13 List of the viceregal household, 1713 (RIA, MS 24.H.22).   14 D.W.

1731–7, 1750–5), who came to Ireland after a long career at court (as groom of the stole and lord steward), from which he had acquired a taste for pageantry, further nourished by having exercised the ceremonial functions of lord warden of the Cinque Ports.[15] Besides personal preference, levels of expenditure and display were also affected by whether or not the viceroy was accompanied to Dublin by his wife (the vicereine). Ormond installed his duchess in the castle in 1703, where they co-hosted social events and briefly created a lively social scene for the *beau monde* of Dublin.[16] But she did not return with him in 1711, when the evidence of his dinner book suggests that evenings were spent with less formality and fewer guests.[17]

Lords lieutenant also differed in their approach to the job, which was essentially one of political management. Some – Pembroke in 1707, Shrewsbury in 1713, or Dorset in 1731–2 – tried to keep the viceroyalty out of the mire of party or factional politics, and to appeal to the loyalty, or at least the goodwill, of all men, much in the way that administrations in England appealed to parliamentarians' sense of duty to the king or queen.[18] This might well involve enhancing the formal aspect of the office: hence Shrewsbury's practice of regular public dining days, complete with musical accompaniment, and grander entertainments on state days; and Dorset's social whirlwind of banquets and balls, during which the state rooms in the castle were decorated with wall hangings, 'paintings and obelisks'.[19] Other viceroys, such as Lords Wharton (lord lieutenant 1708–10) and Carteret (1725–30), who were more experienced in the dark arts of political management at Westminster, and temperamentally better attuned to doing what was necessary, involved themselves directly in the business of persuading and cajoling parliamentary friends and foes. In consequence, the castle became a place for more informal entertaining: 'good words, burgundy and closeting', as Swift primly dismissed such base activities.[20] Entertainment there certainly was, but on a less elaborate scale, which perhaps explains why reconstruction work on the castle was in effect suspended in 1716, and the state rooms, though temporarily smartened up by Dorset in the early 1730s, were not properly refurbished until a decade later.[21]

Hayton, *The Anglo-Irish experience, 1680–1730: religion, identity and patriotism* (Woodbridge, 2012), pp 49–75.   **15** For Dorset, see *ODNB*; John Bridgman, *An historical and topographical sketch of Knole, in Kent: with a brief genealogy of the Sackville family* (London, 1817), pp 113–14; Victoria Sackville-West, *Knole and the Sackvilles* (New York, 1922), ch. 7, esp. pp 153, 159–60; earl of Ilchester (ed.), *Lord Hervey and his friends, 1726–38* (London, 1950), p. 76.   **16** Wilson, 'Vicereines', pp 8–9.   **17** 'Bills of fare for … duke of Ormonde, 1711' (formerly BL, Loan 37/8).   **18** D.W. Hayton, *Ruling Ireland, 1685–1742: politics, politicians and parties* (Woodbridge, 2004), pp 117–18, 255–6.   **19** McParland, *Public architecture*, pp 100–1; Wilson, 'Vicereines', pp 14, 23–7.   **20** 'A letter to the whole people of Ireland' (1724) in *The prose writings of Jonathan Swift*, ed. Herbert Davis et al. (16 vols, Oxford, 1939–74), x, 60. Note, however, Swift's verse 'Apology to the Lady C—r—t' (1725) in *The poems of Jonathan Swift*, ed. Harold Williams (3 vols, Oxford, 1978), ii, 374–80, which depicted the castle in Carteret's time as a forbidding place, thronged with 'powder'd courtiers', 'coxcombs' and 'strutting cornets'.   **21** McParland, *Public architecture*, pp 99–103.   **22** John Dunton, *The*

Every viceroy, however, gave full rein to the ceremonial aspect of the office on the so-called 'state days'. The London bookseller John Dunton published the following account in 1698, when the viceroyalty was in commission, held by two lords justices sent from England, Lords Galway and Jersey:[22]

> They have officers belonging to the household, such as steward and comptroller, who on state days carry white rods as the ensigns of their office: when they go to church, the streets, from the castle gate to the church door ... are lined with soldiers; they are preceded by the pursuivants of the council chamber, two maces ... [and] by the king and pursuivant at arms, their chaplains and gentlemen of the household, with pages and footmen bare-headed: when they alight from their coach ... the sword of state is delivered to some lord to carry before them; and in the like manner they return back to the castle, where the several courses at dinner are ushered in by kettledrums and trumpets ... in these cavalcades the coach in which they rise is attended by a small squadron of horse, after which follow a long train of coaches that belong to the several lords and gentlemen who attend them.

The central feature of these 'state days' was a sermon, marking an important anniversary for which provision was made in the liturgical calendar (the execution of Charles I, the restoration of Charles II, the outbreak of the rising of 1641, the discovery of the Gunpowder Plot), or a major event such as the coronation of a new monarch, a remarkable military triumph, the conclusion of a peace treaty, or a royal birthday.[23]

On such occasions, apart from the celebration of coronations or birthdays, the focus of attention would often be as much on the viceroy as on the monarch. This was even more obvious in relation to the ceremonies attached to the arrival and departure of the viceroy, and the opening and closing of the parliamentary session.[24] It was one of the inevitable consequences of the viceregal system that the person on the spot became a focus for loyal sentiment. Representing the monarch to his or her Irish subjects, the viceroy naturally absorbed in his person some of the loyal sentiment directed towards the sovereign, whether or not he intended to exploit his position to increase his personal prestige.[25] The 2nd duke of Ormond attracted an unusually intense devotion because of his Irish lineage. He behaved in Ireland in a quasi-monarchical fashion, especially when in

Dublin scuffle, ed. Andrew Carpenter (Dublin, 2000), pp 174–5. See also *A description of the city of Dublin in Ireland* ... (London, 1732), pp 10–13. 23 See, for example, *Dublin Intelligence*, 21–8 Oct. 1690. 24 *Dublin Intelligence*, 23–30 Dec. 1690, 16 Apr. 1709, 22 July 1710; Abel Boyer, *The history of the reign of Queen Anne, digested into annals* (11 vols, London, 1703–13), ii, 8; Ld Inchiquin to Sir Donough O'Brien, 5 July 1711 (NLI, Inchiquin papers, MS 45,303/3); *British Mercury*, 4 Nov. 1713; *A description of the city of Dublin*, pp 8–10. 25 As Thomas Wentworth was suspected of doing as Charles I's lord deputy in the 1630s:

residence at Kilkenny Castle, his principal seat.[26] During his first tenure of the lord lieutenancy, in 1703–4 and 1705, he conducted progresses through the country and received the same kind of reception that greeted Queen Anne when she travelled in England,[27] while in Dublin there were banquets and festivities on his birthday, 30 April, which rivalled the celebrations for the queen's birthday.[28] Ormond's return to the viceroyalty in 1711 was celebrated in Dublin by the publication of doggerel verse, with such titles as *Loyalty honour'd ...*, in which the royalist credentials of the duke's family were praised to the skies without a single mention of the queen herself.[29] And, amidst the cannon, fireworks and fanfares of the royal birthday celebrations on 6 February that year, a triumphal arch which featured the queen at the centre also positioned Ormond on her right hand.[30]

III

Specifically royal events, coronations and birthdays, did of course concentrate attention on the monarchy.[31] In King William's reign his and his wife's birthdays (until her death in 1694), and the anniversary of their accession, were marked in Dublin with processions, bells, cannon fire, banquets (complete with musical 'interludes'), balls and entertainments for nobility, gentry and civic dignitaries, and bonfires and illuminations for the city populace, including on one occasion 'a famous firework on St Stephen's Green'.[32] We know of a similar celebration near Tralee in 1700, where gentlemen and ladies were entertained by the county governor, Lord Kerry, to dinner and a ball.[33] Queen Anne's birthday on 6 February was marked in Dublin with the same degree of public spectacle,

---

Dougal Shaw, 'Thomas Wentworth and monarchical ritual in early modern Ireland', *HJ*, 49 (2006), 331–55. **26** Barnard, 'Viceregal court', pp 258–9; Hayton, *Anglo-Irish experience*, pp 51–2; *Post Man*, 18–20 Nov. 1697; Dunton, *Dublin scuffle*, 184. **27** Account of Ormond's progress from Waterford to Lismore, July 1703 (NLI, Ormond papers, MS 993, pp 264–5); Maurice Lenihan, *Limerick; its history and antiquities* ... (Cork, 1866), pp 309, 315; Boyer, *Annals*, ii, 78–80; Edward Southwell to Sir William Robinson, 11 Apr. 1705 (HMC, *Ormonde MSS*, n.s., viii, 149); Sir Richard Cox to Ormond, 21 Apr. 1705 (ibid., 150); Kilkenny corporation minute book 1690–1717, p. 209 (Kilkenny corporation archives; NLI, microfilm P. 5136). **28** BL, Southwell papers, Eg. MS 917, ff 234–8, 244–7. See also Bp John Hartstonge to Ormond, 1 May [1707] (NLI, Ormond papers, MS 2472, p. 130), reporting a festive occasion the previous day in Ormond's 'own city' of Kilkenny, for 'the mayor and all his fraternity' and 'most of the town ladies'. **29** 'F. McD.', *Loyalty honour'd, or a welcome to his illustrious grace James, duke of Ormonde, lord leutenant general and general governour of the kingdom of Ireland* (Dublin, 1711). See also Joseph Trapp, *The church and monarchy secur'd, by the return of his grace the duke of Ormonde, and the change of the late ministry* (Dublin, [1711]); *The Inchiquin manuscripts*, ed. John Ainsworth (Irish MSS Comm., Dublin, 1961), p. 74. **30** *Post Boy*, 20–2 Feb. 1711. **31** This emphasis on the royal birthday followed the practice in England: Sharpe, *Rebranding rule*, pp 623–4. **32** *Dublin Intelligence*, 10–17 Feb. 1690/1, 29 Apr.–1 May 1693; *Flying Post*, 14–16 Nov. 1699. **33** *Flying Post*, 19–21 Nov. 1700.

followed by a banquet and ball (almost always held in the castle state rooms) for favoured guests, and occasionally some other form of entertainment such as a play.[34] In 1704 the duke of Ormond was attended 'in great state' to Christ Church cathedral, where he and a large company of 'the nobility and gentry' were subjected to a sermon by Bishop Smyth of Down and Connor.[35] By 1707 the evening's proceedings had come to feature the formal performance in the castle of a complimentary musical ode in the English court tradition, which after 1708 was transformed into the staging of more elaborate and theatrical 'serenatas', on the Italian model, set to music composed by the chapel master at Trinity College, Johann Sigismund Kusser (Cousser).[36] The ordinary citizens of Dublin were regaled with bells, fireworks, bonfires and illuminations, and 'other diversions'.[37] A detailed account survives in one newspaper of the highly elaborate firework and water display in the capital in 1711: three sets of fireworks – sky rockets, slant rockets, squibs and water squibs – wheels and water wheels, a fountain, and a triumphal arch, all accompanied by 'flourishes' of trumpets and kettledrums, and the firing of the 'great gun' on Aston Quay, and ending with 'eighteen squib-boxes to be thrown among the mob'.[38] After the Hanoverian succession, the same observances were made for George I's birthday, 28 May, though in the absence of the chief governors (the viceroyalty was once again in commission, with two English lords justices) the first anniversary celebrations in 1715 were held in the Tholsel, presided over by the archbishop of Dublin as one of the local lords justices (who deputized for their English superiors), with the benefit of the usual fireworks, and claret made freely available to the attending crowds.[39] The following year (perhaps in response to the failed Jacobite rising in Britain) the government outdid itself, and the corporation also weighed in with its own celebration.[40]

---

34 Ld Rochester to Thomas Keightley, 21 Jan. 1702/3 (*Inchiquin manuscripts*, ed. Ainsworth, p. 72); *London Gazette*, 20–3 Feb. 1703; Edward Southwell to ——, 7 Feb. 1704/5 (TNA, SP 63/365, f. 55); *Dublin Gazette*, 6–9 Feb. 1714.   35 *London Gazette*, 14–17 Feb. 1704; Boyer, *Annals*, ii, 232.   36 *An ode on the queen's birthday, for the year 1706/7* ... (Dublin, 1706); *A serenata to be represented on the birth-day of the most serene Anne ... at the Theatre Royal, the sixth day of February 1709* (Dublin, 1709); *The universal applause of Mount Parnassus, a serenata da camera, to be represented on the birthday of the most serene Anne ... at the Castle of Dublin, the sixth day of February, 1711* (Dublin, 1711); *A serenata theatrale, to be represented on the birthday of the most serene Anne ... at the Castle of Dublin, the sixth day of February, 1712* (Dublin, 1712); *A serenata, to be represented on the birthday of the most serene Anne ... at the Castle of Dublin, the sixth day of February, 1714* (Dublin, 1714). For Kusser, see *DIB*, ii, 920–1; T.J. Walsh, *Opera in Dublin 1705–1797: the social scene* (Dublin, 1973), pp 24–32; H.E. Samuel, 'John Sigismund Cousser', pp 162–3; Owens, 'Cousser, William III and the serenata', pp 7–39.   37 *London Gazette*, 16–18 Feb. 1710; *Evening Post*, 19–21 Feb. 1712; *Dublin Gazette*, 6–9 Feb. 1714; *British Mercury*, 10–17 Feb. 1714. In 1714 the fireworks took place on the Custom House Quay, and in boats or barges on the river.   38 *Post Boy*, 20–2 Feb. 1711. 39 *British Weekly Mercury*, 4–11 June 1715.   40 *Daily Courant*, 6 June 1716. See also *Post Man*, 5–7 June 1718; *London Gazette*, 2–6 June 1719, 4–6 June 1726; *Daily Post*, 8 June 1724, 12 June 1725, 6 June 1727.

Besides the simple entertainment value of these events, they offered an opportunity to present a particular image of monarchy. The triumphal arch set up for the celebration of the queen's birthday in 1711 portrayed Anne as a defender of the Protestant interest, both at home and abroad. She was featured

> with a grand trophy erected over and about her; justice and prudence on each side of her; the glorious sun (in imitation) over her head, and two angels supporting the motto *Fidei defensor* ... the Battle of Saragossa and siege of Aix, with Hercules and Mars on the right, and Pallas and Plenty on the left.[41]

Here were motifs that were widely used in English visual and literary depictions of the queen, associating her directly with the military triumphs of her reign, and through the success of her armies against Louis XIV, with a defence of the reformed religion against the machinations of continental Catholicism. She was frequently portrayed as Pallas Athene, the goddess of wisdom, civilization, and justice, and the companion and patroness of heroic warriors.[42] The same themes were taken up in the odes and serenatas composed for the castle festivities: the ode performed in 1707, for example, rejoiced at the subjection of the armies of the *grand monarque*: 'The haughty Gaul's aspiring fate,/ Submitting to her high command.'[43] The libretti for Kusser's serenatas, four of which survive in printed form, credited Anne with the successes of her field armies against the French, and the achievements of her navy in building a maritime empire. The image of Pallas reappeared, and repeated reference was made to the 'laurels' the queen had won.[44] In this respect her achievements were compared directly with those of Elizabeth I, another persistent theme of English royal propaganda.[45]

These staged demonstrations of loyalty were extremely important to the monarchy in Ireland. For whereas in England, kings and queens (and their advisers) could make use of many different instruments in order to promulgate an image of kingship (or queenship), opportunities in Ireland were more limited. The fact that the viceroy undertook the ceremonial duties which otherwise would have been the province of the monarchy was one important factor. But it was also the case that the visual representations of monarchy, which formed such an important part of the process by which monarchs cultivated what we would now call their 'public image' in England, were less abundant across the Irish Sea. Royal portraits generally arrived in Ireland either as painted copies or engraved prints of English originals. Here too, there was a significant difference between representations of William and Anne. While the image of the victor of the Boyne

---

41 *Post Boy*, 20–2 Feb. 1711.   42 Winn, *Queen Anne*, pp 290, 309.   43 *Ode on the queen's birthday ... 1706/7*.   44 *Serenata* (1709), pp 4, 6: *Universal applause of Mount Parnassus*, pp 5–7; *Serenata theatrale*, p. 10; *Serenata* (1714), pp 3–4.   45 *Universal applause of Mount Parnassus*, p. 6; *Serenata* (1714), p. 5; Sharpe, *Rebranding rule*, pp 547, 575, 609–10, 634; Winn,

took on an iconic character in Ireland, and portraits were to be found in institutions and private houses,[46] depictions of his successor seem to have been few and far between: only two portraits of Anne are known for certain to have hung in public buildings, and there is no surviving evidence that her portrait was held in any private collection (though some must have done).[47] There was a similar pattern in relation to sculpture, though overall even fewer examples: an equestrian statue by Grinling Gibbons was erected to William III in College Green, Dublin, in 1701, another to George I, by John van Nost the elder, on Essex Bridge in the city in 1717, both at the initiative and expense of the city corporation. Quite unlike the situation in England, where Queen Anne was frequently depicted in public sculpture, Ireland possessed no public statue of her.[48] As for the commemorative medals struck for successive sovereigns, they too had been commissioned and struck in Holland or in England, and while some of William's early medals related to his military exploits in the Irish war, their message was primarily intended for his Dutch and English subjects.[49] Finally, the only money coined in Ireland between the Revolution and the controversial patent given to William Wood in 1723, were copper halfpence and farthings produced between 1690 and 1695, which made a minimal impact.[50]

Literary representations of the monarchy were far more common. Although for the most part unsolicited they did reflect the 'official' image conveyed by royal propagandists working more obviously at the monarch's behest. At William's death, Protestant Ireland produced an outpouring of grief that included verse elegies[51] and two printed sermons.[52] Each author proclaimed William's heroic virtues and martial achievements, as a latter-day Joshua in

Queen Anne, pp 282, 310. **46** After the accession of William and Mary the Irish painter Thomas Pooley painted portraits of the two monarchs for Dublin corporation (Toby Barnard, *Making the grand figure: lives and possessions in Ireland, 1641–1770* (New Haven & London, 2004), p. 157). For examples of portraits hanging in private houses, see ibid., pp 160, 170, 177, 182; Elizabeth Mayes (ed.), *Castletown: decorative arts* (Trim, 2011), pp 153–5.   **47** A portrait painted some time after her death still hangs in the Great Hall of the Royal Hospital at Kilmainham; another, by George Bodeley, could be found until 1841 in the hall of the guild of cutlers, painters-stainers and stationers (Guild of St Luke) in Dublin (Anne Crookshank and the Knight of Glin, *Ireland's painters, 1600–1940* (New Haven & London, 2002), p. 11. A third was commissioned in 1713 by Galway corporation but there is no evidence that it was completed (see below, p. 38). For a rare example of pictorial commemoration of Queen Anne in a private residence, her image on a gilt leather hanging at Stackallan House, Co. Meath, see Barnard, *Making the grand figure*, p. 182.   **48** Van Hensbergen, 'Carving a legacy'. **49** Sharpe, *Rebranding rule*, pp 434–43, 606–13; Edward Hawkins, *Medallic illustrations of the history of Great Britain and Ireland to the death of George II*, ed. A.W. Franks and H.A. Grueber (2 vols, London, 1885), ii, 634–723.   **50** John Lindsay, *A view of the coinage of Ireland* (Cork, 1839), p. 60.   **51** *Upon the glorious memory of King William the III, who dy'd the 8th of March, 1701/2* (Dublin, 1702); *Upon the happy and glorious reign and memory of King William the III* (Dublin, 1702); Richard Daniel, *A dream; or, An elegiack poem, Occasion'd by the death of William III, King of Great Britain, France and Ireland* (Dublin, 1702).   **52** James Kirkpatrick, *A sermon occasion'd by the king's death, and her present majesty's accession to the crown* [Dublin, 1702]; Walter Neale, *A sermon preached in St Mary Shandon-church, Cork* ...

defence of religion and liberty, emphasising his particular importance to the survival of Irish Protestants: 'our loss', intoned one clergyman, 'is as unexpressible as it is unparalleled', while to another author he was 'our great deliverer, general, king and friend'.[53] Anne's devotion to the established church attracted praise from High Church clergy, who praised her piety.[54] Others followed the lead of royal propagandists and attributed to her the military successes of her reign, one likening her to Queen 'Eliza', a second portraying her as a warlike dispenser of justice, a latter-day Deborah, and a third as Astraea, the personification of justice, which were all comparisons favoured at her court.[55] This was not simply a matter of imitating English rhetoric, however, for the Irish administration had pointed in this direction by declaring special days of thanksgiving for the successes of the queen's armies and navy: in 1702, 1704 and 1706, when sermons were preached at Christ Church, and in October 1708, when the lords justices led a public celebration for the taking of Lille.[56]

IV

It is easy to see how crown and government benefited from presenting successive monarchs as wise and effective rulers, dispensers of justice, and above all as defenders of Protestantism and liberty. Such propaganda was especially important for both William III and George I, as foreigners taking the British and Irish thrones in defiance of the law of hereditary succession. Of course, William enjoyed a particular advantage in Ireland because of his instrumental role in the defeat of the Jacobite regime, which in the minds of the Protestant population raised him to near-iconic status, and George I could also have expected to receive

---

March the 29th, 1702 ... (Dublin, 1702). **53** Neale, *A sermon preached... March the 29th, 1702*, p. 3; *Upon the glorious memory of King William the III* .... **54** Edward Smyth, *A sermon preached before their excellencies the lords justices at Christ-Church, Dublin, on the 3d of December, 1702* (Dublin 1703) p. 20; idem, *A sermon preached before the lord mayor, and magistracy of Dublin, in St Andrew's church, Dublin, October the 18th 1707* (Dublin, 1708), p. 16; John Echlin, *The royal martyr. A sermon preach'd before their excellencies the lords justices of Ireland, in Christ-Church, Dublin, on the XXXth of January, 1712/13* (Dublin, 1713), pp 21–2; Jonathan Wilson, *A sermon preach'd at Christ-Church, Dublin, before their excellencies the lords justices of Ireland, on Friday May the 29th, 1713, being the anniversary of the happy restoration* (Dublin, 1713), p. 20. **55** Edward Smyth, *A sermon preached ... on the 3d of December, 1702*, p. 20; William King, *A sermon preach'd before their excellencies, the lords justices of Ireland, at the cathedral of ... Christ-Church, on the 7th of September, 1704* (London, 1704), pp 20–1; Francis Higgins, *A sermon preach'd before their excellencies the lord justices, at Christ-Church, Dublin; on Tuesday the 28th of August* (Dublin 1706), p. 14; Edward Synge, *Thankfulness to Almighty God for his more ancient and later mercies and deliverances vouchsafed to the British and Protestants, within the kingdom of Ireland... in a sermon before the Honourable House of Commons, October the 23d, 1711* (Dublin, 1712), p. 19; *Serenata* (1714), p. 6. On Anne as Deborah and Astraea, see Sharpe, *Rebranding rule*, pp 547, 554, 561–2, 564, 566, 584, 634, 665; Winn, *Queen Anne*, pp 312–16, 348, 367. **56** *Dublin Intelligence*, 13 Oct. 1708.

the unequivocal loyalty of his Irish Protestant subjects, for whom a Jacobite restoration was unthinkable. But the propagation of the image of Queen Anne in Ireland was a complicated matter. This was not because of anything the queen herself had done, or failed to do. Indeed, at first glance there appear sound reasons why she ought to have inherited her brother-in-law's mantle. After all, it was in her reign that the decisive victories were won in Britain's long-drawn-out war with Louis XIV, and a vital step taken towards securing the Protestant Reformation and the Revolution settlement through the accomplishment of the Act of Union between England and Scotland (even if, for many Irishmen, this seemed a mixed blessing). It was also in Anne's Irish parliaments that the most severe penal laws were enacted against the Catholic population, the popery acts of 1704 and 1709 being regarded as vitally important in ensuring that the Catholic landed interest in Ireland could not reconstruct itself after the defeat of 1691.

Promotion of the queen's image in Ireland had, however, to contend with two main problems, beyond the fact that she was an absentee (which, after all, did not affect George I's popularity) and that, unlike her male contemporaries (and her predecessor in particular), she was not a battlefield commander.[57] The first difficulty was the very vigorous after-life enjoyed by William III in the Irish public imagination. The practice of toasting his 'glorious and immortal memory' became so popular that in 1713 the bishop of Cork, Peter Browne, was driven to publish a sermon to the clergy of his diocese in which he denounced the practice as theologically wrong-headed to the point of sacrilege.[58] The cult of King William was to wane a little in the 1720s in the face of the energetic promotion of the Hanoverian dynasty, but it revived and by the 1740s had become the cornerstone of that vulgar Whig ideology to which all Protestant Irishmen subscribed.[59] In Anne's reign it was still fresh, and very powerful. The Gibbons statue on College Green was a focus of annual celebrations of William's birthday on 4 November. This was originally an event organized by Dublin Corporation, but quickly metamorphosed into a state occasion: a cavalcade of crown officials and municipal dignitaries, headed by the lord lieutenant or lords justices, would issue from Dublin Castle, proceed along streets lined with soldiers to St Stephen's Green, and thence to the statue, which it would circle three times before departing amidst a volley of gunfire.[60] Evidently the day was also marked by some kind of evening celebration at the Castle. A serenata written for the occasion by Johann Kusser survives, though the date is unknown: it cannot have

---

[57] For the way in which George I's propagandists emphasized his military prowess, in order to associate him directly with William III, see Smith, *Georgian monarchy*, pp 24–5. [58] Lenihan, *Limerick*, p. 311; Peter Browne, *Of drinking in remembrance of the dead ...* (London, 1713). [59] Kelly, '"Glorious and immortal memory"', pp 35–8; Usher, *Protestant Dublin*, p. 107. [60] Kelly, '"Glorious and immortal memory"', pp 30–2; idem, 'Emergence of political parading' , p. 13. As Kelly aptly put it ('"Glorious and immortal memory"', p. 32), the statue became a 'shrine' to the dead king.

been earlier than 1707, when Kusser arrived in Dublin.[61] The proximity of William's birthday to the anniversaries of both the 1641 rebellion and the Gunpowder Plot (coincidentally the same day-date on which William had landed at Torbay in 1688), which were both the long-established occasion of state sermons,[62] extended and consolidated its importance in the Irish public calendar.

The second 'image problem' for the queen in Ireland was the politicization of the monarchy. Early in her reign there emerged a form of party conflict on the English model, with parliament, the constituencies, borough corporations, and indeed Protestant society at large divided by the clash of Whigs and Tories. Given the nature of the ideological division between the parties, it was natural for the Tories to idealize the queen, in effect claiming her as their own. Tories in parliament identified with the established church and gloried in Anne's devotion to its interests.[63] Among the clergy, High Church preachers never tired of expressing their gratitude to 'our most gracious and excellent queen', for her maternal care for the Church of Ireland, while loyal addresses from convocation and from bodies of diocesan clergy focused on her benefactions to 'that most excellent church to which you are such an eminent patron as well as so bright an ornament'.[64] Tories were also less comfortable than Whigs with the idea of resistance to the lawfully constituted monarch, even though Jacobitism went too obviously against their vested interests, and were able to express a fastidious distaste for 'Revolution principles' by glorying in Anne's heredity as the direct descendant not only of James II but of his martyred father. Tory enthusiasm for the queen was evident from the very beginning of her reign, when the author of an elegy on William III went out of his way to praise the new queen and her devotion to the established church, describing her as a new 'Eliza'.[65] Other Tories quickly followed suit. Some of the more enthusiastic, in an attempt to use their praise of the queen as a means of denigrating political opponents, highlighted Anne's hereditary right, ostensibly against purveyors of republican and regicidal principles, but also as a sideswipe at the Whig interpretation of the events leading up to William's accession.[66] At the same time, aware of the dangers of being portrayed as sympathetic to the Pretender and to the Irish Catholic interest, they took pains to glorify the queen as a determined enemy of popery.[67]

It was not easy for Whigs to respond directly to the appropriation of the monarchy for partisan ends. Certainly they could not openly criticize Anne for

---

61 Owens, 'Cousser, William III and the serenata', p. 26, suggests that it might have been performed privately.   62 Kelly, '"Glorious and immortal memory"', p. 30.   63 See, for example, *CJI*, iii, 827–98, 893; *LJI*, ii, 322–3, 367, 424.   64 'Address of the bishop and clergy of Cloyne to the queen, 1711' ed. Edmund Curtis in *Cork Hist. and Arch. Soc. Jnl*, 46 (1941), 140. See also [Henry Joy,] *Historical collections relative to the town of Belfast* (Belfast, 1817), p. 86.   65 *The loyalist: a funeral poem in memory of William III, late king of Great Britain* ... (Dublin, 1702).   66 *LJI*, ii, 322–3, 367, 424; [Joy,] *Hist. collections*, pp 87–8; *CJI*, iv, 46–50. 67 Edward Smyth, *A sermon preach'd in Christ-Church, Dublin, on Saturday the 23d of October,*

fear of appearing disloyal. This did not of course prevent accusations that they were merely pretending to 'love the queen' while refusing to obey her wishes, nor did it deter Tory extremists from concocting fantasies of regicidal conspiracy.[68] During the queen's lifetime Whigs routinely praised her, in a very conventional way, though they often made a point of depicting her as a bastion of the Protestant establishment against the designs of a popish Pretender.[69] This was the theme of the birthday celebration orchestrated during the Whig Lord Wharton's viceroyalty in 1709, an event for which Kusser wrote yet another of his serenatas, focusing on the battlefield triumphs of the queen's reign.[70] It was also a comparatively low-key affair, the banquet being hosted in the Tholsel by Dublin Corporation,[71] and the serenata being performed in a Dublin theatre, which could indicate a strategy of playing down the celebration, though it is not clear how much we should read into the organization of these events, for the birthday fell on a Sunday, the lord lieutenant was not yet in residence and, probably most important, the queen had already forbidden birthday celebrations at court in England because she was still in mourning for her husband, Prince George of Denmark.[72] A theatre may also have been considered a more suitable venue than the castle state rooms for a work requiring stage settings and devices.[73]

Nevertheless, there were other, more subtle and indirect ways in which Whigs could counter what was becoming an element of Tory political campaigning. The most obvious, and most successful, was to promote continued public reverence for King William's memory. This enabled them to focus on the weak point in the Tories' armour, the indiscretions of high-flyers, creating suspicions that the party harboured Jacobite sympathies. In identifying themselves with King William's memory they could also capitalize on his immense popularity. Thus in January 1709, the Low Church clergyman, William Stoughton, a controversial choice to deliver the state sermon on the anniversary of the regicide, went out of his way to use the occasion to praise King William.[74] The serenata performed shortly afterwards, during the celebration of the queen's birthday, also slipped in a reference to 'mighty William', who had arisen in 1689 to stir Britannia to great deeds.[75] Then in the spring of 1710, when a handful of Trinity undergraduates, intoxicated with partisan zeal, damaged the king's statue in a crude political stunt, Whigs in the Irish House of Lords requested the lord lieutenant to issue a proclamation to discover the culprits, in order 'to show the grateful sense this whole kingdom ... have of the great blessings accomplished for that

1703 (Dublin, 1703), p. 22.   68 *The honest citizen's wish* (Dublin, [?1710]); *CJI*, iii, 882–7. 69 William Stoughton, *A sermon preach'd before the state in Christ-Church, on ... the 31st of January, 1708/9* ([Dublin], 1709), esp. pp 16, 24, 34–6. See also Alan Brodrick to St John Brodrick, 17 Feb. 1704/5 (Surrey History Centre, Brodrick papers, 1248/2/169–70). 70 *Serenata* (1709).   71 *Post Boy*, 19–22 Feb. 1709.   72 Owens, 'Cousser, William III and the serenata', p. 27.   73 Murphy, '"Liveridge is in Ireland"'.   74 Stoughton, *A sermon preach'd ... on ... the 31st of January, 1708/9*, pp 18–19.   75 *Serenata* (1709), p. 4.

glorious prince'. The proclamation was followed by an address from the Commons praising 'King William of glorious memory' in even more fulsome terms, and shortly afterwards by the apprehension of the miscreants, who were fined, imprisoned and expelled from the college.[76] But above all, it was public spectacle that renewed William's memory: the celebration of his birthday on 4 November (which, together with the anniversary of the Gunpowder Plot on the 5th, provided two consecutive state days on which Protestants could recall their deliverance) and the anniversary of the battle of the Boyne in July. The latter was a civic rather than a governmental occasion, and therefore under the control of the Whig-dominated court of aldermen in the Dublin Corporation. Although it offered less pomp than the Castle could provide, and was unmarked by a commemorative sermon, it served the same purpose.[77] By this time it seems also to have become common practice for both 4 November and 12 July to be celebrated by 'feasts' in provincial towns attended by the local Whig nobility and gentry.[78]

How were Tories to respond? They were as awkwardly placed in this respect as Whigs faced by celebrations of Anne's queenship. They could scarcely denigrate William's memory, and the repudiation of 'Revolution principles' proved much more difficult in Ireland than in England. Certainly there were some effusions of loyalty on the part of Irish Tories which appeared to take an exalted view of monarchy: the loyal address from the Irish House of Lords in 1711, for example, pledged to make the crown

> descended to your Majesty from your royal ancestors, to flourish upon your sacred head and ... to preserve your prerogative, and those powers with which God has entrusted your Majesty, from being lessened, or invaded, upon any factious pretences whatsoever.[79]

And after the failure of the short-lived parliament of November–December 1713 the party embarked on a campaign of county addresses to the queen, which spoke of her 'sacred person', to her role as 'God's vicegerent', and to the sanctity of the royal prerogative.[80] But only the pathologically indiscreet would have been prepared to question the necessity of the Glorious Revolution, the Tory position being nicely summarized by an MP in 1711 who declared that he and his friends 'believed all there approved of the last [Revolution] and were thankful for it, but that they hoped there would be no more'.[81]

---

[76] Boyer, *Annals*, ix, 221–6; *CJI*, iii, 784, 786.   [77] J.G. Simms, 'Remembering 1690', *Studies*, 43 (1974), 233–6; Kelly, '"Glorious and immortal memory"', pp 31–2.   [78] *The conduct of the purse of Ireland* ... (London, 1714), pp 19–20.   [79] *LJI*, ii, 366.   [80] Hayton, *Ruling Ireland*, p. 175; idem, 'Tories and Whigs in County Cork, 1714', *Cork Hist. and Arch. Soc. Jnl*, 80 (1975), 84–8; Abel Boyer, *Quadriennium Annae postremum; or the political state of Great Britain* ... (2nd ed., 8 vols, London, 1719), vii, 91–2; *CJI*, iv, 46–50.   [81] Newsletter, 10 Nov. 1711 (TNA, SP 63/367, f. 264).

Obviously, one strategy was to emphasize the virtues of the queen and the successes of her reign, and to make the celebration of her birthday, and associated events such as the anniversaries of her accession and coronation, occasions of particular rejoicing.[82] Hence the extraordinary elaboration of the fireworks and entertainments organized by Ormond's administration for the queen's birthday in 1711, after the duke's return to Dublin as part of the ministerial revolution in England the previous year.[83] A second strategy was to downplay William III's anniversaries. Little could be done about the Boyne commemoration, because of its civic nature, but Ormond seems to have attempted to trump the ceremonies on William's birthday in November 1711 by spending more than usual the very next day, when the thanksgiving for the discovery of the Gunpowder Plot was, unusually, accompanied by a day of festivities, beginning in the morning with a ringing of bells, then a state sermon in which the viceroy was attended by the entire House of Lords, the firing of guns at noon, and in the evening a banquet at the castle and the usual round of bonfires, illuminations and other popular entertainments.[84]

V

The activities of the Tory government after 1710 raised the political temperature in Ireland to unprecedented heights and accelerated the growing identification of the queen and her predecessor with rival political parties. Whig concern over the safety of the succession was intensified by the presence of a Jacobite sympathizer at the head of the Irish administration, the English lawyer Sir Constantine Phipps, as lord chancellor and a lord justice for two years in Ormond's absence from the autumn 1711. Phipps' domineering approach to government provoked bitter opposition. By November 1712 he had brought the government of the city of Dublin to a standstill by leading the privy council in an attempt to force a Tory lord mayor on a Whig court of aldermen, part of a more general campaign to exploit the council's powers over municipal corporations in a way that recalled the remodelling of boroughs by Lord Tyrconnell. He had also intervened to halt a prosecution of the news-writer Edward Lloyd for publishing an avowedly Jacobite pamphlet.[85] Unsurprisingly, Whigs chose the annual celebration of William's birthday to mount a public challenge to what they perceived (or professed to perceive) to be a Jacobite

---

82 The queen's accession day and coronation day were marked by ringing of bells, firing of guns and popular illuminations (Kelly, '"Glorious and immortal memory"', p. 31), but the programme was more limited than for her birthday, possibly because of the intimate connexion between these events and the death of William III.   83 Including the erection of a triumphal arch (see above, p. 28), of which there were very few recorded examples in England in Anne's reign (a point I owe to Dr Julie Farguson).   84 *Dublin Intelligence*, [6 Nov.] 1711; 'Bills of fare for ... duke of Ormonde, 1711' (formerly BL, Loan 37/8).   85 Hayton,

tendency in the Castle. Perhaps fearing that the occasion would be exploited for political purposes, the lords justices, Phipps and Archbishop Vesey of Tuam, did nothing themselves to mark the day, but in defiance of this studied neglect 'a number of gentlemen' organized a banquet at the Tholsel, the location reflecting the role of the corporation in spearheading opposition to the Tory administration.[86] As one leading member of the party reported, 225 gentlemen 'din'd ... to remember our glorious deliverer K[ing] William', where they agreed to sponsor an evening performance of Nicholas Rowe's *Tamerlane*, a play which, in the respective characters of Tamerlane and Bazajet, idealized William III and vilified Louis XIV. In addition, they 'bespoke' a reading of the prologue written by Sir Samuel Garth for the first performance in the winter of 1701/2, which had expressly drawn out the analogy with contemporary politics and had urged 'Britons' to unite to fight against a Bourbon succession to the Spanish crown, a clarion-call that resonated a decade later as the Tory ministry in London was going about the business of making peace.[87] Phipps could not be seen to intervene against the play itself, but acted quickly to forbid the reading of the prologue, which had already been banned twice before. His argument showed the extent to which the commemoration had become a political statement, and could be used, at least in Tory eyes, to slight William's successor: 'we all have a regard for his [William III] memory, but 'tis not fit to pay our respects to him by affronting the queen'.[88] Then on the evening of the performance a young Whig squire, Dudley Moore (brother of an Irish MP), jumped on to the stage to defy the ban, succeeded in provoking a riot, and was arrested with several of his friends.[89]

The extent to which the two monarchs, William and Anne, were now being used as partisan symbols was underlined by an incident during the ensuing trial, when Moore attempted to make a political statement by the simple expedient of citing 'the glorious memory' of the late king, only to be cut off by the Tory chief justice with the comment that 'we had all great respect for it'.[90] The controversy over the peace had set up two contrasting images of monarchy: William, the resolute opponent of French absolutism and international popish conspiracy; Anne, the bringer of peace to Europe after a decade of conflict. During the early stages of the War of the Spanish Succession, the queen's reputation had ridden the swell produced by Marlborough's continental victories, with which, as we have seen, she was closely identified: a modern Deborah or Pallas Athene triumphing over the French king.[91] But after 1710, when the Tory ministry of

---

Ruling Ireland, pp 163–5.   86 *Dublin Intelligence*, 8, 18 Nov. 1712.   87 St John Brodrick to Thomas Brodrick, 6 Nov. 1712 (Surrey Hist. Centre, 1248/3/93–4).   88 *CJI*, ii, 991.   89 H.M. Burke, *Riotous performances: the struggle for hegemony in the Irish theater, 1712–1784* (Notre Dame, IN, 2003), ch. 1.   90 Sir Richard Cox's legal notebook, 28 Nov. 1712 (NLI, MS 4245), p. 37.   91 See, in an Irish context, Francis Higgins, *A sermon preach'd ... on the 28th of August*, pp 14–16; Edmund Arwaker, *A sermon preach'd at St Ann's-church in*

Robert Harley, earl of Oxford, began negotiations with the French, the emphasis changed: having achieved the principal objectives of the war, Anne was now depicted as responding to the sufferings of her subjects. Opponents of the peace policy were stigmatized as warmongers and war-profiteers. So, in a passage gratuitously inserted into a state sermon in 1713 on the feast of Charles the Martyr, an Irish High Church parson declared that 'the present war [has] been ... kept on foot ... to impoverish the public, and to raise a moneyed interest in the hands of a few private subjects, which should insult and give laws to the crown'.[92] The conclusion of the peace treaties was marked by addresses from Tory-dominated boroughs, some of which also organized public celebrations, in what appears to have been a concerted effort by Tories to express support for the peace and credit the queen for it.[93] The resources of government were put behind a day of thanksgiving, the highlight of which was a service at Christ Church, in the presence of the lords justices, complete with a *te deum* composed by Kusser and a sermon from a reliable Tory, Swift's friend Patrick Delany, who exalted peace and peacemakers above war and warriors, and declared the Treaty of Utrecht to be 'a peace that demonstrates our prince to be not only the arbiter but the protector also of all the powers in Europe: to whose wisdom they with almost one consent commend their interests, and submit their claims'.[94] The evening was concluded with a theatrical concert, attended by Phipps.[95] There was also the usual public spectacle, though evidently not all participated: the sister of one Whig MP wrote to her brother from Dublin of the rowdiness of the city mob: 'because we did not put out illuminations they broke all our windows'.[96]

By the following autumn a new lord lieutenant had been appointed, the duke of Shrewsbury, with a remit to call a new parliament and effect a consensus between the two parties in order to secure a grant of supply. Unfortunately for Shrewsbury, the general election that took place before his arrival exacerbated the political divisions within Protestant society. It was contested in an atmosphere of near hysteria, Whigs alleging that the Tory ministers in Dublin were intent on bringing back the Pretender, and arousing atavistic fears of Protestants being murdered in their beds, while Tories accused Whigs of attempting to force their views on the queen and her duly elected ministers and

---

Dungannon, on the 31st of December, 1706 (Dublin, 1707), pp 22, 24.   92 John Echlin, *The royal martyr: a sermon preach'd before their excellencies the lords justices of Ireland, in Christ-Church, Dublin, on the XXXth of January, 1712/13* (2nd ed., Dublin, 1713), p. 21.   93 For examples, *Council book of the corporation of Drogheda, vol. I, from ... 1649 to 1734*, ed. T. Gogarty (Drogheda, 1915), p. 318; Lenihan, *Limerick*, pp 315–16; *The council book of the corporation of the city of Cork ...*, ed. Richard Caulfield (Guildford, 1876), p. 366.   94 Samuel, 'Johann Sigismund Cousser', p. 163; Patrick Delany, *A sermon preach'd at Christ-Church, Dublin, before their excellencies the lords justices of Ireland; on Tuesday June the 16th, 1713, being the day of thanksgiving for the peace ...* (Dublin, 1713), p. 11.   95 *Dublin Gazette*, 16–20 June 1713.   96 Mary Dean to Henry Boyle, 23 June [1713] (PRONI, Shannon papers,

of threatening a return to the republican and regicidal days of the 1640s. Nor was there any mood for compromise when the parliament met: it was rapidly dissolved when the Whig majority in the Commons pursued a series of inquiries into the conduct of Lord Chancellor Phipps, which seemed likely to culminate in an impeachment.[97]

At this zenith of party antagonism, the politicization of the monarchy was almost complete. Before the election the Tory majority in Galway corporation made a political statement by ordering that a portrait of Queen Anne should be painted and hung in the town court-house,[98] while Tories in Dublin explicitly picked up a recurrent motif of royal representation in adopting laurel as their party emblem.[99] There was again no government-sponsored commemoration of King William's birthday, though evidently 5 November was still celebrated as a state day; instead, with the lords justices refusing to take part, the high sheriff of Co. Dublin took over the birthday commemoration and led a procession along the customary route.[100]

In the aftermath of the abrupt prorogation of the parliament came the celebration of the queen's birthday in February 1714. After the customary procession and church service, Shrewsbury provided fireworks for the crowds, and an entertainment at the Castle followed by a visit to the playhouse. But the viceroy's event was mainly attended by 'the ladies', and the planned ball had to be postponed. In a metaphor for the lord lieutenant's political isolation, the Tories held a separate evening event at the Royal Hospital in Kilmainham while the Whigs, presumably in order to refute any imputations of disloyalty, held their own banquet at the Tholsel, hosted by the lord mayor.[101] Tories reportedly organized a public demonstration on the day, distributing

> a printed paper in these words: Notice is hereby given to the lovers of our most gracious queen, and present constitution, that they are to meet on College Green at ten of the clock ... each with his laurel in his hat (being her Majesty's birthday) and from thence to march through the city, in order to celebrate the same.[102]

D/2707/A/12/21). **97** Hayton, *Ruling Ireland*, pp 170–6. **98** Galway corporation minute book E, p. 197 (National University of Ireland, Galway, Hardiman Library). For the political background, see James Kelly, 'The politics of "Protestant ascendancy": County Galway, 1650–1832' in Gerard Moran (ed.), *Galway: history and society* (Dublin, 1996), pp 239–43. **99** *The world in uproar, or the hue and cry after the laurels* [Dublin, *c.*1713]; *Come and see, come and see. Or, An account of a cruel monster newly come to town, spew'd up by a Scotch cod near Belfast in the North of Ireland ...* ([?Dublin], 1714), p. 3. **100** Sir Richard Cox to Edward Southwell, 7 Nov. 1713 (BL, Southwell papers, Add. MS 38157, f. 21); Kelly. 'Emergence of political parading', pp 13–14. **101** *British Mercury*, 10–17 Feb. 1714; *London Gazette*, 13–16 Feb. 1714; Sir Richard Cox to Edward Southwell, 6 Feb. 1713[/14] (BL, Add. MS 38157, f. 65); BL, Eg. MS 937, f. 238; Alan to Thomas Brodrick, [Jan. 1714], 9 Feb. 1713[/14] (Surrey Hist. Centre, 1248/3/155–6, 163). **102** Alan to Thomas Brodrick, 9 Feb. 1713[/14] (Surrey Hist.

Outside Dublin, we also know of a celebration at Dunleer in Co. Louth, organized by the Tory sheriff and attended by clergy and 'loyal gentlemen', which 'concluded with bonfires, illuminations, etc.'[103] The rhetoric of these Tory celebrations made implicit comparisons to William. The libretto to the serenata performed at the castle in 1714, which was, if anything, the most extravagantly phrased of all such performances, made reference to her riding in triumph with 'bloodless laurels', the attainment of peace clearly superseding victories in battle, with their massive human cost, while the healths drunk by the Tories at the Royal Hospital included the wish 'that her majesty's reign may be longer, as it has been more glorious, than any of her predecessors'.[104]

VI

The queen was, however, destined to reign for only five months more. At her death Whigs generally showed a degree of restraint in their reactions that was at odds with recent Tory assertions that they had been wishing Anne dead before her time.[105] Admittedly, presbyterians in Ulster, who had suffered increasing persecution under the Tory ministry of 1711–14, culminating in July 1714 in the extension to Ireland of the Schism Act passed at Westminster to suppress Dissenting academies, could not contain their relief.[106] In Carrickfergus (Co. Antrim), it was said that 'some of the Whigs flew to the parish church, and began ringing on its bell a merry peal',[107] while in Belfast George I was proclaimed 'with excessive rejoicings by four hundred inhabitants on horseback'.[108] Although there were a few other reports of unseemly celebrations, as in Cork, where the Whig faction was openly 'joyful, and insolent, drinking "confusion to the clergy"', or in Dublin, where members of the corporation were 'cock a hoop, and cannot contain their joy',[109] these were isolated instances. Nonetheless, while Tories were 'very melancholy upon the death of our good queen', there can be little doubt that few Whigs deeply mourned her passing.[110] One Tory went into

Centre, 1248/3/163). **103** *Post Boy*, 23–5 Feb. 1714. **104** *Serenata* (1714), p. 5; *Post Boy*, 23–5 Feb. 1714. **105** John Winder, *The mischief of schism and faction to church and state. In a sermon preach'd at St Mary's church, Dublin, May the 30th, 1714* (Dublin, 1714), p. 3. **106** J.S. Reid, *History of the Presbyterian Church in Ireland* ... (new ed., 3 vols, Belfast, 1867), iii, 46–56; W.D. Killen, *History of the congregations of the Presbyterian Church in Ireland* ... (Belfast, 1886), p. 167; p. 76; Abp Thomas Lindsay to Arthur Charlett, 8 July 1714 (Bodleian Lib., MS Ballard 8, f. 109); *Pue's Occurrences*, 24–7 July 1714. **107** Samuel McSkimin, *The history and antiquities of the county and town of Carrickfergus*, ed. E.J. M'Crum (2nd ed., Belfast, 1909), p. 77. See also Reid, *Hist. Presbyterian Church*, iii, 59; Sir Richard Cox to Edward Southwell, 19 Feb. 1713/14 (BL, Add. 38157, f. 69). **108** George Benn, *A history of the town of Belfast* ... (London, 1877), p. 572. **109** Cox to Southwell, 17 Aug., 10 Sept. 1714 (BL, Add. MS 38157, ff 110, 119). **110** William Perceval to Arthur Charlett, 10 Aug. 1714 (Bodleian Lib., MS Ballard, 36, f.85). See also *The copy of a letter from a certain gentleman of the High-Church* ... [?Dublin], 1714), a gleeful satire on Tory despair at the Hanoverian succession.

print to denounce Whigs as 'merry mourners' paying no more than lip service to her memory; another, supposedly a septuagenarian gentleman from the King's County (modern Co. Offaly), made the same point in verse: 'in Ireland the men that ate her bread/ Rejoic'd to hear her Majesty was dead'.[111] Certainly, while the occasional message of condolence was prepared in localities where Tory interests were strong,[112] addresses of loyalty to the new king from his first Irish parliament in 1715, a parliament now dominated by the Whigs, were deafeningly silent about the dead queen, in painful contrast to the addresses twelve years earlier welcoming her accession, whose starting point was desolation at the loss of the deliverer of Protestant Ireland.[113] The Commons in particular made no bones about referring to 'those wicked ministers, who by their arbitrary and illegal proceedings, had brought the Protestant interest and our liberties into the greatest danger'.[114] And the healths drunk at a banquet in the Tholsel on King George I's birthday in 1715 toasted 'The glorious memory of King William' but made no mention of the deceased queen other than to praise 'all those gentlemen who were honest in the worst of times'.[115]

The phrase 'the worst of times' quickly became a short-hand method of referring to the period of the Tory administration in England and Ireland, 1710–14, and in Ireland the queen's name became so closely associated with what in retrospect appeared (or was made to appear) a time of trial for the Protestant establishment, that her posthumous reputation was permanently stained. After 1714 she faded rapidly from Irish public consciousness. In the years after the Hanoverian succession some still spoke of 'our late good, gracious and merciful sovereign lady Queen Anne' in order to make a political point,[116] but a decade later only a few kept alive the memory of her reign, most notably perhaps Jonathan Swift, though in his case from nostalgia for her reign, and his part in it, rather than any affection for the woman he had dismissed as the 'royal prude'.[117] There was no institutional trace of the queen in Ireland to last beyond personal memory,[118] and as the generation of Tories and High Churchmen who

---

111 *Britannia's tears: a satyrical dirge by way of a lamentation on the deplorable death of her late gracious majesty Queen Anne, of blessed memory* ... (Dublin, 1714); *The Irish lamentation on the death of Queen Anne* ... ([Dublin], 1714).   112 For example, *Drogheda council bk*, p. 323.   113 *LJI*, ii, 8, 463; *CJI*, iv, 20–1. Note also that the Belfast Presbyterian minister James Kirkpatrick, in *God's dominion over kings and other magistrates: A thanksgiving sermon preach'd in Belfast October 20. 1714, being the happy day of the coronation of his most excellent Majesty King George* (Belfast, 1714), made no reference to the late queen.   114 *CJI*, iv, 20–1. See also ibid., 166.   115 *A list of healths drank at the Tholsel, on the 28th of May 1715* ... (Dublin, 1715). Positive references to Queen Anne in pamphlets or sermons were rare: for one example see Richard Davies, *Loyalty to King George. In a sermon preach'd on the three and twentieth day of October, 1715* (Dublin, 1715), p. 21.   116 *Pue's Occurrences*, 3–7 Feb. 1718/19. See also an anonymous report of a sermon given by the bishop of Waterford in 1716 in which, after paying lip-service to King William's memory, he was 'very copious in Queen Anne's encomium' (— to —, 11 June 1716 (TNA, SP 63/374/295)). I owe this reference to Dr John Bergin.   117 Swift, *Poems*, ed. Williams, i, 193. See also ibid., ii, 567–8; *Prose writings*, ed. Davis, ix, 31; x, 102; xii, 226–7, 266, 273, 286.   118 With the possible exception of the Dublin parish

had been at the forefront of politics in her reign passed away, so too did traces of her historical presence.

Queen Anne's posthumous 'image problem' arose from the fact that her queenship had come to be politicized in Ireland, to be associated with one political party, and from the point of view of posterity the wrong party. She was seen as having been a queen for the Tories, but this had never been her own intention, or the intention of her advisers. In Ireland, however, the monarchy remained sufficiently distant that its prestige could be deployed by viceroys and others for political purposes. Anne's identification with the established church made it natural that she should be lionized by 'the church party'. Nor could she compare with her predecessor, who had not only made himself visible to his Irish subjects but had personally played a key role in the defence of Protestantism and the Protestant interest. Through no fault of her own, Queen Anne became embroiled in an 'image war' in Ireland, but it was a war fought by others using her as an emblem, and against the imperishable memory of a dead hero-king, in which her partisans were never likely to emerge victorious.[119]

---

of St Anne (created by act of the Irish parliament in 1707 (6 Anne, c.21)). [119] I am grateful to Dr Julie Farguson for reading an earlier version of this essay, and for suggesting many improvements. She is not, of course, responsible for any errors of fact or deficiencies in interpretation that remain.

Swift's *Modest proposal* (1729): historical context and political purpose

L.M. CULLEN

Study of the *Modest proposal* of 1729 has been largely confined to Swiftian literary criticism, often devoid of historical sense and self-fulfilling in its analysis of Swift. The pamphlet, of course, poses a challenge, because of its massive literary significance, having been described as 'perhaps the best-known and most often cited satire in the English language'.[1] This has sometimes led to its political context being ignored. The widespread parsing of its exercise in irony adds to the complexity. It can also be viewed as a response to events at the time, or as evidence of a late stage in Swift's state of mind on Irish issues, or, finally, as raising the question of the literary sources which may have provided a model for his writing. The last question is not an easy one to answer as Swift read widely: even the minor question of his brief reference to Japan in *Gulliver's travels* has to be seen in the context of his wide reading of the literature on travel and exploration.[2] Could the *Modest proposal* have been inspired by literary models; for instance, from the literature on cannibalism?[3] It has even been argued that it arose out of a sense of an emerging national debt 'devouring' the nation.[4] However, the metaphorical use of devouring was not in itself necessarily novel or literary: in mid-sixteenth-century England, it was suggested that the spread of pastoral farming had destroyed men's livelihoods and depopulated the countryside, so that, as Thomas More put it, sheep, 'which are naturally mild, and easily kept in order, may now be said to devour men'.[5]

---

[1] *Swift's Irish writings: selected prose and poetry*, ed. Carole Fabricant and Robert Mahony (Basingstoke, 2010), p. 123. [2] L.M. Cullen, 'Gulliver in Japan', *ECI*, 28 (2013), 170–6. [3] On purely literary antecedents for the cannibalism in the *Modest proposal*, see D.F. Passmann, '"Many diverting books of history and travel" and *A modest proposal*', *ECI*, 2 (1987), 167–76. Passmann considered that Swift's proposal to sell babies for consumption was novel. However Ian Campbell Ross has argued persuasively that Swift had a clear-cut model from a descriptive account in the writings of the South-American *mestizo*, Garcilaso de la Vega, probably through a late seventeenth-century translation into English made in Dublin by Paul Rycaut, while serving in 1686–7 as chief secretary (Ian Campbell Ross, '"A very knowing American": the Inca Garcilaso de la Vega and Swift's *A modest proposal*', *Modern Language Quarterly*, 68 (2007), 493–516). This would remain the case, even if, as de la Vega observed, the planned infanticide attributed to Indians was in order to provide a delicacy, whereas Swift's own account proposed infanticide as a source of staple foodstuff (and income) in response to crisis. [4] Sean Moore, 'Devouring posterity: *A modest proposal*, empire, and Ireland's "debt of the nation"', *Proceedings of the Modern Language Association of America*, 122 (2007), 679–95. [5] In *Utopia*, book 1.

Swift's ingenious use of his rich literary sources can at times distract from the underlying purpose of his texts. His wide reading in history and in the story of exploration, his love of parody and irony, and his ease in imaginative formulating of contexts, resulted in texts that lend themselves to several interpretations. The *Modest proposal*, if Ian Campbell Ross' persuasive suggestion of a ready-made model is accepted, is a striking instance of these characteristics. There is a danger of not enough weight being given to Swift's imaginative playfulness, and of meanings being too easily read into his words. Joseph McMinn's observation of 'a dedicated and energetic clergyman who wrote either for pleasure or out of a sense of public duty' should always be borne in mind.[6] In modern writing on *A modest proposal*, there has been little analysis in concrete terms of the political context of Swift's Irish writing in the 1720s, where relevant to his purpose.[7] In the interface between literary criticism and history, there are two problems. The first arises from taking Swift's statements literally (in writing of economic matters his words are often imprecise and sweeping, which explains why he is rarely quoted in economic history); the second arises when interpretation of his texts or underlying arguments, admittedly often a challenging task, is pushed to the outer frontier of realism.

Literary or historical aspects aside, it is also important in reading Swift's imaginative content not to infer his state of mind from his texts. Universally, *A modest proposal* has been seen as a product of despair. For Oliver Ferguson, 'In *A modest proposal*, ten years of warning and exhortation gave way to frustration and despair, as Swift directed the full weight of his wrath not against England, or callous economists, or visionary projectors, but against Ireland herself.'[8] For Carole Fabricant, the pamphlet

> is governed by a central metaphor that for Swift conveyed a definite political and economic – specifically anti-colonial – statement, one that assumed the existence of close ties between Ireland's self-destructive tendencies and England's brutal oppression. As Swift saw it England's lawless seizure of Ireland's earthly produce ... generated a fundamentally anarchic and predatory world founded upon a grotesque chain of devouring.[9]

Swift's most recent biographer, Leo Damrosch, is content to follow this literature: 'Swift's pamphlet is of course a protest against English exploitation of Ireland ... But fundamentally it is a rebuke aimed at the Irish themselves, for complicity in their own exploitation.'[10] He concludes that '*A modest proposal* is a cry of despair'. For Sean Moore, seeking to put the pamphlet in the context of

---

6 *DIB*, ix, 199–200.   7 An exception, reviewing a wide range of aspects of Swift, is Aileen Douglas, Patrick Kelly and Ian Campbell Ross (eds), *Locating Swift: essays from Dublin on the 250th anniversary of the death of Jonathan Swift* (Dublin, 1998).   8 O.W. Ferguson, *Jonathan Swift and Ireland* (Urbana, IL, 1962), p. 175.   9 Carole Fabricant, *Swift's landscape* (Baltimore, MD, 1982), p. 79.   10 Leo Damrosch, *Jonathan Swift: his life and his world* (New

indebtedness, '*A modest proposal* may have evinced consciousness about overpopulation, but it unconsciously reveals a concern with national debt and that debt's relation to financial and rhetorical bubbles.'[11]

Despair is too easily written into Swift's thinking. At first sight, it seems on one occasion to have been expressed in his own words, when in the *Short view of the state of Ireland* (1728) he follows an ironic paragraph, in which he has imagined Ireland's condition as prosperous, by stating that 'my heart is too heavy to continue this irony longer'.[12] Yet this was simply to change key from parody or irony into a description of what he sees as the actual condition of the country. Then, after announcing 'the general desolation in most parts of the kingdom', he makes the totally inaccurate statement that 'the old seats of the nobility and gentry [*are*] all in ruins, and no new ones in their stead'.[13] His despair is to be taken no more seriously than this extravagant statement itself.

A huge literature on Swift, pursued within a learned and somewhat ingrown milieu, develops its arguments in a rich vein of literary and textual criticism. Even in the case of Sean Moore, making a wider argument in the context of fiscal history and national debt, the interpretations are still cast within the straitjacket of Swiftian literary criticism.[14] Moore's work, however, is also flawed by a poor grasp of the Irish economy and its problems.[15] Swift has also often faced the charge that he was in no sense speaking for many; that he was in effect a disgruntled Irishman seeking advancement in England, and hence that his writing did not reflect a deep concern about Ireland or its people. In this regard he is represented in much the same light as Edmund Burke, whose views on Ireland are often seen not as coming from Irish concerns but as those of a man making himself at home in England, and writing even on Ireland in essence as a fair-minded Englishman. In reaction to suggestions that Swift in the Wood's Halfpence pamphlets was addressing only a small circle, Carole Fabricant has made a convincing case that he was articulating the interests of 'a broad spectrum of Irish society'.[16] Though *A modest proposal* has loomed large in all writing on Swift, Irvin Ehrenpreis long stood alone among Swiftian scholars for providing a detailed economic and political context. He saw it as a 'sardonic pamphlet' in which Swift's serious recommendations appear in a paragraph printed in italics.[17] This sober appraisal has been largely ignored in writing in favour of more fanciful interpretations, which draw on an interest in Swift's complex character and on the meaning of his writing at large. Thus James Ward

---

Haven & London, 2013), p. 420. **11** Moore, 'Devouring posterity', p. 687. **12** *The prose writings of Jonathan Swift*, ed. Herbert Davis et al. (16 vols, Oxford, 1939–74), xii, 10. **13** Ibid. **14** Moore, 'Devouring posterity'; idem, *Swift, the book and the Irish financial revolution: satire and sovereignty in colonial Ireland* (Baltimore, MD, 2010). **15** See review by L.M. Cullen in *Business History Rev.*, 85 (2011), pp 831–3. **16** Carole Fabricant, 'Speaking for the Irish nation: the Drapier, the bishop, and the problems of colonial representation', *English Literary History*, 66 (1999), 337–72. See also eadem, 'Swift's political legacy' in Douglas et al. (eds), *Locating Swift*, pp 180–2. **17** Irvin Ehrenpreis, *Swift: the man, his works,*

has found in the tract 'a general satirical dismissal of any serious attempt to alleviate the crisis then affecting the kingdom', finding in it 'an intricate, surreptitious and deeply unpleasant joke' at the expense of emigrant Presbyterian tenant farmers.[18] The ninth symposium on Swift in St Patrick's cathedral deanery in 2010 included a paper by Ian Higgins on 'The politics of *A modest proposal*'. It had a rich scholarly and textual context but paid no attention to the practical issues agitating politics in 1728 and 1729.

In contrast to literary scholars who, whatever one's concern about their historical knowledge, have at least created a huge literature on Swift, historians have too often ignored him. As a historical figure, a man who in his day had a national profile and engaged in public advocacy outside the realm of letters, his stature has declined. Even Lecky, having included him in the first edition of *Leaders of public opinion*,[19] left him out of later editions. The rather poor article on the Wood's Halfpence episode by Albert Goodwin in 1936 remained for sixty years the only significant study of the subject.[20] For want of anything better it was included in a collection of essays on eighteenth-century history in 1966.[21] In the *New history of Ireland*, Swift's Irish pamphlets appear only in a chapter on literature and very briefly.[22] The only fresh ground was broken by James Kelly in a long and comprehensive survey of the economic themes in Swift's writings.[23]

II

Swift's Irish writing appears within a large corpus of publications in the 1720s, which marked the emergence of a vigorous public opinion in Ireland. A literature of this sort, wanting in earlier years, flourished from the beginning of the 1720s.[24] It embraced not only pamphlets, but newspapers: during the reign of George I no less than thirty-three newspapers were launched, and in contrast to the ephemeral journals of Anne's reign, almost half can be regarded as successful ventures.[25] Controversies over the bank proposal in 1719–21, then over the

and the age (3 vols, London, 1962–83), iii, 629. **18** James Ward, 'Which crisis? The politics of distress in *A modest proposal*', *Swift Studies*, 21 (2006), 86. Ward's interpretation is both a forced reading of the pamphlet and an underestimation of the resources of emigrants in 1729. It was the latter circumstance – that tenants were better off and not destitute – that caused government alarm. **19** [W.E.H. Lecky], *The leaders of public opinion in Ireland* (London, 1861). **20** Albert Goodwin, 'Wood's Halfpence', *EHR*, 51 (1936), 647–74. The modern telling is in Patrick McNally, 'Wood's Halfpence, Carteret, and the government of Ireland 1723–26', *IHS*, 30:119 (May 1997), 354–76. **21** Rosalind Mitchison (ed.), *Essays in eighteenth-century history from the English Historical Review* (London, 1966), pp 117–44. **22** J.C. Beckett, 'Literature in English, 1691–1800' in T.W. Moody and W.E. Vaughan (eds), *A new history of Ireland*, iv: *Eighteenth-century Ireland, 1691–1800* (Oxford, 1986), pp 458–9. **23** James Kelly, 'Jonathan Swift and the Irish economy in the 1720s', *ECI*, 6 (1991), 7–36. **24** L.M. Cullen, 'The value of contemporary printed sources for Irish economic history in the eighteenth century', *IHS*, 14:24 (Sept. 1964), 142–55. **25** Idem, *The emergence of modern*

British Declaratory Act ('the sixth of George I') in 1720, and finally over Wood's Halfpence, stiffened political opposition in Ireland. The withdrawal of Wood's patent on the lord lieutenant's advice, on the eve of the 1725–6 session of the Irish parliament, represented a political defeat for Sir Robert Walpole. This surrender was imposed by the strength of public opinion (and was made unavoidable by Irish politicians in government in the Castle falling short in their willingness to support an unpopular policy).

The events moreover turned a former cardboard lord lieutenancy into an active one; a confident parliament made the decision on its own rehousing; and parliamentary sessions did not lose their new-found vigour. *A modest proposal* was part of the political campaign on economic issues in the late 1720s. A much later pamphlet, which received more admiration at the time and in the following century, John Hely-Hutchinson's *Commercial restraints of Ireland*, written for the great Volunteer session of 1779–80 (and having been accorded by posterity, alongside William Molyneux's *Case of Ireland* of 1698, the false accolade of having been burned by the public hangman), is by comparison a mere pedestrian production.[26]

Several propositions can be advanced in regard to Swift. First, he was conservative in his thought generally on social matters. Second, there was an evolution in his thought on economic issues by the late 1720s. Third, the emphasis in his writing in 1728 and 1729 in responding to a growing economic crisis was prompted by real and immediate concern, in contrast to passing and abstract comments in his earlier works. Swift was one of several writers who created an economic literature in the late 1720s which was intended to influence public opinion, and especially opinion within the Irish parliament.

III

Swift was essentially conservative in the sense of seeking the preservation of a familiar world, and of deploring any change. In *Maxims controlled in Ireland* (1729) he lamented that 'the old hospitable custom of lords and gentlemen living in their antient seats, among their tenants is almost lost in England, is laughed out of doors';[27] and in the same pamphlet applied these considerations equally to Ireland:

> The case in Ireland is yet somewhat worse ... These and some other motives better let pass, have drawn such a concourse to this beggarly city that the dealers of the several branches of building have found out all the

---

Ireland, 1600–1900 (London, 1981), p. 30. **26** Idem, 'Economic development, 1691–1750' in Moody and Vaughan (eds), *New history of Ireland*, iv, 126–8; idem, 'Economic development, 1750–1800' in ibid., 188; Beckett, 'Literature in English, 1691–1800', in ibid., 464–5. **27** Swift,

commodious and inviting places for erecting new houses, while fifteen hundred of the old ones, which is a seventh part of the whole city, are said to be left uninhabited, and falling to ruin.[28]

The older districts in Dublin, either in the walled city or just beyond the walls (full of what Swift described as houses 'left uninhabited'), were becoming the residence of tradesmen, while gentry were moving rapidly into new and fashionable districts, around Grafton Street and St Stephen's Green, and on the north side of the Liffey to the east of Capel Street: the line of Abbey Street, which became the location of wine merchants and bankers – an index of wealth – marked the boundary of their colonization of this part of the city. The change was reflected, too, in church building, which not only included rebuilding of existing churches, but the erection of new ones in freshly fashionable districts. There was, moreover, not only a movement of the location of gentry residences within the city, but, even more strikingly, an increase in the overall number of those gentlemen, not permanently resident in Dublin, who spent some or much time in the capital. Members of the Irish parliament were drawn to Dublin by the increasing frequency of sessions after 1692: from the first decade of the new century the parliament met predictably every second year for roughly six months (usually from autumn to spring). For those who did not hold a seat in parliament the increased concourse in Dublin made its social life more attractive or useful. Even if individual gentlemen were reluctant to come to the city, their wives wanted to visit, either to escape the tedium of rural life or to enhance the marriage prospects of eligible daughters. Despite the difficulties of the Irish economy, Dublin grew unceasingly throughout the first three decades of the century. Brooking's map of the city in 1728 glorified its extension in a visual sense, showing the extension of building into virgin fields on the north side, and suggesting in its perspective that on the south side it was moving out towards the high ground below the mountains. The map also included on its margins many vignettes depicting the new buildings in the city.

Swift's writing in the 1720s is an implicit but sustained commentary on a new, enlarged and changing Dublin. But while well aware of the changes, he was not alive to their deeper significance in the way some of his contemporaries were. Some lines from *A short view of the state of Ireland* (1728) reveal this weakness. He declared:

> The lowness of interest, in all other countries a sign of wealth, is in us a proof of misery ... Hence our increase of buildings in this city, because workmen have nothing to do, but employ one another ... Hence the daily increase of bankers, who may be a necessary evil in a trading country, but so ruinous in ours.[29]

Prose writings, ed. Davis et al., xii, 134.   28 Ibid., 134–5.   29 Ibid., 11.

This is an essentially static view. While it shows that even Swift could not but concede the evidence of increased employment all around him, his words emphatically ruled out any benefit in the dynamic features of the physical expansion of Dublin in the 1720s or in the precocious growth of banking in the same decade. Banks were doubly obnoxious to him. They had close ties with government, through dependence on it for some of their custom; and also they were, in the view of Swift and others, the vehicle for replacing the currency with overvalued foreign coins. Swift saw money as needing intrinsic value to give it any worth in its own right, and hence coin was the only true money. On monetary matters he had none of the subtlety of his younger contemporaries, David Bindon and Thomas Prior. In this area he was indeed *the* backwoodsman. However, within the year 1728 his views shifted, becoming somewhat less dogmatic. While early in the year he declared that 'I have often wished that a law were enacted to hang up half a dozen bankers every year',[30] later in the year, in *The Intelligencer*, he accepted the validity of bank notes: he expressed a hope for their wider use and that they 'may not serve as a poor expedient in this our blessed age of paper which as it dischargeth all our greatest payments, may be equally useful in the smaller'.[31]

Swift's views should be contrasted with those of Bishop Berkeley, who regarded luxurious building as beneficial to employment and such expenditure as preferable to money spent on imported consumer goods. Berkeley's view is close to that held in France a generation later by Voltaire, of luxury as a necessary vice. Swift's views contrast, too, with those of Thomas Prior, in economic terms the most perceptive commentator in the 1720s, who also revealed an uncompromising awareness of the utility of bank notes. Swift had a more negative view of economic life. In his view income was transferred by rents into the hands of landlords who spent time and money wastefully in Dublin or, worse, spent their incomes abroad.

As seen by Swift, the expenditure of income, even if it occurred in Dublin and not abroad, paradoxically reinforced the poverty that high or increased rents were in the first instance creating. In other words, in his view such expenditure, even if it financed building, simply reflected the poverty of the country, and the absence of useful outlets for expenditure. But on what could those who held extra income spend their money? Logically, the implication of Swift's writing is that they should return to the countryside and live, and spend their money, among their tenantry. In Japan at the same time, the political philosopher Ogyu Sorai had an identical lamentation: Edo (Tokyo) had become too large: samurai and ordinary people should be returned to the countryside; and daimyo (the great lords) should not reside in Edo. But in neither country was such a pastoral ideal realistic, nor would rural residence by the wealthy have served a purpose

30 Ibid. 31 Jonathan Swift and Thomas Sheridan, *The Intelligencer*, ed. James Woolley (Oxford, 1992), p. 210.

unless it created new employment. Hence, in a sense, the question was one of whether employment would be created in town or in the countryside. Realization of the implications of this lay behind the many – and fashionable – instances of creating industrial villages in the 1720s and 1730s in which textile workers would create a market for local agricultural produce and underpin a rural society always threatened either by low prices for produce, or by hunger.[32] The creation of industrial employment or non-agricultural income in the countryside was not realistic, however: it could not be on a large enough scale, and, if financed by landlords, the capital costs were high and managerial skills either poor or erratic. Many of these enterprises enjoyed a very brief existence. The alternatives were, therefore, stark: income could be spent in Ireland or abroad. If spent in Ireland it would be spent either in Dublin on new building and services catering to the wealthy (in the process drawing people from the countryside into employment in the capital), or, even if gentry resided in the countryside, on new or rebuilt country seats and on imported luxuries such as silks, wine and brandy, items which improvers deplored as they did not create employment within Ireland.

IV

A preliminary point to make in discussing Swift's Irish political writings is that a disservice has been done to him by treating his early works as tracts on economic matters, when their economic content is merely incidental to wider questions. There is an irony in the fact that the Ninth Annual Dublin seminar on Jonathan Swift, intended to mark the 290th anniversary of the publication of *A proposal for the universal use of Irish manufactures*, was devoted to the theme of 'Swift's economics', for despite its title, this was not an economic tract, something that should be evident from its opening theme: 'It is the peculiar felicity and prudence of the people of this kingdom, that wherever commodities, or productions, lie under the greatest discouragements from England, those are what they are sure to be most industrious in cultivating and spreading.'[33] Notwithstanding the English act of 1699, the woollen industry had actually prospered in Dublin, responding to growth in the city and to the wealth of many of its inhabitants. But the woollen manufacture was not the concern of the pamphlet. Harnessing the existing indignation of Swift's readers, its purpose was to attack, from a political perspective, British policies and British administrators in Dublin. The pamphlet endorses the opposition given by Archbishop King to the Declaratory Act of 1720, which asserted the superiority of the Westminster parliament, and in particular to the assumed right of the British House of Lords to act as a court of final appeal for Irish cases, and of the British parliament as a whole to legislate for Ireland. This act of course could not but advert to the 1699

32 Cullen, *Emergence*, pp 38, 51, 74–9. 33 Swift, *Prose writings*, ed. Davis et al., ix, 15.

act banning the export of woollen manufactures, if only because the campaigns of English pressure-groups that culminated in the woollen act had served as a backdrop to Molyneux's tract challenging the right of the English parliament to legislate for Ireland. In *A proposal for the universal use of Irish manufactures*, Swift wrote, 'I have, indeed, seen the present Archbishop of Dublin, clad from head to foot in our own manufacture; and yet, under the rose be it spoken, his Grace deserves as good a Gown as if he had not been born among us'.[34] The key to the thinking in the pamphlet lies in the lines: 'Nothing hath humbled me so much, or shewn a greater disposition to a contemptuous treatment of Ireland in some chief governors, than that high style of several speeches from the throne, delivered as usual, after the royal assent, in some periods of the last two reigns.'[35] Appearing when it did, in May 1720, the pamphlet was a riposte to the recent royal assent (in April) to the Declaratory Act, and a political appeal to Archbishop King, who had memorably made the same point in an address in 1719.

The pamphlet itself is an extraordinarily skilled production, in which all the grievances of Irishmen were marshalled behind the resentment in 1720 against the new act. The appeal to economic matters serves as a mere mantle for the political theme. Its economic themes moreover were not subversive.[36] They would not of themselves have warranted the urge to identify the author and, in default of success in that regard, to prosecute the printer. It was the open challenge, in uncompromising terms, to a law establishing the supremacy of the British parliament which the government could not ignore.

V

We now turn to Swift's economic writings in 1728–9. He visited much of the countryside in the 1720s. Quilca, in Co. Cavan, the residence of his friend Thomas Sheridan, was the place where he 'stayed oftenest and longest'.[37] In a four-month trip in 1723 he visited the south, and also the west (at least Ennis and Clonfert).[38] In the case of Armagh, he visited the MP Robert Cope at Loughgall

---

[34] Ibid., 18. [35] Ibid., 20. [36] But, it should be noted, one change was made in the Faulkner edition on which modern reprintings are based. The celebrated sentence referring to not burning coal and which 'for the latter, I hope, in a little time we shall have no occasion' (Swift, *Prose writings*, ed. Davis et al., ix, 17), is a substitution in the first edition for a clause advocating a wider boycott, 'nor am I even yet for lessening the number of those exceptions [everything except coal]' (Swift, *A proposal for the universal use of Irish manufacture, in cloaths and furniture of houses, &c. Utterly rejecting and renouncing every thing wearable that comes from England* (Dublin, 1720), p. 6). The Dublin coal trade, with its often high prices, was a recurrent source of consumer resentment, and was a subject of repeated legislation intended to halt abuses. In later years Sir James Lowther, proprietor of the Whitehaven collieries, was always uneasy when prices rose during the sittings of the Irish parliament. [37] Damrosch, *Swift*, p. 302. [38] Ibid., pp 345, 475.

in the autumn of 1722, and the Achesons at Markethill for extended stays of eight months in 1728, and four in 1729.[39] Thus he had an intimate knowledge of the country and the worsening situation of rural Ireland in early 1729. His observations on the condition of the people and on high rents reflected not simply his dislike of landlords, but an awareness of the people and of their plight. Beckett was wrong to assert that Swift had 'no sense of national community with the poverty-stricken masses whose cause he was pleading'. Comment in Swift's pamphlets and occasionally in his letters seems sufficiently forthright to ensure that we cannot rule out a real indignation. Beckett supported his assertion by noting that Swift referred to the native Irish as 'our savages'.[40] However, one of the meanings of 'savage' was simply life in a state of nature, without any of the creature comforts of civilization.

Swift's concern, and that of others, was prompted by an alarming deterioration in the economy from 1726 onwards, after a modest cyclical upturn in the early years of the decade. From 1725 there were four bad harvests in a row. The situation became really serious from late 1726, in a worsening of credit conditions. The exchange rate between Irish currency and sterling had deteriorated noticeably in and from August 1726, and in this respect the first months of 1727 proved the most unfavourable of the entire 1720s. The deterioration is even more striking in the usually highly positive balance of trade. In the year ended March 1727 the surplus was replaced by a deficit, almost unprecedented in trade figures, and not to recur until 1782–3. The outcome was better in 1727/8, but two years of contraction in the surplus followed. In the year ended March 1729 the surplus was small; and large imports of grain in the spring and early summer of 1729 ensured that in the year ended March 1730 the surplus was further reduced.[41] Writing to Pope in August 1729 (at the close of a year of famine, more particularly in the north), Swift observed that 'as to this country, there have been three terrible years dearth of corn, and every place strowed with beggars'.[42] The problems were manifold: hunger and even famine, mobility of the poor (graphically described retrospectively by Dobbs in 1731), higher rents as old leases which had expired during the 1720s were renewed, and a surplus which was insufficient to meet external liabilities (including the swollen rentals of absentees). An abrupt rise in migration from Ulster to America was a further and novel feature. The gloomy conclusions for these years, if applied to long-term trends, would have been misleading in their implication of an economy in perpetual crisis. In fact, from the early autumn of 1729 the economy abruptly recovered – there were bumper harvests, and the balance of trade quickly redressed itself.[43] Of course, at the time contemporaries faced with

39 Ibid., pp 347, 435.   40 Beckett, 'Literature in English, 1691–1800', p. 459.   41 L.M. Cullen, *An economic history of Ireland* (London, 1972), p. 46.   42 Swift to Pope, 11 Aug. 1729 (*The correspondence of Jonathan Swift, DD*, ed. David Woolley (5 vols, Frankfurt am Main, 1999–2014), iii, 245).   43 'Our harvest has proved extreamly good': Marmaduke Coghill to

exceptional problems had no grounds for optimism. A sequence of four bad harvests (the fourth resulting in famine by early 1729) was comparable in some respects to the four hungry years in the 1690s in Scotland. Even if the outcome of no single year rivalled the severe famine of 1740–1, the years 1725–8 were certainly the most prolonged run of bad seasons in Ireland during the entire century.

Swift's earlier writings did not deal seriously with the economy. His economic comments, such as they were, were commonplace at the time, and were often superficial. Before 1728, the only pamphlet with a serious social remit was Viscount Molesworth's *Some considerations for promoting the agriculture of Ireland and employing the poor*, published in 1723.[44] Swift knew Molesworth, whose residence was at Brackenstown to the north of Dublin, and who was a cosmopolitan figure, at home in the highest social and intellectual circles of both Dublin and London. One of the *Drapier's letters*, in December 1724, was addressed to Molesworth, and expressed admiration for him:

> Since your last residence in Ireland, I frequently have taken my nag to ride about your grounds; where I fancied myself to feel an air of freedom breathing round me; and I am glad the low condition of a tradesman did not qualify me to wait on you at your house; for then, I am afraid my writings would not have escaped severer censures. But I have lately sold my nag, and honestly told his greatest fault, which was that of snuffing up the air around Brackdenstown; whereby he became such a lover of liberty, that I could scarcely hold him in.[45]

Swift had approved strongly of Molesworth's tract, immediately on its appearance.[46] It had also served as something of a model for Swift's own *Short view* in 1728. The *Short view* was less original than Molesworth's pamphlet (itself modest in its scope, but still the first pamphlet approaching social issues on a broad front). At first sight Swift's pamphlet seems no more than a gathering together of commonplace observations made by himself or others. Swift himself only dimly understood the workings of the economic system. His comments on economic matters were sweeping, often wildly inaccurate, and, where orders of magnitude arose, without exception imprecise. While we must allow that Swift wrote some of his texts without publication in mind, no difference in mode of expression shows between published and unpublished texts. His quarrel with (Sir) John Browne, though having earlier origins, was carried forward in 1728 in criticism of sanguine economic views expressed by Browne in a pamphlet. Yet

---

Edward Southwell, 2 Sept. 1729 (*Letters of Marmaduke Coghill, 1722–1738*, ed. D.W. Hayton (Dublin, 2005) (henceforth *Coghill letters*), p. 72).   44 *Some considerations for promoting the agriculture of Ireland and employing the poor* (Dublin, 1723).   45 Swift, *Prose writings*, ed. Davis et al., x, 93.   46 Carole Fabricant, 'Swift's political legacy' in Douglas, Kelly and Ross,

despite the many and substantive defects in Swift's views, their significance should not be underrated. Repetition of his unqualified assertions in a decade in which economic commentary was in its infancy may have helped to promote a wider currency for commentary on economic matters. Moreover, the *Short view* was a sustained and novel recital of Swift's scattered comments, creating a general economic statement at a time of a growing sense of social crisis. Touching on the paradox of poverty and plenty, he concluded with a broad, blunt – and, for Swift, practical – exhortation: 'We need not wonder at strangers, when they deliver such paradoxes, but a native and inhabitant of this kingdom who gives the same verdict, must be either ignorant to stupidity, or a man-pleaser, at the expense of all honour, conscience, and truth.'[47] The *Short view* was followed by a new periodical, *The Intelligencer*, launched in May 1728 by Swift and (in the words of a government man, Marmaduke Coghill) 'his underling', Thomas Sheridan,[48] which by the year's end had published its nineteenth number. This appeared in the aftermath of the final and most serious of four deficient harvests, and hence 'in the melancholy disappointment of the present crop'.[49] It anticipates the famine, which raged in the early months of 1729. The *Modest proposal* followed logically enough in the autumn of 1729. Joseph McMinn's observation that it was 'one of the few pamphlets of this period he [Swift] was determined to publish' is apposite.[50]

The *Short view* would have served little public purpose in 1726–7, as parliament was not then sitting. It was written at the outset of the parliamentary session of 1727–8. In its somewhat belated public appearance in March 1728, at the end of a highly successful parliamentary session, it proved the precursor of a new wave of writing on economic and social reforms in 1728–9. It is not possible to document Swift's relations with other members of the small group who wrote on economic matters (apart from some detail on the bad relations between him and John Browne, author in 1728–9 of several very good treatises). But the fact that the first pamphlet in 1728–9 was by Swift, and that his *Modest proposal* closed the campaign is suggestive of his central place. The various pamphlets of 1728–9, and of 1731 (for the following parliamentary session), are by far the best economic writings of the century: in no other decade did pamphlets have the same coherence on economic and social matters and they never even remotely approached them in freshness or originality.[51] An arresting illustration of this was the frequent reprinting – in years of economic difficulty – of Prior's *List of the absentees of Ireland* (1729), with an unchanged text, apart from the statistics being brought up to date.[52]

Locating Swift, p. 196.   **47** Swift, *Prose writings*, ed. Davis et al., xii, 12.   **48** Coghill to Southwell, 5 Nov. 1728 (*Coghill letters*, p. 58).   **49** *Swift's Irish writings*, ed. Fabricant and Mahony, p. 102.   **50** Joseph McMinn, *Swift's Irish pamphlets: an introductory selection* (Gerrard's Cross, 1991), p. 183.   **51** For comments on the pamphlets of the 1720s, see Cullen, 'Value of contemporary printed sources for Irish economic history', pp 147–8.   **52** Cullen,

VI

A modest proposal was not a cry of despair, but a logical follow-through to the *Short view* of 1728. Early in the 1729 session (in October) Prior's *List of the absentees of Ireland* set the tone, appearing immediately ahead of the meeting of the committee of the whole House of Commons on the state of the nation. Coghill, high in political councils and freshly appointed as a revenue commissioner, reported that 'we have a bitter book published against absentees. Tho' it has some truths in it, it [h]as many faults and [is] lyable to many objections.'[53] Debate in the Commons opened with a set speech – 'a most elaborate speech of near an hour' – by Lieutenant-Colonel Alexander Montgomery (MP for Co. Donegal), which summarized the concerns of would-be reformers. Montgomery set out

> all the greivances of the nation, our want of publick spirritt, the poverty of the kingdom, the ill consequences of our people goeing to America, occasion'd he pretended by the oppression of landlords by setting their lands too high, and the hardships of collecting tythes, by the luxury of the better sort of people, by the extravagance of the ladies in their silks laces and other vanities, by the irregular and uncertain state of our coyn, by the tricks of bankers and merchants, by our excesse in drinking French wines, by our gentlemen and ladies goeing abroad and living out of their native country, by the neglect of our Laws for tillage, by the continued addition to our establishment ... [54]

Coghill, who disapproved of what he considered over-dramatic and unhelpful patriotic effusions, consoled himself that Montgomery 'concluded without promising any thing, he commended decency, good manners and respect to us all in our proceedings'. Robert Cope (whom Swift had visited in Co. Armagh in 1722) was mentioned by Coghill as a speaker in a more moderate vein. Coghill concluded that, 'if I can Judge right, if Cope and the Tories can be brought off from a representation we shall have no other disturbance, for the angry men find either that they cant concert with any party, or my Ld. Leiut. has found means to stop their mouths'. The *Modest proposal* followed in November, adding to the ill-temper of members of the house.[55] Coghill's hopes of a calm session were

---

'Economic development, 1750–1800', pp 172–3. **53** Coghill to Southwell, 14 Oct. (*Coghill letters*, p. 74). **54** Coghill to Southwell, 23 Oct. (ibid., p. 75). **55** Though the pamphlet is usually said to have been published in October 1729, the fact that Coghill forwarded a copy only on 13 Nov. suggests that it actually appeared a month later. Coghill usually lost no time in sending Swift's writings to England. (*Coghill letters*, pp 10, 55, 58, 60, 89, 91, 94, 98, 100.) It was referred to in the *Dublin Intelligencer* on 15 Nov. Ward's suggestion ('Which distress', p. 80) that Swift's peers 'seem to have looked on the text not as a serious indictment but as a typically eccentric piece' is based on too slight evidence to carry conviction.

dashed. On 5 March he reported that 'The Debates in the House of Commons were carried on with more warmth and boldness than I have ever known.'[56] Things were no better at the end of the session: 'we broke up in a sort of a flame'.[57] Coghill at times betrayed a tone of exasperation with Swift.[58] Frustration in government circles, already high in February,[59] then boiled over publicly in April, when Joshua, Viscount Allen, outraged by the decision of Dublin city corporation to present Swift with the freedom of the city in a gold box, vented his spleen in speeches abusing Swift at the privy council and in the Lords, only to be lampooned by the dean in his turn.[60]

The mood of the House of Commons in the late 1720s was reinforced by several underlying factors. First, a wish to control Ireland's own public destiny had emerged. A sustained and novel engagement of the Commons in economic issues saturated the session of 1729–30. The consequence of a political victory on the scale of that secured in the Wood's Halfpence controversy does not get due recognition in modern literature, and has been ignored in the political narrative, largely because of the long absence of a broad study of Irish politics in the late 1720s, and of Carteret's masterly exercise of his office. The shadow of Goodwin's article lingered long. Goodwin, totally lacking in a vision of the absurdity of an inflated amount of small change as a solution to wider currency problems, saw the outcome of the controversy as the foolish rejection of a meritorious proposal intended to benefit the country. In reality, the scheme had no economic merit, and was a tawdry 'stroke': at heart the dispute was political. The mood of the sessions of parliament in 1727–8 and 1729–30 was thus fuelled by high expectations. The 1727–8 session was marked by the decision to build a new parliament house, and by a political triumph in the acceptance by the British privy council of the heads of a tillage bill, which had not been presented as usual to the lord lieutenant by a small delegation, but by the members of the Commons *en masse*. The following session saw parliament taking still broader initiatives in economic matters.[61]

The second factor was the cumulative effect of the growth in size, wealth and institutions of Dublin in the 1720s, which attracted to the city growing numbers of the landed classes (even many who did not sit in parliament) and kept them there for an ever more lively social season, whether parliament was in session or not. In the mood of 1729 there is something akin to that of Dublin fifty years later, in the great Volunteer autumn of 1779.

The third factor in the popular success of the decade is the evidence of the executive acting under pressure, and creating a more visible and accessible

56 Coghill to Ld Perceval, 5 Mar. 1730 (*Coghill letters*, p. 94).   **57** Coghill to Southwell, 21 Apr. 1730 (ibid., p. 98).   **58** Coghill to Ld Perceval, 5 Mar. 1730 (ibid., p. 94).   **59** For a vivid account, see Coghill to Southwell, 21 Feb. 1730 (ibid., pp 91–2).   **60** Coghill to Southwell, 18 Apr. 1730 (ibid., p. 98). Coghill wrote in a similar tone to Perceval on 23 Apr. (ibid., p. 100). See also Swift, *Prose writings*, ed. Davis et al., xii, 141, 145–6; Ehrenpreis, *Swift*, iii, 650–60.   **61** Coghill's letters between 27 Sept. and 23 Apr. provide an outline of issues and of the mood

presence as a counterweight to the parliament. Proof of this can be seen in Carteret's relatively long lord lieutenancy and his continuous residence at the height of the crisis for an unprecedented period of eighteen months (unprecedented at least since the beginning of the eighteenth century). Under his successor, Dorset, in 1731–6 a brilliant social life was built around the court: the well-known painting in 1731 of a court ball is the first illustration we have of formal Dublin social life. As the parliament was acquiring its parliament house, it became necessary to house the administration in better surroundings. The rebuilding of the run-down and shabby Dublin Castle, seat of government, began in earnest in the 1730s. In a sense the crisis of the mid-1720s created a new political framework for Georgian Dublin, symbolized even monumentally in a new parliament house and a rebuilt Castle.[62]

All the writing of the decade, whether political or economic in approach, had been geared towards parliamentary sessions and influencing them. The timing of pamphlets was bunched in the months before, or at the outset of, the six-month session, which occurred regularly every second year. In the late 1770s this cycle still existed: agitation, both active and literary, occurred in the autumn and spring of 1777–8 because parliament was in session; nothing much occurred in the autumn of 1778 but a climax of agitation was reached in the celebrated Volunteer autumn of 1779 when parliament was meeting again. There was no action of consequence in the autumn and winter of 1780–1, and finally in the following parliamentary session in 1781–2 Grattan's parliament won its modest independence.

The *Short view*, appearing in March 1728, heralded the onset of a concerted campaign of writings on economic matters for the 1729 session. The extension of the work of the Commons to active committees had already created over the decade a small caucus of like-minded politicians. Some of the pamphleteers were MPs, like David Bindon and Arthur Dobbs, and in parliament there were others like Coghill, Henry Maxwell or Agmondisham Vesey, who were chairmen of the growing number of economic committees created by the House of Commons in the course of its work.[63] The political thrust of the writing, even of the economic tracts, accounts for much of the simplification in it: compare, for example, Thomas Prior's *List of the absentees of Ireland*, a great political set-piece giving a simple, crude and even exaggerated picture of the scale of absenteeism and its effects, with the extraordinary sophistication and competence of his *Observations on coin*, also published in 1729, which affords a technical insight into monetary problems and is not a particularly easy read. The *List of absentees* was read closely by contemporaries: ironically, some even complained that their rentals had been underestimated.

of the Commons.   **62** Edward McParland, *Public architecture in Ireland, 1680–1760* (New Haven & London, 2001), chs 4, 7.   **63** D.W. Hayton, *The Anglo-Irish experience, 1680–1730: religion, identity and patriotism* (Woodbridge, 2012), pp 139–42.

Swift's attacks on country gentlemen, coloured though they were by a dislike of gentry who opposed payment of tithes to the church, somewhat crudely argued the case for the exercise of social responsibility. He believed, as indeed others did, that as old leases fell in, rents to tenants were greatly increased on renewal. This was notably the reason for Prior's concern: if rents to gentry rose, remittances to absentees would increase in proportion. The Achesons, Swift's hosts at Markethill, in Co. Armagh, were Swift's ideal, with their rents not above half the value of the land. Swift's writing is part of the working out of the themes of social responsibility to be pursued at national level in parliament and at local level by gentry on their estates. A decade later, in 1738, it was to be spelled out in great detail under a suggestive title, in Samuel Madden's *Reflections and resolutions proper for the gentlemen of Ireland*.

The various pamphlets that appeared within a period of about twenty months in 1728–9, including the dean's own *Modest proposal*, amounted to a concerted campaign to influence parliamentary opinion. The following session, in the winter of 1729–30, was highly successful in economic terms: the Dublin trade in English coal was regulated, a portmanteau 'navigation bill' was passed, establishing the Navigation Board, and the decision was taken to launch the Newry canal, the first true canal in these islands, intended to carry inland coal to the coast to reduce the dependence of Dublin on coal imports.

VII

The *Modest proposal* derives its significance from its position as the climax of a literary barrage. Its immediacy is somewhat disguised by the most commonly reproduced modern text altering the 1729 title. The words 'the children of poor people' become 'the children of poor people in Ireland', and in addition the words 'Written in the year 1729' follow the title. These changes downplay the directness of what in 1729 was conceived as an address to the Irish public (for which the words 'in Ireland' are redundant), and give the pamphlet a less specific purpose.[64] The distinction between the original and later texts is important: it is easy to see the pamphlet – as indeed it has been seen – as 'parodying the many fatuous and ill-informed "proposals" for a solution to Ireland's ills being circulated at the time'.[65] It in no way took issue with this style of writing. Possessing a familiarity with recent literature, it is a parody not of pamphlets but of the way in which good sense represented by proposals for dealing with the economy's plight were not listened to by government. Swift's own proposal was in a vein of mock seriousness, adopting the customary tone of pamphlets,

---

[64] I am indebted for these observations to Ian Campbell Ross. The changes appear in the Faulkner edition of 1735, which serves as a source for modern editions. [65] *Swift's Irish writings*, ed. Fabricant and Mahony, p. 123.

especially of those which seriously addressed economic issues. Having observed that, 'as to my own part, having turned my thoughts for many years, upon this important subject; and maturely weighed the several schemes of other projectors',[66] he launches into his own proposal. He parades in mock seriousness calculations of the cost of rearing the children of the poor to provide from their carcasses a new food source, and his enumeration of the benefits reveals an easy conversancy with the ideas, language and format of arguments of the literature at large.

It was the knowledge that the *Modest proposal* could not be acted on, was indeed outrageous, that ensured its impact. It seemed to suggest that a preposterous measure to guarantee the welfare of the country had more value than more meritorious proposals. However, behind this mock seriousness, the pamphlet explicitly takes into account the themes set out in other writings, not least the new pamphlets of 1728–9.

> Therefore let no man talk to me of other expedients: of taxing our absentees at five shillings a pound; of using neither cloaths, nor household furniture; except what is of our own growth and manufacture: of utterly rejecting the materials and instruments that promote foreign luxury: of curing the expensiveness of pride, vanity, idleness, and gaming, in our women: of introducing a vein of parsimony, prudence and temperance: of learning to love our country; wherein we differ even from Laplanders and the inhabitants of Topinamboo: of quitting our animosities, and faction; nor act any longer like the Jews, who were murdering one another at the very moment their city was taken: of being a little cautious not to sell our country and consciences for nothing; of teaching landlords to have, at least, one degree of mercy towards their tenants. Lastly, of putting a spirit of honesty, industry, and skill into our shop-keepers; who, if a resolution could not be taken to buy only our native goods, would immediately unite to cheat and exact upon us in the price, the measure, and the goodness; nor could ever yet be brought to make one fair proposal of just dealing, though often and earnestly invited to it.[67]

Swift's real purpose is the opposite of what he appears to be advocating: 'Therefore I repeat; let no man talk to me of these and the like expedients; till he hath, at least, a glimpse of hope, that there will ever be some hearty and sincere attempt to put them in practice.'[68]

Some emphasis is necessary, given the widely held view that Irish politics became apathetic in the wake of the Wood's Halfpence affair. According to the *New history of Ireland*, 'Once the furore aroused by Wood's Halfpence died down, there was a lull lasting over twenty years in Irish politics.'[69] There was not.

---

66 Swift, *Prose writings*, ed. Davis et al., xii, 110.   67 Ibid., 116–17.   68 Ibid., 117.   69 J.L.

The affair was a ringing defeat for the government in London. It was never again to propose measures as chimerical as Wood's Halfpence. It no longer vetoed proposed Irish measures as readily as it had done in the past. Ireland had to be managed seriously. This was first done, and with skill, by Carteret, who helped to ensure that the British privy council was aware of the high political cost of frustrating the intention in heads of bills from Ireland. The lord lieutenancy in the following decades was largely entrusted to politicians of experience or stature, some served at a time for more than one session and some reappeared in later times. It faced an invigorated sense of national identity, and in economic matters, a programme of well-defined proposals. In time a division emerged between the calculating great politicians (forced into opposition on occasion but happy to return to the fold) and others both inside and outside parliament who sought a more consistent and less self-serving patriot policy. It was to result without delay from the late 1740s onwards, when revenue soared, in a wide range of economic interventions by parliament.

The Irish parliament in the late 1720s had to create extra taxes to meet debt, and a true national debt has its origins in these years. There had been a loan in 1716; however, the stock was not traded. A land agent writing to his absentee employer in the late 1720s predicted that an increase in the national debt would be likely to lead to 'jobbing' in the style of the London market. To what extent and at what date a market emerged is not clear, and the first reference to stock prices seems to be a retrospective reference to the early 1750s.[70] For a time the increase in what was still a moderate debt was halted by surplus in the late 1740s and early 1750s. Edmund Burke, a critic in many respects of the Irish parliament, had a good word to say for its reinforced economic interventionism. These measures were not in themselves in any way novel. They were part of the programme introduced in the late 1720s, with implementation, given a revenue surplus, now made easier. Economic and infrastructural intervention was, moreover, to remain a central part of the activity of the parliament until its demise in 1800.

The economic and political writings of 1728–9 and 1731 had a relevance that went beyond events in parliament. The writers and their parliamentary supporters provided the backing for the Dublin Society founded in 1731. The crisis of 1728–9 had brought together a number of men of talent, and the informal cooperation of the summer and autumn of 1729 inside and outside parliament was logically formalized in 1731 in the Dublin Society, the first of its

McCracken, 'The rise of colonial nationalism, 1714–60' in *New hist. Ire.*, iv, 114. But see, among more recent writings, R.E. Burns, *Irish parliamentary politics in the eighteenth century* (2 vols, Washington, DC, 1989–90); Patrick McNally, *Parties, patriots and undertakers: parliamentary politics in early Hanoverian Ireland* (Dublin, 1997), chs 6–9; Eoin Magennis, *The Irish political system, 1740–1765: the golden age of the undertakers* (Dublin, 2000), ch. 1; D.W. Hayton, *Ruling Ireland, 1685–1742: politics, politicians and parties* (Woodbridge, 2004), ch. 8. **70** L.M. Cullen, *Anglo-Irish trade, 1660–1800* (Manchester, 1968), p. 185.

kind in Europe. The political background to its rise is reflected in the fact that it first met in the months ahead of the 1731 parliamentary session, and its early meeting place was in the new parliament house, which had been already beginning to take shape during the politically splendid autumn of 1729. These ideas, summarized in the paragraph quoted above from the *Modest proposal*, and already enumerated by Alexander Montgomery in his speech in the Irish House of Commons, were pursued in the later 1730s in Berkeley's *Querist* and Samuel Madden's *Reflections and resolutions proper for the gentlemen of Ireland*, and more modestly in the numerous publications of the Dublin Society. The real significance of the *Modest proposal*, which ranked with Prior's *List of the absentees* as one of the two most effective pamphlets of the age, has become lost in the quest in Swiftian studies for deeper meanings of the text. Swift had simply harnessed his readings in history and geography and his verbal playfulness to a public task. Though the objective was identical, these qualities gave it a sombre ornamentation that contrasted with the prosaic but politically more effective text by Prior.[71]

---

[71] This is a revised version of a paper originally delivered in 1991 at a seminar on Swift in Celbridge Abbey (Vanessa's home), St John of God Order, St Raphael's, Celbridge. A later version was read at the annual conference of the Ireland-Japan Society in Gakushuin University, Tokyo, in 2007. I am indebted to Ian Campbell Ross for criticisms and suggestions, which have greatly reduced the deficiencies of an earlier draft.

Novel spectacle? The birth of the Whiteboys, 1761–2

DAVID DICKSON

No survey of eighteenth-century Irish history, whatever its focus, can ignore the sudden arrival on stage of the Whiteboys, the agrarian protest movement associated with central Munster, which made its first appearance in the winter of 1761–2. Musgrave, in his monumental history of 1798, saw the Whiteboy outbreak as the first malignant step leading towards 'popish insurrection' a generation later, and historians from Madden, Froude and Lecky to Wall, Cullen, Smyth and McBride have all sought to interpret and contextualize afresh those strange events that occurred in the countryside skirting the Galtee and Knockmealdown mountains.[1] A generation ago James Donnelly provided a close reading of Whiteboyism as it evolved through the 1760s, and followed it shortly afterwards with an essay on the rather different but eponymous movement of the 1770s. These essays were followed by Thomas Power's study of Co. Tipperary in the eighteenth century, which revealed the complex links between gentry rivalries at the political level, and subaltern protest and its violent suppression.[2]

The Whiteboys have also lurked, albeit not very prominently, within the eighteenth-century Irish landscape as depicted and elaborated by Sean Connolly. Their story lay just outside the time frame of his *Religion, law and power* (1992), but they featured centrally in his celebrated exchange with Vincent Morley in 2002/3 over whether or not early Whiteboyism was infected by Jacobite sentiment and powered by popular political disaffection.[3] In Connolly's estimation the movement conformed to the European standard model of pre-industrial rural protest in being 'conservative and defensive in character' and

---

1 Sir Richard Musgrave, *Memoirs of the different rebellions in Ireland ...* (3rd ed., London, 1802), pp 27–32; R.R. Madden, *The United Irishmen and their times* (2nd ed., 4 vols, Dublin, 1858), i, 29–89; J.A. Froude, *The English in Ireland in the eighteenth century* (3 vols, London, 1881), ii, 24–37; W.E.H. Lecky, *A history of Ireland in the eighteenth century* (2nd ed., 5 vols, London, 1898), ii, 21–44; Maureen Wall, 'The Whiteboys' in T.D. Williams (ed.), *Secret societies in Ireland* (Dublin, 1973), pp 13–25; L.M. Cullen, *The emergence of modern Ireland, 1600–1900* (London, 1981), pp 122–3; Jim Smyth, *The men of no property: Irish radicals and popular politics in the late eighteenth century* (Basingstoke, 1992), pp 33–45; Ian McBride, *Eighteenth-century Ireland: the isle of slaves* (Dublin, 2009), pp 312–41. 2 J.S. Donnelly, 'The Whiteboy movement, 1761–5', *IHS*, 21:81 (Mar. 1978), 20–54; idem, 'Irish agrarian rebellion: the Whiteboys of 1769–76', *RIA Proc.*, 83 (1983), sect. C, 293–331; T.P. Power, *Land, politics and society in eighteenth-century Tipperary* (Oxford, 1993), pp 174–220, 242–65. 3 S.J. Connolly, *Religion, law and power: the making of Protestant Ireland, 1660–1760* (Oxford, 1992), pp 219, 223, 314; Vincent Morley, 'George III, Queen Sadhbh and the historians', *ECI*, 17 (2002), 112–20; S.J. Connolly, 'Jacobites, Whiteboys and republicans: varieties of disaffection in eighteenth-century Ireland' in ibid., 18 (2003), 63–79. Cf. idem, *Divided kingdom: Ireland,*

'pragmatic', only coming into existence 'in response to actual or threatened change', in this instance 'the enclosure of common lands and the extension of pasture at the expense of small scale tillage'. He highlighted how the victims whose ditches were levelled were a mix of Catholic and Protestant big farmers, that some of those involved were small-town craftsmen, and that the movement's social composition was 'overwhelmingly plebeian'. But perhaps his most telling riposte to Morley, whose critique was based on a review of eighteenth-century Munster Gaelic poetry and its visceral anti-Hanoverianism, was simply to note the absence of direct evidence, observing how striking it was that 'the novel spectacle of large-scale popular protest in the Irish countryside [by the Whiteboys] provoked remarkably little response from among the Gaelic literati'.[4]

What, one might wonder, could possibly remain to be said about this 'novel spectacle', unless some entirely fresh evidence can be brought to light? No such discovery has been made, and first-hand evidence on what was actually going on in the early months of Whiteboy activity (from late autumn 1761 up to April 1762) remains surprisingly thin. Donnelly's principal sources were the Dublin newspapers and magazines, specifically *Faulkner's Dublin Journal*, but even if one looks at the newspaper titles not cited by Donnelly – daily and weekly papers published in London, Cork and Belfast – the same reports, even the same phrases, that appear in *Faulkner's* re-appear there, often with the same colourful details. Faulkner, despite the family's intimate connexions with the then viceroy the earl of Halifax, only began to carry reports about the Munster 'levellers' late in March 1762, perhaps five months after the first incidents.[5] Other types of source are even thinner: judicial records of the special commission that tried Whiteboy prisoners in June 1762 do not survive in any form, and (perhaps more surprisingly) internal archival evidence from the Munster estates affected by early Whiteboy activity is almost entirely missing. Indeed information on the first stages of the protest in autumn 1761 is entirely retrospective, dating from spring 1762 at the earliest. However, from early April until mid-summer of that year the Munster 'tumults' became a huge public issue, grabbing attention both in Dublin and London. Things then died down until early in 1763, when a second wave of incidents occurred in north and north-east Munster, with a second wave of publicity in the press, paralleled by the meteoric appearance of Oakboys in central Ulster, come and gone in a few summer weeks, and in some respects echoing events in the south. But the reverberations of the second and more violent phase of Whiteboy activity continued until the trials of the supposed Whiteboy godfathers in 1765 and 1766, culminating in the hugely controversial prosecution and execution of Father Nicholas Sheehy and three prominent Catholic laymen. Power has suggested that in Co. Tipperary alone

---

1630–1800 (Oxford, 2008), pp 301–5. **4** Connolly, 'Jacobites, Whiteboys and republicans', 73, 75–6. **5** George Faulkner's particular connexion came from the fact that his niece and adopted daughter Mary Donaldson had become (and was to remain) the earl of Halifax's

there were over forty-two agrarian incidents between 1760 and 1766, but so sensational was the Sheehy affair, then and thereafter, that the beginning of Whiteboyism has always been seen through the prism of that prosecution. Here the intention is to keep the focus on that first cycle of protest in 1761/2 for, however incomplete the evidence, it does throw up some puzzling patterns.[6]

II

In the historiography of Irish rural protest, from George Cornwall Lewis' great inquiry in 1836 to Maura Cronin's survey of 2013, the events of 1761–2 have always provided the overture, prefiguring the character and repertoire of agrarian movements to come.[7] But were they really the first manifestation of popular protest? And if not, how did they acquire that reputation? Sean Connolly reminded us a long time ago that they certainly were not the first manifestation. In his two essays on the 'houghing' campaign in Connacht in 1710–12 he investigated an episode that both Froude and Lecky had spotted (using tantalizing state paper and grand jury sources lost in 1922), but he turned their arguments around, seeing the low-key resolution of that protest as at least as important as the brief flare-up itself. Systematic attacks on cattle and sheep began in west Galway in 1710, but many districts further east were not affected until the winter of 1711–12. In its origins it may have been a private vendetta, but the declared aims became far more ambitious: to halt tenurial change and the advance of 'the cattle of the merchants and newcomers that were engrossing the lands'. Emerging out of the 'bad lands' of Connemara, the houghers' agitation swept across the richer limestone pasturelands of east Galway, central Roscommon and beyond. It appears to have been a sudden, short-lived but well-disciplined movement and one that proved fairly resistant to criminal investigation. Military force was deployed, but only a handful of those arrested received capital punishment. Connolly saw it as driven by economic and material grievance, not crypto-Jacobite brigandage, and as innovative in its methods, not least in the use of fictive proclamations. These mimicked the language of the privy council and hinted at a 'moral economy' embracing tenants' rights. And (thanks to Froude) we know of at least one hougher deposition where reference was made to 'an oath of secrecy', something usually assumed to be a Whiteboy innovation; other reports spoke of night-time activity, blackened faces and the wearing of white shirts, all providing a strange foretaste of the 1760s.[8]

---

mistress: *DIB*, iii, 542–3. 6 Donnelly, 'Whiteboy movement', passim; idem, 'Hearts of Oak, Hearts of Steel', *Studia Hibernica*, 21 (1981), 8–22; Power, *Tipperary*, pp 175–6. 7 G.C. Lewis, *On local disturbances in Ireland...* (London, 1836), pp 3–19, 30; Maura Cronin, *Agrarian protest in Ireland, 1750–1960* (Dublin, 2012), pp 2–3, 9–11. 8 Froude, *English in Ireland*, i, 460; Lecky, *Eighteenth-century Ireland*, i, 362–4; Smyth, *Men of no property*, pp 35,

Yet the Connacht houghers were a long way from the Munster Whiteboys, not least because the target for their actions was different: the cattle and sheep of strangers. Nearly all the incidents reported relate to the maiming or killing of large herds of livestock, and while there were precedents for devastating attacks on cattle and especially sheep at times of political breakdown in the seventeenth century, major attacks on animals in the field were to prove very unusual in the eighteenth. There were admittedly some reports of cattle maiming by the early Whiteboys, but it was a minor part of their repertoire. And there is no evidence of large crowds in Connacht – except for the 'hundreds' who came to harvest animal carcasses – whereas the mobilization of large gangs became a central feature of early Whiteboyism, and there was a distinct sense of the theatrical in some of their actions. Then there is the question of leadership and control: the evidence, indirect and problematic as it is, suggests that the houghers' actions were connived at and probably directed by powerful local patrons (or their sons) rather than by lower-status tenants in whose defence the movement was purporting to act (although the speed at which the movement spread across six counties in the winter of 1711–12 does hint at excellent lines of social communication). The identity of Whiteboy leadership in 1761–2 is also uncertain, but there can be no doubt that the *coqs de village* and small-town craftsmen of south Tipperary and west Waterford played a far more prominent role in early Whiteboyism than did their Connacht precursors. And a further point of contrast: the Whiteboys left a powerful legacy and were remembered, but the houghers were forgotten: after 1714 there was no reported aftershock, no delayed recurrence, no memory of the wave of protest.[9]

The publication of the comprehensive *Proclamations of Ireland* in 2014 provides confirmation that no collective protest movement in the Irish countryside caught the attention of Dublin Castle for four decades after the demise of the houghers. However one episode predating 1761 did register in the privy council: the string of incidents that occurred along the Kildare/Meath border during the summer of 1753. These were centred on the neighbourhood of Kilcock and spread eastwards to Maynooth and Celbridge, precipitating three government proclamations in two months. The catalyst was said to have been the

---

43–4; S.J. Connolly, 'Law, order and popular protest in early eighteenth-century Ireland: the case of the houghers' in P.J. Corish (ed.), *Radicals, rebels and establishments: Historical Studies xv* (Belfast, 1985), pp 51–68; idem, 'The houghers: agrarian protest in early eighteenth-century Connacht' in C.H.E. Philpin (ed.), *Nationalism and popular protest in Ireland* (Oxford, 1987), pp 139–62; Neal Garnham, *The courts, crime and the criminal law in Ireland, 1692–1760* (Dublin, 1996), pp 193–6; James Kelly and M.A. Lyons (eds), *The proclamations of Ireland ...* (5 vols, Dublin, 2014), ii, 647–9, 672–3. The Irish act, 9 Anne, c.11, 'to prevent the maiming of cattle' was framed in 1710 with the specific purpose of halting the destruction of the cattle of those 'who are not ancient inhabitants of the baronies west of Galway city'. **9** *An apology for the clergy of Ireland in respect of their civil rights, especially as to agistment for dry and barren cattle* (Dublin, 1738), pp 8–9; Lecky, *Eighteenth-century Ireland*, i, 361–7; Connolly, 'Houghers', pp 139–61; idem, *Divided kingdom*, p. 300; Garnham, *Courts*, pp 193–6.

enclosure of part of the large public commons at Courtown, to the immediate south of Kilcock.[10] The episode came at a time of sharply rising land prices, but why should a town with 'a thriving aspect' twenty miles west of Dublin have been the cockpit for trouble? It was surrounded by some of the finest farmland in Leinster along the Rye Water, and had remained an enclave for cereal farming. It was noted (in the 1770s) that surprisingly large numbers of Kilcock townsmen were fully employed agricultural labourers, who presumably still owned some livestock. But the trigger remains a mystery.[11]

The protest had novel elements: 'proclamations' were posted up in neighbouring towns for several weeks summoning supporters to come out on Whit Monday to demolish ditches on the once-common land at Courtown. And on the day itself there was a public parade, with estimates of the crowd varying from 800 to 1,600, which 'marched in a military manner to the site with colours flying and a person with them playing on an hautboy'. There, the newspapers reported, 'they pull down the piers and hedges, burn the gates ... they go about laying the whole country under contribution'. When the owner of the disputed ground at Courtown rebuilt his ditches, these were demolished a second time, after which no less than five companies of foot and two troops of cavalry were sent from Dublin to scatter the levellers. Little more is known of them other than that the convicted leaders were sentenced to nothing worse than a public whipping. But two features of the episode stand out: the urban identity of the participants – they were clearly described as 'the mob of this town' by one Kilcock correspondent; and their focus on recapturing reputedly communal land (whatever the legalities of that claim), some of which had become gentry demesne; one attack was on the Celbridge demesne of Thomas Marlay, lord chief justice of the king's bench.[12]

Communal attacks on private enclosures were a thing of the distant past in eighteenth-century England, but there was one isolated episode in south-west

10 Kelly and Lyons (eds), *Proclamations*, iii, 416–17, 419–21. A commons beside the town of Kilcock appears on the Down Survey (http://downsurvey.tcd.ie), and 'Kilcock Common' was marked very prominently to the south and west of the town in John Noble and James Keenan's *County map of Kildare*, published in 1752. But by the time of the six-inch Ordnance Survey in 1837–8 the only sign of the Kilcock commons were two townland fragments – 'Commons West', which was a public race-course, and 'Commons South', where there were tell-tale signs of squatter housing [http://maps.osi.ie/publicviewer/#V1,688498,739718,5,7]. Cf. J.H. Andrews, 'The struggle for Ireland's public commons' in Patrick O'Flanagan, Paul Ferguson and Kevin Whelan (eds), *Rural Ireland: modernization and change, 1600–1900* (Cork, 1987), pp 1–23. 11 Charles Vallancey, *A report on the Grand Canal, or, southern line* (Dublin, 1771), p. 25; Thomas Campbell, *A philosophical survey of the south of Ireland, in a series of letters to John Watkinson, MD* (London, 1777), p. 292. Young noted of the Kilcock/Summerhill area in 1776 that 'here are few cottars [i.e. labourers] without a cow, and some of them two': Arthur Young, *A tour in Ireland* ... (2 vols, Dublin, 1780), i, 28. 12 *Faulkner's Dublin Journal* [henceforth *FDJ*,], 16 June, 7 July 1753; *London Evening Post* [henceforth *LEP*], 21–3, 28–30 June, 5–7, 10–12 July, 13–16 Oct. 1753; Kelly and Lyons (eds), *Proclamations*, iii, 416–17, 419–21; Garnham, *Courts*, p. 196. Kilcock and indeed Courtown itself became flashpoints in the

Scotland in 1724-5, which has elements both of the Connacht houghing campaign and of Kilcock. The 'Galloway Levellers', who became active across sixteen parishes overlooking the Solway Firth, had banded together to break down the walls, the 'dykes', enclosing huge 'cattle parks' that had been appearing there over the previous half century. These had been erected by local heritors (gentry) and their kin, many of whom had turned to store cattle production for the English market as a source of income in hard times. Initially much of the stock had been imported from Ireland, and several of the ranching heritors also had Ulster property. But with the closure of that trade they became breeders in their own right. Some of their new parks encroached on common grazing land, but mostly they colonized pre-existing tillage 'farmtouns'. Religious and political tensions specific to south-west Scotland were also present, and these seem to have sharpened the communal fears and economic resentments evident among small tenants and petty proprietors: the Levellers, drawn mainly from dissident Presbyterian communities across what had been the old heartland of Covenanting, made a particular point of attacking the parks of episcopalian and Catholic heritors (some of whom had strong Jacobite links). In Kirkcudbrightshire alone they marshalled more than a thousand men, hundreds of whom were armed with flintlocks. Some cattle were slaughtered, but the main activity remained the destruction of miles of stone walls, against which magistrates were powerless to act until they secured heavy military support (the Inniskilling Dragoons, as it happened). The army remained in the area for at least four months without halting the campaign, but there was only one major confrontation, and no more than one or two fatalities. Meanwhile the Levellers used the printing press to justify their actions and managed to secure political sympathy at the highest level. The crisis passed within a year and without creating martyrs. The most severe punishment meted out was transportation.[13]

When compared to Irish protest movements the Levellers seem tactically more astute, making full use of friendly patrons, disaffected clergy and parish-based structures (including the selection of 'captains'). There was talk of covenants and manifestoes. And seen from Edinburgh or London (where they attracted considerable publicity), they were a perplexing rather than an ominous lot. Their actions were never copied or repeated. That seems all the more remarkable given the profound structural changes under way in the countryside across lowland Scotland. But there are tantalizing parallels with the Kilcock levellers thirty years later: a large military presence was required to smother the

1798 rebellion: Seamus Cullen et al., *Fugitive warfare: 1798 in north Kildare* (Clane, 1998), pp 15-19, 57-60. 13 T.C. Smout, *A history of the Scottish people, 1560-1830* (London, 1972), pp 304-10; I.D. Whyte, *Scotland before the industrial revolution: an economic and social history, c.1050-c.1750* (London, 1995), p. 145; Alistair Livingston, 'The Galloway Levellers: a study of the origins, events and consequences of their actions' (MPhil, University of Glasgow, 2009), pp 30-1, 49-61, 69-79; Robert Dodgshon, 'The clearances and the transformation of the Scottish countryside' in T.M. Devine and Jenny Wormald (eds), *The Oxford handbook of*

protests in each case, yet there was no exemplary terror, and there is evidence in both episodes of a deliberately light touch in the manner of suppression. And despite growing social divisions between farmer and agricultural labourer in both societies, there was no subsequent expression of communal grievance (until, in the case of north Kildare, the 1790s, when agrarian and political grievances intersected).[14]

III

The Whiteboys of 1761–2 had therefore several precursors. So why was their impact and legacy so much greater? After all, their geographical reach was less than the houghers, a radius of thirty-five miles at most, and the duration of the first wave of incidents, about six months, was similar. The numbers openly involved were obviously greater; indeed the business of levelling walls and filling in ditches in a single day or night required huge communal participation. But Whiteboy crowds (from 100 to 600) were not so different from the numbers involved in the most serious urban food riots (such as in Belfast in 1756), the worst election scuffles, or perhaps some of the affrays with the revenue.[15]

Donnelly's history of Whiteboyism was, as we have noted, heavily dependent on newspaper evidence, which remains the richest source of detail. But there are some puzzling features about that evidence. If, as commentators subsequently maintained, the Munster levelling campaign began around November 1761, it is strange that no newspaper notice of what was happening appeared until the end of March 1762, after which time there was an abundance of reports, and in the London press some of these appeared in the first column of the front page.[16] The story, whatever it was, broke late. A second oddity is that commentary in the newspapers and monthly magazines chose to focus on incidents in the north-east corner of Cork and the Blackwater bend in west Waterford, rather less on south Tipperary, and very little on Limerick, whereas other, albeit more tentative, evidence suggests that activity in north Cork was late in coming and was less extensive than in the Golden Vale, the Maigue valley or along the corridor between the Galtees and Knockmealdowns. There may indeed be a link between the particular attention devoted to Cork and west Waterford and the delayed public commentary.

modern Scottish history (Oxford, 2012), pp 143–4. **14** In the case of Kilcock, the gaoler in Naas employed to whip those convicted only went through the motions; in Galloway, the army commander, having arrested some 300 levellers after a major confrontation, allowed all but twenty of his prisoners to escape before any legal process: *LEP*, 13–16 Oct. 1753; Livingston, 'Galloway Levellers', p. 83.   **15** Power, *Tipperary*, p. 178; Eoin Magennis, 'In search of the "moral economy": food scarcity in 1756–57 and the crowd' in Peter Jupp and Eoin Magennis (eds), *Crowds in Ireland, c.1720–1920* (Basingstoke, 2000), pp 198–207.   **16** For example: *LEP*, 21–3 Apr. 1762.

Here the political context becomes relevant. Five years into the Seven Years War, a major expansion of the military budget had been the top priority when the earl of Halifax and his ambitious chief secretary William Hamilton arrived at Dublin Castle in October 1761. Thereupon, in order to drum up parliamentary support for an increase in the Irish army establishment, Halifax quite deliberately chose to emphasize the risk of imminent French invasion, playing on fears among MPs already heightened by earlier invasion rumours in 1759 (that were not without foundation), and by Thurot's brief landing at Carrickfergus in 1760. Halifax did, however, appear to believe in the possibility of invasion and was concerned at the vulnerability of the south-west. By securing from parliament greater flexibility over the Irish military budget he won his point, and during the winter of 1761-2 unprecedented numbers of troops on the Irish establishment (over 2,000) were gathered in Cork for trans-shipment to America.[17] At such a juncture it was hardly 'paranoid' (as some have suggested) for Irish Protestants to be fearful lest the great conflict overseas be carried onto Irish soil, and that would mean Munster soil. Protestants in that province were far more sensitized to the dangers of Catholic *revanche* than their co-religionists in the capital, and they were decidedly unsettled by signs of a new Catholic assertiveness.[18]

This had been evident in the challenges within several towns and cities as to the legality of quarterage demanded by the craft guilds, which in Cork had culminated in a temporary victory for unfree Catholic craftsmen in 1758 and the humiliation of the city's mayor. Then came the hint of a veiled Catholic interest in several constituencies in the autumn general election in 1761, most notably in Thomas Mathew's campaign to take one of the seats for Co. Tipperary. As Thomas Power has demonstrated, Mathew's success in mobilizing the votes of freeholders of doubtful religious conformity had been greatly helped by out-of-door support that was unambiguously Catholic. And although his victory was overturned, the local aftershocks continued throughout the first cycle of Whiteboy activity.[19]

17 *St James' Chronicle or the British Evening Post* [henceforth *SJC*], 27-30 Mar. 1762; earl of Halifax to earl of Egremont, 29 Nov. 1761, and Egremont to Halifax, 5 Dec. 1761 (*Cal. HO papers, 1760-5*, pp 82, 84); Eoin Magennis, *The Irish political system, 1740-1765: the golden age of the undertakers* (Dublin, 2000), pp 158-62; A.P.W. Malcomson, *Nathaniel Clements: government and the governing elite in Ireland, 1725-75* (Dublin, 2005), pp 148-9. The duke of Bedford, Halifax's predecessor, had warned William Pitt in 1759 that Munster was 'so full of disaffected inhabitants that the enemy [on landing] would not be in want, either of supplies or provisions or succours and intelligence of any kind': Bedford to William Pitt, 22 Aug. 1759 (A.P.W. Malcomson (ed.), *Eighteenth-century Irish official papers in Great Britain: ii* (Belfast, 1990), p. 226). On Halifax's fears of invasion, see Halifax to Egremont, 18 Dec. 1761 (*Cal. HO papers, 1760-5*, p. 87). 18 On the supposed incidence of Protestant 'paranoia' and 'hysteria', see Donnelly, 'Whiteboy movement', 40, 54; Morley, 'George III, Queen Sive', 114; T.P. Power, 'Publishing and sectarian tension in South Munster in the 1760s', *ECI*, 19 (2004), 97; idem, 'Father Nicholas Sheehy (*c.*1728-1766)' in Gerard Moran (ed.), *Radical Irish priests, 1660-1970* (Dublin, 1998), p. 69. 19 F.H. Tuckey, *The county and city of Cork remembrancer*

Then, at the beginning of March 1762, it became known that Halifax's government was supporting two initiatives that would directly affect the status of Irish Catholics: first, the 'elegit' bill, a measure designed to remove ambiguity as to title on land mortgaged to Catholic lenders, and, second, the measure to raise five regiments to be officered and manned by Irish Catholics but to be paid for and commanded by the king of Portugal, albeit after their declaring due allegiance to George III. This news added to the fears of the fearful, and it played into the hands of those who sought to profit from displaying their true-blue Protestant credentials. Political opposition to both measures developed during March, but it only became publicly visible in early April. Viscount Boyle, son and heir of the ageing earl of Shannon and recently elected as an MP for Co. Cork, together with his older brother-in-law, the earl of Carrick, began to mobilize Munster Protestant opinion against these proposals. The Shannon estates were principally in east Cork, but the family's political power rested on their dominant influence in a string of boroughs across south Munster, including Youghal. Carrick's estates were in Kilkenny and east Tipperary, but his political standing, such as it was, depended on his alliance with the Boyles.[20]

Halifax had been informed of strange disturbances in the south of the country in January 1762; in early March the Co. Limerick gentry, at Halifax's invitation, conveyed their views to the Castle; and on 17 March the Irish privy council finally issued a proclamation against 'the levellers', referring specifically to events in Co. Limerick. There was no reference in the proclamation to any political dimension, but rumours were already circulating that the disturbances were directly connected to the war, that French money and French-trained military officers were involved, and that it related to some larger French plan.[21] The story grew and travelled, and by April even George III was giving credence to the idea. Halifax was remarkably slow to brief Whitehall against such an

---

(Cork, 1837), pp 137–8, 350–1; W.P. Burke, *History of Clonmel* (Clonmel, 1907), p. 366; Power, *Tipperary*, pp 248–51; David Dickson, *Old world colony: Cork and south Munster, 1630–1830* (Cork, 2005), pp 105, 276–7. Another unwelcome development was unprecedented recruitment in Cork city 'for the land and sea service', including both Protestant and Catholic: *Cork Journal*, 15 Feb. 1762; *Sleator's Public Gazette* [henceforth *SPG*], 27 Feb.–1 Mar. 1762. **20** *SPG*, 9–13 Mar. 1762; [Hibernicus], *Some reasons against raising an army of Roman Catholicks in Ireland. In a letter to a member of parliament* (Dublin, 1762); Halifax to Egremont, 18 Dec. 1761, [?6] Feb., 14 Mar. 1762 (*Cal. HO papers 1760–5*, pp 87, 154, 165); Egremont to Halifax, 26 Dec. 1761, 23 Feb 1762 (ibid., pp 91, 159); *Catholic Ireland in the eighteenth century: collected essays of Maureen Wall*, ed. Gerard O'Brien (Dublin, 1989), p. 119; Power, *Tipperary*, p. 255; L.M. Cullen, 'The Blackwater Catholics and County Cork society and politics in the eighteenth century' in Patrick O'Flanagan and C.G. Buttimer (eds), *Cork: history and society* (Dublin, 1993), pp 565–9; idem, 'Burke's Irish views and writings' in Ian Crowe (ed.), *Edmund Burke: his life and legacy* (Dublin, 1997), p. 64; Magennis, *Irish political system*, pp 164–8. On the Shannon electoral interest, see *Lord Shannon's letters to his son*, ed. Esther Hewitt (Belfast, 1982), pp xxxii–xli. **21** Jeremiah Jackson to Baron Carbery, 8 Mar. 1762 (Bisbrooke Hall, Uppingham, Rutland, Carbery papers, B/3/9); Lecky, *Eighteenth-century Ireland*, ii, 23; Kelly and Lyons (eds), *Proclamations*, iv, pt. 1, pp 27–8, 29–31.

assumption, but from the second week of April there was a government counter-offensive, first in College Green and soon evident in the press. Just why Halifax and Hamilton came out so strongly against the political interpretation remains unclear: did Edmund Burke, Hamilton's private secretary and confidant, play the pivotal role in elaborating a counter-argument within Dublin Castle, even to the extent of writing Hamilton's bravura Commons speech on 12 April? Burke's robust and very well-informed views as to what was happening in Munster and who was responsible are not in doubt, but his movements and his actions during that critical spring are almost completely unrecorded, and some of the most telling evidence comes from decades later. The case for Burke's decisive role is strong, but not conclusive. What is incontrovertible is that Halifax, having helped to sow Francophobic fears in November, was from late March championing the view that there was no subversive political 'contagion' spreading in Munster and that it was simply 'the blind effect of a rabble destitute of employment and wretched in condition'. He had his own political reasons for adopting such a posture. He was anxious to bring the parliamentary session to an uncontentious conclusion and to get back to the political hothouse of Westminster, where there was now intense friction at court and within the British cabinet over the future conduct of the war. Halifax had ambitions for senior office, and a murky French plot in Munster could quite plausibly have been used by his Westminster enemies against him.[22]

Meanwhile Boyle and Carrick, with or without prompting from London, managed to stir up a major storm in both houses of the Irish parliament, on the one hand orchestrating opposition to the Catholic regiments and demanding that Halifax present any relevant papers, on the other seeking a Commons committee to investigate 'the causes and progress of the subsisting Popish insurrection in the province of Munster' (this was appointed on 5 April). However, in the following weeks the government won tactical victories over Carrick in the Lords and Boyle in the Commons. Halifax reported emolliently on 8 April to the earl of Egremont, secretary of state for the southern department, that things were now settling down and that there was absolutely no French dimension, only to be sharply informed that Whitehall had heard otherwise from prominent Munster proprietors based in England: several had been briefed from the scene of action to the effect that 'French officers have been employed in disguise to corrupt the minds of the lower class'.[23] However, Halifax seems to have convinced cabinet

22 Charles Jenkinson, to [George Grenville], 13 Apr. 1762 (*The Grenville papers...*, ed. W.J. Smith (4 vols, London, 1852–3), i, 439–40); Halifax to Egremont, 17 Apr. 1762 (*Cal. HO papers 1760–5*, p. 174); *The correspondence of Edmund Burke*, ed. T.W. Copeland et al. (10 vols, Cambridge, 1958–78), i, 144; Conor Cruise O'Brien, *The great melody: a thematic biography and commented anthology of Edmund Burke* (London, 1992), pp 44–7; Power, *Tipperary*, pp 257, 267; Cullen, 'Burke's Irish views', pp 64–5; Magennis, *Irish political system*, p. 166.
23 Thomas Waite to Sir Robert Wilmot, 10 Apr. 1762, Wilmot to Waite, 5 [?*recte* 15] Apr. 1762 (PRONI, Wilmot papers, T/3019/4323–4); Jenkinson to Grenville, 13 Apr. 1762 (*Grenville*

allies in London of the correctness of his judgment, and departed Ireland at the beginning of May, ruffled but not, it seems, politically damaged by the turn of events. (Carrick and his Munster allies were to have better luck with Halifax's successor in the next parliament in 1763/4, but that is another story.)[24]

But why were there such efforts to influence opinion in London in April and May and what incentive, amidst a fast-moving war, was there to elaborate on the 'tumults and riots' in 'some distant quarters' (Halifax's wording) in the neighbouring kingdom? One reason was that the elegit bill was still alive, the 'heads' having been quietly assented to in both houses in Dublin and sent across the water before the opposition had been mobilized. One can assume that the focus of the Boyle group was now to secure its defeat in London at the British privy council stage of the process. Broadcasting news in London of a Munster plot, spiced with Jacobite embellishments, must have seemed a far more effective way of spiking the bill than making further parliamentary waves in Dublin. And the plan for the Catholic regiments, which lay outside the control of parliament, was still in the air in mid-April. But both initiatives were subsequently halted and later abandoned. The prospect of peace was certainly a factor changing political calculations in Whitehall, but the 'Munster insurrection' story seems to have played a part as well.[25]

The sequence of publications discussing events in Munster supports such a political reading. There were only four pamphlets directly commenting on early Whiteboyism, and none of these was printed or reprinted in Dublin, which is quite against the eighteenth-century norm; two were printed (without the printer being identified) in Cork, and two in London (see the Appendix, below). All rejected the Munster plot theory. Two (those appearing in 1766 and 1767) can be confidently attributed to John Curry, the Dublin-based physician and co-founder of the Catholic Committee, who courageously chose to print in Cork in the wake of the Sheehy trial when there was still danger of a further witch-hunt. But neither of the authors of the pamphlets appearing in 1762 are known: *An*

papers, i. 439–40); *LJI*, iv, 242–3; *CJI*, vii, 154, 161, 173; Halifax to Egremont, 8, 13, 17 Apr. 1762, Egremont to Halifax, 13, 27 Apr. 1762 (*Cal. HO papers 1760–65*, pp 171, 173–4, 175, 177); Matthew O'Conor, *The history of the Irish Catholics from the settlement in 1691...* (Dublin, 1813), pp 282–5; Lecky, *Eighteenth-century Ireland*, ii, 33–4; Cullen, 'Burke's Irish views', pp 64–5; Magennis, *Irish political system*, pp 166–8.   **24** Ld Carrick to ———, 28 May 1766 (*Corresp. of George III*, ed. Fortescue, i, 312); Cullen, 'Blackwater Catholics', pp 569–70; idem, 'Burke's Irish views', p. 66; Magennis, *Irish political system*, pp 166–8. The address presented by the Lords to Halifax at the end of the parliamentary session on 27 Apr. congratulated him on the 'wise and seasonable exertion of his power, in support of the civil magistracy, suppressing without opposition those accidental though very criminal gatherings of a rash and outrageous populace', the wording a reflection of the (temporary) eclipse of the 'insurrectionist' lobby: *LJI*, iv, 259–60.   **25** Waite to Wilmot, 17 Apr. 1762 (PRONI, T/3019/4327); *CJI*, vii, 173; *London Chronicle* [hereafter *LC*], 27–30 Mar. 1762; [John Curry], *A parallel between the pretended plot in 1762, and the forgery of Titus Oates in 1679. Being a sequel to the candid enquiry into the causes and ...*(Cork, 1767), p. 36; O'Conor, *Irish Catholics*, pp 291–3; O'Brien, *Maureen Wall essays*, p. 119; Magennis, *Irish political system*, pp

alarm to the unprejudiced and well-minded Protestants was an attempt to re-work Berkeley's *Querist*, and it appeared late in the summer (and it would be no surprise if a link between it and Curry's Catholic Committee co-founder Charles O'Conor can be established). However the authorship of *The late tumults in Ireland considered*, by 'An Englishman', published in London in the third week of April, is more intriguing. It had the mark of a seasoned pen. Moreover, within days large sections were reprinted in several London newspapers, and its argument was abstracted in the April issue of the Dublin edition of the *Gentleman's and London Magazine*.[26] It gave an unusually insightful analysis of the current stresses within rural Munster and their distant origins, discounted the plot theory and ridiculed some of the bombastic accounts, not least the reports of 'the petty services of the Youghal militia, as it is called' against the Whiteboys. It was scathing about rumour-mongers, instancing the widely publicized Whiteboy oath: 'any one that has common discernment may see this oath was made for them in Dublin, at least, if not on this side of the water'. A Munster rather than an English author seems likely, and one who was no friend of the Shannon interest. It chimed remarkably neatly with the Dublin Castle argument.[27]

Meanwhile newspaper coverage relating to the Whiteboys ran strongly through April and May, detailing a variety of incidents, army movements, arrests, the first judicial examinations, and the special commission in June where over a hundred cases were tried. But there was a sharp division of interpretation as to the meaning of events, some correspondents endorsing the plot theory and reporting on French officers, Spanish Franciscans, and shadowy figures with gilded swords and gold watches, others rubbishing such accounts and arguing that the movement was entirely driven by the material grievances of smallholders and was not exclusively Catholic (in Co. Limerick that was true, but not it seems elsewhere). Locally the *Cork Evening Post* (not extant for these months) seems to have been a major source for Jacobite rumours, but the Catholic-owned *Cork Journal* (for which some issues survive) walked an understandably discreet path. The commentary in *Faulkner's*, the most widely read Dublin paper, was unexceptional until 20 April when it launched an attack on those London newspapers that had been publishing 'lying letters from Dublin, and other parts of Ireland' that reported a Jacobite plot. In suggesting that such wild talk might affect London's continental diplomacy, Faulkner was either a very insightful observer of court politics, or else was taking a cue from his friends in Dublin

---

166–8; McBride, *Eighteenth-century Ireland*, p. 314.   **26** *Gentleman's and London Magazine* [hereafter *GLM*], 31 (1762), 198–200; *LC*, 22–4 Apr. 1762; *SJC*, 24–7 Apr. 1762; *Lloyd's Evening Post*, 7–10 May 1762; Power, *Tipperary*, pp 254–5; idem, 'Publishing and sectarian tension', pp 95–6.   **27** 'An Englishman', *The late tumults in Ireland considered* (London, 1762), p. 7. It is unlikely but not impossible that Burke may have been involved with this publication; the author was familiar both with Munster and with the promotion of the linen industry. Sir Richard Cox (1702–66), given his literary energy and enthusiasms, is another possibility, but

Castle.[28] Was there deliberate news management at work, in Dublin or London? It seems likely. One anonymous Dublin critic of the conspiracy theory closed his letter to the *London Chronicle*,

> is it not for some such purpose that all the dirt is thrown which infernal malice can invent, that some of it may stick to those destin'd victims, the Papists; by which false artful, and calumnious methods, the ancestors of those were forc'd into a rebellion, and by being so removed from any connection with the establish'd government, room was left for the fanatic wolves of those angry times, like the wolves in the fable, to devour the sheep and the dogs separately?[29]

IV

Word spread that Good Friday, 9 April 1762, was to be the day for the great rebellion and massacre, or perhaps it was to be Saturday night. The Whiteboys would rise and attack their Protestant neighbours. That was the rumour that spread across the south from Kilkenny to Kerry. There were ancient precedents for such moments of *grande peur*, but like them this one was entirely without foundation, even though Lord Carrick was still setting out details of the plot four years after the event. But the fact that isolated Protestant families rushed to urban safety reveals the sense of vulnerability that a great many of them felt during wartime, and insofar as the rumour was passed on by JPs and army officers 'sent by government express', it had a measure of credibility. The correspondence of Jeremiah Jackson, the Carbery agent living near Adare, Co. Limerick, reveals the very mixed feelings of one minor Protestant functionary at what was happening: acceptance that 'the poor people are grieved' and were attacking the right targets, yet fear of 'almost ... open rebellion. A few foreign troops, which it's believed they expect, would make it really so.' Whether the massacre rumour was started innocently – in reaction to the increasingly brazen behaviour of the Whiteboys – or was a sinister provocation, the Good Friday scare succeeded in ratcheting-up communal tensions in parts of Munster.[30]

---

his views on the 'plot' are not known.   **28** *Pue's Occurrences*, 30 Mar.–3 Apr., 6–10 Apr. 1762; *FDJ*, 17–20 Apr. 1762; *Cork Journal*, 22 Apr. 1762; *GLM*, 31 (1762), 308, 371–3; Power, 'Publishing and sectarian tension', pp 77, 90. On the *Cork Evening Post*'s political alignment, see 'Verax', 'To the editor of the *London Chronicle*, Dublin April 28' (*LC*, 6–8 May 1762). The most extensive coverage in London appears to have been in the *London Chronicle*: 8–10, 10–13, 17–20, 20–2 Apr., 6–8 May 1762. On Charles O'Conor's annoyance at the exaggerated accounts in the London press of the Whiteboys and the groundless speculative explanations, see O'Conor to John Curry, 4 June 1762 (O'Conor, *History of Irish Catholics*, pp 287–8). **29** 'Verax', 'Letter'; 'Fidelis', 'Extract of a letter from Dublin, May 20' (*LC*, 29 May–1 June 1762).   **30** Jackson to Carbery, 25, 30 Mar., 8, 24 Apr., 13 May, 21 July 1762 (Carbery papers, B/3/12-15, 20, 27); Thomas Hutchins to Revd Thomas Orpen, 7 Apr. 1762, Orpen to Arthur

At the beginning of April there were a series of huge public meetings in Cork city to establish 'an association for their defence against the attempts of private or foreign enemies', which attracted the signatures of some 2,000 Protestant citizens and led to the establishment of a new militia; subsequent meetings passed resolutions offering rewards for the arrest of Whiteboy leaders and, in particular, the author of an anonymous letter threatening to march 15,000 of Queen Sive's men into the city. At this time, and apparently on government orders, there were arms searches of their fellow Catholic citizens, which revealed almost nothing. In alarmed response a group of a 111 Cork city Catholics announced rewards for the capture of 'levellers', specifically for whoever 'acts as chief to said assemblies'.[31]

Meanwhile a counter-rumour spread through the districts where the Whiteboys were active: that the army was coming and that vast numbers of country people would now be rounded up for some terrible punishment, an alarm perhaps created by the early excesses of Lord Drogheda's regiment of light horse who arrived in Limerick on Palm Sunday, fresh from enforcing the revenue laws in Ulster, before marching into Tipperary and setting up camp at Clogheen. There were recurring, if vague, stories of mass flight, of an exodus to the hills or to neighbouring counties. But whatever about the behaviour of the soldiery, the range and intensity of the manhunt was unprecedented (and, as Cullen has noted, there was no other security operation carried out on this scale during the century, even in the 1790s, until the actual outbreak of rebellion). Through April and May 1762 the press carried incessant reports of small companies of soldiers, usually accompanied by local magistrates, fanning out in search parties from Cork, Clonmel and Limerick to arrest suspected Whiteboy leaders, and of their success in capturing small and sometimes quite large numbers of suspects.[32]

Herbert, 9 Apr. 1762 (NAI, Herbert papers, M1857); David Landes to Baron Brandon, 10 Apr. 1762 (TCD, Crosbie papers, MS 3821/248); 'Fidelis', 'Extract of a letter'; *An alarm to the unprejudiced and well-minded Protestants of Ireland* ... (Cork, 1762), pp 24–5; 'Short narrative of some disturbances', p. 24; Ld Carrick to [——], 28 May 1766 (*Corresp. of George III*, ed. Fortescue, i, 311–12); Donnelly, 'Whiteboy movement', p. 45; James Kelly, '"We were all to have been massacred": Irish Protestants and the experience of rebellion' in Thomas Bartlett et al. (eds), *1798: A bicentenary perspective* (Dublin, 2003), pp 315–16.   31 *LEP*, 10–13 Apr. 1762; *Cork Journal*, 12 Apr. 1762; *LC*, 20–2 Apr. 1762; *GLM*, 31 (1762), 373; Halifax to Egremont, 17 Apr. 1762 (*Cal. HO papers 1760–5*, p. 174); Power, 'Publishing and sectarian tension', 95, 97; Neal Garnham, *The militia in eighteenth-century Ireland: in defence of the Protestant interest* (Woodbridge, 2012), pp 73–4. On Edmund Burke's possible role in encouraging such an arms search to weaken insurrectionist theories: Cullen, 'Burke's Irish views', pp 64–5.   32 Waite to Wilmot, 15 Apr. 1762 (PRONI, T/3019/4325); Halifax to Egremont, 17 Apr. 1762 (*Cal. HO papers 1760–5*, p. 175); *GLM*, 31 (1762), 239, 373; *CJI*, vii, 173; 'Copy of a letter from Dublin, April 1' (*LC*, 10–13 Apr. 1762); *LC*, 17–20, 20–2, 24–7 Apr. 1762; *SJC*, 1–4, 18–20 May 1762; *Lloyd's Evening Post*, 19–21 Apr. 1762; [John Curry], *A candid enquiry into the causes and motives of the late riots in the province of Munster* ... (London, 1766); p. 23; Cullen, 'Blackwater Catholics', p. 568.

V

By that stage the Whiteboy movement, now nearly six months old, had undergone several stages of evolution. At least three phases can tentatively be suggested: a 'Kilcock' phase in the mid-autumn of 1761, when the issue was access to *public* commons from which town-based craft workers and village-based labourers were excluded after these had been 'enclosed by neighbouring gentlemen', thereby contributing to a shortage of land for potato cultivation and for grazing their few beasts. Edmund Burke's information was that it was in and around Kilmallock, Co. Limerick, that the first protests, very similar to the Kilcock affair, had been the catalyst, encouraged by an eccentric Protestant attorney, William Fant. It seems that they then spread to the hill village of Kilfinane and around the edge of the Galtees to the small towns of Clogheen and Ballyporeen, both of them worsted-spinning centres hosting clusters of combers and 'clothiers' who put out large volumes of wool for spinning within their district. One of the Whiteboy captains who narrowly avoided punishment was James Hyland, a big Clogheen clothier. And the parish priest in that parish was the socially well-connected but 'giddy and officious' Nicholas Sheehy, 'with a quixotic cast of mind' (in John Curry's judgment), who was at least a passive supporter of local protest from an early stage.[33]

The second phase had begun by New Year 1762, as the agitation against recent enclosure moved from public to private commons and from predominantly town- and village-based protests to actions by cottiers and partnership tenants and under-tenants across south Tipperary and east Limerick, reaching Mitchelstown and the great Kingston estate. Two decades previously these cottier/smallholders, hanging on in what were predominantly ranching districts, had lived through the 1740–1 famine that had been particularly destructive in the region. Edward Willes commented on the extreme poverty of lowland Tipperary as he journeyed through it in 1760, but by then the cottier smallholders on the poorer soils had begun to improve their circumstances, rearing cattle on the more marginal soils in what was mainly a zone of very fine grassland. Most cottiers probably held annual tenancies, but the lease-holders among them were likely to be active reclaimers, progressively breaking in the coarser soils through potato cultivation.[34]

---

33 'Copy of a letter from Dublin, April 1'; *LC*, 20–2 Apr. 1762; *LEP*, 13–15 Apr. 1762; Ld Chief Justice Aston to William Hamilton, 24 June 1762, and 'An unfinished paper of Mr Burke's relative to the disturbances in Ireland' (*The works and correspondence of the rt. hon. Edmund Burke*, ed. Charles William, Earl Fitzwilliam and Sir Richard Bourke (2nd ed., 4 vols, London, 1852), i, 20, 23); Madden, *United Irishmen*, pp 34, 36; Lecky, *Eighteenth-century Ireland*, ii, 12–13; Burke, *Clonmel*, pp 365, 368–9; Donnelly, 'Whiteboy movement', 43; Power, *Tipperary*, pp 184, 261–2; idem, 'Nicholas Sheehy', pp 62–78. Public commons existed close to Kilmallock and Kilfinane at the time of the Down Survey, but do not appear on the 1st edition of the six-inch Ordnance Survey maps (http://downsurvey.tcd.ie; http://maps.osi.ie/publicviewer/#V1,560960,627783,5,7). **34** Young, *Tour in Ireland*, ii, 141–2; *The letters of*

Cottier cattle depended disproportionately on 'common', the boggy, rocky or high-altitude ground once deemed of so little value (other than for turf-cutting or summer grazing) that it carried no quit rent and was left as a common space to be shared between the residents of the contiguous townlands. But with rent levels rising from the late 1740s, the value of once marginal land was being re-priced, reflecting the growth of both beef and butter prices. The early stages of the Seven Years War had been highly profitable for beef exporters, and some of the benefits trickled down to the small players selling store cattle to the big graziers, who fattened bullocks for the slaughterhouses in Cork. Cattle prices had taken a severe jolt late in 1761, but a more critical problem in 1762 was grass: a dry spring was followed by a near rainless summer throughout Munster.[35]

Some of the big cattlemen and sheep-masters had been encroaching on private commons for decades, draining and ditching it. In so doing they had not breached the terms of their leases; indeed they may well have received encouragement from landlords or estate agents so to do. Yet for the under-tenants affected, the rolling back of common land could mean a drastic loss of a customary perquisite at a time when the value of that perquisite was rising. It seems that only a small number of ranching tenants and a smaller number of landowners in south-west Tipperary (those with large deer-parks) were targeted in these early months, and it is possible that these were the most energetic enclosers.[36]

Levelling spread through the countryside and became a great night-time activity – 'five hundred men, some say eight hundred' was one Co. Limerick estimate – implying group discipline and the general, perhaps universal, adoption of white outer clothing. Oaths of association may already have been there in the first phase but it is more likely that they only became universal as more ambitious levelling work drew in greater numbers of volunteers and strangers. Oath-taking may have been inspired by a near-universal familiarity with formal and informal judicial processes (and, as we have seen, there may even have been an earlier oath of secrecy used among the houghers), but alternatively the template for the Whiteboy oath may have been the secret oath

---

the Lord Chief Baron Edward Willes to the earl of Warwick, 1757–1762, ed. James Kelly (Aberystwyth, 1990), p. 52; David Dickson, *Arctic Ireland* ... (Belfast, 1997), pp 67–9. The distinction between public and private commons was missed in the otherwise well-informed discussion of commonage in 'An enquiry into the causes of the outrages, committed by the *Levellers* or *White-boys*, in the province of Munster', *Dublin Magazine*, Apr. 1763, p. 196. **35** Jackson to Carbery, 18 Nov. 1761 (Carbery papers, B/2/19); *LC*, 15–17 July 1762; John Rutty, *A chronological history of the weather and seasons, and of the prevailing diseases in Dublin* ... (London, 1770), pp 268–71; Tuckey, *Cork remembrancer*, p. 139; Dickson, *Old world colony*, pp 195, 218–23, 648.   **36** Power, *Tipperary*, pp 174–7, 184–5. There was also the suggestion that some tenants who had failed to secure a renewal of their leases were encouraging former under-tenants and cottiers to make trouble against new tenants: 'Letter from Dublin, April 1'. On Arthur Young's active management of reclamation and enclosure on the southern flank of the Galtees while he was agent of the Kingsborough estate in the late 1770s, see Young, *Tour*

of association used by journeymen in the larger towns in their wage-protecting societies or 'combinations' (and the Whiteboy movement was sometimes referred to as a 'society'); such oaths promised dire consequences for those who betrayed secret knowledge.[37] There was, however, at least one novel element in the Whiteboy oath, however much it may have been embellished in the retelling: fealty to Queen Sive [*recte* Saedhbh], the fictive counter-symbol to royal authority. She may have been invoked in jest to begin with, but this practice was represented in hostile reports as something quite sinister. In Co. Limerick, the fictive name of Joan Meskel, or Shevaun, had appeared on warning notices, but Sive was more enduring. She was, however, a late appearance, chiefly associated with the third evolutionary stage of the movement.[38]

That stage came by the end of January 1762 as Whiteboyism spread south across the Knockmealdowns to the Blackwater and Bride valleys and to the upland communities overlooking them. This was firmly dairying country, which meant the survival of far greater numbers of small stock-holding partnership farmers than in Co. Tipperary, some of them renting their cows but most owning their dairy-herds. The constant search for grass was at least as compelling as in Tipperary, but the range of grievances was now wider, touching on tithe, lease renewal, disputed debts, and the demolition of pounds and mills. And with their greater numbers they had stronger collective capacity to organize. Furthermore, as butter producers who went to market they had a more intimate knowledge of the big city than did Tipperary smallholders, although even here intermediaries associated with the yarn trade, like Dennis Conner of Tallow, played a leading role. The Waterford author of the 'Short narrative' [Appendix, no. 6] provided for his London readers startling, if highly coloured, evidence as to the level of Whiteboy organization, and some unusual details, claiming that in west Waterford 'at least 30,000 perches of fences' – some 120 miles – had been levelled between January and April, and he described how the movement had grown from thrice-weekly gatherings and specific levelling assignments to the

in Ireland, ii, app., pp 69–71. 37 Jackson to Carbery, 8 Mar. 1762 (Carbery papers, B/3/9); 'The statement of Lawrence Geghane of Borrisoleigh, 11 March 1763' (PRONI, T/3019/4533); *LC*, 4–6 May 1762; Burke, *Clonmel*, p. 363; Donnelly, 'Whiteboy movement', 26–7, 39; Power, *Tipperary*, pp 184, 215; McBride, *Eighteenth-century Ireland*, p. 315. A letter sent to Dublin Castle from Co. Tipperary 'as early as January 1762' was noted by Lecky in the then Public Record Office of Ireland; the writer maintained that 'all the able young fellows from Clonmel to Mitchelstown' frequently assembled at night, seizing horses, levelling and issuing threatening letters; they called themselves 'fairies' (not it seems Whiteboys) and imposed regulations on farmers who employed servants and shepherds (Lecky, *Eighteenth-century Ireland*, ii, p. 23). In the 'Letter from Dublin, April 1', it was stated the Munster rioters had 'at first called themselves Fairies, because they appeared at night only, and ... departed before day-light. They afterwards took the name Levellers, and declared they would restore the property of the poor, oblige landlords to set their lands on reasonable terms, and reduce the price of meat and grain' (*LC*, 10–13 Apr. 1762). The terms 'fearraidhes' had been used to describe the gangs of retainers employed by Daniel Mahony in south Kerry in the 1720s (M.A. Hickson, *Selections from old Kerry records*, ser. 2 (London, 1874), pp 157–9, 181).

situation in March when local Whiteboys were engaging in public display and had become 'so audacious as to march at night with music playing disaffected and treasonable tunes, [and to] give regular orders of command, draw up in form and fire shots', which culminated in a series of night-time public marches 'invading' Lismore, Tallow and Cappoquin, to steal horses and liberate prisoners in the name of the fictive queen.[39]

The response of senior Catholic clergy to such provocative behaviour was cautious in the extreme. Bishop Kearney of Limerick came out early with a pastoral on 8 March that warned about meetings of levellers, 'who if I am rightly informed make incursions into this district and county, particularly into Kilfinen [sic]', turning up lea ground, houghing cattle and writing 'menacing letters', and noting that 'gentlemen of our communion, who [have] exerted themselves in inveighing against their conduct, have not been free of their menaces'. But three weeks later, Bishop John O'Brien of Cloyne, with a diocese that straddled the newly disturbed districts in north-east Cork, issued a long pastoral and noted how 'profligate disturbers of peace and tranquillity' from adjoining counties had now infested parishes 'on the frontiers' and were gaining ground every day; he rejected a plea from priests in these areas to delay imposing 'spiritual penalties' until similar sanctions were applied in neighbouring dioceses. The shrill denunciation gives the impression of clerical alarm faced by broad communal support for the 'multitude of dissolute night walkers'. A few days later Bishop Walsh of Cork diocese instructed his clergy to 'excite their respective congregations to the just abhorrence of the infamous practices of the persons called Levellers'. But, despite claims that 'Popish landholders' had been the first to suffer from Whiteboy activity, there were signs that ancestral tensions were being stirred up as Whiteboy companies paraded southwards to within sight of Youghal, a 'true-blue' town with an embattled sense of Protestant vulnerability.[40]

---

38 One Cork correspondent claimed that Sive 'was a woman who, in the last rebellion, headed a party of rebels, and defended a castle against the English until she was killed', a reference perhaps to Lady Roche who had held out at Castle Widenham (in the next parish to Glanworth) before being captured and hanged in 1652 (*LEP*, 13–15 Apr. 1762). On 'Joan Meskell', see Jackson to Carbery, 25 Mar., 21 July 1762 (Carbery papers, B/3/12). Cf. Máirín Nic Eoin, 'Secrets and disguises? Caitlín Ní Uallacháin and other female personages in eighteenth-century Irish political poetry', *ECI*, 11 (1996), 44–5.   39 'A succinct account of a set of miscreants in the counties of Waterford, Cork, Limerick, and Tipperary, called Bougheleen Bawins (i.e., White Boys) ...' (*LC*, 10–13 Apr. 1762); *LC*, 17–20 Apr. 1762; 'A short narrative of some disturbances which happened in the counties of Limerick, Cork, Tipperary and Waterford, from the months [sic] of November 1761 to the month of April 1762' ('The Whiteboys in 1762: a contemporary account', ed. James Kelly, *Cork Hist. and Arch. Soc. Jnl*, 94 (1989), 22–6); Lecky, *Eighteenth-century Ireland*, ii, 22; Donnelly, 'Whiteboy movement', 41; Dickson, *Old world colony*, pp 220–3. In the upland parish of Ardagh north of Youghal, 'a notorious Leveller who had attested the greatest part of [the] parish' was convicted of 'breaking the enclosures of Mr William Hall ... in company with about 60 levellers' and jailed for two years: *LC*, 24–7 Apr., 19–22 June 1762.   40 *Cork Journal*, 15 Feb., 25 Mar. 1762; *SPG*, 23–7 Mar. 1762; *LC*, 8–10, 17–20 Apr. 1762; 'Verax', 'To the editor of the *London*

It was also evident in Lismore, where on 4 June, his Majesty's birthday, 'the effigy of Queen Sive was burned ... and great rejoicings were made there on that occasion'.[41]

Then came the controversial judicial aftermath. Commencing in late April, government law officers toured the four affected counties to assess the evidence against the five hundred or so prisoners held in the jails in Clonmel, Limerick, Cork and Waterford. By the time they had finished examining the vast number held in the Cork county gaol, it became clear that they were not going to bring charges of 'rebellious practices' or treason against anyone; thirty of the Cork prisoners who had been originally arrested by the Youghal militia around Tallow were sent by ship back to Waterford to face trial, but 'as they passed the Exchange they huzza'd, and behaved with the utmost insolence'. Across the four counties it seems that more than two-thirds of those who had been arrested for Whiteboy activity were released.[42] One of the law officers, Godfrey Lill, MP for Fore (Co. Westmeath), was a close ally of Anthony Malone, who with the English-trained Lord Chief Justice Aston had been one of the regular assize judges on the Munster circuit; the latter were now appointed to conduct a special commission in each of the four counties. Neither the ruggedly independent-minded Malone nor the younger Aston was in any way beholden to the political heavyweights in the province.[43] They conducted the commission over three weeks in June, after which most of the remaining prisoners were released without charge, a small number were imprisoned, and capital verdicts were given against two in Limerick, three in Cork, none in Clonmel and seven in Waterford, all for specific property crimes (arson and cattle maiming), but in no case for treason – or for levelling ditches. Although nothing appeared in print to suggest it, the grand juries of Cork and Waterford were disconcerted at the outcome, and 'at both places spoke their minds very freely to the judges, to no purpose'.[44] Aston, in his subsequent private report to Hamilton, was adamant that there had been no political tincture to the protests and that their oath was merely 'to be true to one another, and not to discover what was done, or by whom', adding 'that when an oath was imposed on any, it was to be true to Sive and her children; and not to discover any of the Whiteboys, her children'. The 'dying words' of Darby Browne, one of the Waterford men executed, was the only statement from a

---

Chronicle, Dublin, April 28' (*LC*, 6–8 May 1762); [Viscount Taaffe], *Observations upon the affairs of Ireland examined and confuted...* (Dublin, 1767), pp 20–1; O'Conor, *History of Irish Catholics*, app., pp xxvi–xxix. On the delay by the privy council in issuing proclamations, Halifax observed in mid-April that 'it was not until a short time ago that a single affidavit could be procured of any outrage that had been committed, on which a proclamation could be grounded': Halifax to Egremont, 17 Apr. 1762 (*Cal. HO papers 1760–5*, p. 175).   41 *SPG*, 12–15 June 1762.   42 *FDJ*, 20–4 Apr. 1762; *LC*, 22–4 Apr. 1762; *Pue's Occurrences*, 18–22 May 1762; *Gazetteer and London Daily Advertiser*, 1 June 1762.   43 *SPG*, 1–16 Feb. 1762; *GLM*, 31 (1762), p. 308; Cullen, 'Burke's Irish views', pp 66–7.   44 Jackson to Carbery, 21 July 1762 (Carbery papers, B/3/27); *GLM*, 31 (1762), 369–71; Cullen, 'Burke's Irish views',

condemned Whiteboy to emerge, and it was published without comment in both Irish and English newspapers. It said publicly what Aston confirmed privately, and its chaste account set out how, as a small cattle-owning tenant, he had become involved at Candlemas. With its simple explanation of how a Whiteboy unit was entirely innocent of political intent and how it drew heavily on traditional associational culture (specifically the Mayboys), Browne's statement has justly become famous.[45]

Browne and those convicted with him were executed far from their native parish at the gallows outside Waterford city, with little if any ceremony. The three Cork Whiteboys received very different treatment. The specific charges against two of them related to a great Whiteboy assembly organized near Glanworth in late March where a mock trial of the horse of an unpopular local JP had been conducted and the creature sentenced and killed; Robert Stackpole, a Whiteboy captain on whom had been found 'a long list of names', was charged with being master of ceremonies, and Pierce Moore, a tiler, for playing a fiddle during the proceedings, together with Pierce Bailey, a mason, for burglary. That they were major figures in levelling escapades in north Cork seems likely, but the charges brought against Stackpole and Moore were bizarrely inconsequential. Nevertheless the trio were sentenced to be hanged in their home parishes in north-east Cork. Moore and Bailey nearly escaped during their post-trial detention, and Stackpole had made an abortive effort to have a statement of his case published by a journeyman printer. A senior city priest, Father Standish Barry, tended to them before they were brought in two hackney chairs to their places of execution – Mitchelstown, Fermoy and Glanworth – attended by a huge convoy: some 325 soldiers, plus Emmanuel Pigott's newly embodied city militia of 50 gentlemen. Contemporary accounts suggest a theatrical display of local Protestant intent and an implied protest at 'the great lenity shown by the judges'. Perhaps the strangest feature was the decision by those in charge to place white shirts on each prisoner at the gallows.[46]

The elaborate choreography of these executions in north Cork must have heightened their shocking effect. Yet Curry, Madden and many later historians have been understandably mesmerized by the fate of Father Sheehy and his co-

---

p. 66; Power, 'Nicholas Sheehy', p. 69. The possibly apocryphal story that Aston and Malone were feted by crowds along the road 'for above ten miles' after they left Clonmel on their return to Dublin was first recorded in William Crawford, *The history of Ireland* (2 vols, Strabane, 1783), ii, 316–19.   **45** Darby Browne's declaration appeared (inter alia) in *GLM*, 31 (1762), 436–7; *LC*, 20–2 July 1762; *Pue's Occurrences*, 10–13 July 1762. Cf. Ld Chief Justice Aston to William Hamilton, 24 June 1762 (*Works and correspondence of Burke*, ed. Fitzwilliam and Bourke, i, 20–1). On the production of a false 'dying declaration' by the Limerick Whiteboy John Banyard, see *Cork Journal*, 24 June 1762.   **46** Waite to Wilmot, 22 June 1762 (PRONI, T/3019/4346); *GLM*, 31 (1762), pp 37–41; *LC*, 1–4 May, 26–9 June, 1–3, 3–6 July 1762; *Lloyd's Evening Post*, 23–6 Apr., 25–8 June 1762; *LEP*, 6–8 May, 26–9 June 1762; Tuckey, *Cork remembrancer*, p. 351; Donnelly, 'Whiteboy movement', 47; Power, *Tipperary*, p. 258. On Pierce Bailey's reported rebuttal that he was a Protestant, see *Lloyd's Evening Post*,

accused in 1766, ignoring these earlier instances of exemplary retribution. Little is known of the social status of Stackpole or his friends but it is most unlikely that they had gentry connexions, unlike Father Sheehy and the trio who were executed in Clogheen in front of 'several thousand spectators' in 1766.[47] Whether the Cork victims became instant heroes in death, as happened with Sheehy, is not recorded. But Abraham Devonsheir, the Cork county sheriff, in choosing to stage such powerful judicial theatre near the victims' homesteads (and not far from his own Palladian *dacha*) made a signal contribution in fashioning the white shirt as a formal icon of protest. Neither Devonsheir and his allies, nor the notorious clique of magistrates in Tipperary that four years later pinned charges of treason on innocent Catholic gentry, can be credited with inventing 'Whiteboyism', but by politicising the phenomenon they managed to invest it with a potency that had previously existed only in their imaginings.[48]

VI

Charles Tilly's comparative study of 'contentious performances' may offer a useful way of reassessing the longer story, an approach which he used to examine the evolution of popular protest in England from the 1750s (and tried with less success to apply to Ireland). Following Tilly, we can see that the first levellers in Tipperary inherited, borrowed and adapted a repertoire of actions and symbols to articulate their grievances, but as with other episodes of social protest they acted using a fairly narrow range of props. Yet, as Tilly has argued, every performance of social protest has its own character, reflecting both the multiple choices of protagonists as to which elements of the repertoire to use and the type of response chosen by their antagonists, whether local or external; both have agency. In 1761 there were, as we have seen, precedents for neighbourhood groups going about and demolishing walls and ditches, maiming livestock and cutting down ornamental trees. However, there were no rural precedents for communal oath-taking, mass meetings at night, the universal use of uniforms, mock trials, threatening letters, disciplined marches, or the discharge of *feux-de-joie*. Yet these were all adaptations of existing social or recreational practices, or were mimicking the formal processes of civil or military authority. And within this repertoire there were some politically charged symbols: it should come as no surprise if there were many Jacobite allusions amidst the badinage and melody-making evident at the bigger Whiteboy gatherings, allusions which outsiders

23–5 June 1762. 47 *Cork Journal*, 5 May 1766; Power, 'Nicholas Sheehy', p. 76. 48 Ian McBride was the first to highlight these Cork executions and to argue that early Whiteboyism was intensely political, albeit in terms of local power relations: *Eighteenth-century Ireland*, pp 312–13, 316–17. Cf. Madden, *United Irishmen*, pp 38–87; Power, *Tipperary*, pp 260–6. On Abraham Devonsheir and his links with the Shannon interest, see Edith Mary Johnston-Liik, *History of the Irish parliament* (6 vols, Belfast, 2002), iv, 53–4.

could misjudge, or choose to misjudge. Tilly warned against looking for epochal shifts and revolutionary changes of script in the history of such contentious episodes. Perhaps if there were to be a fuller audit of such incidents across eighteenth- and early nineteenth-century Ireland, it might be possible to determine when and where there were critical innovations in the repertoire of protest-and-response and critical adaptations in performance routines. But for the moment it seems reasonable to conclude that 1762 was indeed one such instance when the scripts were changed, thanks to all the players who became involved.[49]

APPENDIX

A check-list of contemporary essays, memoranda and pamphlets relating to the Whiteboys, 1762–3 (published and unpublished), in likely order of composition and/or appearance

1 [Hibernicus], *Some reasons against raising an army of Roman Catholicks in Ireland. In a letter to a member of parliament* (Dublin, 1762).[50]
2 'Copy of a letter from Dublin, April 1' (*London Chronicle*, 10–13 Apr. 1762).
3 'A succinct account of a set of miscreants in the counties of Waterford, Cork, Limerick, and Tipperary, called *Bougheleen Bawins* (i.e. White Boys). Being an extract of a letter from a gentleman residing in Youghall to his son in London' (*London Chronicle*, 10–13 Apr. 1762, and subsequently in *Gentleman's Magazine and Historical Review*, 32 ([Apr.] 1762), 182–3).
4 'An Englishman', *The late tumults in Ireland considered, and the true causes of them impartially pointed out with their respective remedies. Together with some hints towards repeopling the deserted provinces of that kingdom, and employing the poor* (London, 1762).[51]
5 'Verax', 'To the editor of the *London Chronicle*, Dublin April 28' (*London Chronicle*, 6–8 May 1762).
6 'A short narrative of some disturbances which happened in the counties of Limerick, Cork, Tipperary and Waterford, from the months [sic] of November 1761 to the month of April 1762' (published as 'The Whiteboys in 1762: a contemporary account', ed. James Kelly, in *Cork Hist. and Arch. Soc. Jnl*, 94 (1989), 19–26).[52]

---

49 Charles Tilly, *Contentious performances* (Cambridge, 2008), pp 4–5, 14, 62–73, 159–60, 168–73. Cf. Donnelly, 'Whiteboy movement', 29–30; Power, *Tipperary*, p. 179. I am very grateful to James Kelly, Jim Livesey and Eoin Magennis for comments and helpful suggestions along the way. 50 Provenanced and dated 'Clonmell, 7 March 1762'. 51 Reported in the *London Chronicle*, 22–4 Apr. 1762 as being 'published on this day'. Cf. *St James Chronicle*, 24–7 Apr. 1762; *LEP*, 7–10 May 1762. 52 On the possibility that Sir Richard Musgrave's father was

7 'Fidelis', 'Extract of a letter from Dublin, May 20' (*London Chronicle*, 29 May–1 June 1762).

8 '"Letter from Cork", 25 May 1762', reprinted from the *Cork Evening Post* [not extant] ([Exshaw's] *Gentleman's and London Magazine and Monthly Chronologer* [Dublin], xxxi (1762), pp 371–3).

9 'Journal of the proceedings at the Assizes for the trials of the Levellers, or White Boys' ([Exshaw's] *Gentleman's and London Magazine and Monthly Chronologer* (Dublin), 31 (1762), 369–71).

10 *An alarm to the unprejudiced and well-minded Protestants of Ireland: Or, Seasonable queries upon the rise, danger, and tendency, of the White-Boys* (Cork, 1762).

11 M.S. Esq., 'An enquiry into the causes of the outrages, committed by the *Levellers* or *White-boys*, in the province of Munster' (*Dublin Magazine*, Apr. 1763, pp 193–200).

12 'Momoniensis', 'Remarks on a piece, entitled, "An enquiry into the causes of the outrages, committed by the *Levellers* or *White-boys*, in the province of Munster. By M.S. Esq"' (*Dublin Magazine*, June 1763, pp 366–8 ['reprinted from the *Cork Journal*']).

13 Letter from Lord Carrick to ——, 28 May 1766 (published in *The correspondence of King George the third from 1760 to December 1783...*, ed. Sir John Fortescue (6 vols, London, 1927–8), i, 310–20).

14 [John Curry], *A candid enquiry into the causes and motives of the late riots in the province of Munster; together with a brief narrative of the proceedings against these rioters, anno 1766. In a letter to a noble lord in England* (London, 1766); (2nd ed., London, 1766); ([? 3rd ed.], London, 1767).

15 [John Curry], *A parallel between the pretended plot in 1762, and the forgery of Titus Oates in 1679. Being a sequel to the candid enquiry into the causes and motives of the late riots ...* (Cork, 1767).

16 'An unfinished paper of Mr Burke's relative to the disturbances in Ireland at the beginning of the reign of George the third' (*The works and correspondence of the rt. hon. Edmund Burke*, ed. Charles William, Earl Fitzwilliam and Sir Richard Bourke (2nd ed., 4 vols, London, 1852), i, 21–3).

17 Revd John Hewetson, 'Account of the Whiteboys' (Thomas Bartlett (ed.), 'An account of the Whiteboys from the 1790s', in *Tipperary Hist. Jnl*, [iv] (1991), pp 140–7).

the author, see James Kelly, *Sir Richard Musgrave, 1746–1818: ultra-protestant ideologue* (Dublin, 2009), p. 28.

'Ravaging houses of ill fame':[1] popular riot and public sanction in eighteenth-century Ireland

JAMES KELLY

On Tuesday and Wednesday, 10–11 May 1768, the city of Dublin was plunged into 'general consternation'[2] by an outburst of riotous violence that resulted in 'several' deaths and the destruction of some forty houses.[3] The immediate cause was a 'quarrel in Smock Alley' on 10 May as a result of which Denis Callan, a butcher from Ormond Market, forfeited his life. According to the coroner's inquest, held on the same day, he was murdered by 'persons unknown'. In ordinary circumstances, Callan's demise would have excited little or no notice outside his immediate circle of friends and family.[4] However, his murder possessed a number of features that distinguished it from the run-of-the-mill unexplained and ill-documented deaths that routinely featured in the pithy reports that were the stock-in-trade of eighteenth-century newspapers. First of all, he was 'murdered in a brothel', and while this was not unprecedented, it was omitted in the initial reports, which focused on the fact that 'the deceased has left a wife with five children, who are reduced to the most affecting distress by this shocking murder'. And second, though Callan's employment was acknowledged, no reference was made to the fact that the butchers of Ormond Market were the main constituent of one of the city's most powerful 'factions' – the Ormond Boys – whose long and ongoing feud with the city's other major faction, the Liberty Boys, was currently in one of its active phases, or that Callan had 'formerly received the punishment of the laws for riotous offences'.[5] The imputation, overt in a later commentary on events, from which this detail derives, is that Callan was a member of the Ormond Boys, and while this can neither be confirmed not corroborated, it chimes with the information in one of the initial accounts that the 'numerous mob' that 'associated for the purpose of

---

1 *Freeman's Journal* (henceforth *FJ*), 14 May 1768. 2 Ibid., 24 May 1768. 3 The 1768 riots have not passed unnoticed. They are mentioned briefly by Patrick Fagan (*The second city: portrait of Dublin, 1700–1760* (Dublin, 1986), p. 214); by Martyn Powell (*The politics of consumption in eighteenth-century Ireland* (Basingstoke, 2005), pp 221–2); and by David Fleming ('Public attitudes to prostitution in eighteenth-century Ireland', *IESH*, 32 (2005), 13). Both Powell and Fleming engage with the episode in the context of a broader exploration of attitudes towards prostitution, while Fagan's fleeting reference is presented in the context of a brief survey of 'lowlife' in eighteenth-century Dublin. 4 See Robert Munter, *The history of the Irish newspaper, 1685–1760* (Cambridge, 1967), passim. 5 James Kelly, *The Liberty and Ormond Boys: factional riot in eighteenth-century Dublin* (Dublin, 2005), pp 41–4; *FJ*, 24 May 1768.

84

ravaging houses of ill fame in this city and suburbs' on 10–11 May was organized.[6]

It was only later also that it emerged that Callan had gone to the brothel in Smock Alley of his own volition on Tuesday morning, and 'falling into bad company, was murdered'. It was not clear to the author possessed of this pertinent nugget of information 'who was the aggressor' in the altercation that led to Callan's death, or who inflicted the fatal injury, but the indication that 'several persons ... of both sexes' were taken up 'on suspicion of being concerned in this atrocious offence' cautions against assuming, as many contemporaries appear to have done, that it was one of the sex workers in the establishment.[7] In practice, it mattered little to the generality of Ormond Boys. They were so conditioned by the culture of violence intrinsic to faction, and by the tradition of popular sanction that deemed brothels a legitimate target when abuses were committed within their walls, that, provoked by 'a just abhorrence' of the manner in which their comrade had fallen, 'they immediately assembled themselves [and] repaired to' Smock Alley in order to make plain their displeasure at events.

What followed was not, as this suggests and the reports of what ensued confirm, an inchoate or directionless act of revenge; the Ormond Boys (like all factions) possessed a cadre of leaders who were well schooled in the practicalities of organizing sorties (albeit on other factions usually), and knowledgeable in the art of marshalling their ranks. They were thus able at short notice to gather a body of men, numbered in the 'hundreds', to repair with them to Smock Alley and, having identified the brothel in which their comrade had breathed his last, to embark on tearing 'the house to pieces'. There is no record, visual or verbal, of precisely what they did, but there is reason to suggest that they did not confine themselves to non-structural destruction, which was customary on these occasions. And, in the estimation of one thoughtful commentator, 'had they been content with the setting a mark on a house, which could harbour such miscreants ... no reasonable person could have condemned their proceedings'. But this was not the case. One may debate their motivation; the benign view was that the 'zeal for revenge immediately transformed itself into a zeal for reformation'. A more dispassionate reading would suggest that having encountered little resistance in Smock Alley, and imbibed the 'vast quantities of liquor' liberated in the brothel that was their primary target, the 'inflamed' and 'virtuous mob' undertook to expand their riotous endeavour to embrace all the 'bawdy houses' in the city and its environs. It is not clear if this was predetermined or a spur of the moment decision, but in a further manifestation of their capacity for organization, the

6 *FJ*, 14 May 1768.   7 Patrick Fagan has claimed that 'the trouble ... was sparked off by the slaying by the prostitutes of ... Callan' (Fagan, *Second city*, p. 214). I have not found evidence for this, and it is not entirely consistent with the sympathy extended to the sex workers in early reports of the incident: see *Faulkner's Dublin Journal* (henceforth *FDJ*), 14 May 1768; Powell, *Politics of consumption*, p. 222.

crowd 'divided ... into different parties' in order better to accomplish their goal, and 'perambulated the town [and suburbs] all night and the succeeding day', 'tearing down doors, windows, partitions, grates etc, turning the unfortunate inhabitants out naked, and carrying off whatever money, plate, clothes, or household goods they could discover in them, as lawful booty'.[8] *Finn's Leinster Journal* provided its readers with an arresting account of what transpired over the course of the two days:

> Tuesday night, and Wednesday, the mob continued to pull down houses ... they began in Smock Alley, and levelled a house almost to the ground. From thence they went to Sycamore Alley, and entirely stripped a house; and burnt the furniture; they likewise gutted one house in Stephen Street, one in Northumberland Court, two in Whitefriar Street, one in Dame Street, two on Hog Hill, one in Anglesea Street, one in Werburgh Street, one in Joseph's Lane, nine on the Blind Quay, one in Fishamble Street, one in Britain Street,[9] one in Dirty Lane, Dame Street, one in Turnstile Alley, three in Marshal Alley,[10] one in Arran Street, one in Cuckoo Lane, two in Mosse Street, one on George's Quay, one in Grange Lane,[11] two in Ringsend, and one on Donnybrook road; in all 37. In Arran Street, one of the villains, being anxious to steal the main beam, the whole edifice fell in at once, by which five or six people lost their lives.[12]

Though these figures were implicitly challenged by those who maintained that the number of 'sacked' houses was greater, there was more agreement on this point than there was on the amount of damage, which was variously estimated at between £10,000 and £30,000.[13] Word pictures provided more telling, if impressionistic, reference points. Invoking a disturbance fresh in the public memory, one author compared the 'devastation' inflicted on the city to 'the memorable military insurrection on the 6th and 7th of August 1765, when Newgate [prison] was broke open and upwards of 70 fellows were let loose upon the public'.[14] Another, opting for a more dramatic analogy, alleged that Dublin resembled 'a conquered city, after being plundered and sacked by the most savage enemy'.[15] This was greatly to exaggerate, of course. The account in the *Public Gazetteer*, which acknowledged that at 'most' locations the crowd targeted 'the windows, frames and shutters, tore down the partitions, wainscot etc, besides carrying off the furniture, and drinking and spilling the liquors', corroborates the impression, conveyed by the reports of the manner in which the 'different parties' traversed the city and its suburbs, that this was not the irrational

8 *FJ*, 24 May 1768.   9 It is not clear whether this refers to Great or Little Britain Street.
10 Otherwise known as Marshal[seas] Alley, which was off Fishamble Street.
11 Grangegorman Lane, off Channel Row.   12 *Finn's Leinster Journal* (henceforth *FLJ*), 18 May 1768.   13 *Public Gazetteer*, 14 May, 1768; *FJ*, 14 May 1768; *FLJ*, 18 May 1768.   14 *FJ*, 14 May 1768   15 *FLJ*, 14 May 1768.

handiwork of a directionless mob.[16] It also explains the perpetrators' voluntary surrender to the authorities when they had 'finished their work'.[17]

Approximately thirty 'fatigued' and 'intoxicated' rioters were taken into custody by the lord mayor and sheriff at Ringsend on 12 May, from whence they were brought to Newgate; a small number of others were taken up separately in the city a few days later. As a result, order was soon restored.[18] A majority of commentators gave credit for this to the lord mayor, sheriff and magistrates, though searching questions were posed by the more thoughtful as to why the authorities knew 'nothing of the proceedings of such a numerous lawless rabble for a whole night and part of the next day', why they had not acted with greater urgency, and why they had neither assembled a civil force nor called upon the military for assistance 'to quell so dangerous an insurrection'.[19] Using as a guide the (controversial) execution of Bosavern Penlez for his participation in the destruction of 'a bawdy house' in London in 1749, implicit comparisons were drawn between the docility of the Irish authorities and the decisiveness of their English equivalents.[20] This echoed the chorus of opinion in Dublin, which deemed it unacceptable that 'a drunken and dissolute mob' should be at liberty to 'inflict…what punishments they please' even if their targets were such socially marginal venues as 'bawdy houses' and individuals whose involvement with the sex industry placed them well beyond the boundaries of respectability. 'We live under a government, and are blessed with a constitution by which the meanest subject, or the greatest criminal, is not to be affected in his liberties, or property, without a legal trial', it was observed.[21]

II

The preparedness of at least some of those who encountered the trail of destruction left in the wake of the brothel riots of May 1768 to engage with the broader implications of the episode for the enforcement of the law was emulated further afield. Horace Walpole cited the fact that the murder of a butcher 'in a brothel in Dublin had raised such a flame, that forty houses were pulled down

---

16 *Public Gazetteer*, 14 May 1768.   17 *FJ*, 14 May 1768.   18 *FLJ*, 14, 21 May 1768; *Public Gazetteer*, 12, 21 May 1768.   19 *FJ*, 24, 31 May 1768.   20 The so-called 'Penlez riot' takes its name from an attack on a brothel, the residence of Peter Wood, on the Strand on 2 July 1749, in which Bosavern Penlez was a participant. Prosecuted under the Riot Act (1715), Penlez was found guilty and sentenced to death. Penlez claimed in mitigation that he was 'in liquor', and entertained reasonable hopes that the sentence would not be enforced given his respectable background (he was 'born of very good parents … his father … was a divine of the Church of England') and the court's recommendation that 'mercy' should obtain in the case. However, mercy was not extended and Penlez was executed. (Trial of John Willson and others, 6 Sept. 1749, ordinary's account, 18 Oct. 1749 (www.oldbaileyonline.org, accessed 2 Feb. 2015); Frank McLynn, *Crime and punishment in eighteenth-century England* (London, 1989), p. 223).   21 *FJ*, 24, 28, 31 May 1768.

by the mob, and several persons killed', in support of his dubious contention that the populations of Britain and Ireland were seized at that moment by 'a mutinous spirit' that inhibited efficient government.[22] Had domestic and external observers pondered the matter longer they might have been less ready to rush to judgement and less categorical with the conclusion they offered. The 1768 Dublin riots, like the execution of Bosavern Penlez in England, was a defining event in the history of brothel rioting in Ireland, but it was also part of a larger and longer lasting tradition of attacking property in the seventeenth- and eighteenth-century Atlantic world. Attacks on brothels and playhouses, and on occasion prisons and private houses, were a common occurrence every Shrove Tuesday in early seventeenth-century London. Then as later the primary participants – apprentices and allied unruly elements – did not engage in wanton undifferentiated destruction: the crowds (ranging from two hundred to several thousand) which carried out the attacks not only targeted specific properties but also differentiated between those they singled out for demolition, and those where the destruction of content, which embraced windows, window frames and wainscoting, as well as furniture, was the priority. Since it was the contention of those who engaged in such activity then that they were motivated by the desire to mitigate the temptation to sin during Lent, historians have argued that the apprentices were indulged in their disorderliness because this was a once a year occurrence and because it was in keeping with 'the ritualized inversionary disorder embedded in traditional holiday celebrations'.[23]

Shrove Tuesday and other festivals anchored in the traditional church calendar survived the accelerated 'Protestantization' of English society in the early seventeenth century, albeit shorn of many of their 'traditional rituals'. The infrequency with which 'bawdy houses' were targeted for attack in London during the Restoration era suggests that this once-familiar Shrove Tuesday tradition was one of the casualties, though the practice of attacking properties persisted. The involvement of apprentices in the destruction of bawdy houses in London on Easter Monday in 1668, and the unusually vigorous response of the authorities, has properly been anatomized for what it says about the opposition to Charles II's attempt to impose religious conformity rather than for what it reveals of the survival of a venerable tradition that accommodated forms of riot. But, the fact that brothels were targeted in 1668, and again in 1680, indicates that the motive that previously impelled apprentices had survived the transformation of the festive calendar in a sufficiently robust form to allow for its animation when circumstances were propitious.[24] The Restoration era provided few such

---

22 Horace Walpole, *Memoirs of the reign of George III*, ed. Derek Jarrett (4 vols, London, 2000), iv, 21.   23 K.J. Lindley, 'Riot prevention and control in early Stuart London', *RHS Trans.*, 5:33 (1983), 109–11; Robert Shoemaker, 'The London mob in the early eighteenth century', *Journal of British Studies*, 26 (1987), 290; Peter Burke, 'Popular culture in seventeenth-century London' in Barry Reay (ed.), *Popular culture in seventeenth-century England* (London, 1985), pp 35–8.   24 Shoemaker, 'London mob in early eighteenth cent.',

opportunities; the contested political environment that followed the elevation of William and Mary to the throne was more conducive, and more examples of mob attacks on houses are to be found in the early eighteenth century.[25] It was a measure of the gravity with which the practice was regarded, and of the politico-religious tension of which it was a manifestation, that the landmark Riot Act passed at Westminster in 1715 included a specific clause targeted at penalizing damage to property. Clause four of the act decreed that 'any persons unlawfully, riotously and tumultuously assembled' who 'shall unlawfully, and with force demolish or pull down, or begin to demolish or pull down any church or chapel, or any building for religious worship ... or any dwelling-house, barn, stable, or other out-house ... shall be adjudged felons, and shall suffer death as in cases of felony, without benefit of clergy'.[26] Because only a modest number of such charges were pursued at the Old Bailey in the decades following enactment, it is tempting to conclude that the act served as an effective deterrent to riotous interventions involving the destruction of buildings, but this would be to give it too much credit. Identifiable elements of the populace continued to believe in the utility of the practice. For example, its appeal to tradesmen was manifest in 1720 when a body of journeymen tailors attempted to pull down a master's 'house of call' during a workmen's strike, and in 1768 when 'one hundred or more' men 'destroyed all the saws and frames, and pretty nearly demolished the brick building that is the counting house' at an enterprise located in Limehouse, London, because it was perceived to threaten the livelihood of traditional sawyers.[27]

If the survival of the sanction of riotously damaging property was assisted by the success with which it adapted from a situation at the beginning of the seventeenth century, when it was invoked by a particular social group on a particular date, to the situation prevailing in the eighteenth, when it was appealed to intermittently by diverse social interests not bound by a comparable festive calendar, its adaptability was even more strongly manifested in its migration with English settlers who ventured overseas. Brothel riots in Boston in 1734, 1737, 1771 and 1795 and in New York in 1793 provide tangible evidence of its successful translation to Britain's North American colonies.[28] The situation in

pp 290–1; Laurence Manly, 'London and urban popular culture' in Andrew Hadfield et al. (eds), *The Ashgate research companion to popular culture in early modern England* (Farnham, 2014), pp 357–71; Tim Harris, 'The bawdy house riots of 1668', *HJ*, 29 (1986), 537–56. **25** Trial of John Love, Thomas Bean, George Purchase and others, 6 Sept. 1716, and trial of John Nash for breaking the peace/riot, 10 Oct. 1716 (www.oldbaileyonline.org, accessed 2 Feb. 2015). Capital verdicts were handed down in both cases. **26** 1 Geo. I, c. 5, sect. 4. **27** Shoemaker, 'London mob in early eighteenth cent.', pp 279–80; trial of Edward Castle for breaking the peace/riot, 6 July 1768 (www.oldbaileyonline.org, accessed 2 Feb. 2015). **28** Jack Tager, *Boston riots: three centuries of social violence* (Boston, MA, 2001), p. 15; P.A. Gilje, *The road to mobocracy: popular disorder in New York, 1763–1834* (Chapel Hill, NC, 1987), pp 86–91; John D'Emilio and E.B. Freedman, *Intimate matters: a history of sexuality in America* (3rd ed., Chicago, 2012), pp 51–2. Brothel riots have also been identified in America

Ireland was similar, though the manner in which it was pursued was more obviously comparable to England. Brothels were the primary object of those who deemed it legitimate to target buildings and their contents in response to perceived and real abuses, but, as identified above with reference to London, the sanction was not confined to those involved in the sex industry or reserved for buildings assigned to that purpose. The houses of merchants engaged in the trade in grain were also targeted, and though the identification of only six instances between 1710 and 1777 suggests that it was resorted to conservatively by food protesters, the order of the sanctions they visited on property was palpably larger when one adds grain stores and mills to the list.[29]

In keeping with the understanding of the practice of brothel rioting provided by seventeenth- and eighteenth-century English exemplars, the first instance recorded in Ireland conformed to the archetype. 'A great mobb', roused to anger by the murder of a man 'amongst the whores in Smock Alley', Dublin, in March 1716, 'pull'd down and destroy'd all the bawdyhouses there'.[30] Further attacks on 'disorderly houses' in the capital followed at irregular intervals in the course of the ensuing decades. Their infrequency suggests that the owners of these establishments were sufficiently alert to the likely consequences to take steps not to provoke the mob, but the fact that 'disorderly' houses were invaded and wrecked in Dirty Lane, Copper Alley and Anglesea Street in 1739, 1745, 1754 and 1760 in response to reports of 'ill use' indicates that the 'lady abbesses' who ran these institutions were not always successful in ensuring they operated beneath the public's radar.[31] It may be that it was all but impossible to prevent incidents of this kind because of the volatility of these spaces and because the people they attracted were predisposed to disorder.[32] Furthermore, there were external factors that could not be legislated for, one of which was the appeal the sanction had for the soldiery billeted in the city. Indicatively, one of the earliest identifiable examples of a property being demolished in Ireland involved soldiers billeted in the Royal Barracks, who joined forces with elements of 'the mob' to 'pull down' a house in Feather Bed Lane, Dublin, in 1727 in revenge for the death of one of their colleagues at the location the previous night.[33] In most

in still greater number in the early nineteenth century, but the most detailed investigation of those that took place in New York between 1825 and 1857 has concluded, based on the fact that they took the form of attacks by small groups of men, that they were a manifestation of male insecurity and resentment at the greater visibility of women in the public realm: T.J. Gilfoyle, 'Strumpets and misogynists: brothel "riots" and the transformation of prostitution in antebellum New York City', *New York History*, 68 (1987), 44–65. **29** This observation about food protesters is based on ongoing work on this subject; see David Dickson, *Old world colony: Cork and south Munster, 1630–1830* (Cork, 2005), p. 379 for the 1710 incident. **30** *Dublin Intelligence*, 10 Mar. 1715/16; Fagan, *Second city*, p. 213. **31** *FDJ*, 18 Sept. 1739; *Dublin Daily Post*, 18 Sept. 1739; Burke to Richard Shackleton, 12 Mar. 1745 (A.P.I. Samuels, *The early life, correspondence and writings of Edmund Burke* (Cambridge, 1923), pp 68–9); *Public Gazetteer*, 8 Mar. 1760; *FJ*, 13 June 1799. **32** As illustrated by reports in *Pue's Occurrences*, 19 July 1755, 25 Sept. 1756; *Hoey's Publick Journal*, 9 June 1773; *FJ*, 8 June 1773. **33** *Faulkner's Dublin Post Boy*,

instances, however, the priority for those targeting brothels was to break up furniture and to tear the 'inside' to pieces. Even the evidence of cases reported in the press in which rioters did not cease activity at that point – somewhere between three and six buildings were 'pull'd down' or 'nearly demolished' between 1727 and 1760 – does not invalidate the conclusion that damage was typically prioritized over destruction, and that the crowds who engaged in riotously attacking brothels and other buildings only proceeded to pull them down when the offence was more than usually grievous or when the failure of the authorities to intervene was interpreted as an authorization to continue.[34]

The skeletal character of the identified reports of the riotous destruction of property dating from the first half of the eighteenth century precludes confident analysis of either the thinking or motivation of those who engaged in such activity. Yet some conclusions can be ventured. The participation of elements of the Dublin 'mob' with soldiers of Lord John Kerr's regiment in the demolition of a number of houses in 1727 suggests that those who engaged in such activity believed they possessed a moral entitlement, possibly a moral authority, to apply this sanction. The implication, that it was appropriate to punish certain transgressions by destroying the material goods of those who infringed the prevailing popular code, up to and including their place of residence, was also firmly held. And in the case of brothels, it derived further legitimacy from history: those who applied the sanction could reasonably point to the fact that they were observing a tradition that had been pursued by their forbears for generations.

While the authority of custom and practice must not be underestimated, the fact that it possessed less weight in Dublin than in London may have facilitated the 'mob's' engagement in other practices which, by reason of the fact that they too targeted buildings – primarily residences – can be considered allied pursuits. The select destruction by food protesters of the houses of merchants and traders engaged in the exportation and sale of food has already been mentioned. A more particular sanction, pursued intermittently throughout the country, involved laying the body of an executed felon at the 'door or house' of the person who had pursued the prosecution that culminated in a capital conviction.[35] This practice could, and did, take different forms. The populace of Cork was sufficiently persuaded in 1767 that Jeremiah Twomey, who had been executed for robbery, was 'innocent' of the charge, that they 'brought his body from the gallows, in his coffin, to the prosecutor's door, where they bled him, took the rope off his neck, threw it in the window, besmeared the door and window shutters with blood, whilst showers of stones were pelted at the windows from every quarter'.[36]

5 June 1727. **34** *Dublin Intelligence*, 10 Mar. 1715/16; *Faulkner's Dublin Post Boy*, 5 June 1727; *Pue's Occurrences*, 9 Mar. 1745; Samuels, *Early life of Edmund Burke*, pp 68–9; *Public Gazetteer*, 8 Mar. 1760. **35** *FJ*, 24 Dec. 1782. **36** C.B. Gibson, *History of the county of the city of Cork* (2 vols, Cork, 1861), ii, 204–5; James Kelly, 'Punishing the dead: execution and the executed body in eighteenth-century Ireland' in Richard Ward (ed.), *A global history of*

Another example, which better illustrates the link between this activity and the targeted destruction of property, concerned Oliver Deacon, who was executed at St Stephen's Green in Dublin in 1747 for robbing 'his master', William Le Fanu, of 'several sums of money'. Because he had confessed 'his guilt', the public expectation was that Deacon's death sentence would be remitted, so when he was hanged, 'a mob', more than five hundred strong, removed his body from the scaffold and

> laid the same at the door of [William Le Fanu's] house [on Stephen's Green], and with great shoutings and out-cries, attempted the door of the said house, and, with stones and brick-batts, broke all the windows in the front of the said house, and put the said William LeFanu, his wife and family in fear and dread of their lives, several declaring that they would take away the pallisadoes of the said house, and that they would not leave a brick of the said house standing.

The intervention of the 'main guard' prevented the mob from making good their threat in this instance, but the incident brought the matter closer than was comfortable for the residents of Dublin's fashionable streets, who normally regarded such matters from a safe distance. Anxious that this should not set a disagreeable precedent, the privy council offered a reward of £30 for the apprehension and conviction of John Deacon of Ormond Market, who was credited with orchestrating the event, and sums of £20 and £10 for up to ten unnamed participants.[37]

Nothing is known of John Deacon other than what we can glean from the documentation generated by the attack on Le Fanu's house. The fact that he was from Ormond Market encourages speculation, even if he and his brother were not active members, that the Ormond Boys may have been actively involved in the symbolic deployment of Oliver Deacon's body and in the threat to destroy William Le Fanu's place of residence. It certainly took organization, as well as bravura, to threaten popular sanction against one of Dublin's elite. Yet, lest one conclude that that was a unique occurrence, both features were again in evidence in 1754, when Isaac Drury, a well-connected commissioner of the peace, was so perturbed by a threat emanating with the 'city mob' to come 'to my house to pull it down', because he had accompanied the unpopular lord lieutenant, the duke of Dorset, to his embarkation for England, that he deemed it prudent 'to keep a guard' on his home.[38] Drury's costly precautions were not tested, but when his

---

execution and the criminal corpse (Basingstoke, 2015), pp 37–70. 37 James Kelly and Mary Ann Lyons (eds), *The proclamations of Ireland, 1660–1820* (5 vols, Dublin, 2014), iii, 359–60; *FDJ*, 2 Jan. 1748. 38 Isaac Drury to Ld George Sackville, [21 May 1754] in James Walton (ed.), *The king's business: letters on the administration of Ireland 1740–1761, from the papers of Sir Robert Wilmot* (New York, 1996), pp 90–1. Drury was put to such additional expense that he sought compensation from the Irish administration. He was subsequently in receipt of a

experience and that of William LeFanu are taken together, and we factor in that the crowd was mustered in Dublin to the beat of a drum, in the same manner as in London, it is apparent that brothel riots are not best understood when viewed in isolation.[39] By extension, the links that can be drawn between such events and other comparable displays of public protest, far from being fortuitous or coincidental, are indicative of a pattern of popular behaviour, which reveal that the crowd possessed the confidence as well as the capacity to apply its 'law'.[40] Viewed from this perspective, the practice of attacking brothels was but one manifestation of a code of behaviour shared by the populace which deemed it legitimate to sanction individuals and interests who had transgressed by attacking their property with destructive intent. Indeed, it was part of a behavioural and attitudinal continuum that countenanced activities as well known as the 'food riot' (long perceived as the quintessential manifestation of a 'moral economy'), the abduction of women in order to acquire control of their economic assets, the throwing of vitriol on women wearing imported clothing, and popular sanctions as ordinary as the ducking in and pumping with water, and dragging women through the gutter (or kennel) for various offences including kidnapping children in order to steal their clothes.[41]

Viewed as a collective of comparable, rather than individual (and idiosyncratic) behaviours, all of which were fuelled by a concept of 'popular justice', it is apparent that the practice of attacking brothels not only possessed moral authority among the Anglophone population of Dublin and Cork, who were its primary exponents in Ireland, but also drew on a reservoir of support that was much broader than the incorrigible tendency of the respectable to dismiss it as the handiwork of an ignorant and uncultured mob. This may have been correct in respect of the 'party of rioters' who attacked a house in New Street, Dublin, in 1759, in the course of which 'several ... were desperately wounded', but it is hardly tenable when it comes to those 'charged with breaking windows and otherwise destroying the house of Mr John Bower, linen weaver', of Blackpool, Cork, in 1769, and still less those responsible in 1757 for pulling down the house of a gentlemen in Mallow, who had prompted intervention when he bested another gentleman in what appears to have been an affair of honour.[42] Indeed, one can go further and query the utility of the term 'mob', since it was primarily used by those who were well removed from the social interests they described,

---

small pension (£100) on the Irish establishment: *Gentleman's Magazine*, 33 (1763), 539.
39 Shoemaker, 'London mob in early eighteenth cent.', p. 289; *Public Gazetteer*, 16 Aug. 1763; *FJ*, 13 Aug. 1789.   40 The practice of laying bodies 'at the prosecutor's door' continued: see *Hibernian Journal*, 10 Jan. 1776; Eden to Loughborough, 20 Oct. 1781 (*The correspondence of William Eden, Lord Auckland*, ed. Bishop of Bath and Wells (4 vols, London, 1861–2), i, 317).
41 *Dublin Gazette*, 30 Sept. 1740; *Hibernian Journal* (henceforth *Hib. Jnl*), 12 Aug. 1776, 10 July 1779; *Dublin Chronicle*, 20 Oct. 1789; James Kelly, 'The abduction of women of fortune in eighteenth-century Ireland', *ECI*, 9 (1994), 7–44; idem, '"An infamous trade": the kidnapping of children, *c*.1730–*c*.1840' (forthcoming).   42 *Public Gazetteer*, 26 June 1759; *Hibernian Chronicle*, 23 Oct. 1769; *Pue's Occurrences*, 26 Apr. 1757.

and in a manner suggesting little understanding of the gradations within the 'lower classes' or sympathy for their way of life. Yet despite the imprecise manner in which it was reflexively resorted to by the commentators on whose accounts we are disproportionately reliant, the word 'mob' is not without its uses. The fact that it was employed so persistently by contemporaries is obviously significant. Moreover, its value and utility are not inconsiderable so long as it is acknowledged that it was deployed loosely in order to denominate the various interests below the respectable whose patterns of recreation as well as protest challenged, when they did not simply offend, the sensibilities of those above them in the social order.[43] It was an imprecise term, used imprecisely, because it never possessed a defined sociological meaning. On the contrary, it embraced a diversity of employments and interests in the lower occupational categories which possessed a shared world-view, permitting them to coalesce in pursuit of certain objects and to differ with no less intensity when they disagreed. Whenever a mob assembled, whether it comprised the dozen persons prescribed in the Riot Act, the score or more that may have combined to attack a single property, or the hundreds required to sustain a major episode such as that of 10–11 May 1768, it is improbable that it was representative of the lower social orders from which most 'mobs' emanated. Rather, every such gathering may more accurately be characterized as a self-selected sample of the populace at large, animated by particular concerns, that struck a chord with the populace at large.

III

It will not come as a surprise that 'mob' gatherings for the purpose of breaking into and either wrecking or demolishing brothels, houses and, on occasion, places of work, increased in the wake of the events of 10–11 May 1768, given the broad support they enjoyed among the populace, and the tolerance they were shown by the authorities during the first half of the century. In comparison with the number of riotous confrontations involving the military and public, revenue officials and counterfeiters, even political and electoral riots, they were not especially numerous, but they spanned the range of riotous activity that the category permitted. The easiest to engage with is the classic brothel riot. This may be illustrated by the mob which was prompted to rise up by an assault perpetrated in the summer of 1774 on a 'young man in liquor', who was 'decoyed into a house of ill fame in the Blind Quay' where he was 'seriously cut and abused'. As a result, 'all the furniture belonging to the house, with the sashs, window shutters etc.' were 'destroyed' and thrown into the street.[44] The

---

[43] See James Kelly, *Sport in Ireland, 1600–1840* (Dublin, 2014), especially introduction and conclusion.   [44] *Hib. Jnl*, 27 June 1774.

destruction of 'two houses of ill-fame' in the summer of 1780, and an attempt at another in 1787, demonstrates that the populace of Dublin was not disinclined to impose a sterner penalty when it was deemed appropriate, but it is notable that demolition was a sanction more identifiable with the military. Indeed, in two separate incidents in October 1775 soldiers were responsible for the destruction of three brothels – two on Anglesea Street, and one at the back of Blind Quay – in Dublin in a six-day period.[45] What was even more noteworthy among instances in which the 'mob' was the driving force was their greater willingness to co-operate with the civil authorities. This commonly took the form of handing over to the city sheriffs sex workers encountered in the course of an intervention.[46] Officials too now tended to be more interventionist. The most revealing illustration of this trend was provided by the mayor of Cork, John Harding, who responded to the actions of 'a riotous mob' that 'pulled down and destroyed several dwelling-houses' in that city in the winter of 1779–80 by issuing a municipal proclamation in which he explicitly asserted that those responsible were guilty of 'high treason' and offered a reward of £10 'for the first person who shall be taken and prosecuted to conviction for said riot'.[47] The outcome, paradoxically, was not a decline in the number of riotous attacks but an increase, since it coincided with a greater readiness to target 'houses of ill fame' based on uncorroborated 'reports'. Examples recorded in the press include an account dating from 1774 to the effect that 'an innocent girl was inveigled into a brothel in Anglesea Street', Dublin; from 1776, that 'a young gentlemen' had been 'assassinated' in 'a noted brothel' on the same street; and from 1781, that 'a young girl had been strangled' in a comparable establishment on Little Boater Lane, also in the capital.[48] In a number of instances, the mob was persuaded to disperse by the intervention of the sheriff before major damage was inflicted, but this was not always the case.[49] Moreover, such incidents were not without import. Besides the disruption they inflicted on the operation of the brothels themselves, and the incentives they provided for certain madams and ordinary prostitutes to relocate,[50] they were eagerly seized upon by the vocal minority which believed that legislative intervention was necessary if attacks on 'bawdy houses' were to be eradicated and some redress provided to the problems caused by the growing number of street-walkers and brothels, which it was alleged already exceeded, by a factor of four, the number in London.[51] There was no basis in fact for these numerical claims, and virtually no prospect of the legislature taking up the suggestion floated in 1791 that Ireland should follow the example of 'most countries in Europe' and take steps to prevent 'assaults on houses of ill fame' by improving their security, thereby 'rendering them less

45 *FLJ*, 21, 25 Oct. 1775; *Hib. Jnl*, 7 June 1780; *FJ*, 7 July 1787.   46 *Hib. Jnl*, 27 June, 12 Oct. 1774, 7 June 1780.   47 *Hibernian Chronicle*, 3 Jan. 1780.   48 *Hib. Jnl*, 12 Oct. 1774, 12 Apr. 1776; *FJ*, 16 Oct. 1781.   49 *Hib. Jnl*, 27 June, 12 Oct. 1774, 12 Apr. 1776; *FJ*, 16 Oct. 1781.   50 See *The memoirs of Mrs Leeson, madam*, ed. Mary Lyons (Dublin, 1995), p. 145.   51 *FJ*, 16 Oct. 1781; *FLJ*, 20 July 1774; Fleming, 'Attitudes to prostitution', pp 4–5, 10–11.

dangerous, and ... obliging them to contribute to the good of the community by paying for that protection'.[52] It may be, as David Fleming has pointed out, that there were some in the upper ranks of society, 'prompted by ideas of genteel piety, charity and growing evangeliszation', who were willing to perceive prostitutes as victims, but they were in a minority among the lawmakers, and still more thinly represented among the populace, who shared the slowly appreciating suspicion with which prostitutes and those engaged in the sex trade continued to be regarded.[53]

Indeed, a case might be made that this attitude was not limited to prostitution or to abuses perpetrated within brothels, based on the comparable increase in the number of instances in which individuals with no connexion to the sex industry were threatened with a visitation with destructive intent to their place of residence. One may point to the threat issued by a 'mob' in 1793 that they would 'pull down' the Dame Street residence of a man named Busby on foot of rumours that he had contributed to the death of one of his three daughters 'by stinting them of food'.[54] The rumour was false and no attack was mounted, but this is less significant in the scheme of things than the demonstration of intent that was manifest, then and on other occasions, when individuals were deemed to have behaved 'illegally or oppressively' in the public's estimation.[55] Moreover, as previously demonstrated in the 1750s, the mob was no respecter of social rank. Their targets extended up the greasy pole of preferment to include members of the judiciary. A threatened action against the residence of an 'unpopular judge' was not proceeded with in 1781, because the judge was living in borrowed quarters, but others were not so fortunate. They included a farmer, who was forced to witness his windows, doors, roof and part of the walls being broken; a Church of Ireland clergyman, Patrick Crawley, whose house on Digges Lane was 'almost demolished' because he had dismissed an abusive servant; a householder in the Bailey Fields, whose furniture was burned in the street and his house partially demolished; and an 'industrious person', whose ribband 'factory' in upper Church Street was seriously damaged by 'a desperate mob' fearing for their livelihoods.[56] As these cases suggest, there were instances when attacks on private premises masked what, at this remove, seems like simple intimidation with neither customary nor popular legitimacy. The committal to Newgate prison in 1789 of Jack Finegan, alias Jack Slap, for 'having threatened several inhabitants of Cannon Street with the mob that would demolish and destroy their shops and properties', is still more clear cut; it provides a revealing insight into how one unscrupulous individual may have used the sanction to his advantage. Moreover, it may have been resorted to more widely in the late

---

52 *Clonmel Gazette*, 30 July 1791; *Ennis Chronicle*, 1 Aug. 1791.   53 Fleming, 'Attitudes to prostitution', p. 16.   54 *FJ*, 28 Mar. 1793; *Dublin Chronicle*, 28 Mar. 1793.   55 *FJ*, 20 Feb. 1772.   56 *Hib. Jnl*, 5 Aug., 19 Oct. 1781; *FLJ*, 3 Feb. 1779; *FJ*, 11 May 1784. Patrick Crawley (*d*. 1802) was vicar of St Doulaghs, 1774–83 (J.B. Leslie and W.J.R. Wallace, *Clergy of Dublin*

eighteenth century given the increased frequency with which it was articulated that the mobs which attacked property were more interested in looting than destroying houses and their contents. The handful of such cases that have been identified also suggest it was more usual in rural areas than in Dublin, which is in keeping with the identifiable fluidity of the phenomenon previously described, and the manner in which, outside the major urban areas where it was primarily practised, it intersected with agrarian protest.[57]

Fluid or not, the defining target of house rioters was the brothel, and this was underlined in the 1790s, when, for the second time in the eighteenth century, the city of Dublin was significantly disrupted by a serious, and in this instance unusually enduring, phase of protest, which peaked in the summers of 1791 and 1795. There was little indication in the spring of 1791 that the populace was any more disquieted than usual with the activities of the 'mother abbesses' who ran the city's many brothels or with the sex workers who touted for work on the streets. However, the capacity and intent of those sections of the populace which believed abuses in brothels should not pass unpunished had grown with the city and they demonstrated both in a vigorous response in April to a report emanating from 'a house of ill fame in Ross Lane' that the daughter of a poor woman had been 'decoyed into the above mentioned house, and ill-treated and detained by the mother abbess', identified as Norah Beatty. The damage inflicted was consistent with the sanction usually invoked in these cases. Having 'totally demolished the windows and wood work, [and] proceeded to destroy the furniture', the mob was only prevented from 'pulling down or destroying the house' by the intervention of the city police – a new, and controversial, addition to the forces of law and order, which was soon to assume the initiative in such instances.[58] The crowd at first resisted the attempt by the police to take control of the situation, and while this almost certainly mirrored the difficult relationship then obtaining between the police and the people, it is highly significant that an attempt by 'a number of apprentice boys, with persons of low description, assembled in Stephens Green' to target other 'bawdy houses' later the same day was only interdicted by the apprehension of one of the 'ringleaders'.[59] This action secured only a temporary respite, however, for when on Sunday, 24 July, two troopers were embroiled in an altercation at a house of 'ill fame in Fleet Lane', as a result of which one of the soldiers was left 'in a bloody condition', the mob was quickly roused. Observing the resistance encountered by the small body

and Glendalough (Belfast, 2001), p. 519). **57** *FLJ*, 9 Mar. 1776; *Dublin Morning Post* (henceforth *DMP*), 5 July 1785; *Volunteer Evening Post*, 27 Oct. 1785; *Dublin Chronicle*, 4 June 1789. **58** *FJ*, 26 Apr. 1791; *Hib. Jnl*, 27 Apr. 1791; *Dublin Weekly Journal*, 30 Apr. 1791. The destruction was described as follows by the latter: 'the temple was completely pillaged, and the shrines and other necessary appendages of the religious mysteries of the place – beds, bedding and mirrors – were involved in a common destruction'. For the Dublin police, see, inter alia, S.H. Palmer, *Police and protest in England and Ireland, 1780–1850* (Cambridge, 1988), pp 92–104, 119–35. **59** *FJ*, 26 Apr. 1791.

of soldiers which had 'sallied out of the barracks' to avenge their injured comrade, a 'prodigious mob' estimated (almost certainly wrongly) at 'at least five thousand men' joined forces with the soldiers, and, 'proceeding by the graduation usual when not immediately checked', not only wrecked the brothel at the heart of the dispute but also entered 'several other houses'. Reports varied as to the damage that was caused. According to one account, the mob 'stormed every house in Fleet Lane but one, breaking the very walls and demolishing beds, desk tables, chairs and every sort of furniture'; another reported that 'in about one hour every house in the neighbourhood [of Fleet Lane] was completely gutted of the few articles of furniture they contained, and the doors and windows completely demolished'. Whatever the precise sequence of events, the result was that the brothel at the heart of the incident was 'left unfit for the occupancy of even those wretches who were their ordinary inhabitants'. Some of the furniture tipped onto the street was 'carried off', but the beds, like the windows on many such occasions, were targeted for particular attention; they 'were ripped up with knives', with the result that 'the whole street appeared perfectly whitened with feathers when the mob dispersed'.[60]

The intervention of the police watchmen at this point would, in normal circumstances, have brought this episode to a conclusion, except that the mob refused to disperse. They forced the watchmen 'to retire before the clouds of stone and brickbats which were showered upon them'. This fusillade provided 'another party of the mob' that was 'engaged in gutting and plundering two [or three] houses of ill-fame in Crown Alley' with the time to achieve this object. Their 'intention was to proceed in the same manner [as the mob on Fleet Lane] and level every house of that description to the ground' but they proved less disciplined than their colleagues; it was alleged that 'plunder seemed to be their real object', with the result that their actions were interrupted by the arrival of a detachment of the horse guard, followed, shortly afterwards, by a detachment of foot, which initially encountered 'very severe resistance'. Obliged finally to beat a retreat in the face of disciplined military action, the mob dispersed, only to reassemble the following morning, Monday, 25 July, and they were already embarked on pulling down one of the houses in Crown Alley when they were once again 'prevented by the timely interference of the military'. They were also prevented from gaining access to Fleet Lane by the presence of a strong guard 'at both ends' of the street. In the normal course of events this would have represented the end of the matter, but even the arrest of a number of rioters did not have the desired impact. Later that day various groups were spotted on New Street, at the Coombe and on Townsend Street where they had gathered 'for the purpose of rioting', but they revised their plans when they were made aware 'that

---

60 *DMP*, 25 July 1791; *FJ*, 26 July 1791; *Dublin Chronicle*, 26 July 1791; *Hib. Jnl*, 27 July 1791; *FLJ*, 30 July 1791; *Cork Gazette*, 30 July 1791; *Clonmel Gazette*, 30 July 1791; *Ennis Chronicle*, 1 Aug. 1791.

not only the police watch guards, assisted by the army, were, on the first sign of tumult, ready to apprehend them, but also the citizens and inhabitants were determined, on the first appearance of any noise, to join in bringing them to punishment'. The serried ranks arrayed against the rioters proved sufficient, finally, to bring the episode to a conclusion, though an incident on 2 August when the furniture, beds and bedding of 'a house of bad repute in the Barley Fields' was targeted in response to the theft of a 'pair of boots' from 'a shoemaker' demonstrated that the public 'indignation' that fuelled such interventions was far from quieted.[61]

The events of 24–5 July 1791 – one of the three notable instances of brothel-breaking in eighteenth-century Ireland – served to reinforce the increasing realization by the municipal authorities that it was no longer strategically appropriate or socially acceptable to turn a blind eye and allow such *émeutes* to burn themselves out, which was their preferred response to that point. They were encouraged to arrive at this conclusion by speculation, relayed in the press in the aftermath of the July riots, that 'the success of the populace in ravaging the brothels in Fleet Lane and Crown Alley has induced them to extend their operations to houses of the same description in other parts of town'.[62] No attempt was made to do so, but the thrust of the commentary indicates that, as with such demotic 'sports' as bull-baiting and throwing at cocks, the respectable were increasingly disinclined to indulge the 'riotous impetuosity of the mob'.[63] The authorities were also increasingly disposed to take action. Three of the five men taken up for 'riot and affray ... at the house of Norah Beatty' on Easter Monday were found guilty of riot (but not assault) at the Dublin commission of oyer and terminer in early August, while the alertness of the authorities a week later saved a house in Liberty Street from the hostile intentions of the mob which had assembled 'to demolish it'.[64] More generally, calls upon the commissioners of police 'to rid the streets' – and specifically Dame Street, George's Lane and College Green – of the 'prostitutes and their dangerous followers' who made parts the city disagreeable at night suggested that the tolerance of prostitution was also wearing thin, though the police were still disinclined to pursue an organized crackdown.[65]

If the pattern of events played out in 1791, and the direction of public commentary, imply that the authorities and respectable opinion had arrived at a point when they were no longer prepared to tolerate those who engaged in wrecking brothels, they were to have little opportunity to demonstrate their strengthened resolve, as there were no major incidents of this kind in either 1792 or 1793. This readiness to take a harder line with brothel-breakers might have

61 *DMP*, 25 July 1791; *FJ*, 26 July 1791; *Dublin Chronicle*, 26 July 1791; *Hib. Jnl*, 27 July 1791; *FLJ*, 30 July 1791; *Walker's Hibernian Magazine*, Aug. 1791, p. 190. 62 *DMP*, 6 Aug. 1791; *Clonmel Gazette*, 30 July 1791; *Ennis Chronicle*, 1 Aug. 1791. 63 See Kelly, *Sport in Ireland, 1600–1840*, pp 216–18, 228–33. 64 *Dublin Weekly Journal*, 6 Aug. 1791; *DMP*, 6 Aug. 1791; *Ennis Chronicle*, 15 Aug. 1791. 65 *FJ*, 12 May 1792; Fleming, 'Attitudes to prostitution', pp

worked to the advantage of the owners of the city's many brothels if they had been able to sustain this situation and to ensure that their enterprises were conducted in a manner that did not elicit hostile attention. They were not in a position to do so, however, and when, at the end of April 1794, the proprietor – Mrs Fetherstone – of a brothel on Great Britain Street 'beat one of her girls so inhumanly that she was on the point of expiring' the mob was quick to spring into action. As the latest in a series of beatings to come to public notice 'within' the calendar year, the mob was determined there should be no doubt as to its position in such cases. The damage inflicted on Mrs Fetherstone's property – broken windows and ruined furniture – was restricted by the timely intervention of the city sheriff, but the populace did not conclude from this that they should refrain from such activity for the future. Six weeks later, another 'Cyprian temple' in nearby Capel Street was subjected to a similar assault.[66]

Viewed in isolation, these incidents in 1794 were comparable to the brothel attacks that had taken place intermittently during the 1770s and 1780s. The difference on this occasion was that having demonstrated the capacity to pursue an organized and destructive campaign in the face of more determined opposition in 1791, the mob assumed that they could do so again when and if they chose, and to greater effect. Their capability was displayed in January 1795 when, in a demonstration of profound public unease with the intensified activities of recruiters, a mob forced its way into 'two rendezvous houses' in Fleet Street, which they 'completely gutted, destroying beds, furniture, windows etc'.[67] Though the 'rendezvous houses of recruiting parties' were rarely targeted in this manner, the result was emboldening, and some months later, on Sunday, 5 July, 'a daring mob assembled about a house in Strand Street, and under pretence of its being a house of ill fame, proceeded to demolish its windows, furniture etc'. Since this episode was directly comparable to any one of a number of brothel riots, there was no reason to conclude at the time that it was anything other than an isolated event. But, encouraged by the failure of the police to get involved, the same 'mob' reassembled on the following day, when they 'entirely gutted' a premises on Liffey Street which was, they maintained, a 'house of ill fame'. The intervention of the authorities in this instance resulted in the arrest of 'some of the ringleaders', but it was too little and too late to put the genie of protest back in its bottle, and on Thursday, 9 July, 'parties of this most daring mob', numbering three or four hundred persons, proceeded to 'demolish different houses in Trinity Street, Cope Street, Fleet Street, Townshend Street etc.' Appropriate preventative measures instituted by Alderman William James, a police commissioner, ensured that there were no further incidents over the weekend of 10–12 July, but the mob was not ready to retire from the fray. Recognizing that they still possessed the upper hand in this game of tactical

12–13, 14–15. 66 *DMP*, 1 May 1794; *Hib. Jnl*, 30 Apr. 1794. 67 *FJ*, 31 Jan. 1795; *Ennis Chronicle*, 5 Feb. 1795.

cat-and-mouse, they orchestrated a further attack on Monday, 13 July, when they broke the windows and doors, 'shattered the furniture, destroyed beds and bedding, and put the inhabitants to flight' from 'the house known as the Thatched Cabbin on Ship Street'; and on Tuesday, 14 July, when a number of brothels were attacked and Alderman James was injured endeavouring to 'quell a riotous mob who had assembled to pull down a house in Wood Street'.[68] Ten sackings in ten days encouraged speculation that Dublin was about to experience its own Gordon Riots, which had resulted in the death of more than two hundred people and the destruction of hundreds of properties in London in 1780.[69] Such comparisons were unwarranted, as a mere five (out of six) persons taken up for their part in the attack on Wood Street were committed to Newgate to wait trial. Furthermore, the arrests were sufficient, together with the heightened police presence on the streets, to put an end to the longest sequence of organized brothel rioting to strike the city of Dublin to date. The next identifiable episode of this kind did not occur until mid-August when the mob responded to an incident in a rendezvous house in Essex Street by forcing their way in, and, having liberated those inside, by gutting the building.[70] They sought to go further in December and to pull down a brothel in Kennedy's Lane following the discovery there of the body of a 'woman of the town', but the intervention of the sheriff, William Stamer, prevented its destruction, and brought the curtain down on an eventful year.[71]

The attacks mounted in July 1795 were the last major brothel riots to take place in Ireland in the eighteenth century. They were not the last interventions of this kind, however. A local mob attacked, and devastated, 'Mother McLean's temple at Sandymount' in August 1796 out of exasperation at the example set this 'genteel' community by the indiscreet behaviour of the 'vestals' working in the house.[72] Three years later a mob attacked a brothel on Strand Street and a house in Jervis Street, though the intervention of the authorities served partially to frustrate the intentions of the rioters in both instances.[73] It was clear then that rioters would no longer be afforded the liberty they once enjoyed to sanction those employed in the sex industry when unacceptable abuses were brought to the public's notice, as it echoed the increased disposition of the authorities to respond promptly and with appropriate force. The impulse to target brothels was not easily eradicated, however. The arrest by town-major Swan of two 'ruffians' in 1801 who had 'collected a number of person together for the purpose, as they termed it, of "tattering kips",[74] and had proceeded with that intent to Dame Court', captured the conflicted state of affairs. On the one part, it indicated that

---

68 *FJ*, 11, 14, 16, 18 July 1795.   69 *FJ*, 14 July 1795; Ian Heywood and John Seed (eds), *The Gordon riots: politics, culture and insurrection in eighteenth-century England* (Cambridge, 2012). 70 *Hib. Jnl*, 12 Aug. 1795; *Ennis Chronicle*, 17 Aug. 1795; *FJ*, 18 Aug. 1795.   71 *Hib. Jnl*, 14 Dec. 1795.   72 *Ennis Chronicle*, 11 Aug. 1796.   73 *FJ*, 30 May 1799.   74 Meaning destroying houses of ill fame.

the belief in the justification of attacking brothels had not just persisted into the early nineteenth century but was sufficiently firmly anchored in popular culture to possess its own distinct terminology.[75] On the other, the fact that the two men were intercepted before they could embark on their depredatory course and that the town-major was intent on pursuing a prosecution, signalled that this was a popular practice that would no longer be accommodated. Now increasingly identified with lawlessness and criminality, brothel rioting lived on, on borrowed time.[76]

IV

The persistence of the practice of attacking and sacking houses in the eighteenth century, whether brothels or the residences of individuals who were deemed to have transgressed the customary code of behaviour accepted by the populace, attests to the strength and enduring nature of the popular belief that the 'mob' possessed a moral authority, independent of the law, to determine and administer sanctions they deemed apposite. In so doing they were asserting their conditional acceptance of the claim by the state that it alone was entitled to determine the punishments meted out to law-breakers, and the manner in which they should be administered. The significance of this assertion was not lost on contemporaries. Commenting on this very point, one percipient observer pleaded in the aftermath of the 1768 riots that 'a drunken and dissolute mob may not be entrusted with the liberty of determining, what are to be deemed bawdy houses, and inflicting what punishments they please, not only on the immediate occupiers, but even on many innocent persons'.[77] Justified as such commentary may have seemed in the wake of events in 1768, 1791 and 1795, when brothel rioting peaked, it nonetheless requires contextualization. The number of offences that generated opprobrium sufficient to induce the 'mob' to intervene to administer its brand of punishment was small. It embraced pickpocketing in church, the kidnapping of children, and a variety of transgressions perpetrated by women and informers. Furthermore, the range of acceptable popular punishments was limited; it included being ducked (mildly or severely) in water (the River Liffey primarily) or given a 'good drenching' under a pump; being dragged in the gutter or rolled through the kennels; and the administration of physical punishments, which might involve being 'pelted with stones' or, on occasions, body mutilation (such as having one's ears cropped). The destruction of the furniture, fittings and, sometimes, the fabric of a house was of a different order. Yet it too possessed popular legitimacy, with the result that as well as brothels, mobs also deemed it reasonable to attack and, sometimes, to destroy the

---

75 *Cork Advertiser*, 10 Oct. 1801.   76 Ibid.; *DMP*, 1 May 1794; *Hib. Jnl*, 30 Apr. 1794; *FJ*, 11, 16, 18 July 1795, 30 May 1799.   77 *FJ*, 24 May 1768.

houses and the places of work of those, merchants and shippers included, who were deemed to have infringed the norms of what the populace deemed appropriate behaviour. In numerical terms, such attacks were exceeded by the number of attacks on brothels. Even together, they cannot be said to represent a major type of riot. But modest though such events may appear in the grander scheme of things, they had a distinct impact upon the communities in which they took place. Moreover, since the attitudes of the early-modern populace can be better divined by studying the actions of the crowd than the words of their betters, it provides an opportunity to explore how they applied the moral authority that was integral to their view of the world and their relationship with those who claimed to be their social superiors.

Educating eighteenth-century Ulster

T.C. BARNARD

The authorities in Ireland regarded education as essential to good order, productivity and – increasingly from the sixteenth century – Anglicization and the spread of Protestantism.[1] Endowed grammar schools were conspicuous elements in the early seventeenth-century Ulster plantations. Yet, the positive measures have attracted less attention than the repressive ones. The survival and successes of clandestine schools for Catholics and Protestant dissenters, legally proscribed between the 1690s and 1780s, are known.[2] Either explicitly or implicitly their existence has been linked with the persistence of Catholic beliefs among a majority of the population and the emergence of a vigorous nationalism, both cultural and political.[3] If romanticizing about fortitude marks some of the accounts, others seek to measure what dame, hedge, petty and other elementary schools achieved, especially in relation to functional literacy.[4]

Education may be seen as integral to the survival and re-emergence of a distinctive Irish Catholic nationalism. In contrast, its role in making Ireland either 'British' or 'English' (and as a corollary or pre-condition, Protestant) has been sketched rather than probed.[5] The results of teaching for the politics, society and culture of Protestant Ireland are strangely neglected.

Recent developments in writing about seventeenth- and eighteenth-century Ireland suggest that accounts of tuition and schooling could profitably be amplified. As the necessities and accessories of daily life multiplied, education

---

1 S.J. Connolly, *Divided kingdom: Ireland, 1630–1800* (Oxford, 2008), pp 317–18; Timothy Corcoran, *State policy in Irish education* (Dublin, 1916); Raymond Gillespie, 'Church, state and education in early modern Ireland' in M.R. O'Connell (ed.), *O'Connell: education, church and state* (Dublin, 1992), pp 40–59, 104–7; Michael Quane, 'The diocesan schools, 1570–1870', *Cork Hist. and Arch. Soc. Jnl*, 66 (1961), 26–50; Victor Treadwell, 'The Irish court of wards under James I', *IHS*, 12:45 (Mar. 1960), 1–27. 2 Connolly, *Divided kingdom*, pp 199–200; idem, *Religion, law and power: the making of Protestant Ireland, 1660–1760* (Oxford, 1992), pp 151–2; 'Report on the state of popery, Ireland, 1731', *Archivium Hibernicum*, 1–4 (1912–14). 3 Martin Brenan, *Schools of Kildare and Leighlin, AD1775–1835* (Dublin, 1935); P.J. Dowling, *The hedge schools of Ireland* (Dublin, 1935); Hugh Dorian, *The outer edge of Ulster*, ed. Breandán Mac Suibhne and David Dickson (Dublin, 2000); Antonia McManus, *The Irish hedge school and its books, 1695–1831* (Dublin, 2002); eadem, 'The Irish hedge schools and social change' in Deirdre Raftery and Karin Fischer (eds), *Educating Ireland: schooling and social change, 1700–2000* (Dublin, 2014), pp 1–21; Philip O'Connell, *Schools and scholars of Breiffne* (Dublin, 1942). 4 J.R.R. Adams, 'Swine-tax and Eat-him-all-Magee: the hedge schools and popular education in Ireland' in J.S. Donnelly, jr and K.A. Miller (eds), *Irish popular culture, 1650–1850* (Dublin, 1999), pp 97–117. 5 T.C. Barnard, *Cromwellian Ireland* (Oxford, 1975), pp 183–212; Nicholas Canny, *Making Ireland British, 1580–1650* (Oxford, 2001), pp 9–10, 31–2, 52–5, 252, 331, 406; Jane Ohlmeyer, *Making Ireland English:*

was among them.[6] The demand for schooling itself enlarged commercial opportunities; it also stimulated the local printing, import and sale of school books and texts intended for children (or the childish). Education reflected gender. Convention and practice typically destined women for domestic and informal roles. The female curriculum was geared towards housewifery, marriage and motherhood. The necessary knowledge might be learned within the family, home or neighbourhood. Yet, there were factors – religious, moral, cultural and practical – which recommended systematic education for girls. Oversight of a household, care of children, conjugal and social duties all required a confident literacy and numeracy.[7] One *paterfamilias* originally from Ulster worried about the occupations of daughters. John Black urged the girls still at home near Belfast to avoid idleness through the 'useful exercise of their needles, a good book', walking in clement weather, and friendly visits to neighbours.[8] Unfortunately Black did not specify the titles of the books to be read. Also, it is unclear whether reading aloud was routinely combined with embroidery and sewing as it might easily be. Indeed, Charles Rollin, whose translated works appeared in Dublin during the 1730s, imagined a sewing circle in which what had been read aloud would then be discussed.[9] A portrait of two Ulster girls captures this division of labour in female domesticity.[10]

Here, by way of a tentative exploration, some of the issues and puzzles will be considered. To make the discussion manageable, it will be confined to eighteenth-century Ulster. Immediately, it can be objected that Ulster, owing to its confessional and socio-economic demography, is unlikely to be representative of all Ireland. True enough, but a start has to be made.

II

In 1738 a landowner, reviewing the education available in north-eastern Ireland, concluded, 'people will send children where they are best taught'.[11] Such stark utilitarianism explained why establishments flourished or dwindled until extinct. Schools were differentiated, both in theory and practice, by what was taught and how and how well. A sequence of reading, writing and arithmetic was accepted

---

the Irish aristocracy in the seventeenth century (New Haven & London, 2012), pp 433–42. 6 Toby Barnard, *Making the grand figure: lives and possessions in Ireland, 1641–1770* (New Haven & London, 2004); Padhraig Higgins, *A nation of politicians: gender, patriotism and political culture in late eighteenth-century Ireland* (Madison, WI, 2010); Martyn Powell, *The politics of consumption in eighteenth-century Ireland* (Basingstoke, 2005). 7 Charles Rollin, *The method of teaching and studying the belles-lettres* (4 vols, Dublin, 1742), iv, 429–31; idem, *New thoughts concerning education* (Dublin, 1738), pp 76–84. 8 L.M. Cullen, John Shovlin and T.M. Truxes (eds), *The Bordeaux–Dublin Letters, 1757: correspondence of an Irish community abroad* (Oxford, 2013), p. 99. 9 Rollin, *New thoughts concerning education*, p. 76. 10 William Laffan (ed.), *Ireland: crossroads of art and design, 1690–1840* (Chicago, 2015), p. 196. 11 Edward Southwell to Richard Daniel, draft [Sept. 1738], (BL, Southwell papers, Add. MS 20131, f. 103).

as the essential foundation. What then was added depended on the future for which the child was destined: useful labour, trade, clerking, the armed forces, seafaring, a lettered profession, the inheritance and management of property, matrimony, or public life. Prolongation and supplements also depended on parents' means. Increasingly too, social and cultural aspirations – to pass muster in polite, refined and respectable society – mattered.

Arguments developed as to what subjects were indispensable, and to whom. In particular, there was questioning of the usefulness of intensive study of 'dead' languages (Greek and Latin). Equally vehement disagreements arose over the best methods to achieve success. Innovators, frequently promoting their own schools, insisted on the superiority of their systems. Most improvements recommended in eighteenth-century Irish establishments derived ultimately from Quintilian, John Locke, Charles Rollin and a host of bustling English schoolmaster-authors. By the mid-eighteenth century, educationalists based in Ireland were publicizing their ideas in the hope of popularizing their establishments: Thomas Sheridan; David Manson; James Gough; Samuel Whyte.[12] Later, onlookers such as Henry Brooke and the Edgeworths expressed opinions.[13]

A school's repute owed much to a dynamic teacher. No matter how generously a school might have been endowed or how detailed and precise were the regulations, success rested on the instructors. Popularity with parents, if not with pupils, can usually be traced to the attentiveness of the master and, sometimes, of his spouse, who looked after the pupils' welfare. The first judgment was subjective: beyond acquiring functional literacy and writing a clear hand there were few agreed measures. Then, too, highly regarded teachers might move, retire, or decline into dotage or drunkenness.

What was wanted from schooling by the paying parents and guardians varied. Practical qualifications – appending a shaky signature to a document, deciphering a posted notice or summons, to read verses of the Gospels and newspapers, printed almanacs and chap-books, and casting orderly accounts – competed with ornamental ones. By the 1730s, it was felt 'that one can make but a poor figure in the world without reading almost incessantly'.[14]

Many overseers, while allowing that tangible qualifications were desirable, rated nebulous virtues more highly. How the latter were to be instilled meant close scrutiny of the attributes and attitudes of masters and mistresses. Those running boarding establishments routinely proclaimed the vigilance with which

---

12 *A general account of the regulation, discipline course of study, and expences, attending the education of youth* (Dublin, 1758); James Gough, *A practical grammar of the English tongue* (Dublin, 1760); *The Irish spelling-book; or, instruction for the reading of English, fitted for the youth of Ireland* (Dublin, 1740); Thomas Sheridan, *An oration pronounced before a numerous body of the nobility and gentry* (Dublin, 1757); Samuel Whyte, *Modern education, respecting young ladies as well as gentlemen* (Dublin, 1775).   13 Maria Edgeworth and Richard Lovell Edgeworth, *Practical education ...* (London, 1798); Anne Markey (ed.), *Children's fiction, 1765–1808* (Dublin, 2011), pp 22–4.   14 James Bruce to James Trail, 24 Aug. [c.1730] (NLI,

morals were overseen. Away from home, children were prey to temptations.[15] In addition, given the high levels of childhood mortality, there was anxiety about physical health, especially in boarding schools. Elders varied in their view of the discipline to which those of tender years should be subjected. Even the writer most associated with the more benign opinion, John Locke, allowed that the wilfully obstinate should be corporally punished.[16] How far belief in innate sinfulness had been wholly superseded by one in innate reasonableness, particularly among rigid Calvinists, can be doubted.[17]

Almost all expected an ethical training which derived ultimately from Christian and classical precepts. But further refinements might be sought, reflecting confessional affiliations. So it was that establishments opened that were committed to inculcating loyalty to either the Church of Ireland, the Roman Catholic faith, Presbyterianism or one of the several other brands of Protestant dissent. From the 1690s to the 1780s all but the conformist Protestant teachers operated outside the law and necessarily acted discreetly.

III

Notionally, at least, the educational hierarchy in Ulster was headed by the royal and diocesan schools. From their inception, the royal schools fluctuated in their fortunes. A primatial visitation at the opening of the eighteenth century recorded that the master at Dungannon was 'well approved', but that his counterpart at Armagh did not please.[18] The generous stipend attached to the headmastership tempted the ambitious as much as the able. Where nomination rested still with the lord lieutenant, appointments were subject to the same jobbery as other offices in the gift of the crown. The passing of the right of appointment in Armagh and Dungannon to the archbishop of Armagh may have done no more than introduce different but equally grubby pressures.[19] Both viceroys and primates tended to install clerics as a consolation for lack of preferment to a bishopric or deanery. Several such nominees – Thomas Sheridan, appointed to Cavan in 1735, Charles Carthy (Armagh in 1740) and William Dunkin at Portora (1746) – proved themselves to be effective schoolteachers. They were also talented poets. An ample salary did something to compensate for enforced

---

Bruce papers, MS 20,868). **15** *Belfast News-Letter* (henceforth *BNL*), 30 Apr. 1765, 4 July, 30 Sept. 1766, 30 Aug., 6 Dec. 1768, 13 Apr. 1771, 15–19 Sept. 1775. Cf. John Locke, *Some thoughts concerning education* (9th ed., Dublin, 1728), pp 76–7, 81–2, 221. **16** Locke, *Some thoughts concerning education*, pp 45–6, 49–59, 95, 99, 156–7, 247. **17** G.M. Ashford, 'Children and childhood in eighteenth-century Ireland' (PhD thesis, St Patrick's College, Drumcondra, 2 vols, 2011); Rollin, *New thoughts concerning education*, p. vi. **18** William King, 'Observations on the primatial visitation of the province of Armagh, 1700' (PRONI, DIO/4/29/1/2/2). **19** *Report of her majesty's commissioners appointed to inquire into the endowments, funds and actual conditions of all schools endowed ... in Ireland*, [PP 2336–1], HC

removal from Dublin, where they had been prominent in literary circles, but never altogether reconciled them to the northern billets. For Sheridan, Swift's friend and collaborator, a salary of £80 *p.a.* was a considerable drop from the £800 he was said to have earned from his Dublin teaching. After three years, he sold his remaining tenure of the mastership for £400, and came back to the capital.[20] Dunkin remained at Portora from 1746 until 1763. He was subsequently accused of having enriched himself and his family from the endowments of the school: a salve for a missed mitre.[21] Ironically, Charles Carthy, the butt of Dunkin's and his circle's sallies during the 1730s, had become head of the Armagh Royal School in 1740. Carthy had ingratiated himself with the administration with loyal odes to celebrate British victories overseas. Once ensconced in Armagh, he also preached in the cathedral against the Jacobite uprising in Scotland.[22]

Whether or not Dunkin, Carthy and Sheridan nurtured the poetical talents of their charges, their appointments directly flouted John Locke's advice against the prevalence in grammar schools of a competitive imitation of Latin and Latinate verse. Locke was further disregarded when, in 1774, the trustees of the Erasmus Smith bequest applied their funds to a series of prizes for Greek, Latin and English compositions for which pupils in the Irish grammar schools would compete.[23]

Masters with more conventional scholastic credentials enhanced the reputations of royal schools. The Revd William Murray had taught in Lord Clanbrassil's prestigious school at Dundalk before coming to Dungannon, said to be worth £500 p.a.[24] At Armagh, several factors combined to elevate the Royal School. A flourishing academy, accommodated in impressive new buildings, formed part of Archbishop Robinson's vision for an archiepiscopal capital, worthy of a prince bishop in Germany or Austria. The administrative, commercial and recreational centre of a prospering region, Armagh supported an assortment of schools and teachers. It justified the presence there of a printer as well as bookseller, William Dickie.[25] (He printed Headmaster Carthy's sermon.) Much also rested with the capabilities of the headmaster – from 1754 to 1786, Revd Dr Arthur Grueber.[26] An alumnus of the 1780s later recalled that

---

1857–8, xxii, pt 1, pp 48, 52.   **20** Jonathan Swift and Thomas Sheridan, *The Intelligencer*, ed. James Woolley (Oxford, 1992), pp 6–16.   **21** Michael Quane, 'Portora Royal School, Enniskillen', *Clogher Record*, 6 (1968), 509–10; Catherine Skeen, 'Introduction' in William Dunkin, *The parson's revels*, ed. Catherine Skeen (Dublin, 2010), pp 19–44.   **22** Charles Carthy, *A sermon preached in the cathedral of Armagh. December 15, 1745. On occasion of the present rebellion* (Armagh, 1745).   **23** *BNL*, 20–3 Sept. 1773; W.J.R. Wallace, *Faithful to our trust: a history of the Erasmus Smith Trust and The High School, Dublin* (Dublin, 2004), p. 71.   **24** Sir James Caldwell to Lady Caldwell, [8 Feb. 1778] (John Rylands Lib., Bagshawe muniments, BAG3/29/61); Trevor Parkhill (ed.), *The castle and the crown: the history of the Royal School Dungannon, 1614–2004* (Belfast, 2004), p. 9.   **25** Robert Munter, *A dictionary of the print trade in Ireland, 1550–1775* (New York, 1988), p. 75.   **26** Grueber had been a pupil of Sheridan in Dublin: G.D. Burtchaell and T.U. Sadleir, *Alumni Dublinenses* (Dublin, 1935),

the Armagh school had gained the reputation of being the Eton of Ireland.[27] This was not entirely through its record of putting boys into Trinity College Dublin.[28] Ethos might count for more than examination results. Something of this renown beyond its immediate Ulster hinterland can be gauged by the decision of the O'Briens of Co. Clare to enrol sons there. Lady O'Brien, a devout mother attentive to her children's upbringing, had sent the eldest to Portarlington, run by French Protestants, but after four years transferred him to the Royal School in Armagh. Another O'Brien followed to Portarlington, but he and a younger brother were also removed to Armagh.[29]

By the later 1760s, the popularity of the Royal School meant the employment of assistant masters, who then lodged boys in their houses.[30] Personal oversight of this kind guarded against the physical and moral dangers in sending youths from home, of which Locke had warned. In addition, the presence of the scholars encouraged specialists who offered supplementary lessons in music, drawing, dancing, fencing, mathematics. Joseph Holland moved from Coagh to Armagh city to teach mathematics. Holland gave lessons to the 'young gentlemen' in Armagh School.[31] Soon he was accepting the overflow of boarders that could not be accommodated by the assistant masters.[32] By 1773, another mathematics master had opened a school in Armagh.[33] For the humble and indigent there were charter and charity schools.[34]

The royal foundation was complemented by girls' schools. The smartest in Armagh was run by Mrs Ivory, a Swiss. She emphasized the healthy situation of the school and her care for the moral well-being of her charges. What she offered herself – French, English, history, geography, needle and tambour-work – could be expanded with music, dancing and writing. Masters in each of these arts would attend thrice weekly. Boarding at Mrs Ivory's was advertised in 1773 at £20 p.a. but two years later the fee fell to £16.[35] Also, Mrs Wallace and her daughter had a girls' school in Armagh, where they taught needlework.[36] By 1764, a new assembly room was announced, where musical entertainments could be staged.[37] In 1768, at least one dancing master was based in the town.[38] By 1775, 'Dumont', boasting of past performances (as principal) at the courts in London, Dublin, Paris and elsewhere, was prepared to teach the girls at Mrs

p. 350.   27 Tom Duncan, 'History of the Royal School Armagh' in Jonathan Bardon (ed.), *The 1608 Royal Schools celebrate 400 years of history, 1608–2008* (n.p., 2007), pp 50–4. 28 M.L. Ferrar (ed.), *Register of the Royal School Armagh* (Belfast, 1933), pp 8–16.   29 Anne French, memoranda (TCD, MS 5096); James Fortescue to Sir James Caldwell, 10 Apr. 1767 (Rylands Lib., BAG3/16/94); Duncan, 'History of the Royal School Armagh', pp 15–82; C.E.B. Brett, *The buildings of County Armagh* (Belfast, 1999), pp 222–3.   30 *BNL*, 8 Aug. 1769, 19 Feb. 1771, 19–22 Dec. 1775, 2–5 Jan. 1776.   31 Duncan, 'History of the Royal School Armagh', pp 15–82.   32 *BNL*, 15 Mar. 1768, 19 Feb. 1771.   33 Ibid., 23 Feb. 1773. 34 Catherine McCullough and W.H. Crawford, *Armagh* (Irish Historic Towns Atlas, 18), p. 19. 35 *BNL*, 9 Mar. 1773, 19–22 Dec. 1775.   36 Ibid., 14 Mar. 1766.   37 Ibid., 7 Sept. 1764. 38 Ibid., 21 Apr. 1767. Cf. L.A. Clarkson, 'Armagh, 1770: portrait of an urban community' in David Harkness and Mary O'Dowd (eds), *The town in Ireland: Historical Studies* xii (Belfast,

Ivory's school to dance.³⁹ He was also engaged to instruct two daughters of the Annesleys from Castlewellan.⁴⁰ Dancing, far from a frivolous diversion, had been advocated by Locke and other theorists. By teaching a controlled and graceful demeanour, it guarded against 'clownishness': the proficient would henceforth carry themselves in a manner that proclaimed good breeding.⁴¹

Appointment to head any of the Ulster royal schools was an official grant, subject to the same lobbying and intrigues as other forms of patronage. In 1774, the lord lieutenant appointed the Revd James Cottingham to the Cavan school. Cottingham announced that he would 'give an effectual but not a slavish attendance' to the post. A deputy was essential (as a curate was to an absent or casual rector or vicar). A master from Westmeath was persuaded to come as second master at Cavan. The inducement was a salary (paid by Cottingham) of £110 *p.a.*, to which would be added fees from the boarders for extras. The deputy was assisted by his wife in supervising the boarders. At this time, the inmates were charged a standard twenty guineas plus £5 entrance.⁴²

IV

The concentration of educational and recreational facilities in Armagh was unusual if not unique. No single landlord could hope to replicate it. Seventeenth-century landowners had appreciated the value of a prestigious school in their bailiwicks. Some who founded schools aimed high; others contented themselves with institutions that offered the rudiments of reading, writing and arithmetic and, particularly for girls, weaving and sewing. Among examples of the more ambitious type are Lord Weymouth's foundation at Carrickmacross and the Hamiltons' in Dundalk. At Carrickmacross, the master was required to teach 'religion, virtue and learning in Latin, Greek and Hebrew; also oratory, poetry, antiquities; and arithmetic, geography, surveying and other parts of practical mathematics'. Scholars had to compose in English and Latin, and to translate frequently from both languages.⁴³

Similarly ambitious was the Hamiltons' Dundalk establishment (begun in 1725), which thrived under the direction of the Revd John Skelton. In return Skelton was said to have made a 'decent fortune' from the mastership.⁴⁴ Particular emphasis was placed on the preparation of pupils for entry to Dublin

1981), pp 100–1.   39 *BNL*, 17 Apr. 1772, 19–22 Dec. 1775; J.C. Greene, *Theatre in Belfast, 1736–1800* (Cranbury, NJ, 2000), pp 133–4.   40 Account, 1775 (PRONI, D/619/12/A/175). 41 Locke, *Some thoughts concerning education*, pp 71, 215, 301; Barnard, *Making the grand figure*, pp 112–13, 353, 357.   42 James Cottingham to Sir James Caldwell, 10 July 1774, 15 Nov. 1777 (Rylands Lib., BAG3/17/16, 16a); Parkhill (ed.), *Castle and crown*, p. 9. 43 Michael Quane, 'Viscount Weymouth Grammar School, Carrickmacross', *Royal Soc. of Antiquaries of Ire. Jnl*, 86 (1956), 35–8.   44 Sir James Caldwell to Lady Caldwell, 4 Oct. 1772 (Rylands Lib., BAG3/29/30; *BNL*, 15 Apr. 1766; Samuel Burdy, *The life of Philip Skelton*,

University. Indeed, the pedagogical methods had been approved by the provost and senior fellows. For boarders, the annual charge was eighteen guineas, and four guineas on entry. Day boys, however, were charged only a yearly four guineas. Visiting masters provided lessons in French and dancing. Dumont included Dundalk as well as Armagh in his circuit.[45] As extras to a curriculum oriented towards the university, writing and mathematics could be taught.[46] In 1770, a new boarding house close to the schoolroom was built. It was calculated to please parents of prospective boarders since there was 'no communication with the town'. The contagion, physical and moral, against which Locke warned, would be avoided.[47] In the light of these developments and with a thriving town and promising catchment, other teachers were attracted to Dundalk. More prosaically, the Hamiltons wanted to equip tenants' children with practical skills, especially once they opened a cambric factory in the town. To this end, in common with other proprietors, they utilized the system of charter schools being established across the island.[48]

Notwithstanding the acclaim for the Clanbrassil school, the reminiscences of one former pupil caution against too rosy a view. The future Sir James Caldwell from Fermanagh was sent to Dundalk. He remembered being examined by Skelton – successfully – on Horace.[49] Yet, to a son, Caldwell confided that, having attended several schools, he could never learn Latin or Greek. Even so, 'what is still more extraordinary, I have wrote many vols & never could learn to spell nor cannot now write a common letter without looking ten times in the dictionary'. To his son, he suggested, 'if he never knew or heard any thing more of me, he would reckon me an idiot'. But he had been able to take degree at Trinity with credit and then got enough French to prosper in armies abroad.[50]

Relatively few of the grammar schools in Ulster could be traced to landlords' initiatives. The latter generally favoured the avowedly vocational charity schools, which proliferated in the first couple of decades of the eighteenth century and some of which were subsumed into the network overseen by the Incorporated Society after 1733.[51] As early as 1708, Henry Conyngham, proprietor of Mount Charles in Donegal, was planning to endow a school for seven girls. They would be taught to read and spin.[52] Lifford and Ardstraw benefited from similar educational benefactions.[53] Michael Ward in Co. Down proposed to bequeath

---

ed. Norman Moore (Oxford, 1914), pp 37, 51.   **45** *BNL*, 17 Apr. 1772.   **46** Ibid., 28 Apr. 1767.   **47** Ibid., 23 Feb. 1770.   **48** Ibid., 24–8 Apr. 1767; Harold O'Sullivan, *Dundalk* (Irish Historic Towns Atlas, 16), pp 4–5, 20; Michael Quane, 'Dundalk Grammar School', *Co. Louth Arch. Soc. Jnl*, 16 (1966), 91–102.   **49** Sir James Caldwell to Philip Skelton, 17 Apr. 1778 (Rylands Lib., BAG/3/17, 75).   **50** Sir James Caldwell to Josiah John Caldwell, *c.*1779 (ibid., BAG3/13/133).   **51** D.W. Hayton, 'Did Protestantism fail in early eighteenth-century Ireland? Charity schools and the enterprise of religious and social reformation, *c.*1690–1730' in Alan Ford, James McGuire and Kenneth Milne (eds), *As by law established: the Church of Ireland since the Reformation* (Dublin, 1995), pp 183–6.   **52** Thomas Knox to William Conolly, 11 Aug. 1708 (Irish Architectural Archive, Conolly papers, box 57).   **53** Visitation, Derry,

£20 p.a. to the charter school of Killough in order to educate twenty children in the Protestant religion and to buy spinning wheels. Constructively he allowed that some of the funds could be spent on fishing tackle, apprenticeship fees and books.[54] Sophia Hamilton at Bangor and Lady Ann Dawson in Co. Monaghan were remembered for their exertions to educate tenants.[55] The Boyds, proprietors of Ballycastle, were behind the charter school opened there.

Lists of the books sent from Dublin to the charter school at Ballycastle indicate the limited scope of the schooling. The majority of the pupils who found employment did so in local crafts and manufactures (pre-eminently of linen), agriculture and domestic service. It was thought that they had no need to go further than the first steps. Indeed, it was deemed dangerous to equip them for more, since it might excite unrealizable expectations and thereby breed frustrations which could find subversive outlets. Accordingly, the diet of print consisted of horn and spelling books, primers, Bibles, prayer books, approved Church of Ireland catechisms, psalters, and the *Whole duty of man*. By 1797, Hannah More's pious tracts were added.[56] The requirement of the children regularly to attend Church of Ireland worship explained the despatch (in 1741) of a dozen copies of 'select singing psalms'.[57]

At Coleraine, responsibility for the school in the town was split between the Irish Society in London and the corporation. The absent Society had high ambitions for a grammar school. In the event local demand was too weak to sustain it. Lack of willing pupils was worsened by negligent masters. By 1740, the Irish Society agreed to give the school a more vocational focus, preparing entrants for trade and crafts rather than for the lettered professions.[58] In Ulster, in contrast to the Puritan colonies of North America, there was no attempt to compel sizable townships to provide instruction in reading.[59]

The most visible schools perhaps inevitably subscribed to and inculcated the tenets and attitudes of the established Church of Ireland. The charity school in Belfast established during Queen Anne's reign was conceived as a bridle on aggressive Presbyterianism.[60] More generally, the terms of the bishop's licence, without which a teacher could not legally act, stipulated that 'the art of

---

c.1733 (RCB, GS 2/7/3/34). **54** Francis Lascelles to Michael Ward, 6 May 1737, 3 Mar. 1739[/40], 14 Apr. 1740 (PRONI, Castle Ward papers, D/2092/1/4, 138; D/2092/1/5, 61, 64); Michael Ward, draft will, 16 June 1749 (ibid., D 2092/1/7, 209); Walter Harris, *The antient and present state of the County of Down* (Dublin, 1744), pp 17–19. **55** Proposal of Sophia Hamilton (PRONI, D/2092/1/2, 42); John Burns, *An historical and chronological remembrancer* (Dublin, 1775), p. 286; Harris, *Down*, p. 61; *A sermon preached at the funeral of the right honourable Lady Ann Dawson, at Ematress ... March 8th, 1769* (Dublin, 1769), pp 7, 16–17; John Stevenson, *Two centuries of life in Down, 1600–1800* (Belfast & Dublin, 1920), pp 215–16. **56** 'Goods delivered at Ballycastle', 1770–97 (TCD, MS 5609). **57** Incorporated Society, account book, 1733–78, at 14 Feb. 1740[/1] (TCD, MS 5419, f. 52). **58** T.H. Mullin, *Coleraine in Georgian times* (Belfast, 1977), p. 43. **59** E.J. Monaghan, *Learning to read and write in colonial America* (paperback ed., Amherst & Boston, MA, 2007), pp 19–45. **60** William Tisdall, *An account of the charity school in Belfast* ([?Belfast], 1720).

grammar' form part of the course. The licensed were required to 'expound such good Latin and Greek authors as are approved and usually taught in the grammar schools'. Catechizing was also included. In addition, approved masters had to obey the statutes of the individual schools and subscribe to the first four canons of the church.[61] Strict oversight coupled with the expense and inconvenience of acquiring the licence deterred many from doing so.[62]

Evasion of the statutory requirements worsened the danger of potential anarchy, with teachers able to set up with little more than a space in which to operate. Teaching was a final resort for some, who had exhausted other possibilities of earning a livelihood. Sometimes, it was a phase in a varied career, which might have included service in the army.[63] The master of the free school in Coleraine, John Searson, had previously been a merchant in New York and admitted that he had fallen on hard times, which included imprisonment.[64] Whatever his merits as a merchant, Searson had few as a teacher. When complaints about his neglects and brutality multiplied, he was dismissed in 1793.[65] James Baillie, escaping a sentence of banishment delivered in Scotland, was reported to be teaching a school in or about Belfast.[66]

For women, schoolteaching was an occupation that combined respectability with the chance of an income.[67] In 1757, Grizel McKewn, a clergyman's widow, rented a house in Belfast with the intention of accepting female pupils. She intended to engage an assistant from Dublin. In time, Mary Cochran, who assisted Mrs McKewn for nine years, started a school in Belfast on her own account, as did another McKewn pupil.[68] Miss McDonnell, on the strength of having tutored the Misses Fortescue of Ravensdale, Co. Louth, for six years, opened a boarding school in Drogheda. Similarly, Mrs Paton used her experience as a tutor in private families to establish a school at Lisburn.[69]

On occasion teaching was combined with other occupations, particularly by married couples. In Belfast, Mary Miles supplemented the household income by teaching plain work while her husband (ominously) made whips.[70] Another combined teaching simple sewing with selling snuff and haberdashery. Mrs Dickinson ran a succession of smart schools in Belfast, Co. Antrim, and Newry, Co. Down, while her husband offered to train would-be entrants into commerce.[71] Less alluring is the sound of yet another Belfast school: Mary

---

61 Form-book of Bp Thomas Fletcher of Dromore, 1744 (RCB, M/31, f. 16). 62 Visitations, Derry, c.1733, Clogher, c.1733 (ibid., GS 2/7/3/34). 63 Toby Barnard, *A new anatomy of Ireland: the Irish Protestants, 1649–1770* (New Haven & London, 2003), p. 105. 64 John Searson, *Poem on Down-Hill ...* (Coleraine, 1794). 65 Mullin, *Coleraine in Georgian times*, pp 44–5. 66 *BNL*, 17 Feb. 1767. Cf. Adams, 'Swine-tax and Eat-him-all-Magee', p. 109. 67 Barnard, *New anatomy*, p. 77. 68 *BNL*, 5–8 Oct. 1773, 10–13 May 1774. 69 Ibid., 2, 9 May 1769. More generally, see S.J. Connolly, 'A woman's life in mid-eighteenth-century Ireland: the case of Letitia Bushe', *HJ*, 43 (2000), 433–51; John Logan, 'The dimensions of gender in nineteenth-century schooling' in Margaret Kelleher and J.H. Murphy (eds), *Gender perspectives in nineteenth-century Ireland: public and private spheres* (Dublin, 1997), pp 36–49. 70 *BNL*, 8 Apr. 1766. 71 Ibid., 14 May, 23 July 1771, 17 Apr. 1772, 29 Jan. 1773, 21–5 Feb. 1777.

McKee and Christian Wilson, when not overseeing the girls' sewing, made shrouds and laid out corpses.[72]

Surveyors readily joined their work to teaching. John Thomson, in Belfast, was busy in both field and classroom instructing in mathematics.[73] His repute was enough for William Douglas, a pupil, to bill himself as his successor.[74] A few surveyors and accountants, wishing to spread their skills further (and make more money), compiled manuals.[75] In Belfast, James Morphett gave evening classes in mathematics during the winter. Arriving from Tullamore in King's County in 1758, he took boarders at the yearly rate of £16. He intended to have his schoolroom painted around the walls with all the propositions of Euclid, 'geometrically, algebraically and fluxionally demonstrated'. There were maps and globes as well.[76] Morphett had written a 'Compleat practical scheme of surveying', for which he was seeking subscribers.[77] Some who taught acted as scriveners, interpreters of abstruse print, even as composers of laudatory verses or begging letters.[78] Those skilled in numbers were prone to pretensions and sometimes enveloped themselves in mumbo-jumbo.[79] Manipulating and interpreting numbers led through measurement and astronomical observations into astrology.

Common as a form of occupational diversification was the clerical tutor. Recent graduates and those awaiting their first benefice or call put what they had learnt so laboriously to profitable use. A strong sense is conveyed that for many entrapped in teaching, such as Carthy and Dunkin, it was a *pis aller*. Thomas Williams, having lived at Castle Caldwell as the family tutor, was subsequently employed in two other households before serving as usher in the diocesan school in Derry. He was awaiting ordination and a curacy: they would come four years later.[80] Williams wrote resignedly, 'I can't say that this sort of life is my choice, but I have been obliged to yield to the vicissitudes of fortune, when it was not in my power to gratify my taste'.[81]

Personal recommendation by word of mouth was the preferred mode by which parents and guardians identified trustworthy tutors and good schools. Advertising smacked of desperation. However, by the middle of the eighteenth

---

72 Ibid., 10 Jan. 1764, 21 Feb. 1769, 10–14 Jan. 1777.   73 Ibid., 29 Apr. 1760.   74 Ibid., 9 Mar. 1764, 11 Nov. 1768, 30 Apr. 1773.   75 Barnard, *New anatomy*, p. 103; J.B. Cunningham, 'William Staratt, surveyor-philomath', *Clogher Record*, 11 (1983), 214–25; William Kelly, *The merchant's companion; being a complete system of book-keeping* (2 vols, Cork, 1774); William Staratt, *The doctrine of projectiles* (Dublin, 1730). Cf. David Dickson, 'Philip Ronayne and the publication of his *Treatise of algebra*', *Long Room*, 8 (1973), 13–18.   76 *BNL*, 18 Aug. 1758, 23 Sep. 1760.   77 Ibid., 21 Mar. 1760. There is no evidence that it was published (J.H. Andrews, *Plantation acres: an historical study of the Irish land surveyor* (Belfast, 1985), p. 432). 78 Richard Edgeworth, accounts, 23 Sept. 1736 (NLI, MS 1511); Adams, 'Swine-tax and Eat-him-all-Magee', pp 110–16.   79 William Carleton, *Traits and stories of the Irish peasantry* (5 vols, London, 1836), ii, 151–2.   80 D.W.T. Crooks, F.W. Fawcett, and J.B. Leslie, *Clergy of Derry and Raphoe* (Belfast, 1999), pp 102, 172, 308.   81 Thomas Williams to Sir James Caldwell, 13 Oct. 1750 (Rylands Lib., BAG3/16/398).

century, the columns of the *Belfast News-Letter* were crowded with notices of schools and teachers. The abundance of institutions and instructors indicated a buoyant market for education, but it was a competitive world. Rivals stressed the superiority of the regimen and accommodation, good results, modest fees, convenience of times, and salubrious location. Mathematics masters insisted on the utility of what they offered. John Dennis was making a point perhaps when he itemized 'writing, arithmetic, book-keeping, elements of geometry with its practical applications ... to *real* trade and business'.[82] Gilbert McClure's school in Ballymena covered writing, merchants' accounts, book-keeping and mathematics. McClure boasted of 'the great number of finished clerks that has come from his hand'.[83] One who had been through such a regime himself advertised in the *Belfast News-Letter* for a job as a clerk.[84]

An extreme example of disparaging rivals came from James Derby, or as he styled himself 'famous James Derby'. He alleged that other 'ABC teachers' had condemned his writing of scripts. He retaliated by asserting that his copperplate was the best in the kingdom.[85] Derby's confidence in the excellence of his methods led him to promise that if the pupils did not progress according to 'the most sanguine expectations of parents and friends', he would not expect to be paid.[86] Similarly bold was Dunlop Adams, another Belfast writing master. He asserted that any scholar aged ten who took his lessons for six to eight months would then be able to write a good hand.[87] More diffident was Samuel Barr, a newcomer to the calling. He kept his charges low until he was better known: five shillings for a quarter year.[88]

Those wanting education sometimes appealed through printed advertisements. In 1768, the parish of Tynan sought a schoolmaster. He had to be a Protestant of the Church of Ireland and be certified as being of good moral character. He would be required to teach reading, writing and the five common rules of arithmetic.[89] Seven years later, Hillsborough was advertising for a schoolmaster, promising an annual salary of £20. The requirements were that he be Protestant, and able to teach English grammar, writing and mathematics.[90] In 1777, Ballintoy needed a master for its 'very numerous school'. The salary would be a yearly £15; candidates had to be of upright moral character and members of the Church of Ireland; reading, writing and arithmetic were the subjects listed.[91] Also in 1777, the Belfast poor-house was seeking a master or mistress who could teach reading, writing and the five common rules of arithmetic. The mistress would teach knitting, sewing and spinning.[92]

Fathers occasionally sought tutors through a newspaper advertisement. One, living near Newry, wanted a middle-aged man, 'recommended for sobriety', who

---

82 *BNL*, 31 May 1768. Emphasis added. 83 Ibid., 24–8 Dec. 1773. 84 Ibid., 22–5 March 1774. 85 Ibid., 4 Oct. 1768. 86 Ibid., 10 Jan. 1769. 87 Ibid., 12 Dec. 1752. 88 Ibid., 20 Apr. 1771, 19 Oct. 1770, 12 Dec. 1772. 89 Ibid., 16 Aug. 1768. 90 Ibid., 12–16 May 1775. 91 Ibid., 7–11 Mar. 1777. 92 Ibid., 26–9 Mar. 1776.

could teach reading, writing, English grammar and arithmetic.[93] In Lisburn, a 'decent well-behaved woman' was sought to teach reading, needlework and knitting. An additional requirement was to be able to pronounce English well and to be Protestant.[94] Another private arrangement that may have been common, particularly in country districts, was revealed when Mr Alexander of Springhill near Castlereagh announced that he had engaged a tutor in Latin for his children. He sought other boys who would come as paying guests to share the tuition.[95]

Teachers told of the subjects that they offered; more rarely of the methods employed. Parents' choices were constrained by the prospective futures of offspring, by sometimes subjective impressions of abilities (of both the child and the teacher), reputation, ambience and atmosphere, and (above all) by finances. Boarding a child (female and male) cost a basic £16 to £20. Supplementary lessons added to the bills, as did schoolbooks, stationery and presents at Christmas or the New Year for teachers and servants. Such spending was beyond the means of most. If undertaken, careful inspection to ensure value for money was likely. Dissatisfaction and also changes in family circumstances help to explain why so many youths were moved frequently from one school to another. Progression with age also necessitated shifts to more appropriate establishments.

Sizable economies could be achieved by attending on a daily basis rather than as a boarder. Then the yearly charge came down to four or five guineas, although the supplements had still to be paid. Daily attendance as well as saving money kept children from the physical and moral contagions in a strange residence. To overcome parental reluctance, boarding establishments (as we have seen) emphasized the strict care of moral welfare. Often physical arrangements were also mentioned as baits: small classes; boarding houses in which no more than four or five would be lodged; new buildings; healthy situation; isolation from the temptations of the town.

Only the rich could maintain a living-in tutor, since the annual wage was usually £20. However, if several pupils were to be tutored, a resident could be a cheaper option since the minimum fee for a single child at a top school was much the same. Hopefuls did advertise their services, but more reliable were recommendations from relations and acquaintances or from the dons at Trinity College. If this stratagem failed for want of suitable candidates or if it was felt that the softness of home-life needed to be replaced by a plunge into a larger and rougher world, then prosperous parents could reduce the risks. Samuel Waring, a squire from Co. Down, had been educated locally at Lisburn before matriculating at Trinity. For his sons he first employed a tutor, but in the 1720s sent them to a Dublin school.[96] They were accompanied by the tutor and put into lodgings.[97] Meanwhile, the father, as a member of parliament, needing to be

---

93 Ibid., 25 May 1765.   94 Ibid., 15 Dec. 1772.   95 Ibid., 11 Nov. 1766.   96 Burtchaell and Sadleir, *Alumni Dublinenses*, p. 859.   97 Samuel Waring to Richard Waring, 8 Oct. 1723

in the city, took rooms nearby.[98] The outlay was considerable: teaching alone was £9 4s., entrance money of £2 6s., and £1 3s. to the usher. Lodgings and diet added £54. Then the pair had to have their own desks; presents were given at Christmas. A writing master was paid separately. Books and paper (16s. 6d.) were a lesser expense than clothes (£3 5s. 6d.). The tutor still had his annual salary of twenty guineas. However, these expenses were eclipsed when one of the sons sickened and died. The medical bills amounted to £63.

Dublin was also chosen for the schooling of two young Savages from Portaferry. An aunt approved the decision, 'as they will have by much a better opportunity of learning everything that is necessary for them than they could possibly have in the north'. Indeed, the capital had been the preferred option for the male Savages' education from at least the early eighteenth century.[99] One of the boys was regarded as precocious in his ability to read. However, the mother lamented that he spoke 'nothing but Irish, which I fear will prevent his being a scholar so soon'.[100] Whether the problem was Irish-speaking servants at home or their strong brogue is not clear. Other parents worried about their children acquiring the brogue, and teachers in the north explicitly addressed the problem, suggesting that it was seen as a bar to social and economic advancement.[101]

Frequently mothers were active in selecting schools for children.[102] In the 1770s, much of this business fell to Lady Caldwell because her husband was preoccupied elsewhere. Lady Caldwell held strong opinions of her own, some of them deriving from the Irish episcopal household in which she had been reared. She turned for advice to a brother. Sir John Hort criticized Sir James Caldwell's neglect and his grandiose notions.[103] Hort appreciated that the young Caldwells were not destined for 'subalterns, foxhunters and tenants', but nor were they to be 'milo[rd?] men or idle gentlemen'. He cautioned Lady Caldwell against removing to Dublin to allow the children better chances. The danger was that she would 'hawk them about to every review and every junketing house in the purlieus of the town'.[104]

As with many families of similar circumstances, the Caldwells tried a mixture of educational strategies. The variations reflected changed opportunities – schools and then teachers went in and out of fashion or repute, new ones opened – and also the inclinations and attributes of the individual child. At least two tutors had been employed at Castle Caldwell.[105] One, Major George Ridlesdale,

(private coll., Co. Down).   98 Samuel Waring to John Waring, 11 Sept. 1725 (private coll., Co. Down); Burtchaell and Sadleir, *Alumni Dublinenses*, pp 859, 860.   99 Savage accounts (PRONI, Savage/Nugent papers, D/552/B/3/1/13A), pp 147, 152.   100 Barbara O'Reilly to Andrew Savage, 21 Aug. 1744, 7 June 1746 (ibid., D/552/A/2/7/11, 13). G.F. Savage-Armstrong, *A genealogical history of the Savage family in Ulster* (London, 1906), pp 141, 147–8. Cf. deposition regarding A. Savage, *c*.1716 (PRONI, D 2092/1/2, 29).   101 Barnard, *Making the grand figure*, pp 328–9.   102 'The diary of Anne Cooke', *Co. Kildare Arch. Soc. Jnl*, 8 (1915), 115–18.   103 Sir John Hort to Lady Caldwell, 9 May 1767, 20 Sept. 1771, 'Good Friday' 1773, 5 Oct. 1773, 3 Apr. 1774, 24 June 1775, n.d. (PRONI, Hort papers, D/1634/1/47, 55, 66, 68, 72, 75, 83).   104 Sir John Hort to Lady Caldwell, 'Good Friday',

may have served his employer best by composing verses for theatrical and musical entertainments to which Sir James Caldwell was addicted. Caldwell made use of his friendship with John Hawkesworth, an English *littérateur* who had also assisted with his compositions. At least one young Caldwell spent time with the Hawkesworths at Bromley in Kent, where Mary Hawkesworth ran a successful school.[106] Another child was removed from Cashel to the more convenient Royal School at Dungannon.[107]

V

Notions of what constituted a fitting education had always varied according to social status, finances, gender and intentions for adulthood. In the eighteenth century, they were altering thanks to the writings of popular educational pundits and the requirements for both prestigious and profitable employments. To cater for the changing needs, schools and teachers proliferated. In part because of a greater choice, but also under the pressures on the fashionable, polite and respectable to differentiate themselves sharply from inferiors, members – or aspirants to be members – of the elite deserted the local schools run by the clergy, sometimes the nearest diocesan school. As well as a growing trend to look further afield within Ireland for the right school, there are signs among those who could afford it of contemplating schools in Britain, Oxford and Cambridge, and study as well as cultural tourism in continental Europe.[108] By the 1760s, a correspondent decreed that a spell at Oxford was 'absolutely necessary to the accomplishment of a gentleman of family and fortune'.[109] One estimate from this decade warned that attendance at Oxford or Cambridge cost a minimum of £300 *p.a.*, whereas for a continental university an annual budget of £200 might do.[110]

Choices open to the Caldwells and Warings were closed to most. Day-schools saved money, but here too the many alternatives confused. Instructors boasted of efficacious, even novel, methods. The subjects taught mattered. Many provided only the rudiments; some, what was wanted by those who aspired to gentility and the lettered avocations; more insisted on what qualified for trade, accountancy and clerking. Times and terms for classes were adjusted, ostensibly to suit the convenience of customers. The advertisements for Belfast practitioners convey a strong impression, not just of hopefuls wishing to better themselves,

1773, [1774] (ibid., D/1634/1/66, 75). **105** Thomas Williams to Sir James Caldwell, 13 Oct. 1750 (Rylands Lib., BAG3/10/398). **106** John Hawkesworth to Sir James Caldwell, 11 Dec. 1767 (ibid., BAG3/10/769–7); Charles Hamilton to same, 11 Sept. 1769 (ibid., BAG3/10/947–9); J. L. Abbott, *John Hawkesworth: eighteenth-century man of letters* (Madison, WI, 1982), p. 13. **107** Lady Caldwell to Sir James Caldwell, [1773] (Rylands Lib., BAG3/29/57). **108** Balfour accounts, 20 May 1740, 20 May 1741 (NLI, MS 11,922). **109** Reginald Heber to B. Townley Balfour, 27 June 1763 (NLI, Townley Hall papers, MS 10,367). **110** John Bourke to G. Brabazon, 2 Feb. 1762 (Barber MSS, box II, private coll.,

but of teachers catering to, and maybe trading on, this impulse. John Livingston, who taught book-keeping and arithmetic as well as spelling and reading, was one of several to hold an early-morning class, in his case between seven and nine.[111] Others were scheduled before and after work and even in the middle of the day, when a break from drudging work might be allowed.[112]

The craving for self-improvement, palpable from some advertisements, is confirmed by at least one memoir. John Tennent, apprenticed to a grocer in Coleraine, resented his master's unwillingness to allow him time for continued schooling, as their agreement had stipulated.[113] A hostility to books and reading, and indeed schooling, on the part of a shopkeeper-master constituted the grievance of an apprentice. Tennent struggled to read secretly in bed. The son of a Presbyterian minister, he had evidently been taught more than the rudiments while at home near Ballymoney during the 1780s. In Coleraine, he relied on volumes procured from relations, snatched days at school, and long passages of poetry by Milton, Dryden and James Thomson that he had memorized. Some may have been learnt from printed texts; more through recitation and repetition.[114]

The tuition on offer was inflated with hyperbole, already the convention of advertising. The realities and results are harder, usually impossible, to gauge. For practical and utilitarian teaching, no formal qualifications were demanded. Teachers set out, and maybe exaggerated, their credentials. They proclaimed success elsewhere or tutelage under a better-known avatar. It is hard now to separate the competent from opportunists and adventurers, but at the time the hopeless and derelict were soon spotted and avoided. Other than in the grander schools, premises may not have impressed. Rooms above shops or in private houses could be hired for classes. A sometimes unduly optimistic view is taken of how little extreme heat or cold, smoke, smell, gloom, and physical discomfort retarded learning.[115] Tired and ill-nourished youngsters, dashing from bed, workshop, office or lodging to a lesson for which they had paid, may not always have comprehended fully (or even heard clearly) what was being expounded. The fact that some teachers stressed the smallness of the groups which they accepted indicates that personal attention was valued.[116] A leading Belfast educationalist, David Manson, boasted that he split the pupils (only twenty and of both sexes) into three classes, each with its own teacher and room. Thereby the confusion when all were taught in a single space was avoided. Manson's practice contradicts William Carleton's later assertion that the melee of a single, large class (perhaps of forty) was beneficial since it obliged individuals to concentrate.[117]

Physical arrangements influenced parents' choices and, no doubt, were

London). 111 *BNL*, 5 May 1769, 11–14 May 1775. 112 Ibid., 7 Nov. 1766, 4 Oct. 1768, 3 Apr. 1772, 17–20 Aug. 1773. 113 'The journal of John Tennent, 1786–1790', ed. Leanne Calvert, *Analecta Hibernica*, 43 (2012), 76–128. 114 Ibid. 115 Emily Cockayne, *Hubbub: filth, noise and stench in England* (New Haven & London, 2007), pp 127–30. 116 *BNL*, 2 May 1769. 117 Adams, 'Swine-tax and Eat-him-all-Magee', pp 114–15; *BNL*, 29 May 1767, 15 Jan. 1773;

reflected in the fees that they were paying. Adults, having themselves been responsible for the early nurture of the young, including the start of reading, might pay attention to the methods professed by prospective school-teachers. How many were guided by educational pundits such as John Locke, Charles Rollin, David Fordyce and (later) Rousseau cannot be guessed. Irish editions of their works were published and, even without the locally produced versions, they were easily obtained in Ireland.

Locke's influence in eighteenth-century Ireland is acknowledged to have been strong. It might be expected to extend beyond his ideas on society and government to education.[118] His *Thoughts concerning education*, published originally in England in 1693, was first reprinted (apparently) in Dublin only in 1728. Locke's ideas, if they insisted on the need to excite a child's curiosity and to nurture reason, are credited with popularizing gentler attitudes. Yet, while sparing in the occasions when corporal punishment could properly be inflicted, Locke did not ban it, especially to eradicate wilful stubbornness.

Locke criticized the grammar schools, with their focus on Greek, Latin and formal logical exercises. He emphasized instead moral foundation and conduct consonant with good breeding. His recommendations, entrusting the main tasks to parents, were not ones easily undertaken by most. Nor was his preference for a resident tutor of high moral calibre practicable in most families. Suitable governors were few and the cost high: a minimum of £20 *p.a.* An alternative occasionally adopted in Ulster was for a tutor to be shared by a small group of boys, who would come to live in one house with the instructor. Enterprising schoolmasters stepped in. Small numbers of boys were lodged with them, so that their moral formation could be overseen minutely and their physical care entrusted to a house-keeper, typically the master's spouse. In Armagh, the lack of supervision was avoided by what were in essence hostels kept by assistant masters.

Only a handful of the establishments advertised in eighteenth-century Ulster professed to follow Locke's formula; most adhered to the conventions that he had berated. A target of his sharpest barbs was the obsession in grammar schools with composing themes and verses in Latin and Greek. He rejected the defence that thereby rhetorical and oratorical skills useful in public and professional lives were perfected. Imitating classical poets was positively dangerous. Adepts were hailed as wits and, flattered by praise, neglected their estates and took to gaming. Despite Locke's strictures, grammar schools in Ulster, as elsewhere in Ireland and Britain, focused on the classics. Moreover, some masters, notably Carthy and

---

Dorrian, *Outer edge of Ulster*, pp 101–4, 107–8.   118 Ashford, 'Children and childhood in eighteenth-century Ireland'; Marianne Elliott, *Wolfe Tone: prophet of Irish independence* (New Haven & London, 1989), p. 20; I.R. McBride, *Eighteenth-century Ireland; the isle of slaves* (Dublin, 2009), pp 63–8; R.B. McDowell and D.A. Webb, *Trinity College Dublin, 1592–1952* (Dublin, 2004), pp 70, 72–3.

Dunkin, themselves personified the addiction to versifying if not to its ruinous consequences.[119] The benefaction from the Smith trust embedded the habit even more deeply in the Irish grammar schools. In 1788, when a fly publisher in Derry promised a medal for the best poem in celebration of the siege a century earlier, the competition attracted fifteen submissions from across the province.[120] One product of the school system in Ulster, John Black, a wealthy exile in France, displayed precisely the trait that Locke had reprobated. A letter of 1757 was interlarded with Latin tags. Proud rather than abashed, Black observed, 'you see that I recollect now & then ... some occasional pedantic scraps of my Belfast education above 60 years ago'.[121]

Few teachers in eighteenth-century Ulster mentioned a debt to educational theorists and reformers, although indebtedness can often be inferred. A particularly effective self-publicist was David Manson, who detailed his system in print. Manson sugared the pill of learning by trying to make it fun, thereby heeding the advice of Locke and Rollin. Manson termed his Belfast establishment, set up about 1752, 'a play-school'. Eschewing physical punishment, he aimed to kindle enthusiasm through exploiting urges such as emulation, shame and honour. He devised elaborate games to teach and then improve reading, spelling and pronunciation. In the lowest of the three classes he had tables of monosyllabic words printed and framed on large sheets, which were then hung from a wooden box in the centre of the schoolroom. Recreation and fresh air were integral to his regime. Even when boys were playing on the bowling-green, they were encouraged to test one another with spelling and grammatical puzzles.[122]

Important in Manson's regime were the separation of pupils into three classes, each with its own teacher and room. For a time one of the teachers was Manson's sister, Jane Rabb, who subsequently opened her own reading school.[123] Manson seems to have created a pedagogues' quarter. Lessons were scheduled so that those who had been studying for part of the day in one of the other nearby schools could catch up with their reading.[124]

Manson owed much in approach and detail to Locke, Rollin and Fordyce.[125] He happily availed of popular texts by others, usually English in origin and sometimes reprinted in Belfast. He himself constructed a bulky 'pocket dictionary'. It included spelling lessons, a formidable dictionary, and guides to

119 Locke, *Some thoughts concerning education*, pp 257–63. For defences: Paddy Bullard, *Edmund Burke and the art of rhetoric* (Cambridge, 2011), pp 52–78; Marilyn Francus, *The converting imagination: linguistic theory and Swift's satiric prose* (Carbondale, IL, 1994), pp 6–18; W.B. Stanford, *Ireland and the classical tradition* (Blackrock, Co. Dublin, 1984), pp 211–14. 120 *The Poliorciad: or, Poems on the siege of Derry* (Derry, 1789), pp iv–vi; I.R. McBride, *The siege of Derry in Ulster Protestant mythology* (Dublin, 1997), pp 39–40. 121 Cullen, Shovlin and Truxes (eds), *Bordeaux-Dublin letters*, p. 99. 122 *BNL*, 31 May 1768. 123 Ibid., 29 May 1767, 15 Jan. 1773. 124 Ibid., 7 Nov. 1766, 31 May 1768, 23 Feb. 1770, 30 Apr. 1773, 26–30 May 1775; David Manson, *A new pocket dictionary* (Belfast, 1762). 125 David Fordyce, *Dialogues concerning education* (2 vols, Belfast, 1753). Rollin had been spliced to

pronunciation and parsing. He also explained prepositions and terminations and the rules of syntax, with examples of bad grammar. Most innovative, although traceable to Locke and Rollin, were Manson's sets of alphabetical and numerical cards through which, it was hoped, children would learn reading and counting. The hand-book which accompanied the packs of cards (priced at 2s. 8d.) ran to over fifty pages. Manson, with a note of weary asperity, insisted that the rules of the increasingly complex word and number games could be readily understood by 'any sensible person'.[126] Pupils humiliated by being labelled as 'sluggards' or sent home branded as 'dunces' may not have flourished under his playful approach. Moreover, the public readings within the school's 'parliament', with the rigmarole of a chancellor, vice-chancellor, privy council and fellows of the Royal Society, implanted hierarchical notions, albeit altered from those that prevailed in most schools. The number of Manson's scholars was small. But teachers who advertised teaching 'without the rod' throughout Ulster may have been spelling out their indebtedness to 'the much esteemed and ingenious' Manson.[127]

Female education was widely available. Although not geared to university, the professions and office-holding, in variety of content and price it matched tuition for boys. The most expensive establishments — Mrs Fossette's at Moy, Mrs Ivory's in Armagh or Mrs Dickinson's in Newry — wooed the same social and economic clientele as did the best grammar schools.[128] Mrs Fossette operated a boarding school, and took day pupils. Moy, on the river Blackwater, was easy of access but avoided the dangers of larger towns. Other than English, taught 'grammatically', an impressive range of needlework was offered, together with cooking, the economy of the table and starching. Making pastry, preserves, pickles, jellies and 'blomage' were specified. Given the annual fee of sixteen guineas, a pupil might reasonably expect to be mistress of a household in adulthood. Yet, the skills would allow not only distant direction but activity in the kitchen. They matched the requirements for a servant in the Townley Balfour household in the 1760s: to 'work and clear starch, and make paste very well, jelly, blancmange, soups and made dishes of all sorts, puddings'.[129] Fossette's prospectus told of tending manners and minds so that the pupils would emerge 'happy in themselves and useful to society'.[130]

Advertisements alone seldom disclose the denominational affiliation of masters and mistresses. The best established and amply endowed were associated with the Church of Ireland.[131] Given legal prohibitions, teachers belonging to

---

Locke's *Thoughts concerning education* in a Dublin edition of 1738. **126** David Manson, *Directions to play the literary cards: invented for the improvement of children in learning and morals* (Belfast, 1764); *BNL*, 21 Feb. 1769, 2 Jan. 1770. Also, reprinted in America (1769): Edwin Wolf II, *The book culture of a colonial American city: Philadelphia books, bookmen, and booksellers* (Oxford, 1988), p. 64. **127** *BNL*, 5 Apr. 1768, 5 May 1769, 2 Jan., 9 Mar. 1770, 16–19 Nov. 1773. **128** Ibid., 14 May, 23 July 1771, 17 Apr. 1772, 29 Jan. 1773, 21–5 Feb. 1777. **129** — to Mrs Townley Balfour, 17 Mar. 1767 (NLI, MS 10,367). **130** *BNL*, 15–18

other confessions acted circumspectly. During the Tory reaction in the later years of Queen Anne's reign conspicuous Presbyterian teachers, such as John McBride in Belfast, and the philosophy school at Killyleagh were inhibited.[132] Not until the 1780s was information published about the academy at Strabane run by a Presbyterian or Prospect Hill outside Lisburn, a Quaker school.[133]

In 1768, Revd William Crawford, a 'new light' Presbyterian and Glasgow graduate, was taking a few boys as boarders in Strabane and would teach them languages and mathematics at a standard £20 p.a.[134] Gradually his teaching evolved into an academy, the rules of which were printed in 1785.[135] Concurrently, Crawford had been compiling a *History of Ireland*: it appeared in 1783, propelled into print on the Volunteering surge, in two volumes and by subscription.[136] The academy sought to instil practical skills, the capacity for abstract thinking, civic dutifulness and a strong moral sense. By implanting 'decent civility', it prepared students for 'domestic life ... friendship and society'. Crawford's and his supporters' intention was to provide what had hitherto been lacking in the locality and to stop the exodus to more distant schools. Above all, Crawford subscribed to the doctrine that 'man is formed for improvement'. Agreeing with Locke, he acknowledged that the way that the classical languages were taught was off-putting. Those who did master the technicalities tended towards pedantry and to empty declamations. Priding themselves on the accomplishment, the 'vanity of the vain' was further inflated. But, as the examples of Newton, Dryden, Pope and Shaftesbury demonstrated, classical learning helped towards scientific knowledge and the appreciation of the sublime and beautiful. Crawford advocated the study of mathematics, geography and astronomy, again for their applications and reminders of the immensity of creation.[137] His 'philosophical liberality and fidelity' were communicated more widely thanks to their endorsement in the 1789 edition of William Guthrie's *Geography*, a compendium popular in Irish schools.[138]

V

Mar. 1774. 131 Clogher diocesan papers (RCB, D.1/72, 2–5); visitations, Derry, c.1733, Clogher, c.1733 (ibid., GS 2/7/3/34). 132 James Kirkpatrick to John Stirling, 13 Mar. 1703[/4] (Glasgow Univ. Lib., Stirling papers, MS Gen. 207/118); James Trail, autobiography (PRONI, D/1460/1). 133 William Crawford, *Regulations of the Strabane Academy* (Strabane, 1785); John Gough, *A collection of narrative pieces from ancient and modern history* (Dublin, [?1790]). 134 *BNL*, 30 Aug. 1768. 135 Crawford, *Regulations of Strabane Academy*. 136 William Crawford to earl of Charlemont, 5 Oct., 21 Dec. 1781 (RIA, Charlemont papers, 12 R 11/91, 94); HMC, *Charlemont MSS*, i, 389–90; Norman Vance, 'Volunteer thought: William Crawford of Strabane' in D.G. Boyce, Robert Eccleshall and Vincent Geoghegan (eds), *Political discourse in seventeenth- and eighteenth-century Ireland* (Basingstoke, 2001), pp 259–60. 137 Crawford, *Regulations of Strabane Academy; Records of the General Synod of Ulster* (3 vols, Belfast, 1898), iii, 69, 76; J.A. McIvor, *Popular education in the Irish Presbyterian Church* (Dublin, 1969), pp 54–5. 138 William Guthrie, *An improved system of modern geography* (Dublin, 1789), pp 409, 486.

Good schools were good for towns. Indeed, any school brought benefits, especially if it had boarders. It was not only that townspeople wanted their children to be instructed and that traders and craft-workers wanted apt apprentices and employees, capable of reading, writing and counting, but schools and their scholars demanded commodities and services. A garrison quartered in or near a town created even greater demand, but was liable to wreak more havoc.

One specific need in schools was print. Establishments were publicized in the newspapers' pages; so too were the latest books. The use of print to broadcast scholastic triumphs, pioneered by Charleville School in Cork, seems not to have been copied in eighteenth-century Ulster.[139] Not just in ambitious schools, such as in Armagh, but in Manson's too, specified texts were conned and exercises with pen and paper were routinely set. Few printed in Ulster towns have survived.[140] Schoolbooks were handed down from generation to generation or sibling to sibling. Small and flimsy, the volumes eventually disintegrated. When new copies or recommended 'improved' editions were wanted, they were ordered as easily from Dublin booksellers or directly from London and Scotland, as from retailers in Belfast, Newry and Armagh. Yet the stable presence of a grammar or Latin school may have encouraged and sustained specialist booksellers, stationers and printers.

In Armagh, the successive businesses of William Dickie and James Reilly hardly relied on the custom of pupils, despite their regular orders. Masters, notably Carthy, with literary pretensions, added to jobs. When an ambitious Dublin edition of the multi-volume *The universal history* was announced in 1745, Dickie ordered eight copies. His investment equalled that of a Derry operator but was surpassed by the sixteen taken in Newry and ninety by three Belfast booksellers.[141] A more elaborate effort to satisfy and perhaps enlarge literary tastes was the construction of the Public Library and its lending of books. Between 1796 and 1802, the title most in demand was Gibbon's *Decline and fall*.[142] Its popularity may have owed something to a fascination with classical history acquired at school. However, its notoriety alone aroused curiosity.

Gibbon belonged to a cultural world distinct from that in which the bulk of readers in eighteenth-century Ulster were immersed.[143] Educationalists worried over the effects of a diet of the fabulous, picaresque and salacious.[144] Christian and moralizing texts were offered as alternatives. Gibbon illustrated the dangers

---

139 *The magazine of magazines* (Limerick, 1751), p. 188.   140 Other than Belfast printings, copies of an *Accidence* (Londonderry, 1789), and of Daniel Fenning, *Universal spellingbook* (Newry, 1780) are recorded. Cf. Dorian, *Outer edge of Ulster*, p. 105.   141 *The universal history* (20 vols, Dublin, 1745).   142 R.C. Cole, *Irish booksellers and English writers* (London, 1986), pp 29, 130–47, 247; John Killen, 'The reading habits of a Georgian gentleman, John Templeton and the book collections of the Belfast Society for Promoting Knowledge' in Bernadette Cunningham and Máire Kennedy (eds), *The experience of reading: Irish historical perspectives* (Dublin, 1999), p. 103.   143 J.R.R. Adams, *The printed word and the common man: popular culture in Ulster, 1700–1900* (Belfast, 1987).

of secularism and scepticism detected by critics in the overly classical – and pagan – curriculum to which the elite was subjected. Pessimists feared that the blinkered regimen of many schools, while imparting a functional literacy, bequeathed an aversion to books. Such evidence as there is – usually autobiographical – suggests that an adult appetite for reading could be traced to haphazard instruction in home and neighbourhood.[145] Also, among the few who retraced their steps in learning, autodidacticism was powerful.

Schooling helped to create a population in which a majority could cope with the daily encounters with written words and numbers. Moreover, literate skills were acquired by those who did not need them for employment.[146] On the evidence reviewed here, there was no shortage of teachers. Populous towns offered choice. But the extent to which schooling either embedded or transcended denominational, local and regional attachments cannot be evaluated. Texts, recounting sacred deeds and parables, legends and romances, initiating in spelling, multiplication, mensuration, penmanship and navigation, were common, not just across Ireland and Britain, but in Continental Europe and North America.[147] Education based on print tended towards homogenization; regional and confessional particularity was fostered in the family, at worship and work, by talk and song rather than through reading.

---

144 For example, R. Humphreys, *The amusing instructor* (Dublin, 1769), sig. B[1]. **145** Adams, *Printed word and common man*. **146** Cormac Ó Gráda, 'School attendance and literacy in Ireland before the Great Famine: a simple baronial analysis' in Garret FitzGerald, *Irish primary education in the early nineteenth century: an analysis of the first and second reports of the commissioners of Irish education inquiry, 1825–6*, ed. James Kelly (Dublin, 2013), pp 113–14. **147** Roger Chartier, *Lectures et lecteurs dans la France d'ancien régime* (Paris, 1987); François Furet and Jacques Ozouf (eds), *Lire et écrire: l'alphabétisation des français de Calvin à Jules Ferry* (Paris, 1977); Monaghan, *Learning to read and write*; V.E. Neuburg, *Popular education in eighteenth-century England* (London, 1971).

'So many wheels within wheels':[1] the 1793 Catholic Relief Act revisited

THOMAS BARTLETT

'Revisited' may be too strong a term, for the fact of the matter is that, to date, the 1793 relief act has received relatively little attention from historians. This is puzzling for, as a result of the act, Irish Catholics were admitted to vote in county elections on the same terms as Irish Protestants, most of the barriers to the civil professions were removed and, not least, the way was opened for Catholics to serve openly in the ranks and gain commissions in the armed forces of the crown. Taken together, these were momentous changes that, cumulatively, greatly shook the Irish political structure. Irish Catholics were now indisputably within the 'circle' of the constitution (as Speaker John Foster called it) and, since they had gained the vote, it was argued that permission for Catholics to sit in the Irish parliament, if they were elected, could not be long delayed. Given the large preponderance of Catholic numbers in Ireland, supporters of 'Protestant ascendancy' were undeniably alarmed at such a prospect, and it may be justly claimed that the beginnings of Irish unionism should be dated to the passing of the Catholic Relief Act of 1793. Moreover, as is well known (though rarely emphasized), it was the Catholic forty-shilling freeholder, admitted to the franchise by this act, who was to be the instrument that Daniel O'Connell deployed to secure Catholic emancipation some thirty years later.

Militarily too, the act was of surpassing importance and it was no coincidence that it received the royal assent within weeks of Britain and France going to war with each other. The act cleared the way for the military mobilization of Irish Catholics in the wars against the French revolutionary regime, and subsequently against Napoleon. From a low base – in theory there ought to have been no Catholic soldiers in any British regiment before 1793 – within a year twenty-two regiments overwhelmingly filled by Irish Catholics had been put on the Irish military establishment.[2] In addition, an Irish militia, designed primarily as a defence force, was set up in the spring of 1793. Its rank and file largely consisted of Irish Catholics balloted into the service, while its officers were mostly drawn from the Irish Protestant elite. By the time of the Union, 30 per cent of the British army was Irish, and when emancipation was conceded in 1829 that proportion had grown to 42.2 per cent. It remained disproportionately high

---

1 Westmorland to Dundas, 14 Feb. 1793 (TNA, HO 100/42/287–90). See also Westmorland to Pitt, [?Feb.] 1793 (ibid., Pitt papers, PRO 30/8/331/191–4).   2 J.E. Cookson, *The British armed nation, 1793–1815* (Oxford, 1997), p. 126.

down to the First World War.³ As in politics, so in military matters, the 1793 act was quietly, quickly and startlingly revolutionary. All in all, the 1793 Catholic Relief Act, next to the Union itself, was arguably the most significant piece of legislation passed by the Irish parliament in the eighteenth century.

And yet, explanations for this massive turn-around vis-à-vis Irish Catholics have been lacking. It might have been expected that such a seismic shift, from a policy of firm rejection of Catholics to an (apparently) warm embrace, where politics and the constitution were concerned, and from exclusion to inclusion – even forcible inclusion – in the armed forces of the crown, would have attracted the attention of any number of historians. But this has not been the case. The earliest historical writing surrounding the act was almost entirely dominated by a desire to establish Daniel O'Connell as the only begetter of emancipation. This requirement necessarily meant that the achievements of others, such as Edmund Burke, John Keogh, Edward Hay, Theobald McKenna, Theobald Wolfe Tone and Denys Scully, had to be played down, and hence the 1793 act was largely ignored. Subsequent scholarship has been more generous, if sparse. In 1989 Jacqueline Hill offered what she described as an 'imperial perspective' on the progress of Catholic relief from 1763 to 1780, and while her chosen period precluded any discussion of the 1793 act such a perspective on the entire question was undoubtedly a valuable one.⁴ Then, in 1997, Eamon O'Flaherty followed up his earlier examination of that growing Catholic assertiveness which, in his view, had forced London into making the concessions of 1793, with a wide-ranging examination of the progress of Catholic relief in the last decades of the eighteenth century. Here he credited Edmund Burke and his son Richard with 'considerable authority in the shaping of policy towards the Catholics by successive ministries in London' and specifically in the successful outcome to the demands of Irish Catholics.⁵ Lastly, the most detailed account of the passing of the 1793 act, written by the present author over twenty years ago, was skewed towards high politics, and, while it did cite military considerations as a factor, it remains, I fear, rather unconvincing.⁶ Perhaps a fresh look at the Catholic Relief Act of 1793 would be timely.

The origins of Catholic relief, and specifically of the 1793 Act, are to be located in territories far removed from the shores of Ireland – in Pondicherry in India, in the Ohio valley in British North America, in Manila in the Philippine

3 P.J. Marshall, *Remaking the British Atlantic: the United States and the British empire after American independence* (Oxford, 2011), p. 136; H.J. Hanham, 'Religion and nationality in the mid-Victorian army' in M.R.D. Foot (ed.), *War and society: historical essays in honour of J.R. Western* (London, 1973), p. 161. 4 J.R. Hill, 'Religious toleration and the relaxation of the penal laws: an imperial perspective, 1763–1780', *Archivium Hibernicum*, 44 (1989), 98–109. 5 Eamon O'Flaherty, 'The Catholic Convention and Anglo-Irish politics, 1791–3', ibid., 40 (1985), 14–34; idem, 'Burke and the Catholic question', *ECI*, 12 (1997), 7–27 (quotation at 7). There is a valuable account in O'Flaherty's MA thesis: 'The Catholic question in Irish politics, 1774–1795' (University College Dublin, 1981). 6 Thomas Bartlett, *The fall and rise of the Irish nation: the Catholic question, 1690–1830* (Dublin, 1992). See also, idem, '"A weapon

Islands and in the Caribbean. And the timing was indissolubly connected to the success of British arms during the Seven Years War. By 1763, when that war officially ended, a new worldwide British empire had been established. Its formation would put in motion a series of innovations in governance, lead to a reappraisal of defence needs, and ultimately to a reformulation of the ideology of empire. Where previously, what passed for the British empire had been a poorly governed and loosely connected collection of disparate territories, outposts, factories and colonies tied together by an ideology that stressed the centrality of its 'Protestant, commercial, maritime and free' character (in David Armitage's formulation), this new empire, with its massive territorial gains in Asia and America, could no longer stress its predominant Protestant ethos, its trading nature, its naval reach (as opposed to its armies) or even its concern with freedom. A radical reformulation of ideology was required and a thorough reappraisal of hitherto cherished nostrums was needed to take account of responsibilities for new territories, and, especially, for new subject peoples with different religions, cultures and histories. In addition, the Westminster government would seek to exercise imperial powers. Not surprisingly, there was resistance to any such reconfiguration of the ideology or governance of empire, most notably from the American colonists, who quickly began to unpick the links to Westminster, and who in 1775 went to war with the mother country in order to secure their independence, but also from American Indians who were directly threatened by the new dispensation: Pontiac's War of 1763 was only one such manifestation. The Irish, too, or some of them, whether through the Volunteer movement of 1778–82 or even through the activities of the United Irishmen, up to and including the 1798 rebellion, revealed their resistance to imperial dominion. As for the French, they were not at all reconciled to the end of their colonies or factories in India, the Caribbean or North America. In 1778, France would go to war in alliance with the American colonists in order to recoup some earlier territorial losses; and from 1793 to 1815 she would wage the revolutionary and Napoleonic wars to recover even more. It was the battle of Waterloo (1815) that put an end to an imperial rivalry that had begun sixty years earlier in Asia and in North America.

Much of this is well known, but what is less understood is that the emergence of a territorially vast empire with a new governance and a significant ideology encountered strong resistance, not just from the French and various subject peoples abroad but also from those whom we may dub 'Protestant patriots', and who were to be found at home, in Dublin, London and Edinburgh.[7] It was these 'Protestant patriots', with their open hostility to any dilution of the Protestant nature of the British constitution, who would offer the most coherent, effective

---

of war yet untried": Irish Catholics and the armed forces of the crown, 1760–1830' in T.G. Fraser and Keith Jeffery (eds), *Men, women and war: Historical Studies xviii* (Dublin, 1993), pp 66–85.   7 The term was coined in B.H. Jones, '"In favor of popery": patriotism, Protestantism and the Gordon Riots in the revolutionary British Atlantic', *Journal of British*

and sometime violent resistance to the emergence of a new imperial ideology. It is within this context of a struggle for what might be called a pluralistic empire as opposed to an exclusively Protestant one that the 1793 Relief Act for Irish Catholics has to be viewed.

The arguments on both sides of these 'competing visions of empire' had been well rehearsed before 1793.[8] On the one hand, there were those who claimed, when the appropriate government for the former French (and Catholic) colony, Grenada, came up for discussion, that Catholics could never be admitted to the British constitution which prevailed on the island. Notwithstanding this argument, French Catholics in Grenada secured the vote in 1768 and the right to sit in the political and legal institutions of the island. Similar arguments were heard during the stormy debates over the future government of Quebec, but once again those prevailed who claimed that pragmatism rather than prejudice should determine policy. A Catholic bishop, fee'd by the British government, was dispatched to Quebec, French Catholics were allowed to take an oath of allegiance and permitted to sit on an advisory council to the governor. Within a short time, Governor James Murray, hitherto deeply suspicious of French Catholics in Quebec, was hailing them as 'the most faithful and most useful set of men in this American Empire'.[9] None of this prevented a further noisy debate in the House of Commons, and much anti-Catholic rhetoric in the public prints, during the deliberations on the Quebec Act (1774), but, as before, those who argued for expediency in imperial matters had their way and a legislative council was duly established.[10]

So far as tolerating Catholicism in Great Britain and Ireland was concerned, there was what we may call a halting progress. In Ireland, a Test Act was passed in 1774 that permitted Catholics to swear an oath of allegiance to the Protestant king, as well as renounce certain alleged tenets of their faith. And during the Volunteer excitement of 1778–82 two significant pieces of relief legislation were put through the Irish parliament, which together effectively removed the landed and religious elements of the penal laws against Irish Catholics. However, political power, the professions and the armed forces remained closed to them.

With English and Scottish Catholics it was all rather different. True, English Catholics were granted a modest relief act in 1778, but a similar bill proposed for Scottish Catholics led to serious rioting in Edinburgh during which the house,

Studies, 52 (2013), 79–102.   8 Here the pioneering work of Jacqueline Hill is acknowledged: Hill, 'Religious toleration and the relaxation of the penal laws'. See also Jones, '"In favor of popery"'; David Milobar, 'Conservative ideology, metropolitan government and the reform of Quebec, 1782–1791', *International History Review*, 12 (1990), 45–64; Hannah Weiss Muller, 'Subjecthood and the British empire', *Journal of British Studies*, 53 (2014), 29–58; Aaron Willis, 'The standing of new subjects: Grenada and the Protestant constitution after the Treaty of Paris (1763)', *Journal of Imperial and Commonwealth History*, 42 (2014), 1–21. My thanks to Dr Willis for discussing this topic with me.   9 Quoted in Hill, 'Religious toleration and the relaxation of the penal laws', p. 102.   10 Philip Lawson, 'The Irishman's prize: views of Canada from the British press, 1760–1774', *HJ*, 28 (1985), 575–96.

chapel and library of the Catholic bishop George Hay were burned to the ground. No arrests were made. In the face of public clamour in Scotland – hundreds of petitions were drawn up and over 50 tracts denouncing toleration were published – the proposed bill had to be withdrawn.[11] Then, in a delayed reaction to the English relief act, the Gordon Riots of June 1780 took place as a protest against 'popery'. Hundreds died in what was to be the deadliest rioting in modern times in England.[12] Clearly, any attempt at bringing Catholics within the Protestant constitution, even with imperial objectives in mind, could expect serious resistance, both at plebeian and elite level.

The attempt to bring forward English, Irish and Scottish Catholics, to extend recognition to them as fellow-subjects, was of a piece with similar exercises in favour of Catholics in the Caribbean and Canada. At bottom was the realization by some British ministers that if the challenges faced in governing the empire were to be overcome, then the exclusiveness of a Protestant constitution would have to be diluted. More immediately, and certainly more pressing, the manpower needs of the new empire rendered such initiatives imperative. This was certainly the view of Henry Dundas, William Pitt's 'indispensable' ally and friend, and manager at one time of no fewer than thirty-six Scottish MPs.[13] Dundas was to be home secretary at the time of the Catholic Relief Act of 1793, and he can be credited with a central role in the passing of the Act. In some respects this claim may seem surprising. If Dundas is remembered at all nowadays, it is as Pitt's 'Scottish viceroy',[14] a multiple office-holder, who was one of the more venal politicians in late eighteenth-century Britain. Allegedly he was 'a monster of corruption and oppression who ... sold out his country and countrymen to the English', a minister who staunchly resisted the opponents of slavery in the House of Commons, and one who only narrowly escaped a guilty verdict in his impeachment for corruption by the House of Lords in 1806. 'King Harry the Ninth', as he was dubbed by contemporaries, seems altogether unlikely to be the principal benefactor of Irish Catholics in 1793. And yet, Dundas' imperial vision told him that this was the correct policy to pursue. From an early date he had been on record as urging 'equal treatment for every part of the empire' and he had drawn up the ill-fated bill for the relief of Scottish Catholics in 1778–9. He had also supported the repeal of the Disarming Act in 1781, thus allowing the Highlanders to wear their customary attire, and he had lobbied for the restoration of the forfeited estates to former Jacobite families. In addition, he was an enthusiastic supporter of incorporating Scottish Highland regiments into the British army. And in 1793, he was behind the relief act that

---

11 Mark Goldie, 'The Scottish Catholic Enlightenment', *Journal of British Studies*, 30 (1991), 20–62. See also R.K. Donovan, *No popery and radicalism: opposition to Roman Catholic relief in Scotland, 1778–1782* (New York, 1987).   12 Ian Haywood and John Seed (eds), *The Gordon Riots: politics, culture and insurrection in late eighteenth-century Britain* (Cambridge, 2012). 13 See the biographical entry on Dundas by R.G. Thorne in *The House of Commons, 1790–1820* (5 vols, London, 1986), iii, 632–45.   14 The term is Mark Goldie's: 'Scottish Catholic

made Catholic worship lawful in Scotland and secured Catholic property rights.[15]

Dundas' motivation for extending toleration to Scottish Catholics stemmed partly from his belief that the Highlands could provide a sizable body of recruits to the British army. And there is no doubt that Bishop Hay encouraged this notion of trading relief in return for recruits; Hay even promoted the settlement of Catholic Highlanders on Dundas' estates in Canada.[16] There are, however, grounds for arguing that Dundas' views were rather more expansive than this. After all, Scottish Catholics barely numbered 30,000 in the 1780s, and there was a limit to what could be recruited from that demographic base. What Dundas sought in fact was 'Catholic relief all round', in England, Ireland and Scotland, and while he certainly hoped for recruits for the armed forces, he saw military service itself both as an integrator and as a cure for disaffection in Scotland and Ireland. He forecast that 'an aggrieved elite', whether Scottish Jacobite or Irish Catholic, if given a role in recruitment in Scotland or Ireland, could be 'converted into a loyal service class in order to remove a dangerous particularism within the state', a particularism that threatened imperial unity.[17]

It was this conviction that governed Dundas' correspondence with the lord lieutenant of Ireland, the earl of Westmorland. Appointed home secretary in June 1791, Dundas immediately found himself immersed in the Catholic question in Ireland, for a relief act for English Catholics had just been passed and there were strong signals that Irish Catholics would at least seek parity with their English co-religionists. Ostensibly, British ministers affected to disbelieve that relief for English Catholics could have any direct consequences for Ireland. However, the determination with which the newly appointed Dundas, supported by his colleagues, pressed for parity, and much more, for Irish Catholics must raise doubts about their sincerity. It seems clear that Dundas had from the beginning seen the English concessions as a way to progress Catholic relief in Ireland. This may have been why Sir John Mitford's bill freeing English Catholics from, among other burdens, the double land tax, was allowed to proceed virtually untroubled through the British parliament. Setting an English precedent for Irish Catholic relief had been a tactic successfully pursued in 1778, and, as noted, Dundas had been involved in that earlier business.

Enlightenment', p. 25.   **15** Michael Fry, *The Dundas despotism* (Edinburgh, 1992), pp 70–1. See Fry's entry on Dundas in *ODNB*; and Goldie, 'Scottish Catholic Enlightenment', p. 25 (for Dundas' role in 'making courtiers out of [Scottish] Catholics'). Military historians think rather more of Dundas. J.E. Cookson calls him 'Britain's Carnot' for his efforts in building up the forces during the 1790s (Cookson, *British armed nation*, p. 33). David Brown's University of Edinburgh PhD thesis on Henry Dundas (1989) remains unpublished, but see his 'The government of Scotland under Henry Dundas and William Pitt', *History*, 83 (1998), 265–79. **16** For this idea of 'recruits in return for relief', see R.K. Donovan, 'The military origins of the Roman Catholic relief programme of 1778', *HJ*, 28 (1985), 79–102.   **17** Cookson, *British armed nation*, pp 166–7.

The home secretary initially moved cautiously for, from his Scottish experience, he well understood how speedily 'panics and apprehensions' could be raised over any apparent threat to the Protestant constitution.[18] However, he soon abandoned caution, as the excitable Westmorland was lured into a number of incautious statements and utterances. There were advanced plans, exclaimed Westmorland, for a Catholic-Presbyterian alliance, one founded in admiration for the French Revolution and in a common desire for parliamentary reform. Hence, Catholic demands for concessions ought to be resisted completely because they were accompanied by the threat of violence. In any case, English concessions had no relevance for Ireland, and could set no precedent, as the two countries were entirely different. Moreover, Irish Catholics wanted nothing less than complete repeal of all penal laws, and then would seek 'superiority'. If concessions were offered to Irish Catholics, the Irish parliament would become impossible to control. And did Dundas not realize that all this agitation was the fault of the Burkes, Edmund and his son Richard, the detested (by Dublin Castle) secretary to the Catholic Committee? Finally, Westmorland was confident that he could manage the coming storm over Catholic relief.

Such contradictory and alarmist responses from Westmorland were easily slapped down by Dundas, who soon impressed upon the lord lieutenant that he was minded to go much further in terms of concessions for Irish Catholics than had been on offer for their English counterparts. From an early date, for example, Dundas had raised the prospect of votes for Irish Catholics, a concession that English Catholics had not gained. This was almost certainly a scare tactic adopted by an experienced political 'fixer' to suggest that major concessions far beyond those given to English Catholics were in contemplation (the franchise, possibly seats in parliament), which would then be withdrawn so as to make the earlier claims for more modest advances seem relatively innocuous, even reasonable. In this way, Westmorland and the Irish parliament were brought to put Irish Catholics more or less on an equal footing with English Catholics, something that had initially been ruled out as completely inadmissible.[19]

The resultant 1792 Catholic Relief Act offered little of substance to Irish Catholics. Its significance lay outside its terms. The debates that accompanied its progress through the Irish parliament were filled with vigorous denunciations by 'Protestant patriots' of Catholic aggression, dismissive comments on the social standing of individual Catholic leaders, and fervent promises to uphold

---

18 Ld Grenville to Dundas, 24 Oct. 1791 (HMC, *Fortescue MSS*, ii, 215). 19 Penal laws against Catholics in England and Ireland differed considerably. According to Sir Hercules Langrishe, both English and Irish Catholics were barred from voting in elections or being elected to parliament, while both enjoyed security of property. However, there were wide differences between the English and Irish laws affecting such matters as intermarriage, carrying arms, teaching schools, jury service and practising law. See [Sir Hercules Langrishe,] 'Documents on Catholics' [late 1791] (TNA, HO 100/33/220–32).

'Protestant ascendancy' and the essentially Protestant character of the British constitution. Its passing showed, however, that the 'fears and jealousies' of these 'Protestant patriots', as much as their bluster and posturing, could, with firmness, be swept aside.[20] The patent inadequacies of the relief act were soon revealed, especially as it was known that votes for Irish Catholics, along with a right to bear arms, had been at one time on the table. Ironically, in the light of what was to happen within barely six months, a petition to open the franchise to Irish Catholics was rejected by 208 votes to 25.

The speed with which Dundas returned to the question of Catholic relief in Ireland is surely a clear sign that he had always viewed the 1792 act as a mere stepping-stone on the way to something much more substantial. True, the Catholic Committee in Ireland, in reaction to the disappointing 1792 act, had swiftly begun to implement plans for calling a representative convention – a 'popish parliament' in the eyes of its enemies – to pressurize the British government for further concessions. Even if Dundas had so wished, and there is no evidence that he did, it was evident that the Catholic question would not be allowed to remain 'at rest for some time' as Westmorland had hoped in April 1792.[21] The renewed discussion concerning additional Catholic relief, far beyond that which had been conceded to English Catholics, drew once again a highly agitated response from Westmorland and his chief secretary, Robert Hobart. In a series of despatches and private letters during the autumn and winter of 1792, Westmorland and Hobart forecast an Irish House of Commons out of control, with English government in Ireland 'ruined',[22] reported that arms were being imported by disaffected Catholics and Presbyterians, predicted civil war in Ulster over concessions to Catholics, and announced the revival of the Volunteers of 1782, the latter development being thought well calculated to alarm British ministers.

Their warnings, however, fell on deaf ears. Pitt and Dundas did offer some soothing words to Westmorland and offered an investigation into alleged gunrunning into Ireland from Birmingham, the Isle of Man and Amsterdam. In private, however, Pitt criticized 'the continued obstinacy and, I fear, blindness of the Protestants' and he reassured his close adviser Dundas, that they both 'feel exactly alike on the subject' of Catholic relief.[23] Accordingly, the Castle's demand for tough action against the forthcoming Catholic Convention was turned down. Dundas announced that he was quite prepared to meet and discuss Catholic claims with John Keogh, a leading member of the Catholic Committee (though he refused to have anything to do with Richard Burke).[24] And indeed, when the delegates from the Catholic Convention arrived in London in December 1792

20 Westmorland to Dundas, Jan. 1792 (ibid., HO 100/36/50–5).   21 Quoted in Bartlett, *Fall and rise of the Irish nation*, p. 147.   22 Westmorland to Pitt, 12 Dec. 1792 (PRONI, Additional Pitt papers, T/3319/19).   23 Pitt to Dundas, 8 Nov. 1792 (W.L. Clements Library, Ann Arbor, MI, Pitt papers).   24 Richard Burke to Dundas, 27 Dec. 1792 (*The correspondence of Edmund Burke*, ed. T.W. Copeland et al. (10 vols, Cambridge, 1968–78), vii, 324–8).

armed with their petition, not only did Dundas meet them to discuss the forthcoming relief measures but he presented them personally to George III himself. The 'optics' of this encounter were unmistakable: the major Catholic demand for votes on the same terms as Irish Protestants, and other concessions as well, had been pre-determined. Westmorland eventually came to understand this reality, and so too did his strongly Protestant 'cabinet' of advisers, including the Speaker, John Foster, the head of the Irish revenue board, John Beresford, and the lord chancellor, Lord FitzGibbon, for they all flatly rejected a request to make their views known in person in London. There was simply no point. When Westmorland criticized Dundas for receiving the Catholic delegates and presenting them to George III, Dundas affected to be unaware of any possible objection.[25] He explained that it was not feasible to dismiss the delegates 'in a sullen silence' and, in any case, he wrote, the king could scarcely refuse a petition from 'a great body of his subjects'.[26] (Actually, the king could do just that: two years later, in the aftermath of the Fitzwilliam episode, when a delegation of Irish Catholics arrived in London, once again armed with a petition, the king ignored them, and they were quickly sent packing and advised to transmit their petition through the proper channels, that is, the lord lieutenant.)

With the delegates on their way back to Ireland, Dundas went on the offensive. When Westmorland had complained that the idea of Catholics having the franchise in Ireland was 'an idea quite impracticable', he was curtly told that in 'the present circumstances of this country and of Europe' sweeping concessions were necessary both 'in the interest of the Protestants in Ireland and of the Empire at large'.[27] In January 1793 Dundas reminded Westmorland that votes for Catholics had been considered in 1791 and that it had been Westmorland's fault that 'that experiment was not made' then.[28] He then went on to spell out his 'suggestions' as to what might be offered to Irish Catholics. Their ineligibility for the parliamentary franchise and for sitting on both grand and petty juries would have to be addressed, as would their exclusion 'from every office of trust, civil or military'. He understood that Irish Protestants had no objection to Irish Catholics enlisting in the armed forces and went on to suggest the formation of entirely Irish Catholic regiments (Dundas was a supporter of the Glengarry Fencibles, an all-Catholic Scottish regiment then being recruited, the first since the Reformation).[29] So far as access by Irish Catholics to trade and manufacturing was concerned, Dundas was in favour of the removal of 'all restraints', especially if it turned out that 'Presbyterians and other dissenters'

25 Sir Henry Parnell, *A history of the penal laws against the Irish Catholics from the year 1689 to the Union* (4th ed., London, 1825), p. 110. **26** Dundas to Westmorland, 7 Jan. 1793 (TNA, HO 100/42/128–43). **27** Westmorland to Dundas, 7 June 1792 (ibid., HO 100/37/146-9); Dundas to Westmorland, 17 Dec. 1792 (ibid., HO 100/38/157–60). **28** Dundas to Westmorland, 7 Jan. 1793 (ibid., HO 100/42/128–43). **29** Goldie, 'Scottish Catholic Enlightenment', p. 25. Cookson's observation is apposite here: 'Pitt and Dundas' promotion of Highland service looks much like their promotion of Catholic service in Ireland' (Cookson,

were already admitted to these pursuits. Similarly with education: Dundas felt strongly that Catholics should be educated at home rather than on the Continent. And as for firearms – a matter entirely separate from military service – he and Pitt could 'see no reason why in respect of arms they [Irish Catholics] are to be distinguished from the rest of his Majesty's subjects', adding for good measure that there might be a case for withholding arms from some Protestants.[30]

Almost all the suggestions, or 'heads', that Dundas made were conceded and the 1793 Catholic Relief Act went through the Irish parliament with relatively little opposition. The chief prize that remained beyond the reach of Irish Catholics was the right, if elected, to sit in the Irish parliament. What had begun as a measure intended ostensibly to bring Irish Catholics into line with their English co-religionists had entirely shed this limited aspiration, and had moved Irish Catholics onto an altogether different level where rights were concerned.

In assessing how the act came to pass, the role of the Burkes, father and son, Edmund and Richard, should be played down. Neither figured in the calculations of Pitt or Dundas, though both haunted the fevered imagination of Westmorland and his Irish 'cabinet'. More weight can be accorded to Catholic agency: their organization of the 'Catholic Convention' had compelled the Westminster government to attend closely to their demands, offering a crisis that could plausibly be claimed as necessitating concessions. However, Dundas for one, was already well disposed to listen to Catholic pleas, with or without a convention. And, of course, the threat of a Catholic-Presbyterian alliance in Ireland following the founding of the Society of United Irishmen in late 1791 was much commented on, and it was claimed that such a prospect had apparently spooked Pitt and Dundas into bringing in sweeping concessions in order to head off any such *rapprochement*: though equally, they may have seen in this proposed new departure a further welcome argument in favour of Catholic relief. Again, the worsening military situation on the Continent, the rapid approach to war between France and Britain, and the clear evidence that British and Irish radical thinkers were making common cause with the French revolutionaries, had all boosted the Irish Catholic case for concessions. Similarly, the pressing need for Irish recruits to the armed forces of the crown apparently made necessary the admission of Catholics to all ranks. It should be pointed out, however, that the military authorities had been fighting a losing battle in their efforts to keep Irish Catholics out of the British army, especially since the Seven Years War. The ease with which Irish Catholics rapidly filled the ranks (though not the officer ranks)[31] is testimony to the normality of Irish Catholic military service by 1793.

British armed nation, p. 14). 30 Dundas to Westmorland, 7 Jan. 1793 (TNA, HO 100/42/128–43). 31 Denys Scully was dismissive of the 1793 act in respect of its having facilitated the creation of a Catholic officer cadre within the British army or Royal Navy, asserting that it 'offered little to the hopeful Catholic ensign or midshipman' and adding that 'over twenty thousand military offices were closed to Catholics at this day' (1811) (Denys

In the end, it would appear that it was Dundas' imperial vision, and his conviction that 'local distinctions' had no place if a great empire were to survive, that were the twin spurs for Catholic concessions whether in Scotland, England or Ireland, or Canada, or the captured French islands in the Caribbean. In the specific case of Ireland, he believed 'the practice of three fourths of the country being sacrificed to the whims, prejudices or opinions of the other fourth' was a recipe for continuing strife and division, and this belief explains the tone and content of his numerous despatches to the hapless Westmorland. Extensive concessions for Irish Catholics were necessary, Dundas wrote, 'in the interests of the Protestants of Ireland and that of the empire at large'.[32] However, these favours would not extend to the right to sit in the Irish parliament, for Dundas opposed this last concession. Again, he did so on imperial grounds, for this final boon for Irish Catholics had to be held back as an added inducement to a legislative union between Great Britain and Ireland. To Dundas' dismay, when the Anglo-Irish Union duly passed in 1800 it was not accompanied by a measure allowing votes for Irish Catholics. Indeed, in a memorable scene at George III's levée, the king shouted down Dundas when he sought to bring the matter up. He had no option but to resign along with Pitt and the rest of his ministers. Dundas always maintained that, unlike his other colleagues who resigned out of solidarity with Pitt, he had done so because of the failure to bring in what was, by then, known as Catholic emancipation. With the debacle arising from Earl Fitzwilliam's viceroyalty, and Fitzwilliam's recall to England in February 1795, the 'Protestant patriots' had regained the authority that they had lost in 1793, and subsequently backed by a series of Protestant monarchs were able to delay emancipation for a generation, and so preserve the Protestant character of the empire.

Scully, *A statement of the penal laws which aggrieve the Catholics of Ireland* (Dublin, 1812), pp 120–4). On the question of Irish Catholic soldiers, see Neal Garnham, *The militia in eighteenth-century Ireland: in defence of the Protestant interest* (Woodbridge, 2012), esp. pp 160–3. **32** Dundas to Westmorland 17 Dec. 1792 (TNA, HO 100/38/157–60).

Mary Leadbeater: modern woman and Irish Quaker

MARY O'DOWD

In her memoir of her childhood, Mary Leadbeater recalled her mother's concern at her daughter's talent for writing verse. As a Quaker, Elizabeth Shackleton was fearful that Mary's mind was so absorbed by her literary endeavours that she was in danger of neglecting her religious duties.[1] For his part, Richard Shackleton, Mary's father, was proud of his daughter's talent as a poet but he too advised her as a young adult to give priority to religion, citing the example of Moses who, he suggested, would never have become a 'leader of the Lord's people' if he had devoted himself to honing his poetic skills.[2] Despite her parents' reservations, Mary Leadbeater continued to write. She became one of the most well-known Irish women authors of the early nineteenth century and wrote a best-selling book, *Cottage dialogues*, which appeared in 1811.[3] Leadbeater also maintained a diary for almost sixty years from when she was eleven years of age in 1769 until shortly before her death in 1826.[4]

Mary Leadbeater lived at a time of change for women in Irish society. During her life, middle-class women gained greater access to the public world of commerce, literature and politics. Female literacy rates increased and publishers began to welcome proposals directed at a female readership. A public discourse that supported education for girls widened into a debate on women's societal role and their intellectual equality with men. The woman writer gained a new respectability.[5] Mary Leadbeater was one of the first Irish women writers to benefit from these changes as she developed a public profile as an author, corresponded with other writers and negotiated business terms with printers and publishers. In addition, Kevin O'Neill and Nini Rodgers have traced Leadbeater's involvement in the anti-slavery movement while O'Neill has suggested that Leadbeater was a supporter of republicanism and the United Irishmen.[6] Leadbeater also, like many other women of her generation, became involved in small philanthropic projects, establishing a school for poor children

---

1 Mary Leadbeater, *The Leadbeater papers* (2 vols, London, 1862), i, 116. 2 *Memoirs and letters of R. and E. Shackleton ...* ed. Mary Leadbeater (London, 1823), pp 137–8. See also ibid., pp 102–4. 3 *Cottage dialogues among the Irish peasantry* (London, 1811, 1813; Dublin, 1811, 1813, 1841). 4 NLI, MSS 9292–9346. 5 Gerardine Meaney, Mary O'Dowd and Bernadette Whelan, *Reading the Irish woman: studies in cultural encounter and exchange, 1714–1960* (Liverpool, 2013), pp 13–83; Mary O'Dowd, *A history of women in Ireland, 1500–1800* (Harlow, 2005), pp 210–37. 6 Kevin O'Neill, 'Mary Shackleton Leadbeater: peaceful rebel' in Dáire Keogh and Nicholas Furlong (eds), *The women of 1798* (Dublin, 1998), pp 137–62; Nini Rodgers, 'Two Quakers and a utilitarian: the reactions of three Irish women writers to the problem of slavery, 1789–1807', *RIA Proc.* (2000), sect. C, pp 137–57.

in Ballitore and overseeing the charity premiums awarded by her friend, Melesina Chenevix Trench, to tenants on her Irish estate. Leadbeater was also actively involved in her husband William's expanding mail-coach business and supervised the receipt and dispatch of mail in Ballitore.[7]

Historians of women have generally commented favourably on the Quaker belief in the 'doctrines of the spiritual equality of the sexes'.[8] Women were welcome to speak at Quaker meetings and were eligible to apply for a ministry to preach in public. According to Phyllis Mack, the establishment of separate women's meetings within the Society of Friends in the late seventeenth century gave women a 'formal authority' and created a 'collective identity for women as women'. Mack did note, however, that the supervisory role of the meetings could make them both 'supportive and repressive'.[9] In an Irish context, Phil Kilroy was also circumspect in her judgment. She acknowledged that women in the Society of Friends had a stronger public voice than women in other Christian churches but also noted the limited nature of the business conducted by women's meetings and their supervision by the men's meetings.[10]

In theory, at least, the positive role assigned to women in the Society of Friends and the opening of new opportunities for participation in public affairs should have been complimentary with the wider society gradually embracing partially, at least, the equality message inherent in Quakerism. There was clearly an overlap between Leadbeater's Quaker beliefs and her engagement with Irish public life. As the advice of her parents suggests, however, there were tensions between Leadbeater the Quaker and Leadbeater the modern woman who participated in the public spaces available to women. Within the Society of Friends, Leadbeater was among the more liberal members who welcomed engagement with the outside world and was opposed to a narrow interpretation of the Society's procedures. This led to strained relationships and disagreements with other members of the Society. The aim of this essay is to explore these tensions and identify the ways in which Leadbeater often struggled to conform to the regulations of the Society of Friends. In his case study of another eighteenth-century woman, Letitia Bushe, Sean Connolly noted the tension between 'conventional prescriptions of behaviour and lived reality'. Letitia Bushe did not conform to the ideal of 'domestic docility' and her life veered between relative freedom and independence to live as she chose and the social, legal and financial constraints that limited that freedom.[11] An exploration of Mary Leadbeater's life suggests a similar tension between how she should live

---

[7] *ODNB*; Barbara Hughes, *Between literature and history* (Oxford, 2010), pp 155–7; William Leadbeater to Mary Leadbeater, 7 Mar. 1807 (NLI, MS 8671). [8] Phyllis Mack, *Visionary women: ecstatic prophecy in seventeenth-century England* (Berkeley, CA, 1994), p. 257. [9] Ibid., pp 292, 344. See also Mary Maples Dunn, 'Saints and sisters: congregational and Quaker women in the early colonial period', *American Quarterly*, 30 (1978), 582–601. [10] Phil Kilroy, 'Quaker women in Ireland, 1660–1740', *Irish Journal of Feminist Studies*, 2:2 (1997), 1–16. [11] S.J. Connolly, 'A woman's life in mid-eighteenth-century Ireland: the case of Letitia

according to the Quaker code of behaviour and how she actually lived in the Ireland of the late eighteenth and early nineteenth centuries. In a wider context, Leadbeater's life presents a useful case study of an Irishwoman who benefited from the changing attitudes towards women's involvement in the public sphere.

Daily engagement with Quaker beliefs and lifestyle formed a backdrop to Leadbeater's life as a child and as an adult. In her diary, the young Mary Shackleton described some of the restrictions imposed by the Society's regulations on her childhood and that of her siblings and friends. They were discouraged from mixing with children of other denominations and from participating in entertainment designed for the wider community. She wistfully described how she and her young companions sneaked a peek at the procession through the town by the 'pickle-herring and drum' announcing a puppet show in Ballitore: 'but that's our share of it for we would not be let go to it nor indeed would we desire it'.[12] Despite the inward-looking emphasis of the Society of Friends, Leadbeater spent much of her youth in the company of young men who were not members of the Society. The famous Ballitore school founded by her grandfather, Abraham Shackleton, and maintained by her father, Richard, admitted boys from all Protestant denominations and the occasional Catholic.[13] Some of the boys lodged with Leadbeater's aunt, Deborah Carleton, in whose house Leadbeater and her sisters also lived throughout their teenage years. Leadbeater's early diaries are full of references to the friendships (sometimes flirtatious) that she developed with the boys at the school.[14] Deborah Carleton was frequently ill and the young people spent a great deal of time together, unsupervised by adults. Nor did the friendships end when the boys left the school. Leadbeater maintained contacts with many of the past pupils into adulthood. Some returned to Ballitore to visit their former master and his family, bringing with them news of their employment as soldiers, lawyers and politicians.[15] When Leadbeater began to attend the national meetings of the Society of Friends in Dublin, she frequently made use of visits to the city to meet with her former companions. Edmund Burke was the most famous past pupil of the Ballitore school but the school register also includes the names of boys who subsequently held positions in the Irish academic, legal and political establishment and gave Richard Leadbeater and, later, his daughter, Mary, access to this wider community.[16]

Bushe', *HJ*, 43 (2000), 433–51.   12 29 June 1774 (NLI, MS 9297, pp 13, 15).   13 For a brief history of the school see Michael Quane, 'Ballitore school', *Co. Kildare Arch. Soc. Jnl*, 14 (1966–7), 174–209.   14 Kevin O'Neill, '"Almost a gentlewoman": gender and adolescence in the diary of Mary Shackleton' in Mary O'Dowd and Sabine Wichert (eds), *Chattel, servant or citizen: women's status in church, state and society* (Belfast, 1995), pp 12–21; NLI, MS 9292.   15 See, for example, Feb. 1784 (NLI, MS 9310, pp 14, 16); Aug. 1808 (ibid., MS 9328, p. 56).   16 *Leadbeater papers*, ii, 174.

As noted already, for much of their youth Leadbeater and her sisters lived with their aunt, Deborah Carleton, a single woman who 'looked on us as her children'.[17] Carleton was not a member of the Society and was less strict than her sister in supervising the behaviour of her nieces.[18] In particular, Leadbeater expressed appreciation of her aunt's liberal attitude to books, noting that she had 'indulged' Leadbeater and her sisters with 'books of entertainment' which had to be hidden when their mother visited the house.[19] Leadbeater's mother would have been aware of the strict guidelines of the Society on suitable reading material for children and was clearly concerned to implement them with her own children.[20] Leadbeater in later life recalled that her mother had burnt Samuel Richardson's *Pamela*, her daughter having read one volume of it.[21] The latent conflict between Leadbeater's mother and aunt on enforcing Quaker regulations was to be repeated many times in Leadbeater's life as she struggled with Society members who insisted on a strict interpretation of the Society's rules.

Parents were expected to bring their children to Quaker meetings from an early age. By the time that she started her diary, at eleven years, Mary Shackleton was already attending the thrice-weekly meetings held in Ballitore. As a teenager, in addition to the weekly meetings Leadbeater travelled with her parents, sisters, brother and their extended family to monthly and quarterly meetings in Carlow, Mountmellick and other places in the province of Leinster. She also went to the national meetings in Dublin. In 1784 she accompanied her father to London where they participated in the annual meeting of Quakers from England and Ireland.[22]

The formal structure of Quaker meetings was important for consolidating the Irish community of the Society of Friends as well as for the standardization of regulations. The women's meetings formed an integral part of the church organization. The usual format was that the 'public meeting' of men and women was followed by separate men's and women's meetings. In their analysis of the role of the women's meeting, historians have focused on its supervision of marriage. Couples who planned to marry presented their intention to the women's meeting. Members of the meeting were then appointed to oversee the marriage and to ascertain if the couple had the approval of their parents and family. The women's meeting also discussed 'irregular' marriages, in which one of the partners was not a member of the Society and the service had been conducted by a Catholic or Church of Ireland clergyman. The usual sanction for

---

17 22 July 1778 (NLI, MS 9304). **18** When Deborah Carleton died, her body was not brought to the Quaker meeting-house in Ballitore, which would have been the practice if she had been a member. Mary Leadbeater also noted in her memoir of her aunt that she had not attended meetings. See *Memoirs and letters of R. and E. Shackleton*, pp 87–8; *Leadbeater papers*, i, 61. **19** *Leadbeater papers*, i, 61–2. **20** *Rules and discipline of the yearly meeting of Friends in Ireland, with advice issued and adopted thereby* (2nd ed., Dublin, 1841), pp 16–18. See also J.W. Foster, *The Quaker family in colonial America: a portrait of the Society of Friends* (New York, 1973), p. 78. **21** *Leadbeater papers*, ii, 374. **22** Visit to England, 1784 (NLI, MS 9310,

such a marriage was 'disunity' from the Society but, in addition, it was the responsibility of the women's meeting to enquire if the parents of the offending party had approved or in any way encouraged such a marriage.[23]

Mary Leadbeater's diary suggests, however, that marital affairs did not take up much time at the women's meetings that she attended. In a small community such as Ballitore or the wider provincial group that met in Carlow, the members usually knew the young couples presenting their marriages and would have been aware of the family background and if they had their parents' approval. It was only exceptional or unusual cases that occasionally delayed the meeting.[24] Most of the business of the women's meetings was concerned not with marriage but with answering the 'queries' that were a standard part of each meeting. The 'queries' were a list of questions that were answered on a regular basis at the men's and women's meetings.[25] They dealt with the personal lives of the members as well as the procedures and organization of meetings. They asked about adherence to a plain or simple lifestyle in terms of dress, speech and the performance of marriage and funeral ceremonies; the education of children; and if all members of the community were adhering to the Society's policy of not paying tithes to the Church of Ireland. The phrasing of the answers to the queries could provoke considerable discussion. Leadbeater frequently complained in her diary about women's meetings being 'unreasonably and unnecessarily long'.[26] Meetings could last up to seven hours and might be adjourned until the following day. Leadbeater noted, for example, the 'very long' women's meeting in Dublin in 1790, which was due she thought to too 'much time being spent about matters of little moment'.[27]

The atmosphere at the women's meetings was particularly tense in the years 1799–1802 when there was a theological disagreement within the Irish Society of Friends concerning the status of the Scriptures. Leadbeater's brother, Abraham, was involved in this dispute and was eventually disowned by the Society.[28] The controversy filtered into the women's meetings with Leadbeater clearly, if tacitly, supporting her brother and expressing impatience at the attitude of some of the women members.[29] Noting the censuring of her brother and other women Friends in 1801, she recorded her disapproval: 'Now all these things were matters of conscience and these misdeeds ... committed by some of the worthiest characters we have. It is a day of treading down indeed when such are trampled under foot.'[30]

pp 96–8).   23 Kilroy, 'Quaker women in Ireland'; Mack, *Visionary women*, pp 246–7, 284–9. 24 For an exceptional marriage involving the Leadbeater family, see below, p. 142.   25 For a list of the queries see William Rathbone, *A narrative of events, that have lately taken place in Ireland among the society called Quakers with corresponding documents, and occasional observations* (London, 1804), app.   26 Carlow meetings, July, Sept. 1802 (NLI, MS 9324, pp 102, 128). 27 Dublin meeting, May 1790 (NLI, MS 9315, p. 114).   28 Hughes, *Between literature and history*, p. 162; May, July 1801 (NLI, MS 9324, pp 63, 79).   29 May, June, July 1801 (NLI, MS 9324, pp 63, 79).   30 July 1801 (NLI, MS 9324, p, 79). See also Rathbone, *A narrative*

Disagreements concerning the phrasing of the answers to the queries were still evident at the national women's meeting in Dublin in 1802 when some of the senior women, unhappy with the formulation of the answers to the queries, proposed the formation of a separate committee to draw up more orthodox responses. The suggestion was contrary to the spirit of the women's meeting as a collective unit and underlined the divisions within the Society concerning the Scripture debate. Leadbeater and her Ballitore friend and employee, Mary Doyle, left the meeting early, with Leadbeater expressing her frustration in her diary at the 'much settling of words'.[31]

Only occasionally was Leadbeater explicitly critical in her journal of the authority or the procedures of the Society of Friends. Journals were often read out loud or shared between Friends and their authors were obliged to write cautiously in case they offended a reader or laid themselves open to censure.[32] A careful reading of Leadbeater's diary reveals that she often used brevity or the omission of any comment as a vehicle for criticism. A good example occurred in 1812 when her daughter Deborah secretly married a first cousin, Ebenezer, in a Church of Ireland service. Leadbeater and her husband had refused the couple permission to marry and were shocked by the marriage. Not surprisingly, along with Ebenezer's parents, they quickly found themselves under scrutiny from the Ballitore community as 'reports all over the village' began to spread.[33] Despite the formal disownment of Deborah and Ebenezer by the Society, the extended family joined together to support the young couple and refused to condone the criticism directed at them: 'We made a vow to keep our minds quiet and have not much to accuse ourselves of thou' it appears that we are accused.'[34] Leadbeater and her husband were questioned about their daughter's marriage by a small group of Friends. Leadbeater was careful to acknowledge in her diary that the visitors were 'honest ... sincere and simple ... judging for themselves' but she also tersely noted the more hostile 'feelings of other perhaps prejudiced persons'.[35]

Although members of the Society of Friends believed in the 'spiritual equality' of men and women, there was, nonetheless, a hierarchy of officeholders within the women's meeting with those who had been formally appointed as elders or ministers speaking with greater authority than others. Literate women were nominated as clerks to record the minutes of the meeting and others read out the queries and reported the responses to the men's meetings. Many of the ordinary members of the meeting appear not to have spoken at all.

As an educated woman, Leadbeater frequently acted as clerk at the women's meeting in Carlow but she rarely contributed to the meetings as she suffered all her life from a speech defect which made reading out loud difficult even in a

---

of events ..., pp 50–6, 71–2, 79, 80–3.   **31** Dublin meeting, April 1802 (NLI, MS 9324, pp 49, 51).   **32** Hughes, *Between literature and history*, p. 188.   **33** Aug. 1812 (NLI, MS 9332, p. 70).   **34** Ibid.   **35** Oct. 1812 (ibid., MS 9332, p. 80).

family circle.³⁶ When she did venture to speak at a meeting, she did so nervously and with considerable anxiety: 'my heart beat, and my blood flashed in my face ... the sense of my infirmity of speech prevailed'.³⁷ In 1790 Leadbeater noted that, as the person nominated to read the answers to the queries, she had given a wrong answer at a monthly meeting in Mountrath. She was very reluctant to speak out and explain her mistake:

> I thought the beating of my heart could be heard and dreading that I would not do it... I did get up, and acknowledged the wrong answer I had given ... Anne Paisley told me after that she was glad to hear my voice though she knew not what I said. No one else took any notice to me of it, so I was ashamed to enquire if anyone else heard me.³⁸

There were particular, personal reasons for Leadbeater's preference for silence at meetings, but in her diary she also described the reluctance of other women to speak or accept nomination as clerk. This was partly a product of false modesty, as women denied their ability to take on the task of writing or communicating with the men's meeting. Many women, however, felt uncomfortable assuming a public role even within the confines of the Quaker meetings.³⁹ Some women, when they did venture to speak, acknowledged how difficult they found it.⁴⁰ Leadbeater's diaries suggest that the women's meetings were usually controlled by a small group of office-holders. In the tense atmosphere of 1799, for example, Leadbeater wrote of the trembling of a woman who spoke in defence of another woman who had been expelled from the Society. She was contradicted by one of the more senior figures at the meeting, or the 'great woman', as Leadbeater cynically described her.⁴¹

As a single woman, Leadbeater accepted her role as clerk and was a willing, if anxious, representative at provincial and national meetings.⁴² After she married and had children, however, Leadbeater found attending meetings and taking on the task of clerk or official representative more challenging and a source of tension between her responsibilities as a mother and wife and her religious duties. The Society of Friends did not prioritize a mother's domestic tasks over her spiritual obligations and regular attendance at meetings as well as active involvement in church business was expected of both single and married women.⁴³ Leadbeater's mother and sister had each put aside their domestic

---

36 Hughes, *Between literature and history*, p. 147. 37 Dublin meeting, 30 Oct. 1789 (NLI, MS 9314, p. 164). 38 Mountrath meeting, Feb. 1790 (ibid., MS 9315, p. 40). 39 In 1792 at a meeting in Ballitore, Mary's sister, Sally, encouraged women to speak up if they disagreed with any of the responses to the queries that she had formulated (ibid., MS 9317, p. 97). See also Dublin meeting, Apr. 1806 (ibid., MS 9326, pp 35, 40). 40 See, for example, Carlow meeting, Apr. 1797 (ibid., MS 9321, pp 41–3). 41 May 1799 (ibid., MS 9323, p. 59). 42 See, for example, Carlow meeting, 1778 (ibid., MS 9304); Jan. 1784 (ibid., MS 9310, p. 5); Apr. 1791 (ibid., MS 9316, p. 27); 13 Mar. 1791 (ibid., pp 38, 40). 43 In January 1790, for

responsibilities to engage with church business. Elizabeth Leadbeater was very active in the Leinster Quaker community and travelled frequently with her husband to meetings in Carlow and elsewhere. In addition, she also helped run the Ballitore school and delegated the care of her daughters and stepdaughters to the children's aunt. Leadbeater's older sister Margaret was also involved in church affairs and was for a time a travelling minister, which obliged her to leave her children in the care of her husband. Margaret was initially unsure about abandoning her children and asked her father for guidance. Richard Shackleton wrote to Margaret that although he was not 'for dragging thee from thy domestic concerns ... But ... if Thou has heard his [God's] call GO FORTH, according to Heavenly direction'.[44] Margaret followed her father's advice and spent long periods of time away from her children and husband. When, however, two of her children died during one of her absences, Margaret decided to leave her ministry work and remain at home.[45]

Following the birth of her daughter, Elizabeth in 1791, Mary Leadbeater was clearly at times torn between attending meetings and staying at home to care for her. In her diary she frequently recorded missing meetings, and noted in 1792, when she went to Carlow for a provincial meeting, that she was worried about Elizabeth who 'seemed somewhat indisposed when I left her and I felt I was a mother, but got a favourable account of her today'.[46] Mary also attempted to decline nominations to office-holding but found that this provoked criticism from other members at the women's meetings. At the Carlow quarterly meeting in 1793, she noted that 'it was said I hurt the meeting by refusing to be clerk and causing debate about it'. She was then 'overawed' to speak against her nomination as clerk to a subsequent meeting.[47] Leadbeater continued to be clerk in the following year even though she was about to give birth to her second child, 'fearing to protract the meeting by offering to resign it'.[48]

Another source of tension within the Quaker community in the late eighteenth century was the relationship between the men's and women's meetings. By the last quarter of the eighteenth century, publications endorsing women's intellectual equality with men and their right to education proliferated in Ireland and England.[49] Leadbeater was aware of the debate and took considerable interest in the education of girls. She sent her daughters to the newly opened school for Quaker girls in Mountmellick, and served as a member of the school committee.[50] In 1784 she was present at the London meeting of the

example, the women's meeting at Carlow discussed the absence of members (ibid., MS 9315, p. 8).   44 G.W.S. Grubb, *The Grubbs of Tipperary: studies in heredity and character* (Cork, 1972), p. 77.   45 Ibid., p. 78.   46 Carlow meeting, Jan. 1792 (NLI, MS 9317, p. 4). 47 Carlow meeting, 29 Dec. 1793 (ibid., MS 9318, p. 156).   48 Carlow meeting, 27 Dec. 1794 (ibid., MS 9319, p. 152). See also Edenderry meeting, 26 Sept. 1794 (ibid., p.114). She was still clerk in March 1795 (ibid., MS 9320, p. 34). Unlike his father-in-law, William Leadbeater appears to have also wished his wife to stay at home as much as possible. See correspondence between him and Mary in ibid., MS 8671.   49 Meaney et al., *Reading Irishwomen*, pp 13–53. 50 Apr. 1807 (NLI, MS 9327, pp 26–7); Mar. 1808 (ibid., MS 9328, pp 20–2); July 1807 (ibid.,

Society when English women requested the right to establish a formal national women's meeting as they believed that 'a greater part in the service of the Church was due to the women'. In her diary Leadbeater recorded her 'joy' that the men's meeting had agreed to this proposal.[51] Back in Ireland, she wrote of her irritation at men usurping their authority vis-à-vis the women's meeting. In the midst of the controversy of 1799, she was clearly annoyed that the Carlow women's meeting was 'unreasonably detained' by 'alteration of endorsements in the men's meeting which had been drawn by women friends'.[52] Other breaches of the regulations concerning the respective jurisdiction of the men's and women's meetings were also recorded in her diary.[53]

Although the meetings of the Society had a religious and organizational purpose, the pages of Mary Leadbeater's diary suggest that the spiritual satisfaction that they provided was less of an attraction for her than the social network that surrounded them. Her diaries are a strong testimony to the social dimension of Quaker meetings. She particularly enjoyed the national meetings in Dublin, which were usually followed by a round of tea parties, dinners and sociable breakfasts. Before, and sometimes after, she married, Leadbeater shared lodgings and, often, a bed with other women, with whom she talked and exchanged news and gossip until late at night.[54] In 1781 she described how she attended a meeting in Dublin but she could give no account of it, as 'I was too much engaged with the delightful hopes of my many dear friends' company ... to consider properly my business to the meeting.'[55]

Leadbeater took full advantage of the expansion of the public spaces of the capital city to visit places which would not have met with the approval of the more orthodox members of the Society. For example, when she attended the national meeting in Dublin in May 1782 she went shopping; viewed the parade of the lord lieutenant through Dame Street to Dublin castle; went to a toy warehouse, where she and her companions 'feasted our eyes with a variety of toys'; and took an evening stroll in St Stephen's Green.[56] Despite the disagreements evident at the national women's meeting in 1802, Leadbeater enjoyed her visit to the city that year, commenting on how 'pleasant' it was to see Dublin 'so handsome and so busy, new houses building, fewer beggars'.[57] On other visits to Dublin, Leadbeater toured a wax works in Exchequer Street, visited an art exhibition in the Rotunda, and saw a lion on display in his den.[58] She also made use of her contacts with the past pupils of her father's school to visit Trinity College Dublin on a number of occasions.[59]

MS 9327, p. 53); July 1808 (ibid., MS 9328, pp 50–1). **51** Visit to England, 1784 (ibid., MS 9310, pp 96–8). **52** Carlow meeting, Oct. 1799 (ibid., MS 9323, p. 141). **53** Ibid., MS 9316, p, 32. **54** See, for example, 19 Jan. 1781 (ibid., MS 9307, p. 1); Feb. 1784 (ibid., MS 9310, p. 36). **55** June 1781 (ibid., MS 9307, p. 49). **56** Dublin meeting, July 1782 (ibid., MS 9304). **57** Dublin meeting, Apr. 1802 (ibid., MS 9324, p. 55). **58** Dublin meetings, 1805, 1806 (ibid., MS 9326, 1805 diary, pp 12–13; 1806 diary, pp 13–21). **59** Dublin meeting, 1778 (ibid., MS 9304); 5 June 1780 (ibid., MS 9306); 18 Dec. 1780 (ibid.); Sept. 1807 (ibid., MS 9327, p. 94).

Although the Society's regulations frowned on extravagant displays of wealth in domestic interiors and the use of art work to decorate walls, Leadbeater expressed her excitement at visiting big houses in the city and its vicinity to view paintings, furniture and interior decorations.[60] When she spent several weeks in Dublin in the summer of 1782, Leadbeater noted guiltily that she had indulged her 'passion for painting against which I must one time or other make war'.[61] She visited the house of John Corballis, whose grandsons had attended the Ballitore school, where she viewed a large collection of paintings. She noted in her diary the large number of religious pictures, but 'what struck me the most was a Cleopatra sitting on a couch – a man's eyes were fixed on her with the greatest astonishment presenting the asp to her'.[62] A few days later Leadbeater made an appointment to see the public rooms in Leinster House where she again admired the many 'fine paintings'.[63]

Leadbeater was aware that she often enjoyed the occasion of Quaker meetings for the wrong reasons. In her diary she admitted that her 'motives to attend these solemn assemblies were too little what they should be'.[64] Similarly, in a letter to Melesina Trench, she noted that although the 'meetings are professedly attended on a religious account … the imputation of hypocrisy need not be incurred if this be not always the sole motive'.[65]

Leadbeater's interaction with the wider world outside the Quaker network as a reader, and later as a writer, led her to interpret the rules of the Society with considerable flexibility. Her journal-keeping habit was within the Quaker tradition, as members were encouraged to write down their spiritual thoughts and to record speeches and testimonials delivered at meetings. Leadbeater's diary/journal did not, however, always fall within the guidelines for Quaker journals. As already noted, the early volumes were frank about the lives of young teenage boys and girls in Ballitore. When she reached her late teens, her writing became more cautious, as she divided her record into two parts: the left-hand pages being usually reserved for accounts of Quaker meetings and the right-hand pages consisting of diary entries about Leadbeater's domestic life, along with references to visitors and social occasions. As she settled into a busy life as a mother, wife and published author, she focused more on her private life. She continued to include accounts of Quaker meetings but in a less detailed and less regular manner. Thus only for a relatively short part of her life did Leadbeater's writing fulfil the aim and purpose of a Quaker journal. Instead, her priority in keeping a diary seems to have been to record family affairs and perhaps, as Barbara Hughes suggests, to write down events and anecdotes that might be of use for her published work.[66]

---

60 See *Rules and discipline of the yearly meeting of Friends in Ireland*, p. 204. On the difficulties that the Society had enforcing the regulations on 'plainness' see M.J. Wigham, *The Irish Quakers: a short history of the Religious Society of Friends in Ireland* (Dublin, 1992), pp 41–2. 61 Sept. 1782 (NLI, MS 9308, p. 85). 62 Ibid., pp 85–7. 63 Ibid., pp 88–97. 64 Dublin meeting, 1784 (NLI, MS 9310, p. 168). 65 *Leadbeater papers*, ii, 231. 66 Hughes, *Between*

The rules of the Irish Society of Friends included a section on books, which outlined the type of literature that was considered suitable for members of the Society. The focus was on religious and morally uplifting texts.[67] From childhood, Leadbeater noted that she read books that would not have been approved by the Society's regulations. Her aunt continued to provide her with books when Leadbeater was in her teenage years. In 1790 she remorsefully related how while staying at an inn, she had come across a novel and tried to avoid reading it as would have been in accordance with the Quaker advice on reading. Yet she admitted that she picked up the volume and devoured it:

> why did I so unaccountably and perversely return to the book again and pore over it till I grew so stupid that I cast it down in disgust and then felt so much remorse for such waste of time that I hope it determined me never to open such a volume again.[68]

Leadbeater continued, however, to read widely throughout her life, copying into her diary extracts from some of the most popular writers of the day. She was familiar with the expanding number of publications by women writers including Madame De Staël (whose *Courinne ou l'Italie* (1807) Leadbeater read in French), Elizabeth Carter, Hannah More and Lady Mary Montagu.[69] In addition, she kept up to date with periodical publications and frequently referred to the latest reviews and articles in her correspondence.[70] In short, Leadbeater's reading appears to be very similar to that of other middle- and upper-class Protestant women in late eighteenth- and early nineteenth-century England and Ireland.[71] It was, therefore, far beyond the limits set by the guidelines of the Society of Friends.

The business affairs of William Leadbeater were an important conduit through which the Leadbeaters made contact with society outside Ballitore. Shortly after his marriage in 1791, William opened an inn at Ballitore, where coach travellers going to and from Dublin frequently stopped. William subsequently expanded his business interests to provide mail coaches and became involved in the expanding postal service, using part of the family home as a post office.[72] By the 1790s Ballitore was well known as the place where Edmund Burke was educated. Informed lodgers at the inn were sufficiently intrigued to walk through the village and were often encouraged by their innkeeper to call on his wife, who had met Burke in London in 1784. This was how Leadbeater first encountered Thomas Lewis O'Beirne, Church of Ireland bishop of Meath, and his wife Jane, who took a great interest in Leadbeater's

---

literature and history, pp 133–8.   67 See *Rules and discipline of the yearly meeting of Friends in Ireland*, pp 16–17.   68 Hughes, *Between literature and history*, p. 140.   69 *Leadbeater papers*, ii, 153, 160–1, 170–1, 213, 215, 217, 252.   70 See, for example, ibid., 165, 225, 378.   71 For Leadbeater's correspondence with Trench see ibid. See also Hughes, *Between literature and history*, p. 168.   72 The business affairs of William Leadbeater can be traced through his

writings, encouraged her to publish her work and suggested the title of *Cottage dialogues* for Leadbeater's most famous publication.[73] Another guest at the inn was the writer, Melesina Chenevix Trench, who became a lifelong friend of Leadbeater's and later read drafts of her work and sent her perceptive comments on it. Both Trench and Jane O'Beirne corresponded with Leadbeater about literature and sent her copies of the latest publications that they had enjoyed or thought she should read.[74]

Leadbeater's emergence as a published author gave rise to unease among some within the Quaker community. As in many other aspects of her life, her publications can be divided between those which won approval within the Society of Friends and those which appealed to a much larger audience. Her first book, *Extracts and original anecdotes for improvement of youth* (Dublin, 1794) consisted of extracts from texts, many of them authored by members of the Society in North America or England. Its primary purpose was as a textbook in Quaker schools and it may not have been circulated widely to the general public.

Leadbeater included some of her own poetry at the end of the volume, but her major work of poetry appeared fourteen years later in 1808. This book was clearly important to Leadbeater as a writer rather than as a Quaker. It was a substantial volume of over 400 pages. It began with an English translation of a fifteenth-century Latin text, the thirteenth volume of the Aeneid by Maffaeus.[75] This was followed by Leadbeater's own poems, many of which were addressed to family and friends, among whom was Edmund Burke. One long poem described the village of Ballitore and is similar in format to the prose account that was included in Leadbeater's 'Annals of Ballitore'.[76] She shamelessly exploited her family connexion with Burke to draw attention to her book. In addition to addressing poems to him, she inserted into the volume letters from Burke to herself expressing his appreciation of poems that she had sent him. The content of the letters was not of great significance but their inclusion guaranteed publicity for the book. The London edition of *Poems* (1808) also included a frontispiece engraving of Burke.[77]

Leadbeater invested a considerable amount of time and money in the publication of her poetry. In 1807 she spent several months in Dublin negotiating terms with printers and publishers. She purchased the paper and visited the printer on a daily basis, carefully overseeing the book's production. She had initially planned 'on the advice of several intelligent friends' to finance the book through subscription and had prepared an advertisement which she

wife's diary.   **73** See Feb. 1802 (NLI, MS 9324, p. 17); *Leadbeater papers*, ii, 189, 319; July 1808 (NLI, MS 9328, p. 47).   **74** Jan. 1810 (NLI, MS 9330, p. 9); Mar. 1814 (ibid., MS 9334, p. 19). See also Hughes, *Between literature and history*, p. 168.   **75** *Poems by Mary Leadbeater (late Shackleton) to which is prefixed her translation of the thirteenth book of the Æneid; with the Latin original, written in the fifteenth century, by Maffæus* (Dublin, 1808). Leadbeater used a 'literal' translation by her father for her verse rendition of the original Latin text.   **76** *Leadbeater papers*, i, 6–55.   **77** See also Hughes, *Between literature and history*, p. 172.

sent to London to be circulated.[78] The volume attracted just over five hundred subscribers, most of whom were friends and relatives of the extended Leadbeater family. Most agreed to take just one copy of the volume. Leadbeater and her husband were disappointed by the subscriber response as the money raised did not cover the printing costs. They were particularly disappointed by the lack of interest in England. A Quaker friend, Anne Pimm, reneged on a promise to secure five hundred English subscribers, possibly after she realized that the content of the book was not directed at a Quaker readership as Leadbeater's previous volume had been.[79] William, while supportive of his wife's publication project, was reluctant to provide the necessary cash subsidy of £120 but eventually arranged to borrow the money on short-term loans.[80] Although William advised his wife on financial matters and gave his opinion on how many copies of the book should be published, it was Leadbeater herself who travelled to Dublin, conducted the negotiations with the printers and agreed the final terms. Her dealings with paper-makers, printers and publishers are striking evidence of the manner in which the Dublin print industry was following the example of London and beginning to welcome women authors.

Poems was not well received by reviewers, who were patronizing about Leadbeater's literary talent and dismissive of the value of her verse translation.[81] She was clearly disappointed by the lack of interest in her poetry and attempted unsuccessfully to publish another volume of verse in 1817.[82] As she noted herself, 'in prose I had better success'.[83]

It was, however, a particular form of prose. Leadbeater's next book was *Cottage dialogues*, which was written in the form of a dialogue between two young women.[84] The volume was intended as 'instruction of the lower classes'.[85] The message was that the rural poor should live frugally and soberly and abstain from wasting money on unnecessary luxuries such as drinking tea or manufactured clothes. Unlike her previous volumes, it was a commercial success. As Leadbeater herself acknowledged, this was partly due to the patronage of the O'Beirnes, who encouraged subscribers and, most importantly, sent the manuscript volume to Richard Lovell Edgeworth and his daughter, Maria. The former penned the advertisement for the book and negotiated a contract with his London publisher. Richard Edgeworth also undertook to sell five hundred copies of the volume, enlisting his mostly female friends to distribute them among the poor.[86] In addition, Maria Edgeworth wrote an introduction and extensive notes to the London edition to explain the Irish speech idioms to an English audience.

78 *Leadbeater papers*, ii, 309; Feb.–Mar., Sept.–Nov. 1807 (NLI, MS 9327, pp 13–20, 91–110). 79 William to Mary Leadbeater, 7 Mar., 1, 7, 10, 24 Oct., 7 Nov. 1807 (NLI, MS 8671). 80 Same to same, 1, 7, 10, 27 Oct. 1807 (ibid.). 81 See, for example, reviews in *Belfast Monthly Magazine*, 1:2 (Oct. 1808), pp 137–40; *Eclectic Review*, 4 (1808), pp 816–17. 82 *Leadbeater papers*, ii, 344. 83 Ibid. 84 *Cottage dialogues among the Irish peasantry. Part second. With notes and illustrations* (Dublin, London, 1813), p. iv. 85 *Leadbeater papers*, ii, 172. 86 Ibid., 191–4.

There were only 164 subscribers for the first edition of *Cottage dialogues*, far fewer than for *Poems* but, unlike the subscribers for *Poems*, many agreed to purchase twenty or more copies. In total, the subscribers had agreed to purchase 2,289 copies which ensured that the Leadbeaters would incur no financial loss on the publication.[87] The contract with the London publisher, Johnson, permitted Leadbeater to publish a separate Irish edition, and again she spent time in Dublin negotiating suitable terms with a printer and agreed a print run of another 2,000 copies.[88]

The initial appeal of *Cottage dialogues* may have been due to the involvement of the Edgeworths;[89] however, its success can also be attributed to its accessible format. The book was written in an engaging manner and communicated its moral messages in a simple style that made it easily comprehensible. Leadbeater's publications never referred explicitly to religion or to the beliefs of the Society of Friends; instead, they incorporated the general message of evangelical Protestantism that the poor could improve their lives through self-help: working hard, saving money and living sober lives. It was the convergence of Leadbeater's views with those of other Protestant denominations that strengthened the commercial appeal of her book and enabled non-Quakers to recommend it.

Leadbeater's diary conveys her pride and satisfaction in being recognized as a writer. She was delighted that Maria Edgeworth and her father had offered to sponsor *Cottage dialogues*. She enjoyed the fame it bestowed, as visitors called on her as the author of a best-selling volume rather than as a woman who had met and corresponded with Edmund Burke.[90] It is also clear, however, that some members of the Society were uncomfortable with the time that Leadbeater spent on her writings. In 1786 she recorded in her diary that one of the elders, Jane Watson, echoed the reservations of her parents and told her that the other senior women in the Carlow women's meeting had

> observed how much the life of religion had been hurt by so much writing, ... that they had been remarking on me last sixth day, and thought how much more useful I might have been, had I not devoted my talents too much to other things.[91]

A similar comment was made in 1810 by another senior woman in the Leinster Quaker community, Anne Shannon, shortly after Leadbeater had sent the manuscript of *Cottage dialogues* to the printer. Shannon and some other elders paid a formal visit to the Leadbeater household. Such visits were a regular part of Quaker life, their primary purpose being to ensure that the inhabitants were

---

87 Ibid., 212, 216.   88 Hughes, *Between literature and history*, p. 157.   89 *Cottage dialogues ... Part second*, pp v–vi; Jan. 1810 (NLI, MS 9330, p. 45).   90 See, for example, May 1802 (NLI, MS 9324, p. 44).   91 8 Jan. 1786 (ibid., MS 9311, p. 70).

following the Society's regulations on the use of plain furniture and house decoration and to sit in prayer with the family. On this occasion, when the family meeting had ended, Shannon requested to speak with William and Mary alone: as Leadbeater recorded, 'me, she recommended not to encumber myself so much with writing'.[92]

Despite this advice, Leadbeater quickly followed up *Cottage dialogues* with four other volumes using a similar dialogue format and conveying broadly similar messages. Part two of *Cottage dialogues* was a series of conversations between two men who had also featured in part one. *The landlord's friend* took the form of a series of dialogues between Irish-based landlords while *The pedlars*, which also used a similar format, was commissioned by the Kildare Place Society, presumably for distribution in schools. All three volumes were subsequently marketed together by Leadbeater's Irish publisher in one volume.[93]

Although this list of publications might suggest that Leadbeater chose to ignore the recommendation of Anne Shannon, a close reading of her diary and letters indicates that this was not the case. Following the publication of *The landlord's friend* in 1813 Leadbeater began to work on volumes which fitted more comfortably into a Quaker bibliography than her dialogues. In 1822, she published *Memoirs and letters of Richard and Elizabeth Shackleton, late of Ballitore, Ireland*. Printed by the London-based Quaker publisher, Harvey and Dunton, the volume was very different in tone to her dialogue volumes. It was at one level a homage to her parents, particularly her father. It was also, however, a publication that conformed to the Quaker guidelines on books. Leadbeater selected and edited her father's letters to focus on his religious guidance to members of his family and other Friends. Harvey and Dunton also published Leadbeater's next volume, *Biographical notices of members of the Society of Friends who were resident in Ireland* (London, 1823). This was based on a considerable amount of research in Quaker journals and related documentation. Both books would have met with the approval of those who were concerned that Leadbeater's writing distracted her from her religious responsibilities. In these volumes, which demanded far more time and study than her dialogues, Leadbeater was clearly using her writing talent to serve the Society. As she explained to her friend, Melesina Chenevix Trench, she did not expect the memoirs of her parents to be of interest to 'any out of the Pale of our own Society'.[94]

A concern to keep within the Quaker guidelines for writing and reading may have been the reason why Leadbeater never published the work for which she is best remembered: her 'Annals of Ballitore', which was edited posthumously for

---

92 Aug. 1810 (ibid., MS 9330, p. 55). 93 *The landlord's friend. Intended as a sequel to Cottage dialogues* (Dublin, 1813); *The pedlars* (Dublin, 1826); *Cottage dialogues. Parts I, II, III* (Dublin, 1822); *Cottage dialogues among the Irish peasantry ... The three parts now first published in one volume* (Dublin, 1841). 94 *Leadbeater papers*, ii, 317.

The Leadbeater papers in 1862. The first part of the 'annals' was an imaginative and original tour through the village, describing the buildings and their occupants. The remainder of the text consisted of an account of events in the village, mainly focused on the extended Shackleton/Leadbeater families. Leadbeater drew on her diary entries for much of the material. The text of the introductory section was completed in the 1790s and the 'annals' were in circulation among friends and family in 1808.[95] By 1822 Leadbeater noted that her 'annals' comprised 'three bulky volumes', but she also indicated that she did not want the manuscript published until after her death.[96] In 1862 her niece Elizabeth Shackleton collaborated with the printer Richard Webb to prepare the volumes for publication, along with selected items from Leadbeater's correspondence with the writers Melesina Chenevix Trench and George Crabbe.[97] The fact that the 'annals' referred to people who were still alive may have been one reason why Leadbeater was reluctant to distribute them more widely during her lifetime, but the censure that was likely to come from the elders in the local Quaker community may have been the most compelling reason why she decided that her most creative work should not be published until after her death. It was a secular publication which unlike her other prose publications had no social purpose.

Mary Leadbeater lived at a time of change for middle-class women in Ireland. She relished the new opportunities for women writers to have their work published, and welcomed and enjoyed the new public spaces opened to women in large cities such as Dublin. She lived all her life in the midst of the Quaker community in Ballitore, but participated in the 'republic of letters' through her correspondence with other authors and her wide-ranging reading. The entry of women to the modernizing world of the early nineteenth century did not sit easily with the rules and discipline of the Society of Friends, which narrowly defined the intellectual activities of the ideal member. Leadbeater defied these regulations to read and write books that were not within a strict interpretation of the regulations. Her diaries and correspondence suggest that she was aware of the tension between her desire to participate in the public world of writing and publishing and her concern to conform to the regulations of the Society. Phyllis Mack has noted the 'supportive and repressive' nature of Quaker women's meetings.[98] The Leadbeater diaries hint that the Irish meetings shared similar characteristics as they were controlled by a small group of activists who closely monitored the behaviour of the women in their communities. Historians have focused on the spiritual equality granted to Quaker women but the restrictions imposed on women members, particularly in the early nineteenth century, when ideas about women's role and status in society were changing, also merits

---

[95] Aug. 1808 (NLI, MS 9328, p. 57). Magda and Rolf Loeber are editing a complete transcript of the 'Annals' for the Irish Manuscripts Commission.   [96] *Leadbeater papers*, ii, 320–1.   [97] *DIB*, v, 376.   [98] Mack, *Visionary women*, p. 285.

attention. More widely, a study of Mary Leadbeater's life reveals how she interacted with the wider world outside of the Quaker community. A central theme in Sean Connolly's writings has been a questioning of the notion that Ireland was an exception to general developments in European society. Irish historians have tended to view the large Quaker archive as only of value to ecclesiastical historians, as it is concerned with a small, exceptional community. Mary Leadbeater's diary reveals the extent to which members of that small community responded to changes in society in ways that were less exceptional than might be assumed.

Migration, mission and identity: Presbyterian fundraising and the evangelization of the Irish Catholic diaspora, c.1840–70

ANDREW R. HOLMES

Sean Connolly has devoted a significant proportion of his career to analysing the interaction between religious reform and identity politics in the nineteenth century. He has argued that the emergence by the 1880s in Ireland of two political traditions, each expressing their identity through religion, was a contingent and complex process. Building upon these foundations, the present essay will explore the interaction between migration, missionary activity and identity between 1840 and 1870. It concentrates on two deputations sent by the General Assembly of the Presbyterian Church in Ireland to America in 1848–9 and 1859 to raise funds to finance missions to convert Catholics in Ireland. These deputations were products of a tradition of emigration from Ireland that began in the eighteenth century as well as the more immediate stimulus provided by the Great Famine. Furthermore, they appealed to a shared concern among evangelicals on both sides of the Atlantic about the potential dangers of large-scale Irish Catholic emigration. It is important to note from the outset that this was a new departure in Irish emigration experience. Emigrants from Ireland during the eighteenth century were mostly Presbyterians, and they did much to shape religious and political developments in the thirteen colonies before 1776. By the 1840s, their descendants faced an influx of new Irish immigrants – starving Catholics fleeing the ravages of the Famine. In the decade after the Famine Ireland's population declined by a third, and between 1847 and 1854 an average emigration was 196,000 persons *per annum*.[1] Evangelicals in the United States were fearful that Protestant America would be undermined by so-called priest-ridden and feckless Irish Catholics. As a consequence, they were eager to support Presbyterian missions in Ireland as a means of counteracting this threat at its source. Significantly, the American Presbyterians who often facilitated this fundraising were themselves first- or second-generation descendants of Irish emigrants, most notably George Hay Stuart and Nicholas Murray, better known by his pen name, 'Kirwan'. These Protestant Irish or 'Scotch-Irish' supporters were keen to distinguish themselves from the recently arrived Catholic Irish and to draw attention to the social and moral improvement which they claimed their

---

[1] Based on the figures given in N.C. Fleming and Alan O'Day (eds), *The Longman handbook of modern Irish history since 1800* (Harlow, 2005), pp 489, 499.

brand of evangelical Protestantism produced. A prominent theme of the material discussed below was the claim that Presbyterianism promoted the prosperity of Ulster and that its propagation could improve the rest of Ireland and, by extension, the United States. As a consequence, this essay offers an instructive case study of the interaction of missions and migration between and within the large Protestant and Catholic diaspora from Ireland. It illustrates the importance of personal contacts in facilitating the movement of ideas, funds and persons across the North Atlantic world. It also highlights the contribution of missions and migration to identity formation and, especially, the persistence of anti-Catholicism on both sides of the Atlantic.

II

Before 1800, Presbyterians had shown fitful interest in the conversion of Catholic Ireland. Stimulated by the spread of evangelical missionary activity throughout the North Atlantic world, individual Presbyterians began to become prominent in interdenominational missionary societies during the first two decades of the nineteenth century.[2] Eventually, the Synod of Ulster and the Secession Synod established their own denominational societies, first to scattered Presbyterian communities in the south and west and then specifically to Catholics. By the time both synods had united in 1840 to form the General Assembly of the Presbyterian Church in Ireland, missions to Irish Catholics were an established goal and a Home or Irish Mission was instituted. The two-hundredth anniversary in 1842 of the formation of the first presbytery in Ireland resulted in the establishment of a Bicentenary Fund to finance the construction of churches in the south and west, 'to afford protection to converts from Popery', and to aid 'such other special objects as are included in an extraordinary effort for the benefit of the Roman Catholics of Ireland'.[3] The moderator that year was John Edgar – professor of the theology for the church in Belfast, pioneer of the temperance cause in Ireland, and enthusiastic advocate of missionary and philanthropic activity – and Edgar's name would be synonymous with the cause of Irish mission until his death in 1866.[4] The fund eventually realized £14,000, the largest sum gathered by the church to that point.[5] A prominent theme of the bicentenary commemorations was how Presbyterianism promoted the prosperity of Ulster and how its extension could have the same impact upon the rest of Ireland. The Presbyterian newspaper, the *Banner of Ulster*, pointed to the 'singular coincidence' of the progress of Presbyterianism and economic and

---

[2] A.R. Holmes, 'The shaping of Irish Presbyterian attitudes to mission, 1790–1840', *Journal of Ecclesiastical History*, 57 (2006), 711–37. [3] J.S. Reid, *History of the Presbyterian Church in Ireland* (2nd ed., 3 vols, Belfast, 1867), 3, p. 485. [4] D.W. Miller, 'Edgar, John (1798–1866)' in *ODNB*. [5] W.D. Killen, *Memoir of John Edgar, DD, LLD* (Belfast, 1867), p. 151.

social progress in Ulster. 'There is strong and unimpeachable evidence in these facts, that the easiest mode to improve any country is to improve its people; and that the surest method of making a people free, and keeping them free, is to implant amongst them a knowledge of the Gospel, and preserve it in its purity and truth.'[6] The emphasis on improvement would be a recurring theme throughout this period. The Twelfth Annual Report of the Assembly's Home Mission in 1852 declared that when their forefathers came to Ulster from Scotland in the 1620s and 1630s, 'they came to make agriculture flourish, and civilization spread, and truth and righteousness triumph'; ministers also came with the 'one grand aim of their lives, to fix in the conscience and heart of all, that glorious Gospel of the blessed God, which enlightens, reforms, and saves'. 'What they made Ulster we are desirous to make Leinster, Connaught, and Munster.'[7]

The desire to convert and improve Catholic Ireland was given deadly urgency by the catastrophic famine of the 1840s. Though Presbyterians were convinced that the Great Famine was God's way of providing an opportunity for the conversion of Irish Catholics, in the first instance they prioritized material assistance rather than religious conversion. At a meeting in May Street church, Belfast, on 23 September 1846, Edgar rejected the 'species of heartless philosophy' that saw the famine as the means of modernizing Irish society.[8] Though he hoped soon to have 'an opportunity of directing public attention to spiritual famine in Connaught', their 'effort now is to save the perishing body'. 'Our brother is starving, and, till we have satisfied his hunger, we have no time to inquire whether he is Protestant or Romanist.'[9] Through his efforts around £20,000 was collected for famine relief and the Belfast Ladies' Relief Association for Connaught was established to maintain industrial schools in the west.[10] Edgar presented the annual report of the Home Mission to the Assembly in 1847. Despite the awfulness of the experience, he claimed that the failure of Catholic priests to deal with the distress had opened the hearts of ordinary Catholics to Protestant missionaries and the Presbyterian Church must seize the initiative. 'Let it go forth, then, this day, to all the Church, and to all the world, that the God who brings order out of confusion, and light out of darkness, has overruled the famine in Ireland, to open up Ireland for Protestant missions.' Significantly, Edgar noted that many former pupils in the Irish schools established by the mission had emigrated, bringing with them 'the way of salvation through Jesus'. Instead of spreading the power of Rome in the Mississippi valley or the far west,

---

6 'The bicentenary of Irish Presbyterianism', *Banner of Ulster*, 10 June 1842. 7 'Twelfth annual report of the Assembly's Home Mission', *Missionary Herald of the General Assembly of the Presbyterian Church in Ireland* (henceforth *Missionary Herald*), Aug. 1852, p. 1052. 8 Killen, *John Edgar*, p. 209. 9 Ibid., pp 217, 218. 10 For Presbyterian famine relief in Connacht see, D.W. Miller, 'Irish Presbyterians and the Great Famine' in Jacqueline Hill and Colm Lennon (eds), *Luxury and austerity: Historical Studies xxi* (Dublin, 1999), pp 165–81.

'they have gone to assert the liberty of Christ's freemen for themselves, and to teach America to give freedom, religious and civil, to all her slaves'.[11]

The emigration of starving Irish Catholics to the United States and Scotland was seized upon as an opportunity to gain support for Presbyterian missions in the south and west. Evangelicals in both areas were motivated to do so by what they perceived to be the baleful effects of the growing Irish Catholic diaspora. Members of the Free Church of Scotland were especially supportive and in October 1847 the Board of Missions had appointed a deputation to meet the Free Church to discuss missions in Ireland.[12] Generally speaking, financial contributions from Scotland comprised a significant proportion of the funds available to Presbyterian missions in Ireland.[13] The agent of the Irish Mission, Edward Marcus Dill, noted that fundraising in Scotland had gained £980 14s. 5d. in 1846–7 and £1,643 7s. in 1847–8 – an increase of £662 12s. 7d. and within £318 of their own annual collection.[14] Scottish support was forthcoming, largely because to many Scottish Presbyterians, 'Popish tendencies seemed to be everywhere. Culturally, Scotland seemed to be in danger. To fevered imaginations, a mass of poor ignorant but well-disciplined Catholics, increasingly enfranchised, posed a major challenge.'[15] This challenged the Presbyterian basis of Scottish identity and led evangelicals to form missions to Irish immigrants in Edinburgh and Glasgow, areas already dislocated by urbanization and industrialization. As a consequence, according to Bernard Aspinwall, 'Scottish anti-popery shows marked similarities to American nativism.'[16] Indeed, nativism and anti-emigration in the United States had emerged during the 1830s and intensified during the Famine era as Irish immigrants consolidated their hold on the Catholic Church. This prompted Protestant reaction and nativism 'grew to fever pitch' in the 1850s, when it assumed a political form in the 'Know Nothing' movement.[17] Playing upon this concern among Americans, in May 1847 Edgar issued an appeal to evangelicals in the United States to support missions in Ireland. The 'terrible scourge' of the Famine provided the opportunity 'to break the chain by which the Romish priest so long led his devotee captive, and to set the prisoner free'. The address discussed explicitly the family links between Ireland and the United States. Though emigration had brought thousands of Presbyterians to 'the Western Continent where they have found a home', others had remained to enlighten 'our benighted fellow-countrymen'. More

---

11 'Seventh annual report of the Assembly's Home Mission', *Missionary Herald*, Aug. 1847, p. 458.   12 'Resolutions of the General Assembly regarding the Home Mission' in ibid., Oct. 1847, p. 494.   13 R.J. Rodgers, 'Presbyterian missionary activity among Irish Roman Catholics in the nineteenth century' (MA thesis, Queen's University Belfast, 1969), pp 258–61.   14 'Substance of Dr Dill's Missionary Report, presented at the last meeting of Assembly', *Missionary Herald*, Oct. 1848, p. 606.   15 Bernard Aspinwall, 'Popery in Scotland: image and reality, 1820–1920', *Records of the Scottish Church History Society*, 22 (1986), p. 236.   16 Ibid., p. 238.   17 Kevin Kenny, *The American Irish: a history* (Harlow, 2000), p. 113. Katie Oxx, *The nativist movement in America: religious conflict in the nineteenth*

immediately, 'What Romanism is even America is beginning to learn', and Edgar pointed as evidence to the difference between 'the *Northern Scotch-Irish* emigrant, and the *Southern Roman-Irish* emigrant'.[18]

In one respect, this appeal came at an inopportune moment, as relations between the Irish church and the Old School Presbyterians in the United States was under significant strain. In 1843 the Irish Assembly, prompted in part by Edgar's wholehearted opposition to slavery, made its abolitionist position crystal clear: 'That we consider the enslavement of our fellow-creatures subversive of the natural rights of man, opposed to the spirit and precepts of the Gospel, and ruinous to the temporal and eternal interests of multitudes of the human race.' As 'an oppressive system of slavery exists in America, and particularly in many parts of the United States, where the knowledge of Christianity might have been expected to destroy so great an evil', and as they had an opportunity to address their co-religionists on the issue, 'we do, in our communications to them, earnestly recommend their taking such practical steps as may tend to abolish an evil of such awful magnitude'.[19] Such declarations were not well received, and the Old School response to another letter from the Irish Assembly in 1846 dismissed as ignorant their understanding of the issues and explicitly noted the failure of the Irish church to convert Catholic Ireland. 'That we have done all we could, much less, all we should have done, we will no more venture to assert, than we suppose you would contend that you had fully discharged your duties during the last two centuries, to the millions of Popish idolaters who dwell around you.'[20] The abolitionist Associate Synod of North America was more positive in its response to the Appeal and noted that the zeal and energy of the mission 'cannot but be most gratifying to all the friends of evangelical truth, and encouraging to those who are immediately engaged in this good work'. It was agreed that the Irish church possessed 'peculiar claims upon our sympathy' and a committee was appointed to initiate correspondence.[21]

III

Despite tensions, a deputation of E.M. Dill and Jonathan Simpson conducted a fund-raising tour in the United States between November 1848 and June 1849. Dill was the missionary agent for the Assembly and would later become Secretary of the Scottish Reformation Society in the 1850s.[22] Simpson had

---

century (London, 2013). 18 *An appeal on behalf of the Home Mission of the General Assembly of the Presbyterian Church in Ireland, respectfully addressed to their Christian brethren of all evangelical denominations in America* ([Belfast, 1847]), p. 2. Original emphasis. 19 *Minutes of the General Assembly of the Presbyterian Church in Ireland* (henceforth *MGA*), i (1843), p. 235. 20 Ibid., i (1847), p. 622. 21 'Minutes of Synod' in *The evangelical repository; devoted to the principles of the Reformation, as set forth in the formularies of the Westminster divines, and witnessed for by the Associate Synod of North America*, vi (July 1847), p. 86. 22 John Wolffe,

already visited America in 1843 on a fundraising trip for his Portrush congregation and while there had remonstrated with slave owners in Nashville.[23] The credentials that Edgar provided for the deputation stated clearly the motivation behind this work and the benefits it would produce on both sides of the Atlantic.

> The Directors, believing that the conversion of Irish Romanists is a matter of deep interest to the whole Christian world, and especially to the New World, injured and oppressed by their immigration, and being deeply convinced that no prosperous sphere of effort should be relinquished till every exertion has been made to maintain it, have deputed their beloved, faithful brethren ... to visit the United States for the purpose of awakening sympathy on behalf of Irish Roman Catholics in their present remarkable condition, and obtaining aid for missions to them.[24]

During their six-month trip, Dill published a series of weekly letters in the *New York Observer* on the state of Ireland and the efforts to counteract popery.[25] They travelled throughout the United States and collected $25,697.54, equivalent to £5,400. Donations in excess of one thousand dollars were collected in New York ($7,968.48), Philadelphia ($7,219.5), Pittsburgh ($3,289.9), Cincinnati ($2,317.23), and Albany ($1,007.15). The money collected was reckoned an inadequate indication of the warmth of the reception they had received from 'native Americans, as well as by Irish residents'.[26]

It was clear that the trip was an arduous one and Dill in his report to the General Assembly enumerated the difficulties he and his colleague had faced. These included their own low profile, donor fatigue in the United States, tensions over slavery, and a 'strong prejudice' against the state endowment of Irish Presbyterianism through the *regium donum*. They responded to such concerns by appealing to the self-interest of Americans. They called attention to 'the difference between the Protestant and Catholic Irish' in the United States and that 'it was for their interest, as well as ours, to enlighten and instruct the people, who are pouring in on them in such masses as threaten to disorganize their country'. In a number of places, 'the opposition was serious' from sections of the press, including 'leading evangelical journals' who accused them of advocating the Home Mission as a pretence for supplementing the stipends of weak congregations to ensure the payment of the *regium donum*, though 'it was the Roman Catholic journals that fired their most heavy artillery at us', most notably the *Pittsburgh Catholic*. That said, they had much to be grateful for,

---

The Protestant crusade in Great Britain, 1829–60 (Oxford, 1991), p. 160. **23** Jonathan Simpson, *Annals of my life, labours, and travels* (Belfast, 1895), pp 126–288 (for Nashville, see pp 214–15). **24** Ibid., p. 304. **25** Ibid., p. 307. **26** 'Abstract report of the deputation to America, on behalf of the Home Mission – July, 1849', *Missionary Herald*, Aug. 1849, p. 694.

including meeting 'representatives of nearly all our congregations' who had emigrated, and the extent of interdenominational support – 'an Evangelical Alliance of the very best kind' – from Old School and New School Presbyterians, Dutch and German Reformed, Associate and Associate Reformed Presbyterians, Methodists, Independents, Baptists, and lay Episcopalians, many of whom were first or second generation Irish immigrants.[27] Despite the range and significance of support, the annual report of the Home Mission noted that frequent applications for funds by the church and individual congregations 'would be not only ungenerous and unjust, but would for ever close the fountain which we have found so full and free'. More importantly, 'If we would be helped by others, we must help ourselves.'[28]

The most important contact the deputation made was with George Hay Stuart, a Presbyterian immigrant who left Ireland in 1831 and had established himself as a successful merchant in Philadelphia.[29] Stuart became an elder in the First Reformed Presbyterian Church in that city and gained national prominence in his connexion with the YMCA and his chairmanship of the United States Christian Commission during the Civil War. According to Dill, Stuart 'had placed at the deputation's disposal his home, his heart, his head, his hands, his influence'. Dill 'felt a patriot's honest pride when meeting with such illustrious representatives of Ireland on a distant shore' and he reminded his American audiences 'that these were all to a man the sons of Bible-reading Ulster, and had felt the Gospel's power'. Such men were not lost to Ireland and their 'removal had only put it in their power to serve her more effectually than had they remained at home'.[30] Stuart was thrilled with the interest awakened in the cause and his close relations with the deputation caused him 'to be regarded as a sort of representative of the Irish Presbyterian Church before the Presbyterians of America'.[31]

Along with Stuart, another central figure in encouraging American support for Irish missions was Nicholas Murray, Presbyterian minister of Elizabethstown, New Jersey. Murray was a Catholic immigrant from Ireland who converted to Presbyterianism and gained notoriety for a series of controversial letters to John Hughes, the first Catholic archbishop of New York, written under his pen name, Kirwan.[32] The impetus to write these letters came from Samuel Ireneaus Prime, a prominent Presbyterian clergyman and editor of the *New York Observer*, after Murray had related to him his early life story in Ireland. They first appeared in the *Observer* in February 1847 and 'made a greater excitement

[27] 'General Assembly of the Presbyterian Church in Ireland', *Belfast News-Letter*, 6 July 1849.
[28] 'Ninth annual report of the Assembly's Home Mission', *Missionary Herald*, Aug. 1849, p. 687. [29] *Dictionary of American religious biography* (2nd ed., Westport, CT, 1993), pp 528–9.
[30] 'Selected articles. Irish General Assembly', *The United Presbyterian and Evangelical Guardian*, iii (1849–50), p. 223. [31] *The life of George H. Stuart, written by himself*, ed. R.E. Thompson (Philadelphia, 1890), p. 66. [32] R.A. Billington, *The Protestant crusade, 1800–1860: a study of the origins of American nativism* (New York, 1938), pp 253–5.

than any series of papers in the religious press of our times'. They were translated into a variety of languages and they 'went in Ireland like wild-fire'.[33] One American visitor to Ireland in May 1847 noted that 'Murray's Letters to Hughes are producing a great sensation; far beyond any thing I can account for. They are read with avidity in kitchens, and will sell by thousands among the Irish.'[34] Belfast editions were published in 1850 and 1851 under the supervision of John Edgar. In the preface, Edgar noted that they were 'now republished in unhappy Ireland, long a stronghold of Romanism', as they were 'brief, clear, practical, and characterized by genuine good nature and politeness'. For Edgar, popery was 'an evil of such enormous magnitude and ruinous character, such an enemy to human rights, and destroyer of human souls, that in all its forms it should be opposed – boldly, vigorously, and unceasingly opposed'.[35] Edgar's introduction to the second series recorded that 5,000 copies of the first series had been distributed and claimed that Murray had 'done as much as any other man in the Western World to breath Protestant life and spirit into the masses of the people'.[36] Murray would later dedicate one of his works to Edgar, the 'learned professor, the untiring philanthropist, the faithful minister, the devoted Christian, the true man'.[37]

Murray believed that Catholicism was theologically corrupt and corrupted the lives of its adherents, especially through the malign influence of a despotic priesthood that forbade access to the Bible. Popery 'degrades man' because it 'takes from him the Bible, the revealed will of God, with all its clear light, with all its high motives to excite the soul to high and holy action; and without which neither civilization nor religion can be long maintained'.[38] The various practical problems and difficulties affecting Ireland were 'but as the dust of the balance when compared with the influences of Popery', which met its adherents 'at the cradle, and dogs them to the grave, and beyond it, with its demands for money'.[39] Murray claimed that Hughes' Catholicism was 'for the benefit of the priest, and not that of the people. Its object is not to spread light, but darkness, – not to advance civilization but to retard it, – not to elevate but to depress man, that he may the more readily be brought under your influence.' Immediately, he underlined the relevance of this to the United States. 'And we have in Ireland a type of what our happy land will be when the priest wields the power here which he wields there.'[40] By comparison, Irish immigrants to the United States would find freedom from both the priest and the established Church of Ireland.

33 S.I. Prime, *Irenaeus letters. Originally published in the New York Observer* (New York, 1881), pp 91, 93.   34 *Forty years' familiar letters of James W. Alexander, DD, constituting, with the notes, a memoir of his life*, ed. John Hall (2 vols, New York, 1860), ii, 68.   35 *Homely truth for honest men. Letters to the Right Reverend John Hughes, Roman Catholic bishop of New York. By Kirwan. With an introductory essay by John Edgar, DD, and notes by Samuel O. Edgar, DD* (Belfast, 1850), pp v, vi.   36 Ibid., pp 5–6.   37 Kirwan, *Parish and other pencilings* (New York, 1865).   38 [Nicholas Murray], *Letters to the Rt. Revd John Hughes, Roman Catholic archbishop of New York*, ser. 1 (Philadelphia, [1851]), p. 41.   39 Ibid., pp 48, 50.   40 Ibid., pp 51–2.

'Protestants here are your friends. You are not taxed to support a religion you hate. Your cow or your pig are not driven from your door to pay your tithes.'[41] Murray consciously spoke as an Irish patriot and criticized both Protestant landlords and the British authorities for trammelling freedom. 'It is the very feeling that prompted the British spies to destroy the speech of Emmet, that now prompts your priests to destroy your Bibles. The one fostered the spirit of civil, the other of religious freedom. The British ministry wished to suppress the breathing of your fathers after civil liberty: your priests wish to suppress the breathings of you, their children, after religious freedom.'[42]

In 1851 Murray visited Ireland as part of a fact-finding tour of Europe to see for himself the impact of popery and what could be done to purify the stream of immigration into the United States. He observed that the priests had made Ireland 'a godless, Christless land, and thus they have debased and cursed it'.[43] Murray used the experience of Ireland to directly address an American audience. He wanted 'to excite a feeling of compassion in the bosom of all Americans toward its swarming emigrants weekly landed on our shores', 'to encourage Popish emigrants here to assert their independence, where there is no priestly power to strike them down', and to warn them about the adverse impact of Maynooth-trained priests on American values and institutions.[44] The importance of combating popery in Ireland as a means of helping American evangelicals was appreciated by Irish Presbyterians. At the General Assembly in July 1851, W.B. Kirkpatrick, minister of Mary's Abbey congregation in Dublin, moved the adoption of the report of the mission to Catholics, noting that 'when we have so much emigration from our country into distant lands, converted Irishmen might become civilizers in every district to which Providence may call them, I feel that we ought to strain every nerve, and employ every energy, in order that the Gospel may be circulated wide and far throughout this land'. Kirkpatrick's point was echoed by Murray in his address to the Assembly in which he lamented the lack of Presbyterian missionaries in the west of Ireland. 'God, in his providence, is causing many to come over to us from the hills and valleys of Connaught, and they are passing in crowds to the Far West of our country. There is a cry to you to instruct these men before they go – there is a loud call upon you to make these men free in the liberty of the Gospel of Christ – to resist the efforts of the priests to keep them in bondage in ignorance, and in sin.'[45] The danger to America of this exodus was stated emphatically by E.M. Dill in his 1852 work *The mystery solved: or, Ireland's miseries; the grand cause, and cure*, which was published in both Edinburgh and New York.

41 Ibid., ser. 2 (Philadelphia, [1851]), p. 88.   42 Ibid., p. 104.   43 Nicholas Murray, *Men and things as I saw them in Europe. By Kirwan* (New York, 1853), pp 253–4.   44 [Nicholas Murray], *Romanism at home. Letters to the Hon. Roger B. Taney, Chief Justice of the United States* (New York, 1852), p. 192.   45 'General Assembly of the Presbyterian Church in Ireland' in *Belfast News-Letter*, 14 July 1851.

Americans, beware! You are yet *confident*, but you know not Popery as well as we do, and God grant you never may! How can you overlook the alarming fact, that the hordes of Irish Papists who are landing daily amongst you, must needs corrupt your moral atmosphere, and that from the nature of your constitution, your country's *only* bulwark is the virtue of its people? Then learn in time from Ireland's RUIN what is AMERICA'S GRAND DANGER![46]

IV

The condemnation of the priesthood and Catholicism as a system evident in the rhetoric cited above was always balanced in the mind of Murray and Irish Presbyterians with a hope that liberty in America would have a positive influence on immigrants and a conviction that popery was destined to collapse. In his first series of letters to Hughes, Murray was positive about the imminent destruction of Catholicism. 'My dear sir, the days of Popery are numbered. The Bible is against it. Civilization is against it. The mind of the world is against it. Good people now pray for its downfall as earnestly as they do for that of Mahometanism.'[47] The annual report of the Home Mission presented in June 1852 noted that the loss of two million Catholics as a consequence of disease and emigration had made the religious demography of Ireland more manageable and the prospect of missionary success more hopeful. Despite having to close Irish schools in Co. Tyrone and 'the persecuting spirit and conduct of the Romish mob, under the influence of their priests in Tralee', those who ran the mission were confident of future success.[48] The following year, the report declared, 'A brighter day has dawned. No true preacher of a free salvation deems Romanists hopeless now; the veil of separation has been rent; the Romish caste, like the Hindoo caste, has been broken.'[49] The annual report of the Home Mission in 1855 noted that though emigration had led to a decline in attendance at their schools in the west of Ireland, 'we cannot regret a change which has placed many of our promising pupils beyond the power of the persecuting priest' and a 'besotted, slavish public opinion which gives weight to the words of the altar-curse, and nerves the despot's arm'. Though Connacht was still dominated by Rome, even there 'light and happiness are yet in reserve; the growing empire of Emmanuel shall spread over it; the pollutions and all the abominations of its anti-Christian service shall yet be no more'.[50]

---

[46] E.M. Dill, *The mystery solved: or, Ireland's miseries; the grand cause, and cure* (Edinburgh, 1852), p. 299. [47] Murray, *Letters*, ser. 1, pp 43–4. [48] 'Twelfth annual report of the Assembly's Home Mission', *Missionary Herald*, Aug. 1852, pp 1051, 1054. [49] 'Thirteenth annual report of the Assembly's Home Mission', *Missionary Herald*, Aug. 1853, p. 2072. [50] 'Fifteenth annual report of the Assembly's Home Mission', *Missionary Herald*, Aug. 1855,

By the late 1850s, the desire to convert Catholic Ireland was reinforced by a remarkable outbreak of religious revival in the United States that began in 1857 and was enthusiastically followed in the local and denominational press in Ireland.[51] In its report on the annual meeting of the Irish General Assembly in June 1858, the *Irish Presbyterian* noted, 'If we come together with one heart and one mind, who can tell but God may pour out upon us and on our churches such blessings as are falling on our American brethren. This is what we need. We have all the appliances of a church; what we need is the spark of the heavenly fire, the baptism of the Holy Spirit.'[52] In millennial language, a pastoral letter issued by the General Assembly in November hoped God would 'make a short work upon the earth, and even in our own times to subdue nations in a day to the obedience of faith'.[53] A deputation from the General Assembly visited British North America and the United States from July to November 1858, collecting both information about the ongoing revival and contributions to missionary funds. One of the deputation, William Gibson, published in March 1859 a report of his personal experiences in the previous autumn as an introduction to an account of the revival in Philadelphia by the YMCA.[54] By the time Gibson's account appeared, revival had begun to spread throughout Presbyterian Ulster, transforming lives and leaving a trail of chaos and intense discussion about the character of the movement.[55] Gibson was approached in November by a Boston publisher to produce an account of the revival, which appeared the following year as *The year of grace*.[56] The Assembly of 1859 received the reports of the deputation and it was decided that another should visit North America explicitly to gain funds for missionary activity. As a consequence, John Edgar, Samuel Marcus Dill and David Wilson visited between August and December 1859.

The deputation arrived in New York on 19 September 'after a rough and tedious passage' of seventeen days. They soon met to organize their trip with Murray, who 'manifested an interest in the success of our mission quite as great as our own'.[57] The deputation 'pledged themselves and the Church to two things: *First*, that it should be applied *exclusively* to the Roman Catholic Missions of the Assembly; and *Second*, that it should not be made the occasion of *repressing* the liberality of our own people, but rather the means of *stimulating* them to greater zeal in the cause of Missions'.[58] Their first public engagement was at the Cooper Institute in New York on 22 September. Addresses of welcome were

p. 3014.   51 K.T. Long, *The revival of 1857–8: interpreting an American religious awakening* (New York, 1998).   52 Cited in J.T. Carson, *God's river in spate: the story of the religious awakening of Ulster in 1859* (2nd ed., Belfast, 1994), p. 11.   53 'Pastoral Letter' in *Missionary Herald*, Nov. 1858, p. 209.   54 *Pentecost: or, the work of God in Philadelphia, AD 1858. Prepared by the Young Men's Christian Association. With an introductory statement by the Revd William Gibson* (Belfast, 1859).   55 A.R. Holmes, 'The Ulster revival of 1859: causes, controversies and consequences', *Journal of Ecclesiastical History*, 63 (2012), 488–515.   56 William Gibson, *The year of grace: a history of the Ulster revival of 1859* (Edinburgh, 1860).   57 'The late deputation to the United States', *Missionary Herald*, Apr. 1860, p. 524.   58 Ibid., p. 525.

delivered 'bidding them God speed in their great object of obtaining increased pecuniary resources for the evangelization of Ireland'. An appeal on behalf of the deputation was drawn up and signed by twenty-four prominent evangelicals.

> As one result of the present glorious revival now in progress in Ireland, wide and effectual doors are open to the Roman Catholic population; and from many papal districts there is a cry for help to assist in meeting these daily increasing demands. The General Assembly appeals, through its Deputation, to the Churches of America for aid. Popish emigrants are to America no gain, and to their native land no loss; but if enlightened, and brought to the knowledge of the truth, they would be a rich blessing to both and to the world. Protestants in America should be as much interested in Protestant Missions to these as Protestants in Ireland. And we respectfully but urgently solicit your assistance to aid the Presbyterian Church in its noble efforts to give the Gospel to the entire Roman Catholic population of Ireland.[59]

The twin themes of revival and mission defined the work of the deputation for the next three months. Dill reported to the Assembly that they 'arranged to preach, each three times every Sabbath, and to spend the week-days in addressing public meetings, and making personal calls on parties who might be disposed to contribute to our cause'.[60] Though in Ireland Catholics mainly ignored the revival and the number of Catholic converts was very small, much was made of any conversion in order to appeal to an American audience.[61] For instance, Dill was a minister in Ballymena, the heartland of the Ulster revival, and told a meeting in New York that 'He could not tell how many had been converted, but in Ballymena alone the number was over forty. And the revival was still going on in all directions. It was destined to redeem and disenthrall all Ireland.' In addition, the revival had also led to the decline of sectarian tensions. 'Party spirit was dying out. At their recent anniversary, July 12, instead of a partisan parade with banners, &c., they had a monster prayer-meeting in the fields, and the Orange lodges marched in with Bibles instead of banners.'[62] At the Associate Presbyterian Church's Synod of New York at Coila, David Wilson, minister of Limerick Presbyterian congregation, delivered a number of addresses on 'the Revival in the North, and the Presbyterian Missions in the South and West of Ireland'.[63] At a meeting in Philadelphia in November, Wilson highlighted the benefits to the United States of mission in Ireland and was loudly applauded by his audience. Wilson opposed popery because it demoralized

---

59 'The Irish delegation', *Presbyterian Magazine*, 9 (Oct. 1859), p. 476. 60 'The late deputation to the United States', *Missionary Herald*, Apr. 1860, p. 524. 61 Holmes, 'Ulster revival', pp 510–11. 62 'God's providential and gracious workings. The revival in Great Britain', *Presbyterian Expositor*, 2 (Nov. 1859), p. 593. 63 'Editorial. The Synod of New York', *Evangelical Repository*, 18 (Nov. 1859), p. 376.

individuals by systematically teaching 'the violation of each of the ten commandments', which then 'filled American prisons and alms-houses'. 'Americans, you pay for all that. We desire to act as your servants in the effort to stop this deluge of crime. We carry the war into Italy not with arms of destruction, but with the sanctifying influences of the Gospel of peace. We do ask you to help us in this great work of evangelizing Ireland, and thus of filling America with an enlightened, Bible-reading, liberty-loving People.'[64] A farewell to the delegation was held in St Nicholas Hotel in New York just before Christmas. A letter addressed by the delegation singled out Murray and Stuart, 'these noble sons of old Ireland', whose influence they 'chiefly owe the large and triumphant success which has crowned our enterprise'. The delegation were conscious that missionary activity bound them in a common cause under God that would bring closer together 'the two great Protestant nations of the world, who, with one language, one Bible, one faith, should in love and labour be forever one – one for their common good, one for the establishment of truth and righteousness over all the world'.[65] After three months, they had gained £6,000 and had been 'treated with marked respect by Evangelical Protestants of all denominations'.[66]

The mutual benefits of mission to Irish Catholics continued to be noted during the following decade. In 1860 Murray and Stuart together visited Ireland to ascertain the progress of mission work and the effects of the revival.[67] At a public breakfast in their honour in June, Murray once again noted the reciprocal character of mission work in Ireland. 'In doing for Ireland they felt in America that they were doing for themselves, and it was in that light that he sought to present the claims of the deputation.' The United States 'was flooded with Irishmen, he was sorry to say not from the Presbyterian and Protestant North, for the North sent America her noblest men'. There was 'a different class of Irishmen in America – that class for whom the deputation had gone to solicit aid. They had there the Papal Irish, and they know them everywhere by their garb, their dress, their tone. The[y] looked as if they were brought up to bow to man, and not to God.' These often became 'beggars', 'retailers of spirituous liquors', 'criminals', and it was this 'class of persons for whom the deputation had asked aid; and, in pouring out their money for such an object, they, in America, felt they were doing for themselves'.[68] The Twenty-Fifth Annual Report of the Assembly's Roman Catholic Mission in 1865 enumerated the positive impact of the mission, including that it had 'fitted multitudes for emigration, who, in other lands, are enjoying the fruits of our training, and who supplied means for

64 'Reception of the Irish delegation in Philadelphia', *Belfast News-Letter*, 17 Nov. 1859. 65 'Farewell to the Irish delegation', *Presbyterian Magazine*, 10 (Jan. 1860), pp 42–3. 66 Killen, *John Edgar*, p. 288. 67 *Life of Stuart*, pp 120–6; S.I. Prime, *Memoirs of the Revd Nicholas Murray, DD (Kirwan)* (New York, 1863), pp 330–9. 68 'Public breakfast to Revd Dr Murray and Geo. H. Stuart, Esq., America', *Belfast News-Letter*, 1 June 1860.

emigration to multitudes more, from the fruits of their prosperity in their new homes.'[69]

The specific concern with the Irish Catholic diaspora was related to a more general concern with resurgent Roman Catholicism that would be expressed most forcibly when papal infallibility was promulgated in 1870. In that context, transatlantic Presbyterian cooperation became an important theme in the aftermath of the Civil War and the Irish deputation that visited the United States in 1867 focused on evangelical unity rather than mission to Irish Catholics. John Denham and John Hall stayed in America from May to August 1867 and once more found Stuart to be 'a passport ... to the confidence of American Christians of all evangelical denominations'. In addition to Philadelphia and New York, they visited Indianapolis, St Louis, Springfield, Chicago, Pittsburgh, Lafayette and Montreal. In all these places they assured their audiences of the desire for 'continued peace between Great Britain and America' and Christian unity, and 'neglected no occasion of commending to the good-will of American Christians the emigrants from Ireland, and especially those of our own Church'. Denham noted that they worked closely with Irish immigrants, and he drew a distinction between Fenianism, which most Americans saw as 'an immense, gigantic swindle', and Presbyterian emigrants, 'or the Scotch-Irish', who were 'the bone and sinew of the congregations in which they were found'.[70] The theme of union across the Atlantic had personal resonance for Hall when in September 1867 he accepted a call to become the minister of Fifth Avenue Presbyterian Church in New York.[71]

The desire for united action found institutional expression in 1877 with the formation of the Alliance of the Reformed Churches holding the Presbyterian System, and Irish Presbyterians were among the first to suggest the formation of such an organization.[72] Such a union fitted Presbyterians to be at the forefront of 'resisting Rationalism on the one side and Romanism on the other'.[73] The evangelization of Catholic Ireland remained a feature of these meetings. In 1880 Robert Knox of Belfast reminded British and American Presbyterians that Irish immigrants had become in their respective countries 'a menace or a snare' and urged them to support the conversion of Irish Catholics, which 'cannot be effectually done by dealing with those who are landed on the shores of either country. It must be done at the fountain-head. The salt must be cast into the well's mouth. Irish Romanism must be met and conquered on Irish soil.' Given the historical and religious connexions between Ulster and America, Knox felt that Irish mission had 'a strong claim on the sympathy and help of America'. God had placed Ulster Presbyterians 'in the forefront of the hottest battle; but

[69] 'Twenty-fifth annual report of the Assembly's Roman Catholic Mission', *Missionary Herald*, Aug. 1865, p. 567.   [70] 'General Assembly of the Presbyterian Church in Ireland', *Belfast News-Letter*, 16 Aug. 1867.   [71] T.C. Hall, *John Hall: pastor and preacher* (London, [1901]).   [72] Marcel Pradervand, *A century of service: a history of the World Alliance of Reformed Churches, 1875–1975* (Edinburgh, 1975).   [73] *MGA*, iv (1874), p. 700.

the battle is yours as well as ours', and Knox was assured that his audience would not desert them. 'For your own sakes, and in memory of all you owe to Ulster, "Come to the help of the Lord against the mighty". If we succeed, as by the help of heaven we expect we shall, the richest benefit will be yours, for then you would be receiving, year by year, an influx of free, enlightened, law-abiding Church men and women.'[74]

The two deputations sent to America in 1848 and 1859 in aid of the Irish Mission came at a time when the famine and revival seemed to be creating an opening for the conversion of Catholic Ireland. The unprecedented growth of Catholic immigration from Ireland and the problems this caused in the United States meant that the deputations had a natural support base of Irish Protestant immigrants who were only too happy to deal with their problems at the Irish source. Though the Irish Mission continued its work and individuals like Knox advocated the cause, the urgency of the 1840s and 1850s dissipated. The anti-Catholicism that was such a pronounced feature of the rhetoric of Edgar and Murray was not sustained in missionary activity.[75] In the United States, the personal and family connexions with Presbyterian Ulster laid the foundation for the formation of societies advocating a Scotch-Irish identity, which, in theory at least, were non-sectarian but were dominated by Protestants.[76] In Ulster, anti-Catholicism would be employed in Presbyterian opposition to Irish self-government, which was often referred to as 'Rome Rule'. As a consequence, the lasting legacy of this fundraising activity was not the conversion of Catholic Ireland but the further differentiation of Irish Protestants and Catholics, both at home and overseas.

---

[74] Robert Knox, 'The evangelization of Ireland', J.B. Dales and R.M. Patterson (eds), *Reports of proceedings of the second general council of the Presbyterian Alliance, convened at Philadelphia, September, 1880* (Philadelphia, 1880), pp 424–5. [75] Rodgers, 'Presbyterian missionary activity', pp 210–52. [76] Matthew McKee, '"A peculiar and royal race": creating a Scotch-Irish identity, 1889–1901' in Patrick Fitzgerald and Steve Ickringill (eds), *Atlantic crossroads: historical connections between Scotland, Ulster and North America* (Newtownards, 2001), pp 67–83.

Love, loss and learning in late Georgian Belfast: the case of Eliza McCracken

JONATHAN JEFFREY WRIGHT

On Tuesday, 22 June 1830, the *Belfast News-Letter* reported the marriage of Eliza, 'eldest daughter of John M'Cracken, esq. of Belfast', to Robert James, 'only son of Doctor Tennent'. Conducted by the Revd P.S. Henry, the wedding had taken place just the day before, and appears to have been wholly unremarkable; certainly, there is little to distinguish the calm and formulaic notice of the McCracken–Tennent nuptials from the other marriage notices carried by the *News-Letter*.[1] But while the marriage of Eliza McCracken and Robert James Tennent appears, on one level, as an entirely commonplace occurrence, it takes on a rather different appearance when approached from McCracken's perspective. For McCracken, the marriage marked the quiet culmination of a long and tempestuous courtship, a courtship initially conducted behind the back of her widowed father and charted, in remarkable detail, in a series of closely written letters preserved in the archive of the Tennent family.[2] Penned by McCracken herself, these letters foreground the ways in which her relationship with Tennent was complicated by conflicting feelings of guilt, duty and desire, and detail the complex negotiations which preceded her marriage. Telling of the difficulties she faced, and the unhappiness she experienced, as a young woman trying to exercise a degree of agency in the shaping of her future, they reveal the intricacies of middle-class courtship and provide a rich basis on which to develop a case study of her life as a young woman in late Georgian Belfast.

A model for this sort of study can be found in Sean Connolly's examination of 'the case of Letitia Bushe', in which he explored the 'three-dimensional complexity' of one woman's life in mid-eighteenth-century Ireland and made a convincing case for biographical specificity, asserting that it is necessary to look beyond the particular 'legal, institutional and ideological context' in which women lived and to 'reconstruct the lives themselves'.[3] Adopting a similar approach, what follows is a reconstruction of McCracken's life in the years before her marriage. Needless to say, Bushe and McCracken were two very different

---

1 *Belfast News-Letter*, 22 June 1830.   2 In total, some 301 letters from McCracken to Tennent survive, with 166 dating from the period before the two were married: letters from Eliza Tennent, *neé* McCracken, to Robert James Tennent, 1826–50 (PRONI, Tennent papers, D/1748/G/378/1–301). Henceforth, the abbreviations EM (Eliza McCracken) and RJT (Robert James Tennent) will be used when referencing this correspondence. I am grateful to the Deputy Keeper of Records, PRONI and the Ulster Museum, for permission to use the

women. Whereas Bushe was 'a woman of independent but modest means' who 'aspired to move ... in the inner circles of Irish polite society' and whose emotional life was 'dominated' for some six years by a tempestuous and possibly sexual relationship with Lady Anne Bligh, McCracken was a young middle-class woman whose emotional life was conventionally heterosexual and who appears to have lacked even the modest form of economic independence enjoyed by Bushe.[4] Described thus, McCracken's life might appear mundane. But this should not be permitted to obscure her significance. McCracken, no less than Bushe, offers the historian an opportunity to explore the relationship 'between conventional prescriptions of behaviour and lived reality'. Her letters afford a valuable 'glimpse into the interior life of a woman' and the weighty concerns they address render her case particularly interesting.[5]

Prominent in McCracken's correspondence are the themes of family, love and the difficulties inherent in balancing familial obligations and expectations with individual desire. This, in itself, is far from remarkable: the importance of the family in shaping and, at times, circumscribing the possibilities of women's lives in the eighteenth and nineteenth centuries is, after all, well known.[6] Yet, as Mary O'Dowd has observed, 'extraordinary gaps' remain, in the Irish context, 'in relation to the history of the family, marriage and private life'.[7] Closely related to these areas are those of courtship and engagement. These, too, are issues addressed in McCracken's correspondence, and here also historiographical lacunae have been identified. Lawrence Stone's arguments regarding the rise of 'affective individualism' and romantic marriage have, of course, been the subject of much debate – including in the Irish context, where Connolly has found them wanting.[8] But these wider debates deal, as Katie Barclay has noted, with 'changing values across time'. Below this level, 'the role of love in courtship has received relatively little attention'.[9] McCracken's case thus provides an opportunity to shed light on the under-researched areas of love and family. Added to this, it offers insights into the experience of grief, and on attitudes towards female learning, for McCracken's attempts to grapple with the questions

---

Tennent papers. 3 S.J. Connolly, 'A woman's life in mid-eighteenth-century Ireland: the case of Letitia Bushe', *HJ*, 43 (2000), 451. 4 Ibid., 441, 442, 445. 5 Ibid., 435. 6 Diane Urquhart, 'Gender, family, and sexuality, 1800–2000' in Liam Kennedy and Philip Ollerenshaw (eds), *Ulster since 1600: politics, economy, and society* (Oxford, 2013), p. 245. For two very different studies which locate women in their familial context, see Leonore Davidoff and Catherine Hall, *Family fortunes: men and women of the English middle class, 1780–1850* (rev. ed., London, 2002) and Amanda Vickery, *The gentleman's daughter: women's lives in Georgian England* (New Haven & London, 2003). 7 Mary O'Dowd, *A history of women in Ireland, 1500–1800* (Harlow, 2005), p. 3. See also, Urquhart, 'Gender, family, and sexuality', p. 245. 8 Lawrence Stone, *The family, sex and marriage in England, 1500–1800* (London, 1977); S.J. Connolly, 'Family, love and marriage: some evidence from the early eighteenth century' in Margaret MacCurtain and Mary O'Dowd (eds), *Women in early modern Ireland* (Edinburgh, 1991), pp 276–90. For more on the Stone debate, see Vickery, *Gentleman's daughter*, p. 306. 9 Katie Barclay, *Love, intimacy and power: marriage and patriarchy in Scotland, 1650–1850*

of love and family were complicated by the deaths of her mother and brother, and her correspondence reveals the concerted attempts she made to 'improve' herself by undertaking a course of serious reading in the months running up to her marriage. McCracken's case can, then, be explored by focusing on the general themes of love, loss and learning, but it is first necessary to establish the nature of her world.

II

Most likely born in 1804, McCracken came of age in Belfast during the 1810s and early 1820s.[10] As such, she was a young woman who experienced a world in transition. With the growth of textile manufacturing in the early nineteenth century, Belfast underwent dramatic economic and demographic expansion. From around 19,000 in 1802 its population rose to 37,000 in 1821, and by the 1820s it 'was on its way to becoming Ireland's Manchester'.[11] At the same time, it also experienced religious and political change. In the religious sphere, as was the case elsewhere in Britain, the late eighteenth and early-nineteenth centuries witnessed the spread of evangelicalism and a growing seriousness of outlook both in Belfast and in Ulster more generally.[12] Turning to politics, equally important changes were taking place as those radical Presbyterians who had supported the United Irish movement retreated from the separatism they had espoused in the 1790s. In Belfast, as Connolly long ago observed in an insightful discussion of these developments, 'there remained a recognizable body of protestant radical opinion' long after the 1798 rebellion, and it was not the case that Presbyterians recoiled from 'from the radicalism of the 1790s to a tame acceptance of the established order'. Nevertheless, as 'the long-term consequence of the upheavals of the 1790s worked themselves out', adjustments were required and the radicalism that endured 'was a much modified radicalism, purged of all associations with physical force, republicanism, and separatism'.[13]

(Manchester, 2011), p. 87. **10** Genealogical websites give McCracken's date of birth as 14 May 1804. This date is plausible, but it has not been possible to confirm it with newspaper sources or church baptismal records. **11** S.J. Connolly, 'Improving town, 1750–1820' in idem (ed.), *Belfast 400: people, place and history* (Liverpool, 2012), pp 195, 197. **12** Ian Bradley, *The call to seriousness: the evangelical impact on the Victorians* (London, 1976); David Hempton and Myrtle Hill, *Evangelical Protestantism in Ulster society, 1740–1890* (London, 1992); A.R. Holmes, *The shaping of Ulster Presbyterian belief and practice, 1770–1840* (Oxford, 2006), pp 33–50; J.J. Wright, *The 'natural leaders' and their world: politics, culture and society in Belfast, c.1801–1832* (Liverpool, 2012), pp 192–238. **13** S.J. Connolly, 'Aftermath and adjustment' in W.E. Vaughan (ed.), *A new history of Ireland, v: Ireland under the Union, i: 1801–70* (Oxford, 1989), pp 1, 21, 22. For recent analyses of these political readjustments, see John Bew, *The glory of being Britons: civic unionism in nineteenth-century Belfast* (Dublin, 2009); G.R. Hall, *Ulster liberalism, 1778–1876* (Dublin, 2011); A.R. Holmes, 'Covenanter politics: evangelicalism, political liberalism and Ulster Presbyterians, 1798–1914', *EHR*, 125 (2010), 340–69; Wright, *'Natural leaders'*, passim.

More than mere background, these developments were central to shaping McCracken's world. On an individual level, it is clear that she was influenced by the changing religious temper of the age: 'I know I am far far, from being a christian yet', she lamented, in a letter written in May 1828, 'but I trust I will be one before I am called on to leave this world'.[14] Equally, as a member of a prominent and long-established Belfast family, McCracken was a young woman whose world was impacted directly by the political and economic transformations the town experienced.[15] One of four surviving children of John McCracken, junior, and Eliza McCracken, neé McReynolds, Eliza McCracken was the granddaughter of John McCracken, senior, a successful ship's captain turned businessman, and his second wife, Ann Joy.[16] Joy's family had a connexion with Belfast stretching back to the mid-seventeenth century: her great-grandfather, George Martin, had served as town sovereign in the 1640s and, more recently, her father, Francis Joy, had played an active role in the commercial life of the town, not least as the founder of its first newspaper, the *Belfast News-Letter*. Captain John McCracken played an equally prominent role in the life of the town. As a philanthropist he participated in the setting up of a Marine Charitable Society, but it was as a businessman that he was chiefly known. McCracken's business interests included a ropewalk, a sail cloth factory and one of Belfast's earliest cotton mills, established in 1784 with his brother-in-law, Robert Joy, and a third man, Thomas McCabe. Unlike Joy and McCabe, McCracken remained involved in the cotton industry in the long term. He later opened his own factory and his sons followed him into the industry, with John junior, Eliza McCracken's father, demonstrating a particular aptitude for commercial life and establishing himself as 'one of the most successful cotton manufacturers in the town'.[17] By 1811, John McCracken, junior, was employing some 200 workers and ten ships were kept busy importing the coal required to keep his mill working.[18] Thus, Eliza McCracken was the daughter of a leading player in the commercial life of late Georgian Belfast.

But it was not just in the commercial life of the town that the McCracken family played a prominent role. They were also heavily involved, in the 1790s, in its political life. Although John McCracken, junior, is said to have had no political interests, the same cannot be said for his siblings.[19] His brother, Henry Joy, for example, is well known as the United Irish leader who led rebel forces at the Battle of Antrim and who was publicly executed in Belfast on 17 June 1798. Two other brothers, William and Francis, were also United Irishmen and his sister, Mary Ann, perhaps the best-known Belfast woman of her generation, was

---

14 EM to RJT, 3 May 1828 (PRONI, D/1748/G/378/48). 15 This and the following paragraph draws on Mary McNeill, *The life and times of Mary Ann McCracken, 1770–1866: a Belfast panorama* (Belfast, 1997), pp 21–42; *DIB*, v, 877–81; and *ODNB*. 16 McCracken and McReynolds were married in July 1795 (*Belfast News-Letter*, 3 Aug. 1795). 17 McNeill, *Mary Ann McCracken*, p. 56. 18 Ibid., p. 242. 19 Ibid., p. 56.

an ardent supporter of social and political reform, both during the 1790s and afterwards. The McCrackens were, in short, a family associated closely with reformist politics and one 'whose devotion to their principles had', in Mary McNeill's words, 'run them into serious trouble'.[20] The same might also be said of the Tennents, the family into which Eliza McCracken married. Robert James Tennent's father, Dr Robert Tennent, was a well-known reformer who played an active role in the political life of the town in the 1810s and 20s, and two of his uncles, William Tennent and John Tennent, had been involved in the United Irish movement. William Tennent, indeed, had been present at the founding of the society, and had been imprisoned for several years in the aftermath of the 1798 rebellion, following which he returned to Belfast, revived his business interests and established himself as a leading merchant and banker.[21]

Bearing these social and familial contexts in mind, it is possible to move beyond the identification of Eliza McCracken simply as a young middle-class woman, and to characterize her, more precisely, as a member of late Georgian Belfast's middle-class elite. Through McCracken, a connexion was established between two of the town's most prominent Presbyterian families – families that were intimately involved in its commercial and economic development and which were widely known to have been deeply involved in the unrest of the 1790s. That the families remained prominent in the life of the town, despite the long shadows cast by 1798, testifies to the space that could be found for one-time radicals in post-Union Belfast.[22] However, leaving aside this broader point, the prominence of the Tennent and McCracken families is of particular relevance to Eliza McCracken's story, for it ensured that her privacy was limited and her life was lived in the public eye.

McCracken herself was well aware that this was the case, and her letters contain frequent complaints about the stifling and gossipy nature of middle-class Belfast. At home, she had to contend with the scrutinizing gaze of the family servants, one of whom adjudged Tennent 'a mighty cool lover' on the grounds that he 'does not pay many visits'.[23] But this was nothing compared to the problems faced outside the home. Acutely aware that her behaviour was being scrutinized, McCracken complained that 'there are many in this place, who have no other occupation, & little other pleasure, than in repeating & enlarging stories, that will give pain to others'.[24] Given this awareness of the prying eyes and gossiping tongues of others, she was mortified when, in May 1828, one of Tennent's cousins had entered a bank and 'in a state of intoxication ... commenced a long harangue about me, swore I was the finest girl in Belfast, the

20 Ibid., p. 200.   21 For John, Robert and William Tennent, see Wright, *'Natural leaders'*, pp 13–48.   22 William Tennent's case is particularly significant here: at the time of his death in 1832 he was preparing to stand for election, demonstrating that former United Irishmen were not necessarily required to withdraw from public life (ibid., pp 46–7, 130–1).   23 EM to RJT, 29 July 1828 (PRONI, D/1748/G/378/68A).   24 EM to RJT, 17 Aug. 1828 (ibid., D/1748/G/378/77A).

only one he would marry but that I would not take him, being resolved to have a younger branch of the family'. 'I confess I was greatly vexed to hear of it for several reasons', she fumed, 'to be talked of by any drunken man is dreadful but to have our attachment so very publicly proclaimed, in such a place & in such a manner is really too bad.'[25] What rendered this episode particularly discomforting for McCracken was the fact that her engagement with Tennent had not, at this point, been settled. Yet things scarcely improved when their relationship was set on a more formal basis. If anything, they became worse. Writing in February 1829, McCracken declared Belfast 'extremely disagreeable'. 'If you cannot understand why & how I feel so unhappy at present', she continued, 'you know nothing of a woman's heart, nor of the agony with which she shrinks from the prying & ill natured eyes of the envious & malicious of whom so many are to be found everywhere & with whom it has been my fate this life to meet more than an equal share.'[26]

Such complaints may be read on a number of levels. No doubt many would have shared the disquiet McCracken felt at the prospect of her private business being discussed in public. But McCracken's reference to the fact that she had encountered 'more than an equal share' of the 'envious & malicious' suggests a particular sensitivity to the whisperings of Belfast's gossips. In McCracken's case, such sensitivity was by no means unwarranted. Given her family's recent past, idle gossip could easily spill over into something more sinister, as in June 1829, when her father received a spiteful anonymous letter, commenting on her engagement to Robert James Tennent and making pointed allusion to the two families' involvement in the United Irish movement. The Tennents, the writer observed, were 'Bastards & Rebels, but I suppose the latter seems perfection in your Eyes as it was the disloyalty of the Tennents that threw dust in your Eyes & made you give in your consent.'[27] John McCracken, junior, may well have avoided political activity, viewing it as 'likely to lead one into nasty and difficult situations', but the insinuation that it was the Tennent family's disloyalty that led him to accept Robert James Tennent as a suitable match for his daughter is telling, suggesting that the entire McCracken family lived under the pall of the 1790s.[28]

Political considerations aside, McCracken's sensitivity to the public discussion of her affairs might also have reflected a belief, influenced by contemporary debates concerning women and the public sphere, that it was not appropriate for a woman's life to be the subject of public consumption. The significance of the 'separate spheres' ideology, which sought to limit women to a private, domestic sphere has, of course, been called into question.[29] As Connolly has noted,

---

[25] EM to RJT, 28, 29 and 30 May 1828 (ibid., D/1748/G/378/52).   [26] EM to RJT, 13 Feb. 1829 (ibid., D/1748/G/378/97).   [27] Anonymous letter to John McCracken, enclosed in EM to RJT, 9, 11 and 12 June 1829 (ibid., D/1748/G/378/106B). The reference to the Tennents being bastards arose as a result of William Tennent's numerous illegitimate children, for whom see Wright, *'Natural leaders'*, pp 35–6.   [28] McNeill, *Mary Ann McCracken*, p. 56.   [29] The now classic critique of 'separate spheres' analysis is Amanda Vickery, 'Golden age to separate

scholars have 'warned of the dangers of confusing the prescriptions of contemporary didactic works with actual patterns of behaviour'.[30] Nevertheless, the point remains that didactic writers *did* attempt to proscribe female participation in the public sphere and to encourage women to think of themselves as private beings. Among the most significant of these writers was Hannah More, who chose, for the epigraph of her *Essays on various subjects, principally designed for young ladies*, an extract from the oration of Pericles to the Athenian women: 'As for you, I shall advise you in a few words: aspire only to those virtues that are PECULIAR TO YOUR SEX; follow your natural modesty, and think it your greatest commendation not to be talked of one way or the other.'[31] Whether or not McCracken had read More's *Essays* is unknown, but she did read her later *Strictures on the modern female system of education* and it is possible to detect the influence of More's prescriptions regarding women and the public sphere in the wording of McCracken's complaints concerning the public discussion of her business: 'to have our attachment so very publicly proclaimed in such a place & in such a manner is really too bad'.[32] Moreover, McCracken subscribed to a view of appropriate female character, markedly similar to that upheld by More, who advised women, in Leonore Davidoff and Catherine Hall's words, 'to be quiet, virtuous and meek rather than showy and brilliant'.[33] Thus, discussing Tennent's cousins Isabella and Letitia in a letter penned in June 1829, McCracken revealed her preference for 'wee Letty', explaining that 'her quiet reserve is certainly more to my tastes than Isabella's flourishes'.[34]

McCracken, then, was a young woman who valued quiet and reserve, and who sought to live privately within the context of a close-knit community in which an interest was taken in her personal affairs. This was, at times, a source of deep distress and a complicating factor in her relationship with Tennent. However, as a closer examination of that relationship will reveal, it was just one of a number of factors that troubled their path to marriage.

III

Although the earliest surviving letter from McCracken to Tennent is dated 15 December 1826, it is clear that she was acquainted with him from a much earlier

---

spheres? A review of the categories and chronology of English women's history', *HJ*, 36 (1993), 383–414. But see also, for a response, Davidoff and Hall, *Family fortunes*, pp xvi–xviii. **30** Connolly, 'A woman's life', p. 435.   **31** Hannah More, *Essays on various subjects, principally designed for young ladies* (London, 1777), title page; G.L. Walker, 'Women's voices' in Pamela Clemit (ed.), *The Cambridge companion to British literature of the French Revolution in the 1790s* (Cambridge, 2011), p. 154.   **32** EM to RJT, 28, 29 and 30 May 1828 (PRONI, D/1748/G/378/52). For More, see M.G. Jones, *Hannah More* (Cambridge, 1952); Anne Stott, *Hannah More: the first Victorian* (Oxford, 2003); and Davidoff and Hall, *Family fortunes*, pp 167–72. **33** Davidoff and Hall, *Family fortunes*, p. 170.   **34** EM to RJT, 9, 11 and 12 June 1829

point.[35] For one thing, as a member of an equally prominent Belfast family, Tennent's life was no less public than McCracken's. If anything, it was more so: no anonymous 'face in the crowd', Tennent was a young man whose activities were noted, and there was much to note, for by the mid-1820s he was busily engaged in the process of making a name for himself. In 1824 he and another young Belfast-man, James Emerson, had travelled to Greece to participate in the Greek War of Independence, and in the years that followed he was to play a prominent role in the political life of his home town.[36] Yet it was not just as a public figure or a member of a prominent family that McCracken knew Tennent: the two were personally acquainted. McCracken's initial letter was, indeed, written with the purpose of following up a face-to-face meeting that had occurred between them. Having become aware that he entertained 'sentiments' towards her, McCracken wrote to inform Tennent that she was unable to reciprocate, and to suggest that his romantic feelings would prove fleeting. 'I feel assured your present feelings will soon subside', she noted playfully, 'and in after years you will laugh at this sudden fancy.'[37]

If Tennent's feelings did subside, they did so only momentarily. In the weeks and months that followed McCracken's initial letter, Tennent continued to make his attachment clear, and by August 1827 the pair were involved in an intense and largely clandestine correspondence, centring on the question of engagement. Initially, McCracken proved resistant to Tennent's proposals. 'You ask me tell you "that you are not totally indifferent to me"', she noted in an early letter, 'well then you are not; how could I feel quite indifferent to a man, who has acted towards me as you have done for the last six months? But if you mean that I should say I was attached to you that I cannot say …'[38] Tennent, however, proved tenacious. Seeing evidence of a confused mind in the, at times rambling, rejections penned by McCracken, he ignored her request to 'ask me not again to be engaged to you' and continued to press her for a commitment.[39] Such tenacity provoked frustration on McCracken's part. 'I did hope, I did expect', she wrote at one point, 'that after all I had said to you, you would not put my resolution again to the test, by asking me either to see or write to you.'[40] But such frustration was mixed with a developing sense of attachment. Indeed, McCracken's reference to Tennent's testing of her resolution is significant,

(PRONI, D/1748/G/378/106A). 35 EM to RJT, 15 Dec. 1826 (ibid., D/1748/G/378/1). 36 James Emerson was later to marry Tennent's cousin Letitia (the daughter of William Tennent) and to add her name to his own, becoming James Emerson Tennent. He went on to represent Belfast in parliament and develop a reputation as a man of letters and colonial administrator. For Tennent and Emerson in Greece, see Wright, 'Natural leaders', pp 111–17, and, for Emerson Tennent's later career, idem, 'The Belfast chameleon: Ulster, Ceylon and the imperial life of Sir James Emerson Tennent' in *Britain and the World*, vi (2013), pp 192–219. 37 EM to RJT, 15 Dec. 1826 (PRONI, D/1748/G/378/1). 38 EM to RJT, 12 Aug. 1827 (ibid., D/1748/G/378/4B). 39 EM to RJT, 14 Aug. 1827 (ibid., D/1748/G/378/5). 40 EM to RJT, 16 Aug. 1827 (ibid., D/1748/G/378/6).

indicating, as it does, that her mind was not settled and that her resolve *could* be tested. That this was the case is made clear in her subsequent letter, in which she conceded that her feelings were confused and revealed her growing attachment to Tennent by acknowledging that she knew of no person 'in the world' to whom she would write of her 'faults' and inconsistent feeling as she had done to him.[41] At this point, the pair remained some distance from formal engagement and marriage, but McCracken did succumb, in the long term, to Tennent's attentions. By April 1828 they were discussing the question of *when* they would get married, rather than *if* they would do so, and in September of the same year McCracken reported that her father had given his consent 'to our union at some future period'.[42] From that point onwards, the couple were able to conduct their relationship openly, in full view of their families, and in June 1830 they were finally married.

Described in brief, McCracken and Tennent's courtship appears to have run along well-worn lines. As Barclay has explained, by the late eighteenth century it was expected that women would act as passive recipients of male affection, and courtship 'developed into an elaborate game', during which the 'suitor bombarded his beloved with gifts and declarations of love'. In the face of this lavish affection, women 'expressed reserve and behaved in a non-committal fashion' before eventually giving in, enabling the man to be 'seen as the victor who had wooed and won his sweetheart.'[43] Yet if it conforms in outline to this pattern, the McCracken–Tennent courtship deviates in detail. The pair were, for instance, engaged long before they were married, diverging from the trend whereby women surrendered to the attentions of their suitors shortly before marriage. Moreover, McCracken was far from being an impassive recipient of Tennent's affections. For many, the game of courtship may well have been one which favoured men, with women playing 'a very restricted and prescribed role', but McCracken's correspondence reveals her to have played an active part in the relationship, encouraging Tennent's attentions one moment, discouraging them the next and obliging him, over a long period of time, to satisfy her concerns regarding their chances of future happiness.[44] Taking into consideration these aspects of the courtship, McCracken and Tennent's relationship can be seen to have had similarities with other patterns of courtship. Some similarities can, for instance, be detected with a second, Enlightenment-influenced pattern identified by Barclay, one shaped by 'discourses of rationality', in which participants sought to 'emphasise their choice of partner was rational and their expression of love contained'.[45] More significant, however, are the similarities that exist with the pattern of 'ritualized courtship testing' identified by Karen Lystra in her work on romantic love in nineteenth-century America, whereby women

---

41 EM to RJT, 23 Aug. 1827 (ibid., D/1748/G/378/7).   42 EM to RJT, 21, 25 Apr., 3 Sept. 1828 (ibid., D/1748/G/378/41A, 43, 83).   43 Barclay, *Love, intimacy and power*, p. 90. 44 Ibid.   45 Ibid., p. 92.

manufactured crises in order to 'gauge their partner's emotional commitment'. Such crises could, Lystra argues, take a range of forms. 'Illness, debt, family, other men, religious differences, character flaws, and personal inadequacy all formed the plot material of these private cultural dramas.' The key point is that they were 'more than random troubles in love's path'; they were impediments deliberately placed there, 'obstacles that men had to overcome to prove the emotional depth and sincerity of their love'.[46]

McCracken had ample material with which to construct such obstacles. There was, for example, the question of financial security. Tennent was a young man with prospects, but those prospects were precisely that, prospects, unrealized and unproven. This raised the obvious question as to how he would support a wife. In an early letter McCracken forswore 'mercenary considerations', but she later made it clear that she was unwilling to marry unless it was possible to do so in 'comfort & propriety' and the wedding had to wait until Tennent had finished his legal training in London.[47] Added to this was the question of religion, for McCracken worried that she and Tennent were spiritually incompatible. As early as August 1827, she expressed her fear that Tennent had 'very little religion', and in June 1828 she complained that 'we will never agree on religion, which really vexes me as, I would much rather we should differ on any other subject'.[48] Tennent clearly made no secret of the fact that he disagreed with McCracken in this area. Thus, in a subsequent letter she remarked that 'your opinion of original sin & mine do not by any means coincide'. However, he did succeed in setting her mind at some rest on this score for she went on to remark that she did 'heartily agree' with him in 'thinking that our difference of opinion on this subject will never be a source of quarrel between us'.[49] In the short term, the matter was dropped, though McCracken was to raise religious issues again in October 1829, going back on an earlier pledge 'not [to] speak to you on religious subjects'.[50]

The chief obstacle McCracken threw in Tennent's path was, however, related neither to religion nor to financial security: it was related to the sincerity, or lack thereof, of his affections. Tennent's ill-advised admission, early in the courtship, that 'the difficulty of exciting an interest' had been 'one of the principal motives' of his initial 'pursuit' of McCracken inspired doubts concerning his romantic sincerity, and the haste with which he had declared his interest and pushed for an engagement did little to allay fears on this score.[51] 'For my own part', McCracken noted pointedly, in one of her earliest letters, 'I could not feel attached to any man ... unless I had a knowledge of his character, and, above all, until he had gained my affection, by a great deal of that quiet and unobserved

---

[46] Karen Lystra, *Searching the heart: women, men, and romantic love in nineteenth-century America* (Oxford, 1989), pp 157–8, 166. See also, Vickery, *Gentleman's daughter*, p. 53.   [47] EM to RJT, n.d., 21 Apr. 1828 (PRONI, D/1748/G/378/3A, 41A).   [48] EM to RJT, 23 Aug. 1827, 2, 3, 4 and 6 June 1828 (ibid., D/1748/G/378/7, 53).   [49] EM to RJT, 16 and 17 June 1828 (ibid., D/1748/G/378/55).   [50] EM to RJT, 24 Oct. 1829 (ibid., D/1748/G/378/126).   [51] EM to RJT, 14 Aug. 1827 (ibid., D/1748/G/378/5).

attention, by which I think a man has the only chance of creating an interest in the heart of women, at least of any woman not in her teens.'[52] Confident and self-possessed, McCracken here indicated that she was no impressionable teen, waiting to be swept from her feet. It was not sufficient for Tennent to offer marriage: that marriage had to be based on affection, and that affection had to be cultivated by Tennent in a manner becoming McCracken's perception of herself as a woman. But McCracken was not simply making her own expectations known here. Her comments also had a sharper edge, for in their mid- to late-adolescence Tennent and his associates participated in a seemingly endless round of flirtation and romantic intriguing, and Tennent himself had been engaged to another young woman who he had abandoned.[53] Read in this light, McCracken's comments appear as an assertion that her fate would not be the same and she reiterated the point, more bluntly, in her subsequent letter. 'I cannot forget M.G. and I would dread meeting the same fate', she noted, 'I cannot but blame you, for your conduct towards her ... after you were engaged to her, you had no right to draw back.'[54]

This 'M.G.' was Mary Gray, one of three daughters of James Gray, a well-connected *littérateur*, related, through marriage, to the poet James Hogg. Having been employed, for many years, as classics master at the Edinburgh High School, Gray's father moved to Belfast in 1822, where he served briefly as principal of the Belfast Academy, before taking orders as an Anglican clergyman and travelling to India to take up a chaplaincy at Bhuj, Cutch.[55] In all, the family spent just four years in Belfast, but during this period Mary Gray became attached to Tennent, accepting a proposal of marriage from him. That this proposal was viewed seriously is indicated by the fact that Gray remained in Britain when her family left for India, and when it was ended she was left heart-broken. Her devastation was, indeed, such, that it inspired James Hogg's 'Broken Heart'. When he published this poem in his *Songs by the Ettrick shepherd* (1831), Hogg explained that it had been 'written in detestation of the behaviour of a gentleman (can I call him so?) to a dearly-beloved young relative of my own', and underlined his disgust by appending a verse, 'from another poem written at the same time', in which he condemned Tennent as a 'cold-hearted villain'.[56]

McCracken was not quite so critical, though she nevertheless presented Tennent's treatment of Gray as a major stumbling block. She was, as she wrote in September 1827, 'quite haunted with the idea of poor M.G.', and the regularity with which Gray's name appears in McCracken's letters to Tennent,

52 EM to RJT, n.d. (ibid., D/1748/G/378/3A). 53 EM to RJT, 12 Aug. 1827 (ibid., D/1748/G/378/4B). The romantic intrigues of Tennent's circle are discussed in J.J. Wright, 'Robert Hyndman's toe: romanticism, schoolboy politics and the affective revolution in late Georgian Belfast' in Catherine Cox and Susannah Riordan (eds), *Adolescence in modern Irish history: innocence and experience* (Basingstoke, 2015), pp 15–41. 54 EM to RJT, 12 Aug. 1827 (PRONI, D/1748/G/378/4B). 55 William Steven, *The history of the High School of Edinburgh* (Edinburgh, 1849), app., pp 103–7; *ODNB*. 56 James Hogg, *Songs by the Ettrick*

and the anxiety expressed concerning her, would appear to bear this out.[57] Such anxiety was presented by McCracken as the result of empathy, rather than jealousy. She expressed her horror at the thought that she could, in engaging in a relationship with Tennent, further Gray's suffering and informed him that she could 'well imagine what a feeling mind must suffer, in being treated as you have done M.G.'[58] There is little reason to question McCracken's sincerity in any of this: she emerges from her correspondence as an emotive personality, given to introspection, and she was no doubt aware of the social stigma that could attach to a young woman whose engagement had failed.[59] Nevertheless, it is impossible to escape the conclusion that Gray provided McCracken with a useful means with which to manufacture crises and allay her fears concerning Tennent's romantic commitment. 'As for myself,' McCracken informed Tennent, in September 1827, 'I really could not feel happy, if I knew that my being so made another miserable ... It is best for all parties that you & I should part.'[60] Evidently Tennent successfully negotiated this hurdle, for in her subsequent letter, penned just two days later, McCracken was cheerfully arranging for him to 'pop in' and meet her while drinking tea at her aunt's and imploring him to discuss their relationship with her father.[61] Yet Gray remained a useful negotiating tool and late in December 1827, having actually met her, McCracken utilized her again. Accusing Tennent of having acted with duplicity towards Gray, she came close to breaking off her own connexion with him, reasoning that she 'would not value the affections of any man who could sacrifice his principles for me'.[62] Once again, the relationship survived, but it was not until October 1829, when she learned that Gray had joined her father in India and married 'a man of wealth & high connexions', that the obstacle was removed for good. 'As this is the very first piece of good fortune we have met with since the commencement of our engagement,' McCracken observed, 'so I sincerely trust it is an omen of brightening prospects, at all events I feel relieved of a load of anxiety'.[63]

McCracken's correspondence with Tennent can, then, be framed in terms of the exercise of female agency. Rather than a game fixed entirely in Tennent's favour, the pair's courtship was a negotiation in which McCracken herself exercised a degree of influence. Yet, the extent of McCracken's agency should

---

Shepherd (Edinburgh, 1831), pp 271, 273; Gillian Hughes (ed.), *The collected letters of James Hogg: volume 2, 1820–1831* (Edinburgh, 2006), p. 308. **57** EM to RJT, 16 Sept. 1827 (PRONI, D/1748/G/378/12A). **58** EM to RJT, 12 Aug., 16 Sept. 1827 (ibid., D/1748/G/378/4B, 12A). **59** Vickery, *Gentleman's daughter*, p. 53. **60** EM to RJT, 16 Sept. 1827 (PRONI, D/1748/G/378/12A). **61** EM to RJT, 18 Sept. 1827 (ibid., D/1748/G/378/12B). **62** EM to RJT, 21 Dec. 1827 (ibid., D/1748/G/378/21A). **63** This man of wealth and high connexions was the appropriately named Robert Catton Money, an East India Company official whose 'character and prospects rank very high'. The pair were married at Cutch on 28 Apr. 1829 (EM to RJT, 15 Oct. 1829 (ibid., D/1748/G/378/124A); *Oriental Herald and Journal of General Literature*, 23 (1829), 332; Hughes (ed.),

not be pushed too far. For one thing, not all of the obstacles she placed in Tennent's path worked to her advantage. When, in September 1827, she raised the possibility of a romantic rival, informing Tennent of William Whitmore, an associate of her brother who had, a year earlier, courted her affection and 'made a tolerably deep impression', the balance of power shifted in Tennent's favour.[64] In her subsequent letters, McCracken referred to Tennent's rebuke and reflected, at length, on her feelings for him, conceding that he forbore with her 'more, far more, than I deserve'.[65] Moreover, while McCracken might be said to have exercised agency in her attempts to test Tennent's commitment, the fundamental obstacle to their marriage was one that neither party had any control over. By the late eighteenth and early nineteenth centuries, as Barclay has explained, the marital union 'was increasingly understood to be about meeting the needs of the individual rather than the family'. Nevertheless, the wider family continued to play a role in the settlement of marriages and 'parental permission was to remain an important part of marriage into the nineteenth century'.[66] In McCracken and Tennent's case, such permission was initially withheld: when first apprised of the possibility of a connexion between his daughter and Tennent, McCracken's father initially opposed it and this, more than anything, complicated their relationship.

McCracken's father had learned of the courtship and declared his opposition at an early point. In August 1827, a letter Tennent had addressed to 'Miss McCracken' had been delivered, by mistake, to McCracken's aunts, who had read it and become convinced that the two had been carrying on a clandestine correspondence.[67] This note contained a proposal of marriage and McCracken felt compelled to discuss it with her father who 'was not either ... surprised nor angry merely saying you were a very fine young man & had paid me the highest compliment man could pay to woman but that it would be very imprudent of you to think of marrying for years'.[68] If measured, this response was unequivocal. Thus, the clandestine correspondence McCracken's aunts suspected became a reality and the pair conducted their courtship negotiation secretly, all the while aware that nothing could be settled until McCracken's father had been persuaded to give his consent. This seemed, at times, unlikely. When in July 1828, McCracken's father discovered that the couple had been meeting in secret he responded in a rage, vowing to break the affair off, and it was not until September of the same year that he made it known that he had 'been convinced of the propriety & justice of giving his full consent'.[69] Even then, marriage

Letters of James Hogg, vol. 2, pp 355, 371, 372). **64** EM to RJT, 23 Sept. 1827 (PRONI, D/1748/G/378/14). **65** EM to RJT, 25 Sept., 25 and 26 Sept. 1827 (ibid., D/1748/G/378/15, 16A). **66** Barclay, *Love, intimacy and power*, pp 77, 78. **67** This episode is related in letters which Tennent received from McCracken's cousin Maria McClean: Maria McClean to RJT, 10, 11, 15 Aug. 1827 (PRONI, D/1748/G/369/6, 7, 8). **68** EM, writing in Maria McClean to RJT, 11 Aug. 1827, and EM to RJT, 12 Aug. 1827 (ibid., D/1748/G/369/7; D/1748/G/378/4B). **69** EM to RJT, 5 July, 3 Sept. 1828 (ibid., D/1748/G/378/59, 83).

remained some distance away. Tennent required the agreement of *his* family and, reflecting the fact that 'settlement and marriage remained bywords for bargain and sale', a degree of financial negotiation was no doubt necessary.[70] Nevertheless, a turning point had been reached: the pair's engagement, so long discussed in private, became a public matter and Tennent became a regular caller at the McCracken house.[71]

That McCracken had pursued her relationship with Tennent in the face of her father's objections is not, in itself, particularly noteworthy. Writing of eighteenth-century Scotland, Barclay has noted than 'parental interference was more likely to promote conflict than obedience' and there is little reason to doubt that things were any different in early nineteenth-century Ulster.[72] Yet if such defiance was far from remarkable, it does not follow that McCracken engaged in it lightly. Quite the reverse: her letters reveal her to have been deeply conflicted by the issue of her father's opposition. Writing during what she described ominously as 'the affair of the note', when her father had first signalled his opposition to an engagement with Tennent, she declared herself unwilling to become attached to anyone 'unless I know & am quite sure that my father will approve'.[73] Two days later, however, she complained that 'my wishes were not consulted' and that her father was 'most unreasonable', declaring herself 'indignant, most indignant at the manner in which he has acted towards me'. But this frustration was mixed with a desire to 'check every feeling at variance with my duty towards him' and in a third letter she expressed regret and remorse: 'I am angry with myself for indulging one unkind thought of my dearest father,' she wrote, 'I must have wronged him, I am sure he dearly loves me.'[74] Here, in some of her earliest letters, McCracken articulated a conflicted sense of duty she was to return to again and again in the months to come. In the end, this sense of duty was defeated by her increasing attachment to Tennent, and by April 1828 she had become convinced of her father's selfishness: 'I am so angry with my father that I can scarcely speak to him', she railed; 'if he were foolish or unreasonable in any respects, I could make some allowances for him, but being neither, I have really lost patience, it is no longer my happiness, but his own, he consults'.[75] This shift in attitude arose partly from a conviction that her father had acted equally unfairly in relation to her brother Henry's marriage. Yet it is clear that, in emotional terms, defying her father's wishes cost McCracken much and, to understand the persistence of her sense of duty, it is necessary to turn from the theme of love to that of loss.

---

[70] EM to RJT, 25 July, 18 Sept. 1828 (ibid., D/1748/G/378/66, 84A); Vickery, *Gentleman's daughter*, p. 82.   [71] EM to RJT, 18 Oct. 1828 (PRONI, D/1748/G/378/125A).   [72] Barclay, *Love, intimacy and power*, p. 77.   [73] EM to RJT, 12 Aug. 1827 (PRONI, D/1748/G/378/4B). [74] EM to RJT, 14, 16 Aug. 1827 (ibid., D/1748/G/378/5, 6).   [75] EM to RJT, 5 Apr. 1828 (ibid., D/1748/G/378/35).

IV

In the late eighteenth and early nineteenth centuries, as Davidoff and Hall have observed, middle-class families faced a range of dangers. 'Along with continuing political unrest, the exigencies of poverty, brutality, pressing sexuality, disease and death were all too familiar.'[76] For the McCracken family, political unrest and death were, of course, linked potently in the person of Henry Joy McCracken, who was executed in the aftermath of the 1798 rebellion. For some, the circumstances of this death tarnished the McCracken name, but the family did not forswear his memory. Quite the reverse, his sister, Mary Ann, guarded it, preserving a lock of his hair that she later presented to the historian R.R. Madden, and John McCracken, junior, commemorated his life by naming one of his sons after him.[77] This younger Henry Joy McCracken, Eliza McCracken's brother, was himself to die at a young age in April 1828. The circumstances of this death were rendered particularly tragic by the fact that his wife had died the previous year, and two years before this, on 3 July 1825, his mother, Eliza McCracken, senior, John McCracken's wife of some thirty years, had also died.[78] Thus Eliza McCracken's family was a family over which death cast a long shadow. Hers was a world darkened by grief, and central to understanding her relationship with her father, and the complicated and conflicted sense of duty she felt towards him, was the death of her mother.

The death of Eliza McCracken, senior, had a range of consequences for her eldest daughter. On a practical level, it deprived her, during the period of her courtship, of a sympathetic go-between through which to negotiate with her father and overcome his objections to the relationship with Tennent. As McCracken herself put it, in a passage which reflects neatly her awareness of this want, 'I have no dear mother now to intercede with him'.[79] More broadly, the death of her mother ensured that McCracken was forced to navigate the treacherous waters of love, courtship and sexuality without maternal support. This lack of support was rendered all the more significant by the fact of McCracken's isolation within her wider family network. While she had a number of aunts on her father's side of the family, they provided their niece with little in the way of emotional support. Indeed, McCracken looked on them as a source of emotional and reputational danger, rather than a source of support: 'those old ladys seem to be her evil spirits they will so glory in having anything to tell', remarked a well-disposed cousin, from another branch of the family.[80] Difficult enough at the best of times, this want of female support was rendered all the

---

[76] Davidoff and Hall, *Family fortunes*, p. 357. [77] McNeill, *Mary Ann McCracken*, pp 192, 200, 296. [78] EM to RJT, 27 and 28 Nov. 1827, 16 Apr. 1828 (PRONI, D/1748/G/378/20A and 38A); *Belfast News-Letter*, 8 July 1825; McNeill, *Mary Ann McCracken*, p. 296. [79] EM to RJT, 14 Aug. 1827 (PRONI, D/1748/G/378/5). [80] Maria McClean to RJT, 11 Aug. 1827 (ibid., D/1748/G/369/7).

more serious by the fact that, as her eldest daughter, McCracken stepped into her mother's role as the woman of the house. Such domestic surrogacy was not unusual, and nor was it necessarily without reward. As Davidoff and Hall have noted, it offered 'responsibility, respect and affection without a break from familiar surroundings and the necessity to cope with a new, sexual relationship'.[81] Yet, for a young woman such as McCracken, who *did* wish to break from her familiar, familial surroundings, the role of domestic surrogate could prove frustrating and lead to resentment. 'I know quite well that I must be a very great loss to Papa, no matter at what time he loses me', McCracken wrote bitterly of her father, in September 1827. 'I am so necessary both to his comfort & amusement, but it is selfish of him to prefer his own gratification to my happiness.'[82]

If, however, McCracken resented her father, it is clear that such resentment was balanced by an acute sense of responsibility, and that this sense of responsibility was compounded by a promise made on her mother's deathbed. Conceding early in her correspondence with Tennent that her father's happiness was 'in a great measure' centred on her, McCracken remarked that she was 'bound by a promise, which to me is most sacred, never to displease him' and she later returned to this, explaining 'I promised my dying mother never to displease my father & that promise, no matter at what expense of personal feeling, I shall most religiously fulfil'.[83] Given this, it might well be imagined how difficult McCracken found it to defy her father's wishes and pursue her future with Tennent. That she did so, pursuing a clandestine correspondence and contemplating an engagement before her father had given his blessing to the match, can be taken as an indication of how seriously she viewed her relationship with Tennent, notwithstanding the games she appeared to play when 'testing' his commitment.

Leaving aside the light it shines on her relationship with her father, the death of McCracken's mother – and the fact that McCracken was twenty-one years of age when this occurred, and was therefore old enough to remember her mother and experience her death as a loss – is also significant in understanding the strain of melancholy that recurs in her correspondence with Tennent. In the letter in which she lamented that she had no mother to intercede with her father, McCracken explained morosely that she had 'many dreary hours' and was 'sick of the duplicity & selfishness of this world'.[84] On another occasion, she reflected that 'the future is to me more a subject of apprehension than of hope' and in a remarkable letter penned in November 1827, she detailed a dream she had, during which she had died and 'an angel stood beside my bed, ready to receive my departing soul'. 'I awoke,' she continued, 'awed, but disappointed to find it but a dream, if I were sure of experiencing the same feelings when the hour of

---

81 Davidoff and Hall, *Family fortunes*, pp 346–7.   82 EM to RJT, 25 and 26 Sept. 1827 (PRONI, D/1748/G/378/16A).   83 EM to RJT, n.d., 9 Sept. 1827 (ibid., D/1748/G/378/3A, 9).   84 EM to RJT, 14 Aug. 1827 (ibid., D/1748/G/378/5).

death does really come, gladly would I meet the given monster this very night.' That the recollection of this dream thrilled McCracken's 'inmost soul', leading her to remark that 'in my happiest hours, I never felt anything to equal the rapture I experienced' offers one indication of the deep sense of melancholy that clouded her life. A second is, however, provided by her subsequent reflections: 'I believe I am nervous, everything here so strongly reminds me of the dreadful scenes I have witnessed in this house, every room calls to mind something dreadful, the season of the year, too, is so dreary.'[85] Those 'scenes' must surely have included her mother's deathbed, and it does not require a great leap of imagination to ascribe this melancholy to grief.

Within the context of late eighteenth- and early nineteenth-century Britain, grief had emerged as a permissible emotion. 'In the seventeenth century', Joanne Bailey has observed, 'writers advocated the stoical application of self-control to withstand bereavement. From the mid-eighteenth century, the culture of sensibility approved of a surfeit of feeling so that grief was no longer an emotion that should be entirely stemmed, though it still required management.'[86] Located within this cultural context, McCracken's melancholy, read as the expression of grief, requires little explanation. Yet it is worth emphasizing the extent to which McCracken was troubled by grief, for it was not simply the death of her mother that McCracken had to deal with, but that of her brother, Henry Joy. Detailed in her letters to Tennent, this death affected McCracken deeply. Having become 'wonderfully attached' to Henry Joy following the death of his 'sweet wife' Elizabeth in 1827, McCracken travelled with her father to visit him in Dublin in March 1828, when it was learnt that, en route to Lisbon, he had been 'attacked by a severe spitting of blood'.[87] What she found alarmed her greatly: 'I am worn out by anxiety and fatigue', she wrote on 25 March 1828, 'my brother, my dear & valued brother lies now – perhaps on his bed of death.'[88] By early April, things seem to have taken a turn for the better, and McCracken opened a letter to Tennent brightly, asserting 'I am so extremely happy this morning, I cannot resist telling you of it'.[89] But such happiness proved short-lived. Henry Joy's condition rapidly deteriorated and within a few days he had died.[90] A cruel blow for the family, this was rendered still worse when a Dublin doctor informed McCracken's father that 'every child he had must have a decided tendency to pulmonary consumption'. Reflecting on this, McCracken remarked ruefully that 'I think it most likely my poor father will survive us all, or at least the greater part of us.'[91]

85 EM to RJT, 27 and 28 Nov. 1827, 19, 21 and 24 Nov. 1829 (ibid., D/1748/G/378/20B, 138).   86 Joanne Bailey, *Parenting in England, 1760–1830: emotion, identity, and generation* (Oxford, 2012), p. 40.   87 EM to RJT, 27 and 28 Nov. 1827, 23, 29 Mar. 1828 (PRONI, D/1748/G/378/20A, 25, 28).   88 EM to RJT, 25 Mar. 1828 (ibid., D/1748/G/378/26). 89 EM to RJT, 8 Apr. 1828 (ibid., D/1748/G/378/36).   90 EM to RJT, 16 Apr. 1828 (ibid., D/1748/G/378/38A).   91 EM to RJT, 18 Apr. 1828 (ibid., D/1748/G/378/39A).

Implicit in McCracken's reference to her 'poor father' was a degree of sympathy for his plight: having lost his wife, he had now lost a son and been given to believe that his other children would predecease him. However, in the days that followed McCracken's attitude shifted. Just as he opposed her relationship with Tennent, McCracken's father had opposed Henry Joy's marriage and as she reflected on her brother's death McCracken came to view these facts as connected: 'I am perfectly convinced that the anxiety & misery he suffered from my father's ... unjustifiable opposition to his marriage laid the foundations of that disease which consigned him to an early grave', she wrote darkly. 'I certainly do not believe people die of love – but I am quite satisfied that constant anxiety & wearing out opposition has a most pernicious effect on any frame on which the most remote tendency to consumption can be traced.'[92] Whether McCracken was, in fact, 'quite satisfied' of this, or whether her remarks reflect the rage of grief are open to debate. Nevertheless, it appears that Henry Joy's death served to reinforce the resentment caused by her father's opposition to the relationship with Tennent. In July 1828 his continued opposition led McCracken to write with frustration of his 'unreasonable disposition' and the father-daughter relationship deteriorated markedly.[93] 'My father never speaks to me on any subject except when he cannot avoid it,' McCracken remarked, 'all confidence & affection seem gone.'[94] But just as it reinforced her resentment towards her father, Henry Joy's death also reinforced McCracken's affection towards Tennent. 'I do feel my dear Tennent that all the pain I have suffered has drawn more closely, the ties which unite us', she had written in the days immediately following Henry Joy's death, and in the months that followed the two discussed the question of engagement more earnestly.[95]

Thus grief and loss impacted McCracken and Tennent's relationship in contradictory ways. Whereas the death of her mother rendered it difficult for McCracken to contemplate the possibility of defying her father and pursuing her own happiness, the death of her brother altered her perspective, throwing her father's selfishness into relief and strengthening her emotional bond with Tennent. What is clear is that this was an emotionally costly process and that McCracken and Tennent's courtship was complicated by more than romantic uncertainty and parental opposition; it was complicated by McCracken's experience of grief and her confused sense of duty.

V

Focusing on her troubled courtship and experience of grief, the picture of McCracken's experience presented thus far is not a particularly happy one. Yet

[92] EM to RJT, 22 and 23 Apr. 1821 (ibid., D/1748/G/378/42A). [93] EM to RJT, 5 July 1828 (ibid., D/1748/G/378/59A). [94] EM to RJT, 18 July 1828 (ibid., D/1748/G/378/63A). [95] EM to RJT, 16 Apr. 1828 (ibid., D/1748/G/378/38A).

life did offer some consolations. One obvious source of solace was provided by religion. Evangelicalism is known to have provided succour for those experiencing emotional distress, and evidence that McCracken drew comfort from religious belief can be identified in a letter, penned in October 1829, in which she explained her 'opinion as to the purpose of prayer'. 'When in grief', she wrote, 'I pray for support & resignation to his [God's] will, when in joy, my heart overflows with thankfulness for the author of so much happiness & at all times I implore the divine protection for those I dearly love, & earnestly entreat that in all things at all times, I may be enabled to <u>know</u> & to do my duty no matter how painful that duty may be.'[96] But prayer was not McCracken's only source of consolation: books and learning also provided a form of relief from life's trials.

As a young woman of the early nineteenth century, McCracken lived at a time of increasing literary consumption among women and was a keen reader. It has, indeed, been suggested that her papers offer 'striking evidence of the new image of the educated woman who began to appear in Ulster by the 1820s', and the letters she wrote to Tennent during their courtship bear this judgment out.[97] Books provided a shared interest for the pair, and Tennent encouraged McCracken's literary interests by supplying reading material.[98] Thus, in a letter penned on 26 October 1828, McCracken informed him that she had 'received all the books' but feared that it would be 'a very long time' before she could 'read them all'.[99] This consignment of books appears to have included Hannah More's *Strictures on the modern system of female education*, for within a week McCracken was informing Tennent that she had 'read the greater part of this work', and it may also have included the six volumes of female biography, which she returned in mid-December 1828.[100] This latter work was, presumably, Mary Hays' *Female biography: or memoirs of illustrious and celebrated women of all ages and countries* (1803), a 'daring experiment in history writing', which sought, as Gina Luria Walker has put it, 'to arouse enthusiasm for women's achievements, irrespective of conventional prejudices ... endorsing figures that did not conform to traditional moral codes'.[101] What McCracken made of the work is unknown, but we might suspect that she lacked sympathy towards its wider project, for she had enthusiastically approved More's *Strictures*, informing Tennent that she was 'quite rejoiced to find that she & I agree so well on various matters, particularly in our opinion of French novels & feminine propriety'.[102]

---

96 EM to RJT, 24 Oct. 1829 (ibid., D/1748/G/378/126); Wright, *'Natural leaders'*, pp 205, 210.   97 Mary O'Dowd, 'Women in Ulster, 1600–1800' in Kennedy and Ollerenshaw (eds), *Ulster since 1600*, pp 53–5. See also Gerardine Meaney, Mary O'Dowd and Bernadette Whelan, *Reading the Irish woman: studies in cultural encounter and exchange, 1714–1960* (Liverpool, 2013), pp 65–6.   98 As the nephew of William Tennent, Robert James Tennent had access to one of the largest privately held libraries in Belfast (Wright, *'Natural leaders'*, p. 43).   99 EM to RJT, 26 Oct. 1828 (PRONI, D/1748/G/378/87A).   100 EM to RJT, 1 and 3 Nov. 1828, 19 Dec. 1828 (ibid., D/1748/G/378/88, 91A).   101 Walker, 'Women's voices', pp 156–7.   102 EM to RJT, 1 and 3 Nov. 1828 (PRONI, D/1748/G/378/88).

Given More's reputation as a political and cultural reactionary and an unpholder of 'separate spheres', it might be expected that she sought to place limits on female literary consumption. However, while it is certainly true that More took a dim view of French novelists and their imitators, in particular, female writers such as Hays and Mary Wollstonecraft, condemning their works as 'vehicles of wider mischief' which encouraged 'infidelity and immorality', it does not follow that she was opposed to female education *per se*;[103] quite the reverse, as Jacqueline Pearson has observed, More was a 'key figure in the history of women's literacy' and her political and religious conservatism did not prevent her from supporting women's education.[104] Women, More argued, should be prepared for their roles as daughters, wives and mothers, and this training involved reading. In More's view, the reading of 'dry tough books' inculcated good habits of mind, the study of history proved its value insofar as it provided an opportunity to view the working of providence and a woman with a degree of classical learning made a better match for a man with classical education than the woman without.[105] More approved of middle-class women preparing themselves for marriage with educated men by grappling with serious scholarly work, and it is precisely this sort of disciplined, scholarly reading that McCracken engaged in.

Tellingly, McCracken had asked Tennent in August 1828 for a list of 'good solid improving books' to read, and her letters from the summer and autumn of 1829 reveal her to have undertaken a course of serious reading, heavily orientated towards the classics.[106] Writing in June 1829, for instance, she discussed her reading of Roman history, and by October of the same year she was referring to the Odyssey and the Iliad: she particularly enjoyed the latter.[107] This course of classical reading continued into the following year, with McCracken mentioning her reading of Herodotus in a letter dated 15 February 1830.[108] Alongside such classical reading, her letters also contain references to Shakespeare, to the novels of Maria Edgeworth and to the *Edinburgh Review*.[109] However, it would appear that these texts, like the classical ones, were not read for mere enjoyment, but were consumed seriously, for the purposes of edification and improvement. Indeed, something of McCracken's sober and systematic approach to reading is reflected in her letter of 15 February 1830, in which she informed Tennent that she was returning a copy of the *Edinburgh Review* and explained that 'I did not

---

103 Hannah More, *Strictures on the modern system of female education. With a view of the principle and conduct prevalent among women of rank and fortune* (2 vols, London, 1799), i, 31, 39; Orianne Smith, *Romantic women writers, revolution, and prophecy: rebellious daughters, 1786–1826* (Cambridge, 2013), pp 63–4.   104 Jacqueline Pearson, *Women's reading in Britain, 1750–1835: a dangerous recreation* (Cambridge, 1999), p. 88.   105 These comments are based on Jones, *Hannah More*, pp 114–21 (esp. pp 118–19); Pearson, *Women's reading*, p. 71 and Walker, 'Women's voices', pp 154–5; see also, Stott, *Hannah More*, pp 215–28.   106 EM to RJT, 7 Aug. 1828 (PRONI, D/1748/G/ 378/72).   107 EM to RJT, 9, 11 and 12 June, 24 Oct. 1829 (ibid., D/1748/G/378/106A, 126). See also EM to RJT, 19, 21 and 24 Nov. 1829 (ibid., D/1748/G/378/138).   108 EM to RJT, 15 Feb. 1830 (ibid., D/1748/G/378/143).   109 EM to RJT, 12 and 13 June 1828, 9, 11 and 12 June 1829, 15 Feb. 1830 (ibid., D/1748/G/378/54, 106A, 143).

read the Utilitarian Theory of government as I wish to begin at the beginning of the controversy.'[110] Here, McCracken was referring to the debate conducted between Thomas Babington Macaulay and Thomas Perronet in the pages of the *Edinburgh Review* and the *Westminster Review*.[111] That she was aware of this exchange is significant, highlighting the fact that the parameters of her intellectual world extended beyond classical literature and modern didactic works. But equally significant is her desire to survey the controversy methodically as a whole: here was a young woman who sought to move beyond the 'trivial and superficial education' condemned by More in her *Strictures*.[112]

In addition to reading, McCracken also spent her time developing other, more traditional, feminine accomplishments. 'I am doing wonderfully at drawing', she wrote, with a hint of pride, in June 1829, and her letters also include references to playing the pianoforte and attending language classes.[113] At first glance, this appears to be precisely the sort of activity that advocates of extended female education condemned, but McCracken's attendance at language classes merits further attention. Had the language been French, there would be nothing remarkable about this. However, at a time when such education was beyond the reach of most young women, the language McCracken learnt was Latin.[114] She did so under the tutelage of the Revd Reuben John Bryce, James Gray's successor as the principal of the Belfast Academy.[115] Well-known to the Tennent family, Bryce was an associate of Maria Edgeworth and an educational reformer who advocated the extension of serious education to women and opened the Belfast Academy's courses in mineralogy and geology, logic and the art of education 'to persons of both sexes'.[116] McCracken found Bryce, as a teacher of Latin, 'very good natured and respectful' and while she complained, after one class, that 'my head hurts dreadfully', she derived evident pleasure from her developing accomplishment in the subject.[117] 'I said my Latin extremely well this morning,' she wrote, in October 1829; 'we had several historical points to discuss in which, as usual I had the best of it'.[118]

Intellectual satisfaction aside, the study of Latin also provided McCracken with a means by which to exercise some control over her time. At one point, in a long letter composed over several days in June 1829, she broke off her writing in order to study, and in a later note she instructed Tennent 'to pay your visit to me

110 EM to RJT, 15 Feb. 1830 (ibid., D/1748/G/378/143). 111 See J.E. Crimmins, *Utilitarian philosophy and politics: Bentham's later years* (London, 2011), pp 25–49. 112 Stott, *Hannah More*, p. 219. 113 EM to RJT, 15 and 16 Nov. 1828, 9, 11 and 12 June 1829 (PRONI, D/1748/G/378/89, 106A). 114 Davidoff and Hall, *Family fortunes*, pp 289–90. 115 Hugh Shearman, *Belfast Royal Academy, 1785–1935* (Belfast, 1935), p. 17. 116 *Statement of the constitution of the Belfast Academy; with an account of the history and present state of the system of education pursued in that seminary* (Belfast, 1829), p. 29; *Belfast Literary Society, 1801– 1901: historical sketch, with memoirs of some distinguished authors* (Belfast, 1902), pp 135–6; A.T.Q. Stewart, *Belfast Royal Academy: the first century, 1785–1885* (Belfast, 1985), p. 53. 117 EM to RJT, 3 Oct., 19, 21 and 24 Nov. 1829 (PRONI, D/1748/G/378/120A, 138). 118 EM to RJT, 24 Oct. 1829 (ibid., D/1748/G/378/126).

early as I must say some Latin'.[119] That blunt, decisive 'I must', altogether more assertive than 'I hope to' or 'I would like to', may be read as significant: here, learning and study provided an opportunity to exercise agency. But this point should not be pushed too far, for agency did not equate to independence. As with her reading, McCracken's study of Latin was mediated by Tennent, who assisted her in her studies, and this led her to present her own achievements in a self-effacing manner. Writing in April 1829, she informed Tennent that Bryce 'said he has never had a pupil who could learn so readily', but qualified this compliment heavily, reasoning that her progress was 'no credit to me, as I have two masters.'[120] Tennent's influence is made equally clear in a letter McCracken wrote the following October, in which she discussed the expansion of her studies: 'Bryce wishes us to commence Greek & Logic, will you allow me? (dutiful as usual you perceive).'[121] There is, perhaps, a hint of raillery here; as Amanda Vickery has cautioned, a 'deferential utterance is not an unerring sign of a deferential spirit'.[122] Nevertheless, it is clear that in her intellectual pursuits McCracken sought, and accepted, Tennent's guidance and that this established a precedent for their married life. As late as March 1837, McCracken sought the advice of her then husband, who was away from home, on her reading: 'I am nearly finished Hallam & I do request you will tell me what book I am to begin next,' she wrote; 'I think I heard you say, it was to be Robertson's Charles the fifth, but be sure to tell me.'[123] Hannah More would, surely, have approved: here was a woman reading seriously and pursuing intellectual pursuits, but doing so with a modest spirit and submitting to the guidance of her husband. Here, indeed, was a woman not unlike Lucilla Stanley, 'the ideal wife, literate but modest', of More's influential didactic novel, *Coelebs in search of a wife*.[124]

VI

What, in closing, does McCracken's case tell us about the lives of young middle-class women in late Georgian Belfast? It would, of course, be unwise to extrapolate too widely on the basis of a single woman's experience. Given that she was the daughter of one of Belfast's most successful businessmen, aspects of McCracken's story are, inevitably, atypical. Yet, what is, perhaps, most striking about her case is the extent to which it conforms to broader patterns. At a time when the influence of evangelicalism was becoming widespread, McCracken was a young middle-class woman who worried about spiritual matters and found solace in religious belief. Likewise, at a time when parental support was an important factor in the success or failure of romantic matches, McCracken

[119] EM to RJT, 9, 11 and 12 June, 13 Oct. 1829 (ibid., D/1748/G/378/106A, 123A). [120] EM to RJT, 13 Apr. 1829 (ibid., D/1748/G/378/102). [121] EM to RJT, 24 Oct. 1829 (ibid., D/1748/G/378/126). [122] Vickery, *Gentleman's daughter*, p. 83. [123] EM to RJT, 4 Mar. 1837 (PRONI, D/1748/G/378/185). [124] Pearson, *Women's reading*, pp 88–91.

struggled with her father's opposition to her relationship with Tennent and, against a backdrop of increasing engagement with literature among women, she read widely and seriously in a bid to 'improve' herself. More particularly, in persistently testing Tennent's romantic commitment and placing obstacles in his path to marriage, McCracken employed a recognized courtship tactic and, in worrying about public scrutiny of her affairs and submitting readily to male guidance in her intellectual pursuits, she followed the prescriptions, whether consciously or unconsciously, of conduct writers such as Hannah More. This latter point is, indeed, particularly noteworthy: if conduct writers and didactic literature did not necessarily reflect reality, it does not follow that they were without influence. Overall, then, McCracken demonstrates the extent to which the lives of young women in late Georgian Belfast could – and in her case did – conform to wider patterns. But, perhaps above all, it illustrates the difficulties of courtship and the problems faced by young women in their attempts to exercise agency and strike a balance between individual aspiration, familial expectation and societal scrutiny. Behind the marriage notice which appeared in the *Belfast News-Letter* on 22 June 1830 lay a complex story of negotiation, filial resentment and individual assertion; a story which was surely not unique.

Ireland's clumsy transformation from confessional state to nation state

DAVID W. MILLER

Today the phrase 'confessional state' is a common expression in the political vocabulary of Ireland. The first time that 'confessional state' appeared in Dublin's *Irish Times* (which had been founded in 1859) was in 1970, when an editorial borrowed the term from John Hume, a prominent Catholic politician in Northern Ireland who had used it to describe the southern Irish state.[1] Throughout the next two decades – the most violent period of 'the Troubles' in Northern Ireland – the term 'confessional state' became familiar in the *Irish Times*, and then began to decline in frequency.[2] It was used by Irish Catholics, north and south, who had begun to recognize that their northern Protestant adversaries did have one valid contention: the extraordinary influence of the Catholic hierarchy upon policy in the southern Irish state. Although occasionally Protestant churches' influence on the northern government were mentioned, most of the usage of 'confessional state' in the *Irish Times* referred to the role of the Catholic Church in the south. Popular response to Vatican II by the Catholic laity had contributed to a reconsideration of their own church's political role in the south. Removal from the Republic's constitution of the 'special position' of the Roman Catholic Church in 1973, legalization of contraceptives in 1980, and repeal of divorce prohibition in 1995 were consequences of this growing realization that a confessional state was no longer what many Irish Catholics wanted. News of serious misconduct by priests contributed further to what the historian Louise Fuller has called 'the undoing of a culture' and the journalist Mary Kenny has characterized as 'Goodbye to Catholic Ireland'.[3]

So during the last three decades of the twentieth century many ordinary Irish newspaper readers no doubt became aware of what a 'confessional state' was, and developed opinions as to the advantages or disadvantages of such a state. In the same period several distinguished European historians drew the attention of their profession to confessional concepts: J.C.D. Clark adopted 'confessional state' as a definition of the '*ancien régime*' he discovered in eighteenth-century England. Two German historians, Heinz Schilling and Wolfgang Reinhard,

---

[1] *Irish Times*, 17 Apr. 1970. I use the term 'southern Irish state' for the entity named Irish Free State 1922–37, Éire 1937–49, and Republic of Ireland thereafter. [2] A search for 'confessional state' in the *Irish Times*' digital archive yielded 31 occurrences in the 1970s; 47 in the 1980s; 21 in the 1990s; and 8 in the 2000s. [3] Louise Fuller, *Irish Catholicism since 1950: the undoing of a culture* (Dublin, 2002); Mary Kenny, *Goodbye to Catholic Ireland: a social, personal and cultural history from the fall of Parnell to the realm of Mary Robinson* (London, 1997).

explored what they called 'confessionalization', a project that focused on the social discipline of the state church, primarily from the Peace of Augsburg (1555) to the end of the Thirty Years War (1649), while some of their collaborators adopted the confessionalization paradigm as a basis for explaining later developments in European polities. Although I regard that project to be very important, this essay is not a contribution to the development of the confessionalisation paradigm. Instead of 'confessionalization', as developed by scholars of the early modern period during and after the late twentieth century, I wish to concentrate on another academic term that was conceived during and after the late nineteenth century: the phrase 'confessional state' itself.

II

Because 'confessional state' is a phrase rather than a word, it is not included in the *Oxford English Dictionary* (*OED*), the most obvious source of reference for dated quotations. In order to seek its earliest use I therefore turned to the corpus of digitized primary materials. Electronic searches of *Early English Books* Online (EEBO) and *Eighteenth-Century Collections Online* (ECCO) yielded no return, which would seem to show that the phrase did not occur in any English book printed from 1475 to 1800. For the nineteenth century I searched a collection of some forty-five major British newspapers as well as two Irish papers (the *Freeman's Journal* and *Belfast News-Letter*).[4] Again the phrase did not appear. However, a search in Google Books of periodicals and books published from 1801 through to 1922 revealed 'confessional state' in books or articles written by a total of twelve authors. The earliest was an 1859 English translation of papers presented at an 1857 conference of the German branch of the (British-originated) Evangelical Alliance, by the Revd Th. Plitt, Professor of Theology in the University of Heidelberg. Not only Plitt, but all twelve authors who used the term 'confessional state' in work between 1859 and 1921 were members of the academic profession. I will refer to these academics as 'the dozen'.[5]

What can we learn from these searches? The fact that the *Irish Times* was only one of many (probably all) UK newspapers that never mentioned 'confessional state' in the nineteenth century seems to me to be easy to explain: journalists usually get their political vocabulary from politicians (for example, John Hume), not from academics. However, the fact that 'the dozen', authors hailing from not only the United Kingdom and the United States, but also Germany, Austria, Switzerland, Denmark and France, were discussing the 'confessional state' in texts that found their way into English publications calls for a more reflective analysis.

4 Using *19th Century British Newspapers* (Gale Cengage Learning). 5 The anonymous author in the list was a reviewer of a biography of a German cardinal in *The Catholic University Bulletin*.

Table 1. Authors whose writing of the 'confessional state' appeared in an English book or periodical between 1859 and 1921.

Name	Life-time	Discipline	Cleric?	Nationality	Top academic position	Religious membership
Elisha Benjamin Andrews	1844–1917	political economy, homiletics, history	yes	American	President, Brown University	Baptist
Anonymous				American*		Catholic*
Sir James Donaldson	1831–1915	classics	no	Scot	Principal, United College, University of St Andrews	Congregational
Henry Elias Dosker	1855–1926	church history	yes	Dutch-American	Professor, Western Seminary	Reformed
Hartmann Grisar	1845–1932	church history, archaeology	yes	German-Austrian	Professor, University of Innsbruck	Catholic
Karl Rudolf Hagenbach	1801–74	theology, church history	yes	Swiss	Professor Ordinarius of Theology, Basel University	Reformed
Hans Martensen	1808–84	theology	yes	Danish	Professor Ordinarius Copenhagen University	Lutheran
Iakov Aleksandrovitch Nivokov	1849–1912	sociology	no	Russian-French	Professor, University of Odessa	none*
William Harold Payne	1836–1907	pedagogy, psychology	no	American	Chancellor, University of Nashville.	none*
Martin Rade	1857–1940	theology	yes	German	Professor, University of Marburg	Lutheran
Jakob Theodor	1815–86	theology	yes	German	Professor of Theology, University of Heidelberg	Lutheran*
Ernst Troeltsch	1865–1923	theology, sociology, philosophy	yes	German	Professor of Systematic Theology, University of Heidelberg	Lutheran

*=conjecture

In 1857, when he mentioned '*konfessionellen Staat*' to German Evangelicals in Berlin, Plitt was using a term that had appeared in German books since 1830 and probably had become familiar to those Germans accustomed to attending academic lectures.[6] The sentence in which he used it runs (in translation) 'The confessional state belongs to a bygone age.'[7] That 'bygone age' was, of course,

6 A search of *Google Erweiterte Buchsuche*: 'konfessionellen Staat'. 7 Th. Plitt, 'Religious liberty' in Edward Steane (ed.), *The religious condition of Christendom. Third part: exhibited in*

the period before the French Revolution and the Napoleonic wars that ended the Holy Roman empire and began the unification of Germany. Popular secularization had begun during the Enlightenment, and post-Napoleonic Germany sought a merger of small states into a large state without the complication of the 'bygone' concept of a state church.[8] Undoubtedly many more academics than the dozen were aware of the phrase, for the twelve who used the term generally did not seem to feel it necessary to explain its meaning to their readers – an indication that academics throughout the two north Atlantic continents frequently discussed the meaning of the 'state' in their own lifetime between the 1849 revolutions and the Great War. Study of the 'confessional state' did not become a historical project like 'confessionalization' in the late twentieth and early twenty-first centuries, but it did enable a broader generation of academics in the late nineteenth and early twentieth centuries to describe the massive changes which 'the state' underwent during their lives and those of their parents. But, if the confessional state belonged to the 'bygone age', how would academics describe the new type of the state for their time? That question was answered in the late nineteenth century by the new academic discipline of political science: the 'nation state'.

Most of the dozen were clerics but many had at least one field of study in addition to theology. Perhaps the most interesting of these was Ernst Troeltsch, who adopted sociology while a professor of theology at Heidelberg for about twenty years and was a colleague and neighbour of Max Weber (1864–1920), arguably the most eminent sociologist of his day.[9] Although Weber apparently did not choose to use the term '*konfessionellen Staat*' in his works, he offered a definition of the state that is applicable both to states in his generation and to previous confessional states: 'a human community that (successfully) claims the monopoly of the legitimate use of physical force within a given territory'.[10] Weber's brilliance appears in the phrase 'legitimate use', which can mean legitimacy by *le peuple* in a nation state but by the state church in a confessional state (in confessionalization terms, an example of social discipline).

III

Ireland's transformation from an original confessional state to a nation state is clumsy because its (original) confessional state had more than one state church. Ute Lotz-Heumann has offered a compelling argument that Ireland in the sixteenth and the first half of the seventeenth century experienced 'double

a series of papers prepared at the instance of the German Branch of the Evangelical Alliance and read at the conference held in Berlin, 1857 (London, 1859), p. 278.   8 Thomas Nipperdey, *Germany from Napoleon to Bismarck, 1800–1866* (Princeton, NJ, 1996), pp 356–98.
9 http:people.bu.edu/wwildman/bce/troeltsch.htm.   10 Max Weber, Hans Heinrich Gerth and C.W. Mills, *From Max Weber: essays in sociology* (London, 1991), p. 78.

confessionalization', that is to say the reality of two 'state churches' – Episcopal Protestant and Roman Catholic – because of different religious relationships and commitments within the extended royal family and the fact that during that period the English families that participated in Irish high politics were divided into the largely Catholic 'Old English', who had come to Ireland in the middle ages, and Protestant 'New English', who had begun to arrive during the Reformation.[11] The events following the coronation of the Catholic James II – the 'Glorious Revolution' in England and the 'War of the Two Kings' in Ireland – created an Ireland of neither a single nor even a double confessionalization. Ireland entered the eighteenth century as a state with three churches, each of which claimed the status of a state church: the Catholic Church, which probably served about eighty per cent of the population and two Protestant churches, each of which served about half of the remainder of the population: the (Episcopal) Church of Ireland and the Presbyterian Church in Ulster. Each of the three had its own understanding of its expectation to be a state church. The Church of Ireland was accepted by the king (or queen, in the reign of Anne) in London and Dublin. The Catholic Church was accepted by the exiled James II, who had been deposed in 1688 and, after his death in 1701, by his son James Francis Edward Stuart ('the Old Pretender'). An Ulster Presbyterian (whose ministers regularly received stipends authorized by the crown) would attend the established Presbyterian Kirk if he or she happened to be in Scotland (as would the monarch).[12]

The discipline of theology has done a favour to historians of the present generation. Theologians have long organized doctrines by topic: transubstantiation, for example, may come under the heading of 'sacraments' and predestination under the heading 'grace'. Recently, however, they have begun to study the topic of ecclesiology (Greek for 'church discourse') for beliefs concerning the church itself in a broad range of doctrines, including such matters as politics, society and culture, in which historians are interested.[13] Each of the three major churches in Ireland's eighteenth-century confessional state had ecclesiological doctrines concerning their relationship with the state.

---

11 Ute Lotz-Heumann, 'Church discipline in a biconfessional country: Ireland in a European context' in Herman Roodenburg and Pieter Spierenburg (eds), *Social control in Europe*, 1: *1500–1800* (Columbus, OH, 2004), pp 99–112; eadem, *Die doppelte Konfessionalisierung in Irland: Konflikt und Koexistanz im 16. und in der Ersten Hälfte des 17. Jahrhunderts* (Tübingen, 2000). 12 For analysis of the difference between the English and Irish Protestant dissent, see J.C. Beckett, *Protestant dissent in Ireland, 1687–1780* (London, 1948), pp 13–19. 13 E.g. A.E. McGrath, *Christian theology: an introduction* (2nd ed., Oxford, 1997), p. 461. The term 'ecclesiology' entered English in 1837 as a 'science' of church buildings and their operations, and an Ecclesiological Society focusing on that subject is still active. However, their particular interest is a very minor component of ecclesiology in the academic theological discipline: http://www.ecclsoc.org/ (accessed 5 July 2014). A search of Google Scholar for items mentioning 'ecclesiology' found an average of 6 mentions per year between 1831 and 1950 (presumably largely about church buildings). The number rose to 20 per year in 1951–60 and

Ulster Presbyterianism had received from its elder sister, the Church of Scotland, an anti-Erastian ecclesiological doctrine. Erastianism was the contention that religious authority should be subordinate to secular supremacy.[14] The Westminster Confession of Faith, produced during the civil wars of the 1640s as a creed of the Church of England, but which ended up as that of the Church of Scotland, declared: 'The civil magistrate may not assume to himself the administration of the word and sacraments, or the power of the keys of the kingdom of Heaven.'[15] Had it been written solely by Scottish Presbyterians it would probably have constrained the 'civil magistrate' even more thoroughly. The Revolution settlement gave rise to some apprehension among Scottish Presbyterians, beginning with the conduct of their new civil magistrate from Holland, William III, and continuing during and after the 1707 Act of Union.[16] Ulster-Scot Presbyterians, whose ministers were generally trained in Scottish universities, no doubt had similar opinions about Erastianism. Irish Presbyterianism, having most of its members concentrated in a single province, had no expectation of becoming the established Church of Ireland even if, from about 1672, their ministers received (except during James II's reign and again for a brief period at the end of Anne's) stipends from the king, the so-called *regium donum*.[17] However, the continual influx of clergy educated at Scottish universities, and the emergence of additional Scottish Presbyterian sects such as the Seceders, whose clerics also sought employment, sustained the popular anti-Erastianism of Scotland and Ulster during most of the eighteenth century.

Unlike Ulster Presbyterians, Irish Catholicism had more than one sister state church. Throughout eighteenth-century Europe, Catholic ecclesiologists were concerned less with the relationship between state and church, and more with the pope's relationship with both. There were two such movements: Gallicanism (initially proposed in France), which called for a restriction of papal power by the country's government and its hierarchy; and Ultramontanism ('beyond the mountains', that is the Alps), which argued for complete papal supremacy. Probably because many Irish priests had attended French seminaries, the Irish Catholic Church tended to embrace Gallicanism. So in the final century of the (first) confessional state in Ireland, not only Presbyterians but also Catholics were developing their respective ecclesiological doctrines relative to their situations in a confessional state.

1,180 in 2001–10. **14** The English word 'Erastian' was coined, apparently, during the Westminster Assembly, from the name of Thomas Erastus (1524–83), a Swiss physician and Zwinglian theologian. There is evidence that Erastus' ideas were considerably different from 'Erastianism' as the word was used in the Westminster Assembly and after (N.J. Figgis, 'Erastus and Erastianism', *Journal of Theological Studies*, 2:5 (1901), 66–101). **15** *The humble advice of the assembly of divines, now by authority of parliament sitting at Westminster, concerning a confession of faith, presented by them lately to both houses of parliament* (London, 1646), p. 39. **16** Jeffrey Stephen, *Scottish Presbyterians and the Act of Union 1707* (Edinburgh, 2007), pp 6–8. **17** C.E. Pike, 'The origin of the *regium donum*' in *RHS Trans.*, 3:3 (1909), 255–69.

The Church of Ireland, being a sister of the state church of the predominant country in the archipelago, had a very simple ecclesiological doctrine concerning the Irish state: it was to be governed entirely by members of the Church of Ireland. This continued in spite of the failure of the 1745 rebellion, the death of the Old Pretender in 1766, and the Holy See's refusal to recognize Charles Edward Stuart (the Young Pretender) in his place. Meanwhile, considerable rural disorder unrelated to high politics led in the 1780s to the development of a doctrine of 'Protestant ascendancy', which was advocated by Richard Woodward, bishop of Cloyne, and other influential Anglicans in Ireland.[18]

IV

The French Revolution of 1789–99 prompted the Irish government in 1795 to fund a Catholic seminary in Maynooth, making it possible for students seeking the priesthood to avoid study in France. In 1798 the revolutionaries instigated an unsuccessful Irish rebellion by Catholic and Presbyterian rebels, assisted by French troops. In 1800 enough members of the (all-Anglican) Irish parliament were persuaded (largely by financial inducements) to dissolve Ireland's separate statehood and create a United Kingdom of Great Britain and Ireland. The Act of Union promised

> that the churches of England and Ireland, as now by law established, be united into one Protestant episcopal church, to be called, 'The united church of England and Ireland'; and that the doctrine, worship, discipline, and government of the said united church shall be, and shall remain in full force for ever.

Obviously a parliament (or especially two parliaments, of which one was being eliminated) cannot forever prevent a later parliament from overturning its decisions, as would in fact occur sixty-nine years later, in the form of the Irish Church Disestablishment Act.

In the new Union the Anglican wish for perpetual 'Protestant ascendancy' (that is to say Church of Ireland ascendancy, for in Ireland 'Protestant' was commonly used by Anglicans to mean their own church) continued to face the strife of Catholic gentry and urban leaders who had been seeking Catholic emancipation since the Jacobite future had become dubious. In the 1810s requests for emancipation produced suggestions in parliament that the monarch

---

18 James Kelly, 'The genesis of "Protestant ascendancy": the Rightboy disturbances of the 1780s and their impact upon Protestant opinion' in Gerard O'Brien (ed.), *Parliament, politics and people: essays in eighteenth-century Irish history* (Dublin, 1989), p. 126; Jacqueline Hill, 'The meaning and significance of "Protestant ascendancy"', *Ireland after the Union* (Oxford,

be invested with a veto over papal episcopal appointments, which would of course have been exercised on the advice of the government. Some Catholic bishops, in a spirit of Gallicanism, had approved such a suggestion at the time of the passage of the Act of Union. However, this time Daniel O'Connell, a relatively new leader of the emancipation movement, opposed the veto and the Catholic hierarchy in Ireland agreed. In the 1820s O'Connell developed a remarkable political movement, characterized by huge open-air meetings, which induced in the British government apprehensions of rebellion. He then hit upon the brilliant idea of standing for an election to a seat in the House of Commons, which he duly won. Afterwards (like any devout Catholic) he refused to take the required oath of supremacy thus forcing the English Tory leaders to persuade the king to accept Catholic emancipation rather than risk disturbances in Ireland. Having secured Catholic emancipation and his own seat in the parliament of the United Kingdom, O'Connell turned his attention in 1830 to repeal of the Act of Union. He devoted the remainder of his career to nationalism, but not to nation-statism, for the repeal of the Union would have created an Irish House of Commons with a Catholic majority, under a king directed by a British government.

V

After the Napoleonic Wars, reflective Irish Anglicans realized that their Protestant ascendancy was even less guaranteed than it had been in the previous generation. No doubt few if any Anglican gentry in the 1820s could have explained what had happened during their lifetimes with the perspective of a French historian a century later:[19]

> From the social point of view, the Revolution consisted in the suppression of what was called the feudal system, in the emancipation of the individual, in greater division of landed property, the abolition of the privileges of noble birth, the establishment of equality, the simplification of life.

Nevertheless, they did understand that their social and political world had somehow been transformed, and were especially aware of a development in their cultural world during the previous three decades. Protestant ecclesiology in the early nineteenth century was being modified from church–state doctrines to 'church–church' relationships, primarily because of the emergence of a Protestant movement that was called 'evangelicalism', which the *OED* unhelpfully defines as 'the doctrines and modes of thought peculiar to the Evangelical party' or

1989), pp 1–22. 19 Alphonse Aulard, 'Character of the French Revolution, 1789–1799' in A.A. Tilley (ed.), *Modern France: a companion to French studies* (Cambridge, 1922), p. 115.

'adherence to that party': the earliest quotation given dates from 1831. But a party of what? In the early nineteenth century the Popular Party in the Church of Scotland and the Low Church grouping within the Church of England each became labelled an 'Evangelical party'.[20] Previously, the word 'evangelical' (from Greek, εὐαγγελικός, literally 'of or pertaining to the gospel') had collected various meanings. In the Reformation of continental Europe it had been simply a term for Protestant and later became more specifically a synonym for Lutheran (as opposed to 'Reformed' for Calvinist). However, the earliest practices among Anglophone Protestants that came to be called 'evangelical' had begun in the Covenanter culture of seventeenth-century Scotland and Ulster, which developed outdoor communion services, sometimes in remote places, bringing together members of various congregations. Such worship in Ulster was transmitted to eighteenth-century North America and resulted in the development of gatherings (later labelled 'revivals') in which intensely emotional experiences were understood to be 'spiritual rebirths'.[21] During the eighteenth century similar (though perhaps less dramatic) worship appeared in the Methodist movement begun by a Church of England cleric, John Wesley, who preached in England, Ireland (beyond merely Ulster) and the American colonies. In what we now call a confessional state, the church was a group of parishes (or congregations) each of which was intended to have one or more buildings for worship under the leadership of one official cleric (perhaps with curates). Wesley was attempting to insert evangelical 'preaching houses' and 'local preachers' for his Methodists, who would nonetheless continue to receive communion in the state church. Only after his death in 1791 did the Methodist movement become a Methodist Church. However, the Methodist Church was only one of many churches – including all three of the established churches in the United Kingdom – in which some or all of the clergy considered themselves to be evangelicals.

In 1822 a new Anglican archbishop of Dublin, William Magee, commented in his first charge to his clergy, 'we are hemmed in by two opposite descriptions of professing Christians: the one, possessing a church, without what we can properly call a religion; and the other possessing a religion, without what we can properly call a church'.[22] Although this insult was proclaimed by a leader of the High Church party in the United Church of England and Ireland, the Low Church party – rapidly gaining the name of 'Evangelicals' – would actually attend to Magee's denunciations of both Irish Catholicism and Ulster Presbyterianism during the decade of O'Connell's triumph.

20 S.J. Brown, *Thomas Chalmers and the godly commonwealth in Scotland* (Oxford, 1982), pp 45–8.   21 L.E. Schmidt, *Holy fairs: Scotland and the making of American Revivalism* (Princeton, NJ, 1989); M.J. Westerkamp, *Triumph of the laity: Scots-Irish piety and the Great Awakening, 1625–1760* (New York, 1988).   22 S.J. Brown, 'The new reformation movement in the Church of Ireland, 1801–29' in idem and D.W. Miller (eds), *Piety and power in Ireland, 1760–1960* (Belfast, 2000), p. 181.

Since 1804 London Evangelicals had been providing cheap bibles through the British and Foreign Bible Society, and in 1818 the Irish Society Established for Promoting the Education of the Native Irish, Through the Medium of Their Own Language (usually called simply 'the Irish Society') was established in Dublin.[23] The distribution of bibles and the efforts of several prominent evangelical landowners led to substantial proselytizing of Catholics in the mid-1820s.[24] Stewart J. Brown has suggested that in this period 'there seemed a real possibility that the established church might finally achieve the ascendancy over the religious, moral and intellectual life of Ireland that had eluded it since the Reformation'. However, during 1827–9 this 'new reformation' or 'second reformation' began to disappear, as 'wealthy supporters' became 'sensitive to the accusations of using bribery to obtain converts', and when the Emancipation Act made Catholics 'eligible for most public offices' the brief expectation of a new reformation came to an end.[25]

Unlike Catholics, Presbyterians in Ireland were seldom if ever proselytized individually by Anglican evangelicals. Rather, their principal church (notwithstanding Magee's view that they had no church) was invited into another kind of 'union' – a union of Anglican and Presbyterian churches in Ireland – by an article entitled 'On the advantages of an union amongst Irish Protestants' in the February 1826 issue of the *Christian Examiner and Church of Ireland Magazine*.[26] The anonymous author proposed that the Church of Ireland and Ulster Presbyterians be united as the Established Church of Ireland and endorsed his proposition with evidence presented the previous year to the House of Commons' *First Report of the Commissioners on Education in Ireland* by Henry Cooke – that year's moderator of the Synod of Ulster. From the work of the commission, and his own acquaintance with prominent Church of Ireland clergy and laity, Cooke was apparently becoming aware that evangelical Anglicans in Ireland might consider the admission of Presbyterianism into their ascendancy. However, Cooke also became conscious that they were concerned over the presence of Unitarians in the Synod. He led a struggle against such liberal theologians until 1829, when they left to form their own Remonstrant Synod.[27] A new Belfast periodical, *The Orthodox Presbyterian*, appeared in October 1829. The first sentence of the first issue ran, 'The want of a religious periodical, particularly adapted for circulation among the Presbyterians of Ulster, has long been felt and lamented by the friends of evangelical truth.'[28]

23 Leslie Howsam, *Cheap bibles: nineteenth-century publishing and the British and Foreign Bible Society* (New York, 1991), p. 3; H.J. Monck Mason, *History of the origin and progress of the Irish Society* ... (Dublin, 1844), p. 9.   24 Irene Whelan, *The bible war in Ireland: the 'second reformation' and the polarization of Protestant-Catholic relations, 1800–1840* (Madison, WI, 2005), pp 152–91.   25 Brown, 'New reformation movement', pp 180–208, esp. pp 183, 204–6.   26 *Christian Examiner and Church of Ireland Magazine*, 2:8 (Feb. 1826), 79–90.   27 J.S. Reid, *History of the Presbyterian Church in Ireland*, rev. W.D. Killen (3 vols, Belfast, 1867), iii, 447–63.   28 'Objects and principles of the Orthodox Presbyterian' in *Orthodox Presbyterian*, i (Oct. 1829), p. 1.

So who were those friends and what was their 'evangelical truth'? A term for them appeared in the 1840s and was explained in 1853 by William John Conybeare in an essay that was first published in the *Edinburgh Review*.[29] Conybeare offered a useful analysis of public religious groups in the mid-nineteenth century. He divided church parties into three: Low Church, High Church, and Broad Church, each of which had a 'normal type' and an 'exaggerated type'. In the Low Church his normal type was the Evangelical Party and his exaggerated type was the evangelicals labelled the Recordite Party, who were named after the London newspaper *The Record*, established in 1828. John Wolffe has analysed the role of the Recordites in the mid-nineteenth century and has identified thirty-five Recordites among those whose biographies appear in the *Oxford dictionary of national biography*: they include Henry Cooke.[30] A fellow Recordite, the earl of Roden – a Co. Down landlord who had attempted to proselytize Catholics during the 'new Reformation' and 'who represented a human bridge between Evangelical, Ultra [Tory] and Irish interests' – gave Cooke the opportunity to become a major voice in Recordite circles by inviting him in 1834 to make a speech at an evangelical political meeting in Hillsborough.[31] Eight years after *The Christian Examiner and Church of Ireland Magazine*'s proposal of 'an union amongst Irish Protestants' Cooke announced its arrival:[32]

> I trust I see more in this meeting than a mere eliciting of public opinion, or a mere gathering of the clans. I trust I see in it the pledge of Protestant union and co-operation. Between the divided Churches I publish the banns of a sacred marriage of Christian forbearance where they differ, of Christian love where they agree, and of Christian co-operation in all matters where their common safety is concerned. Who forbids the banns? None. Then I trust our union, for these holy purposes, is indissoluble, and that the God who has bound us in ties of Christian affection, and of a common faith, will never allow the recollections of the past, or the temptations of the present, to sever those whom He has thus united.

In this oration Cooke was announcing the achievement by himself and his fellow Recordites of 'an union amongst Irish Protestants'.[33] However, it is not clear in this quotation whether the wedding that Cooke announced was intended to be a nuptial between the Church of Ireland and the Synod of Ulster or between the Anglican episcopalians and Scottish Presbyterians in the entire archipelago.

---

29 *Oxford English Dictionary* (*sub* 'Recordite'); W.J. Conybeare, *Essays, ecclesiastical and social* ... (London, 1855), pp viii, 57–164. John Wolffe also has edited 'The Recordites (act. 1828–c.1860)' in *ODNB*.   30 John Wolffe, *The Protestant crusade in Great Britain, 1829–1860* (Oxford, 1991), pp 56–108; idem, 'Recordites' in *ODNB*.   31 Whelan, *Bible war in Ireland*, p. 232; Wolffe, *Protestant crusade*, p. 77.   32 J.L. Porter, *The life and times of Henry Cooke, DD, LLD* (London, 1871) p. 277.   33 Cooke's 1834 'banns of a sacred marriage' speech became well known, and is frequently mentioned in academic Irish history. However the origin of that

To understand that issue we must consider another evangelical Presbyterian leader: Thomas Chalmers in Scotland. Early in his career Chalmers had admired the politics of William Wilberforce, a prominent founder of the evangelical Clapham Sect and leader of slave-trade abolition.[34] Throughout his career Chalmers' evangelical politics tended toward the opposite end from Cooke's Recordite 'sect'. In the role of a social scientist as well as a theologian, Chalmers advocated procedures to address consequences of the industrial revolution that were drawing the lower class from rural to urban Scotland, where the geographical and social status of parishes and church buildings were not appropriate for the religious experience of the poor. Among his concerns was the treatment of the Patronage Act of 1712, which gave the right of choosing a minister to the family that had contributed the majority of funds to the parish church. This privilege was treated as property that could be inherited or marketed, and by the late eighteenth century the choice of a parish minister might well be made by a 'patron' who was a wealthy or powerful individual having no connexion whatever to the community of the parish.[35] About a year and a half before Cooke's speech in the Hillsborough meeting, Chalmers had addressed a speech to the General Assembly of the Church of Scotland that expressed Presbyterian apprehension of Erastianism in both Scotland and Ulster.[36] At his suggestion the assembly adopted an act by which a majority of male heads of families would be able to veto the patron's choice.

There followed the so-called 'Ten Years Conflict' in which Scottish evangelicals and their lawyers attempted to gain from the state a recognition of the church's right to determine how a minister would be chosen for a congregation. Meanwhile, in 1840 Cooke had led the process of joining the Synod of Ulster with the synod of the conservative Scottish Seceders in Ireland, thereby producing a General Assembly of the Presbyterian Church in Ireland (no longer claiming only Ulster).[37] As a leader of an Irish assembly comparable to the Scottish assembly, Cooke tried to persuade his Tory friends, including the prime minister, Peel, to respect the Presbyterian understanding of the issue, but with little, if any, success. In January 1843 it was clear that Chalmers had failed, and on 18 May in the General Assembly in Edinburgh more than a third of the ministers, under the leadership of Chalmers, dramatically left the assembly and formed a Free Church of Scotland, thus losing their church buildings, manses and stipends: an event that almost immediately became known as 'the disruption'. Cooke was present, joined in the procession and participated in the

concept in the 1826 *Christian Examiner* has not been thoroughly analysed (probably because of a tendency of Irish historians, including myself, to focus on only one denomination at a time).   **34** Brown, *Chalmers and the godly commonwealth in Scotland*, pp 48, 55.   **35** Ibid., p. 16; J.R. McIntosh, *Church and theology in Enlightenment Scotland: the Popular Party, 1740–1800* (East Linton, 1998), pp 92–124.   **36** Thomas Chalmers, 'Speech delivered in the General Assembly of 1833, on a proposed modification of the law of patronage' in idem, *Tracts and essays, religious and economical* (Edinburgh, 1848), pp 373–94.   **37** Porter, *Life and times*

formation of the new Free Church's General Assembly.[38] However, when the General Assembly of Ireland met, there was an angry debate over a resolution which suggested 'more adequate representation of the principles and interests of Presbyterians in the Legislature of the country'. Cooke interpreted the dispute (correctly) as criticism of himself, and announced that he would not be a member of the General Assembly until the resolution was rescinded. From then until 1847 (when the resolution was cancelled) he did not participate in the assembly. Those four years ended Cooke's politics, both spiritual and secular, and helped provoke the development in rural Ulster of what Andrew Holmes has perceptively called 'covenanter politics' but which Cooke himself had rashly called 'communism'.[39]

VI

The attempted exploitation of multiple denominations to retain Protestant ascendancy had to all intents and purposes finished Henry Cooke as a leader in the 1840s. Other events during the same decade began contributing to the eventual replacement of confessional states by nation states. The most obvious were the revolutions of 1848 in which nationalism became a serious issue in statehood throughout Europe. In Ireland Daniel O'Connell, previously the principal nationalist leader but an opponent of Irish national statehood, had died in 1847, and his rivals, the Young Irelanders, had attempted to join the European revolutionary movement but failed miserably; hardly surprising, given the impact of the most important historical event in Ireland in the 1840s – the Great Famine.

A popular conception among nationalists after the Famine was the supposed memory of Protestants providing food – typically 'soup' – to convert Catholics. Indeed, Recordites early in the dreadful year of 1847 had publicized a 'Special Fund for the Spiritual Exigencies of Ireland' for that very purpose. However, scrutiny of correspondence in the *Record* suggests that few Anglican clergy in the starving areas of Ireland sought to use food to obtain converts.[40] The 'Fund for the Temporal Relief of the Suffering Poor of Ireland', announced by a committee of Belfast Anglicans shortly after the Recordite fund, reflected a difference between evangelical Anglican clergy in Ireland and some in England.[41]

What happened to the ecclesiological doctrines in the two non-establishment denominations as Ireland approached nation-statehood? Ulster Presbyterian

of Cooke, pp 371–6.   38 Finlay Holmes, *Henry Cooke* (Belfast, 1981), p. 156.   39 A.R. Holmes, 'Covenanter politics: evangelicalism, political liberalism and Ulster Presbyterians, 1798–1914', *EHR*, 125 (2010), 340–69; *Londonderry Standard*, 23 May 1850.   40 D.W. Miller, 'Soup and Providence: varieties of Protestantism and the Great Famine' in Enda Delaney and Breandán Mac Suibhne (eds), *Ireland's Great Famine and popular politics* (forthcoming).   41 *Belfast News-Letter*, 8 Jan. 1847.

tenants, having undergone Cooke's union with politically powerful Anglicans, celebrated the failure of Erastianism by joining with Catholics in the Irish Tenant League. About the same time Irish Catholicism, having previously been dominated by Gallican leaders, received an Ultramontanist, Paul Cullen, who became archbishop of Armagh in 1850 (and was moved to Dublin two years later). Instead of Maynooth, Cullen's father had sent him to Rome for his seminary education, and three years after he was ordained in 1829 he had become the rector of the Irish College of Rome. In 1848 he witnessed the Italian nationalists driving Pius IX out of Rome.[42] The extent to which Cullen applied his opinion of Italian nationalism to Irish nationalism is contested, but there is little doubt that Ultramontanism replaced whatever Gallicanism had remained.[43] However, after his death in 1878 the Irish hierarchy returned to paying more attention to Irish politics than to world affairs.

VII

After the 1848 Revolution the confessional state had become 'a bygone age' in Europe, to be replaced by the nation state. Why then after the Great War of 1914–18 did the new Irish state become a confessional state? The late Emmet Larkin gave us half the answer to that question: nationalist politicians in the new state – especially Éamon de Valera – took advantage of an arrangement between the hierarchy and the Parnell party in 1884, about the bishops' concerns on education issues, that he labelled an 'informal concordat'.[44] The other half involves the process from 1912 to 1923 concerning the northern situation that ended with an entity that might be considered a protectorate state, available for southern Protestants who chose to move during the 'troubles' of 1919–23.[45]

---

42 O.P. Rafferty, 'The ultramontane spirituality of Paul Cullen' in Dáire Keogh and Albert McDonnell (eds), *Cardinal Paul Cullen and his world* (Dublin, 2011), p. 67.   43 C.P. Barr, '"An ambiguous awe": Paul Cullen and the historians' in ibid., pp 414–34.   44 E.J. Larkin, *The historical dimensions of Irish Catholicism* (Washington, DC, 1984), pp 111–12, 120.   45 The present author, who lived in a Belfast suburb in 1975–6, had a next-door neighbour who was one of those Protestants that had moved from the southern Irish state to the north.

What's in an Irish surname? Connollys and others a century ago

CORMAC Ó GRÁDA

Níl ionam ach ball de chorp san mo shinsear.
Máirín Feirtéar[1]

How the Old Age Pension Act of 1908 seriously distorted patterns of age reporting in the 1911 Irish census is well known. Still, handled with care, that census has long been a rich, indeed unrivalled, source for social and economic historians. Ethnographer David Symes' study in the early 1970s of farming in two townlands in Ballyferriter in Co. Kerry in the early 1970s seems to have been the first to exploit the individual household enumeration forms. Studies by scholars interested in the comparative history of household structure quickly followed. Over the decades, the census household forms have provided the raw material for many valuable research projects; their digitization in the late 2000s opens up new, exciting possibilities for researching the Irish past – and not just the genealogical past. Topics addressed through using the household enumeration forms range from the age at leaving home in rural Ireland to the determinants of infant and child mortality rates, and from the incidence of intermarriage to the presence of a quality/quantity trade-off in couples' marital fertility strategies.[2] This essay focuses on just one more area where the census sheds some new light.

---

1 Máirín Feirtéar, *Crú Capaill: Dánta Máirín Fheirtéar* (Dublin, 2013), p. 5. The quotation might be translated as 'I am but a limb of my ancestors' body'.   2 Examples include D.G. Symes, 'Farm household and farm performance: a study of twentieth-century changes in Ballyferriter, southwest Ireland', *Ethnology*, 11 (1972), 25–38; Joanna Bourke, *Husbandry and housewifery: women, economic change and housework in Ireland, 1890–1914* (Oxford, 1993); David Fitzpatrick, 'Irish farming before the First World War', *Comparative Studies in Society and History*, 25 (1983), 339–74; T.W. Guinnane, *The vanishing Irish: households, migration, and the rural economy in Ireland, 1850–1914* (Princeton, 1997); Cormac Ó Gráda, 'Did Ulster Catholics always have larger families?', *IESH*, 13 (1985), 79–88; idem, *Jewish Ireland in the age of Joyce: a socioeconomic history* (Princeton, 2006); idem, 'Economic status, religion, and demography in an Ulster town a century ago', *History of the Family*, 13 (2008), 350–9; idem, 'Because she didn't let them in: Irish immigration a century ago and today' (unpublished paper); Alan Fernihough, 'Human capital and the quantity-quality trade-off during the demographic transition: evidence from Ireland' (http://ideas.repec.org/p/ucn/wpaper/201113.html); Yoshifumi Shimizu, 'Transition of the Irish household structure: comparing results from the 1901 and 1911 census returns, with reference to two cases of Glencolumbkille and Clogheen', *St Andrews University Sociological Review*, 47:1 (2013), 1–34; idem, 'Changes

II

The age misreporting in 1911 was prompted by fears that information given on census night might be used as evidence against individuals who had obtained the pension before they were entitled to it.[3] However, the details remained confidential, and the census commissioners allowed those who completed the forms considerable leeway in how they described themselves. Accounts of details such as literacy, occupation, religion, and knowledge of the Irish language were rarely questioned or amended. And so one of Sean Connolly's more famous namesakes, who confided to an associate in 1908 that 'though I have usually posed as a Catholic, I have not done my duty for 15 years, and have not the slightest tincture of faith left', described himself as a Roman Catholic on the household census form in both 1901 and 1911.[4] And although he was born to Irish parents in the Edinburgh slum of Cowgate on 5 June 1868, James Connolly believed – or so he declared – that he had been born in Co. Monaghan.[5] By the same token, although he was certainly no fluent Irish speaker – he moved to Ireland for good only in 1895, although he had served there in the army in his youth – this 'kinsman' described himself as a speaker of Irish and English in both 1901 and 1911 censuses.

III

Connolly is a familiar and relatively common Irish surname. Bearers of the name or variants of it include Scotland's best-known comedian, a Connemara man accused of cannibalism during the Great Famine, one of the most successful Irish politicians of the eighteenth century, and a revolutionary leader and a great Galway hurler in the twentieth. In Ireland in 1911 those with names such as Murphy (56,720), Kelly (46,520), Sullivan/O'Sullivan (38,040), Ryan (30,594), Byrne (28,268), Connell/O'Connell (17,958), Doherty (17,779), Burke/Bourke (17,582), and Kennedy (17,562) easily outnumbered the 11,696 Connollys. But the Connollys were more numerous than the Fitzpatricks (9,617), the Whelans (8,263), the Cullens (7,249), the Gradys/O'Gradys (5,272), and the Lees (4,898).

Some Gaelic Irish surnames get completely lost in mistranslation. Good, amusing examples are Mac Cathmhaoil/Caulfield/Campbell; Ó Síoda/Silke; Mac Taidhg/Montague; Ó Luain/Lambe; Ó Duibhne/Peoples. Some, such as Connolly, encapsulate a range of Gaelic origins and generate multiple versions

in families in Ireland from the nineteenth to the early twentieth centuries', ibid., 2 (2014), 1–23; Alan Fernihough, Cormac Ó Gráda and Brendan M. Walsh, 'Intermarriage in nineteenth-century Ireland', UCD Centre for Economic Research, Working Paper 2014/7. 3 J.J. Lee, 'Irish agriculture', *Agricultural History Review*, 17 (1969), 73. 4 James Connolly to John Carstairs Matheson, 30 Jan. 1908 (quoted in John Newsinger, 'As Catholic as the Pope: James Connolly and the Roman Catholic Church in Ireland', *Saothar*, 11 (1986), 7).

in English. In addition to the 11,742 Connollys, in 1911 there were 1,950 Connellys, 3,013 Conneelys, 206 Conollys, 106 Connolys, and 17 Conneellys. And there were also 622 Kennellys, yet another variant of Connolly, not to mention small numbers of Kinealys and Kineallys. Thanks to the digitization of the Irish censuses of 1901 and 1911 such numbers can now be produced effortlessly.

In Ireland a century ago, surnames were a useful predictor of regional origin.[6] So 4,315 of the island's 10,726 Boyles lived in Donegal; 305 of the 567 Durcans in Mayo; 3,778 of the 6,403 Cronins in Cork; 1,015 of the 1,129 Ferrys in Donegal; 1,176 of the 1,784 McInerneys in Clare; and so on. The Connollys were much more widely dispersed. In 1911 they were most numerous in counties Galway (1,288), Cork (1,136), Monaghan (1,132), Dublin (1,099) and Antrim (733).[7] In relative terms 'Connolly' was most common in Monaghan (15.8 per thousand population), Leitrim (7.3), Galway (7.1), Sligo (5.8), Laois (5.9), and Offaly (5.6). The 1911 census corroborates the findings of Sir Robert Matheson that the Connollys were to be 'principally found' in Cork, Monaghan, Galway, Antrim and Dublin, but provides a somewhat different ranking than his.[8]

Fig. 1 describes the distribution of Connollys at a more disaggregated level, the district electoral division, in 1911. It highlights their strength in Monaghan, but also the presence of concentrated pockets of the surname in west Cork (especially around Glengariff), north Sligo–Leitrim, and Conamara (Clifden, An Cheathrú Rua, and Ceantar na nOileán). But the point about the wide spread of the surname is confirmed.

The problem with Connolly is that it derives from two first names: (i) Congal and (ii) its adjectival derivative Congalach. Congal gives Ó Conghaile, whereas Congalach gives Ó Conghalaigh, and they both fall together as (O) Connolly. The dispersion of the Connollys across so many counties was due to their being descended from distinct Congals and Congalachs. Because the first name is common, the surname is widely distributed, with different unrelated Connolly families. Of these the most distinguished were the Ó Conghalaigh of Airgialla in south Ulster: both revolutionary labour leader James Connolly (1868–1916) and *parvenu* politician William 'Speaker' Conolly (1662–1729) were linked to this clan. Although 'Speaker' Conolly was born in south Donegal, his father, an ambitious miller-cum-innkeeper[9] who had conformed to the state church, was

---

5 Edward MacLysaght, *Irish families: their names, arms, and origins* (New York, 1972), p. 88.
6 Sir Robert Matheson, *Special report on surnames in Ireland* (Dublin, 1909); J.P. Ferrie, 'A new view of the Irish in America: economic performance and the impact of place of origin, 1850–1920' (unpublished paper); M.T. Smith and D.M. MacRaild, 'Nineteenth-century population structure of Ireland and the Irish in England and Wales: an analysis by isonymy', *American Journal of Human Biology*, 21 (2009), 283–9; idem, 'Origins of the Irish in northern England: an isonymic analysis of data in the 1881 census', *Immigrants and Minorities*, 27 (2009), 152–77.
7 The 'Conneely' version of the surname was almost entirely confined to Galway (2,961 of 3,013). Note that totals are liable to change marginally as corrections are made to the data.
8 Matheson, *Surnames in Ireland*, p. 42. 9 Patrick Walsh, *The making of the Irish Protestant*

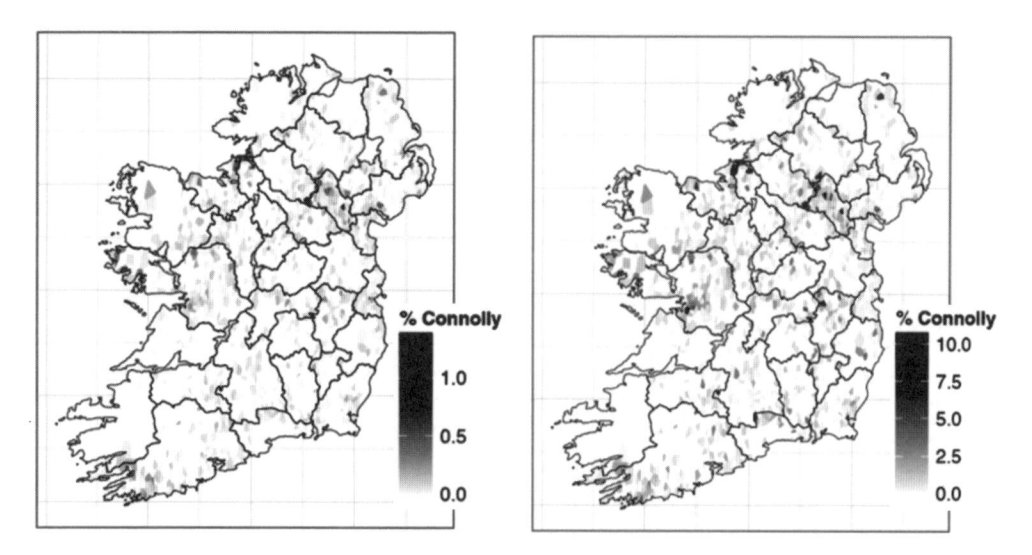

Figure 1. The first map describes the number of the name 'Connolly' in a DED as a percentage of all Connollys in Ireland. The second is the Connollys in a DED as a percentage of its population.

from Monaghan, as was James Connolly's father.[10] The Galway Connollys belonged to the Ó Conghailes, while the Cork Connollys are also of Ó Conghallaigh stock. Whereas the Galway Connollys were concentrated in Connemara, the Cork Connollys were more likely to be found in west Cork.[11] We will return to this topic later.

The 1911 Connolly county rankings are broadly anticipated in the Tithe Applotment Books, which contain lists of landholders liable for tithe payments for the upkeep of clergy of the established church. These books were compiled between 1823 and 1837. Combining Connollys, Conolly, and Conneelys, we find that the surname was most common in Monaghan (328 of 1,369 observations), followed by Cork (166), Galway (120), and Tipperary (92). Co. Dublin (66) came sixth after Leitrim (80).[12] As a source on the relative frequency of surnames, the Tithe Applotment Books are seriously biased against counties such as Galway, however, since they exclude those landless labourers and occupiers of less than one Irish acre of land who were more dominant in the west and south. In Griffith's Valuation, the pioneering and exhaustive survey of land and buildings in Ireland conducted between 1847 and 1864, Galway again leads the way with 727 Conolly/Connollys against Monaghan's 540 and Cork's 469; and 771 of the 784 Conneelys lived in Galway. Here too the data refer to household heads only.

ascendancy: the life of William Conolly, 1662–1729 (Woodbridge, 2010), pp 14–15.   10 Ibid., pp 11–13.   11 The classic source on Irish surnames is MacLysaght, *Irish families*.   12 The data for Cos Antrim and Londonderry are lacking or have not yet been digitized.

IV

Sean Connolly's paternal roots are quite some distance from the Connolly strongholds mentioned above. Sean's father Thomas was born in 1905, not far from Mooncoin in south Kilkenny, or, to be more precise, in the townland of Ballynamona in the civil parish of Dunkitt, barony of Ida.[13] In 1911 Thomas' family was one of three households of the surname in the civil parishes of Dunkitt and neighbouring Rossinan.

These Connollys must have been no blow-ins because the Tithe Applotment Books listed seven occupiers of land named Connolly in Dunkitt in the mid-1820s. They included Thomas Connolly (Skeard) who held 47 plantation acres; John Connolly (Blossom Hill), 16 acres; Richard Connolly (Ballymountain), three acres; and Richard, James, Patrick, and William Connolly (all of Smarts Castle), about 11 plantation acres each. Given that the last four lived in the same townland, and that they held similar amounts of land, they may well have been brothers.

Griffith's Valuation of Kilkenny, which was conducted immediately after the Great Famine, lists nine holders of houses or land named Connolly in the same area. One, William Connolly of Killaspy, was described as 'esq.', and his property was valued at £30. Patrick and William Connolly, both in the townland of Skeard, were valued at £60 each, and held roughly equal holdings of about sixty statute acres. The rest of the Connollys, including two females, were either smallholders or held no land, with valuations ranging from 8s. to £4 12s.

In 1911 Thomas' father and Sean's grandfather, Michael Connolly, was the only householder named Connolly in Dunkitt district electoral division, although 60-year-old Joanna Connolly, a single farmer, lived with her nephew and three servants in Skeard in neighbouring Rossinan district electoral division, and so did 63-year-old spinster farmer Eliza Connolly, her nephew and niece, and three servants. Joanna and Eliza were almost certainly descended from the two strong farming households in Skeard listed in Griffith's Valuation and the Thomas Connolly listed in the Tithe Applotment Books. In 1901 Joanna held the land on which four other smaller dwellings were located, while Eliza was 38-year-old Betsy, then living with her 80-year-old mother Mary Connolly, an Irish speaker, three unmarried siblings (aged between 32 and 52), a niece, and a servant. Betsy/Eliza's ageing by 25 years over the decade is striking, particularly since she was an unlikely candidate for the Old Age Pension.[14] But if their mother was indeed an octogenarian in 1901, it is unlikely that Eliza and her sister Kate (32) were as young as reported in that year's census. Their co-resident niece Mary-Kate aged by only nine years (from 19 to 28) over the decade.

---

13 Private communication, Nov. 2013.   14 On how the pension affected age-reporting see Lee, 'Irish agriculture', p. 73; Cormac Ó Gráda, '"The greatest blessing of all": the old age pension in Ireland', *Past and Present*, 175 (May 2002), 124–62.

Michael Connolly must have descended from the other, less prosperous Connollys: according to the census he was an illiterate 45-year-old farm labourer living in a three-room 'third-class' cottage with his 43-year-old wife Mary, four children, and two relatives. The cottage had a perishable, presumably thatched, roof. Michael and Mary, all born in Co. Kilkenny, had been married 20 years by then, and Thomas was the youngest of their four surviving children; hardship and ill-health is hinted at by deaths of three others before 1911. It is perhaps significant that despite the poverty of the household and Michael's illiteracy, the census form records Mary and their four children – even six-year-old Thomas – as being able to read and write.

I could not find Michael and Mary Connolly in the 1901 census; perhaps they had temporarily migrated to England, where a niece, 25-year-old Mary Synnott, who was living with them in 1911, was born. Twenty-year-old Nicholas Synnott, an agricultural labourer, also shared accommodation with the Connollys in 1911. These are most likely the Nicholas Sinnott and Mary Sinnott, aged ten and 14, who were living in Haresmead, Horetown, in the southern part of Co. Wexford in 1901. Their father – married, perhaps, to Michael's sister – was a labourer and their mother a domestic servant. But no details are given of the Sinnotts' places of birth in the enumeration form. Another Connolly family, headed by 50-year-old Edmond, a farmer, lived in Dunkitt parish in 1901, in the townland of Cappagh. But I could find no trace of Edmond or his family in 1911, in Dunkitt or anywhere else.

South Kilkenny was a very traditional part of the country in many respects. Louis Cullen has drawn attention to the use of the archaic quern there into the 1830s and to the thatching of double-storey houses in more recent times, while Jack Burtchaell has documented the survival of its medieval farm villages.[15] The Irish language clung on there longer than anywhere else in Leinster,[16] with the exception of the Carlingford peninsula. In the Mooncoin area the older generation was still Irish-speaking a century ago.[17] Edmond Connolly spoke Irish, but his wife did not; curiously, their 17-year-old daughter was described as an Irish speaker in 1901, but not their two sons (aged 16 and 14).

Like many other Connollys before him, Sean's father moved to Dublin. A century ago perhaps one-third of Dublin's Connollys had been born outside the city. Two points about these immigrants stand out. First, they were more likely

---

15 Compare L.M. Cullen, *Economy, trade, and Irish merchants at home and abroad, 1600–1988* (Dublin, 2012), pp 33, 100; and Jack Burtchaell, 'The south Kilkenny farm villages' in W.J. Smyth and Kevin Whelan (eds), *Common ground: essays on the historical geography of Ireland* (Cork, 1988), pp 110–23.   16 For a sampling of song and poetry in Irish from the area, see Dáithí Ó hOgáin, *Duanaire Osraíoch: Cnuasach d'Fhilíocht na nDaoine ó Chondae Chill Chainnigh* (Dublin, 1980).   17 Cullen, *Economy, trade, and Irish merchants*, p. 33; Garret FitzGerald, 'Irish-speaking in the pre-Famine period: a study based on the 1911 census data for people born before 1851 and still alive in 1911', *RIA Proc.*, 103 (2003), sect. C, 203; R.A. Breatnach, 'Iarsmaí de Ghaeilig Chontae Chill Choinnigh', *Éigse*, 26 (1992), 21–42.

to have been born in Leinster than in the traditional Connolly strongholds: at least half were born in the eastern province, with Meath and Kildare alone supplying one-quarter of the men, and Wicklow and Kildare supplying one-fifth of the women. Second, about half of both the male and female Connollys returned humble occupations requiring few skills, with domestic service to the fore for women, and occupations such as general or agricultural labourer, gardener, messenger, porter, and shop assistant prominent for men. I could find no latter-day 'Speaker Conolly' blow-in among the elite or managerial classes: a few of the men made it to the status of teacher or clerk, and a few of the women were nurses, but there were no lawyers, no medical practitioners, no engineers, no major employers.

The wide spatial spread of the name Connolly was attributed above to the popularity of Congal and Congalach as first names. Besides those mentioned earlier, there are Connollys, for example, in the Killarney district, as an offshoot of the Éoganacht Locha Léin and in Corcu Duibne, where they became O'Connell (and so ancestors of the great Dan) – but these are two quite different families. The name does not crop up in south Kilkenny in the medieval period. However, there are two families of Ó Conghalaigh who belong to Dál Cais, that is to say collaterals of the O'Briens. The first, Ó Conghalaigh (meic Lorcáin), descended from a brother of Cennétig (father of Brian Bóroimhe). The second, Ó Conghalaigh, descended from Mathghamhain, brother of Brian Bóroimhe. The entry about the second in *An Leabhar Muimhneach* reads:

Ó Mhathghamhain mac Cinnéidigh tángadar na sloinnte seo síos . i. Ó Beolláin, Ó Spealáin, Ó hAnnracháin, Ó Siodhcháin, Mac Innéirghe, Ó Conghalaigh, agus Ó Tuama.[18]

Given the proclivity of the collaterals of the O'Briens to spread widely into east Munster in the eleventh and twelfth centuries, perhaps some of the second group of Dál Cais Ó Conghalaigh ended up in south Kilkenny at that time. But this is only speculation.

V

As Roland Fryer and Steven Levitt (of *Freakonomics* fame) and others have shown, the first names that parents give their children are important markers of religion, social status and aspiration. Similarly, Gregory Clark and Neil Cummins have recently shown how English surnames carry economic information and can be exploited to measure social mobility, or the lack of it, over time.[19] The name

18 Tadhg Ó Donnchadha, *An Leabhar Muimhneach, maraon le suim aguisíní* (Dublin, 1940), p. 236. 19 R.G. Fryer and S.D. Levitt, 'The causes and consequences of distinctively black

Connolly does not carry any obvious socio-economic baggage. But in Ireland people in the past have chosen between Nolan and Nowlan, Smith and Smyth, and Bourke and Burke. What did such choices signify? For example, were the Bourkes 'posher' than the Burkes?

In 1911 Ireland contained 14,251 people named Burke and 4,331 named Bourke. Like the philosopher Edmund Burke, the explorer Robert O'Hara Burke, and Irish scholar Canon Ulick Bourke before them, and Mary [Bourke] Robinson and Chris de Burgh today, they bore the name brought to Ireland by one William de Burgh (*c.*1160–1204), who arrived in 1185 and was awarded vast estates in Leinster and Munster in return for fighting King Henry II's wars. Shortly before his death he 'plundered Connacht, as well churches as territories; but God and the saints took vengeance on him for that; for he died of a singular disease, too shameful to be described',[20] and his son Richard (Riocard Mór) became first baron of Connacht.[21] Although most of William and Richard's humbler descendants in the male line were known as Burkes, some leading members of the family preferred Bourke.

We can turn to the 1911 census for some insight into the choice between Burke and Bourke. A glance at the regional spread of the two variants suggests that the version chosen was in large part determined by county of birth. Between them the counties of Limerick, Mayo, and Tipperary contained nearly two-thirds of the Bourkes, but less than one Burke in four. Galway contained 22.4 per cent of the Burkes, but only 2.1 per cent of the Bourkes.

One relevant and readily estimated measure of the relative status of the two groups is their numeracy. Here we can use age heaping – the tendency for people, particularly in poor countries, to round their age – as a measure of numeracy and, more broadly, human capital. I have employed a common measure of age heaping, the Whipple index, which is defined as:

$$W = [\Sigma(n_{25}+n_{30}+\ldots+n_{55}+n_{60})]/0.2 \Sigma n_i, \text{ where } i = 23, \ldots 62$$

Here n_i is the number of observations for i years of age; only those aged 23 to 62 years are included in the analysis. The measure assumes that people who are only vaguely aware of their age are prone to rounding their estimates to the nearest 0 or 5. By this definition $W = 1$ implies no innumeracy.

names', *Quarterly Journal of Economics*, 99 (2004), 767–805; Gregory Clark and Neil Cummins, 'Intergenerational mobility in England, 1858–1912: wealth, surnames and social mobility', *Economic Journal*, 125 (2015), 61–85. See also Costanza Biavaschi, Giulietti Corrado and Zahra Siddique, 'The economic payoff of name Americanization' (I.Z.A. Discussion Paper No. 7725, Nov. 2013); Claudia Olivetti and M. Daniele Paserman, 'In the name of the son (and the daughter): intergenerational mobility in the United States, 1850–1930' (N.B.E.R. Working Paper No. 18822, 2013). **20** *Annals of the four masters* (http://www.ucc.ie/celt/online/T100005C/text004.html), M1204.3). **21** C.A. Empey, 'Burgh, William de (*d.* 1206)', in *ODNB*.

Table 1. Whipple index values for Bourke and Burke in 1911

Area	Name	Male	Female	All
All Ireland	Bourke	1.40 [1001]	1.41 [939]	1.40 [1940]
	Burke	1.40 [3034]	1.56 [3957]	1.48 [6991]
Dublin	Bourke	1.13 [71]	0.94 [90]	1.02 [161]
	Burke	1.22 [299]	1.47 [351]	1.35 [650]
Tipperary	Bourke	1.47 [231]	1.54 [286]	1.50 [515]
	Burke	1.70 [286]	1.57 [331]	1.66 [617]
Mayo	Bourke	1.41 [167]	1.15 [183]	1.24 [350]
	Burke	1.73 [294]	1.64 [302]	1.69 [596]

Source: derived from 1911 census. Number of observations is given in brackets.

Table 1 reports W values for male and female Bourkes and Burkes in 1911 for Ireland as a whole, and for Counties Dublin, Tipperary, and Galway. In some cases the number of observations is uncomfortably small, and more confidence should be placed in the values for males and females together, rather than for either singly. The pattern for the country as a whole is compromised by the spatial spread of the surnames noted above. However, the results for Counties Dublin, Mayo and Tipperary suggest that in those counties the Bourkes were less prone to age heaping than the Burkes, and therefore probably better endowed with human capital. Still, one can proceed only so far with this kind of exercise, since the spelling for illiterate household heads was often determined by the census enumerators, that is to say the police, perhaps inflating the proportion of the lower-status Burkes.

Data on where Bourkes and Burkes lived in Dublin city and county does not offer much further illumination. By and large, the Bourkes tended to live in the same parts of the city as the Burkes; the correlation between their numbers in Dublin city's wards is +0.74 ($n = 20$); across city and county combined the correlation was even higher, +0.78 (n = 38). In 1911 both Bourkes and Burkes were spread more evenly across the city and county than the Connollys. The representative Burke lived in a marginally more congested and lower-valued ward than the representative Bourke, but there was not much in it. Thus within the city, the average population density where Bourkes and Burkes lived was 60 and 69 persons per acre, respectively; for Connollys it was 57 persons per acre. The average poor law valuation per head for where a representative Connolly lived was £4 4s.; for a Bourke it was £3 4s., and for a Burke £2 9s. The averages for the typical Dublin resident were 64 persons per acre and £3 per head. In city and county combined, the densities were 53, 57, 51, and 48, respectively; the valuations per head £3 3s., £3 2s., £4 8s., and £3 8s. But those numbers reflect the averages where people lived: they are not data based on individual details.

VI

'He has taken the "O"'[22]

In Anthony Trollope's second novel, *The Kellys and the O'Kellys*, where the action takes place in rural Ireland on the eve of the Great Famine, it is the landlord character, Francis O'Kelly, Lord Ballindine, who bears the more Gaelic O'Kelly name while his tenants and distant cousins, Mrs Kelly and her son Martin, stick to the shorter and more Anglicized version. This is the reverse of the pattern exhibited by Trollope's contemporary, Daniel O'Connell, who proudly carried the 'O' at a time when his myriad poorer kinsmen were mere Connells. 'I have heard much about Mr O'Connell's father, Morgan Connell, who kept a huckster's shop in Cahirciveen, and of his pedigree and assumption of the "O" before his name', noted the correspondent of *The Times*, Thomas Campbell Foster.[23] Nowadays the Connells are relatively few, but they were still common a century ago, as were the Learys, Sullivans, and Dwyers.

The 'greening' of such surnames, a gradual process, is evident in the increase in the proportions using the 'O' between 1901 and 1911. If the change is seen as a crude quantification of cultural shift, then few surnames were immune during that decade. The only important examples I could discover were the Briens, most of whom had already made the transition to O'Brien by 1901 in any case, and those named Dea. Why some surnames – such as Connolly – never made the transition is an interesting question without a clear answer. All one can say with confidence is that those with some traction already by 1901 are most likely to have 'taken the O' today.

Neither Sean O'Casey (initially 'Johnny' in his autobiographies) nor Kevin O'Higgins persuaded many other Caseys or Higginses to prefix their names with an 'O'. The 1911 census contains no O'Caseys, although it lists 21 Ó Cathasaighs, including 31-year-old Seághan Ó Cathasaigh, a member of '*Eaglais Protústúnach na h-Eireann*', and a '*sclábhaidhe do lucht an bhóthair iarainn*'. O'Casey, who described himself as '*fear an tighe*', filled the census form in almost flawless Irish on behalf of his mother and brother; perhaps he had received instructions on how to fill the forms *as Gaeilge*. Ten years earlier he was John Casey, a 21-year-old junior delivery clerk, and he knew no Irish. He adopted 'Ó Cathasaigh' in

---

[22] I am grateful to Patricia Fleming for this resonant expression.   [23] T.C. Foster, *Letters of the condition of the people of Ireland* (London, 1846), p. 532.

about 1905 and continued to sign his letters thus until 1923, when he changed to O'Casey when launching *Shadow of a Gunman* at the Abbey Theatre.[24]

The only O'Connollys in the 1911 census were Donal O'Connolly, a 42 year-old grocer's manager living on Gullistan Terrace in Ranelagh, his wife Josephine, and their children Michael and Kathleen. There were no Ó Conghailes or Ní Chonghailes in the 1901 census, but there were 67 in 1911 (32 in Galway, 19 in Monaghan, eight in Antrim, seven in Waterford, and one in Dublin).[25]

The Connollys who switched to Ó Conghaile or Ní Chonghaile for census purposes in 1911 may have been only a tiny fraction of all Connollys, yet they were part of a broader phenomenon. Between 1901 and 1911 the number of Mac Gearailts rose from 3 to 30, Mac Giolla Phádraigs from 1 to 7, Ó Murchadhas from 0 to 85, Ó Briains from 0 to 51, Ó Riains from 0 to 59, Ó Súilleabháins 1 to 46, Ó Broins from 1 to 25, de Búrcas from 0 to 60, and Ó Laoghaires from 1 to 16. The number of males whose surnames began with 'Ua' (an older form of 'Ó') rose from 51 to 1,741. Females were also involved, with the number using 'Ní' leaping from 10 to 656, and that with 'Uí' from 1 to 90. Those using the Irish version of surnames beginning with 'de/De' grew from 2 to 225.

One suspects that these rather remarkable shifts were largely the product of a grassroots campaign organized by the Gaelic League.[26] The increase in 'Ua' among staff and students in St Patrick's College Maynooth – from just two in 1901 to 83 in 1911 – is particularly noteworthy. Overall the disproportionately urban and youthful character of those using 'Ua' in 1911 is consistent with the influence of the Gaelic League. Of the 1,728 individuals for whom ages are available, 322 were aged 0–9 years, 335 aged 10–19 years, 400 were in their 20s, 239 in their 30s, 147 in their 40s, 133 in their 50s, 70 in their 60s, 85 in their 70s, and 17 aged 80 and over.

The rather high proportions of those living in the heavily Irish-speaking pockets of Dunquin/Dún Chaoin (93 of 576), Dunurlin/Dún Urlainn (209 of 799), and Kilquane/Cill Chuáin (98 of 805) in west Kerry who filled in their household forms in Irish – these proportions were much higher than in any other Gaeltacht area – is also worth noting and hints at an organized campaign. On the Great Blasket, by contrast, no household filled in its form – or had it filled in – in Irish in 1911. Sixty-year-old Thomas Crohan – *An tOileánach* – allowed the enumerator to do the filling in, but he signed the form himself in the Gaelic script as Tomás Ó Criomhthain. In 1901, the policeman/enumerator also filled

---

24 Christopher Murray, *Sean O'Casey: writer at work* (Dublin, 2004), pp 77–9; *The letters of Sean O'Casey*, i: *1910–41*, ed. David Krause (London, 1975), pp 105–18. I am grateful to David Fitzpatrick for pointing me towards these references. As David Fitzpatrick notes, Yeats continued to address O'Casey as Casey 'when in patronizing mood, as when rejecting the Tassie' (private communication).   25 The current (2013) Eircom phone directory lists only one O'Connolly, but there are 20 subscribers named Ó Conghaile and 4 named Ní Chonghaile.   26 *Freeman's Journal*, 11 Mar. 1911 (letter to the editor from Patrick O'Daly, secretary of the Gaelic League, stating that arrangements were in place by census commissioners).

Table 2. Adding 'O's to surnames between 1901 and 1911

Name	1901 with/without	% with 'O'	1911 with/without	% with 'O'	Eircom phonebook (% with 'O')
O'Brien	22744/11714	66	24518/12818	66	98
O'Carroll	428/14216	3	568/13788	4	16
O'Connell	6119/10672	36	7286/9277	44	83
O'Connor	14634/16544	47	16876/16543	50	93
O'Dea	1418/625	69	1318/741	64	96
O'Doherty	439/17923	2	632/17779	3	13
O'Donoghue	1219/3691	25	1620/3442	32	78
O'Donovan	622/9319	6	911/8822	9	76
O'Driscoll	1168/4929	19	1690/4378	28	97
O'Dwyer	1275/6711	16	1674/6297	21	66
O'Farrell	617/12784	5	744/12543	6	13
O'Flaherty	646/4143	13	705/3929	15	44
O'Flynn	342/13638	2	524/13561	4	18
O'Gorman	1177/5812	17	1479/5491	21	57
O'Grady	1855/3284	36	2066/3206	39	92
O'Hagan	1221/2480	33	1411/2370	37	75
O'Halloran	1253/2217	36	1342/2169	38	93
O'Hanlon	1168/3623	24	1376/3462	28	58
O'Hara	4116/900	82	4276/912	82	99
O'Kane	2065/6754	23	2208/6207	26	21
O'Keeffe	4356/3589	55	5025/3378	60	100
O'Leary	4474/6486	41	5471/5726	49	99
O'Mahony	1289/8365	13	1955/7660	20	85
O'Meara	931/1717	35	1278/1429	47	99
O'Neill	16994/11954	59	18386/10917	63	97
O'Regan	1183/6432	16	1565/6306	20	65
O'Reilly	3411/20106	15	4566/19551	19	62
O'Rourke	1694/3943	31	2422/3637	40	95
O'Shaughnessy	956/1532	38	1016/1679	38	71
O'Shea	3605/8907	29	4474/7977	36	97
O'Sullivan	7405/31012	19	9167/28873	24	90
O'Toole	1718/3691	32	2221/3504	39	99

Sources: 1901 and 1911 censuses; Eircom online 2013 phonebook (http://www.eircomphonebook.ie/q/name/, Republic of Ireland only).

in the form, but Tomás – then aged only 44! – signed in a fluent hand as Thomas Crohan. In 1911 the constable also filled in the census form of illiterate Blasketman, Patrick Guiheen; his wife Margaret, who presumably could have done it for him, would always be better known as Peig Sayers.[27]

---

27 Lesa Ní Mhunghaile, 'Peig Sayers', in *DIB*, viii, 794–5. My thanks to Alan Fernihough for fig. 1, to Donnchadh Ó Corráin for the information on Congal and Congalach, and to David Fitzpatrick and Peter Solar for some great comments.

Bibliography of the publications of S.J. Connolly to 2014*

1979

'Illegitimacy and pre-nuptial pregnancy in Ireland before 1864: the evidence of some Catholic parish registers', *IESH*, 6, 5–23.

1981

'Catholicism in Ulster, 1800–1850' in Peter Roebuck (ed.), *Plantation to partition: essays in Ulster history in honour of J.L. McCracken* (Belfast: Blackstaff Press), pp 157–71.

1982

Priests and people in pre-Famine Ireland, 1780–1845 (338 pp, Dublin: Gill and Macmillan).

(Compiled) *The rebellion of 1798: facsimile documents* (38 pp, Dublin: Co-ordinating Committee for Educational Services).

(Compiled) *The public record: sources for local studies in the Public Record Office of Ireland* (48 pp, Dublin: Co-ordinating Committee for Educational Services).

1983

'The "blessed turf": cholera and popular panic in Ireland, June 1832', *IHS*, 23:91, 214–32.

'Religion, work-discipline and economic attitudes: the case of Ireland' in T.M. Devine and David Dickson (eds), *Ireland and Scotland, 1600–1850: parallels and contrast in economic and social development* (Edinburgh: John Donald), pp 235–45.

'Religion and history', *IESH*, 10, 66–80.

1985

Religion and society in nineteenth-century Ireland (ii, 69 pp, Studies in Irish Economic and Social History no. 3, Dundalk: Dundealgan Press).

'Law, order and popular protest in early eighteenth-century Ireland: the case of the houghers' in P.J. Corish (ed.), *Radicals, rebels and establishments: Historical Studies xv* (Belfast: Appletree Press), pp 51–68.

'Marriage in pre-Famine Ireland' in Art Cosgrove (ed.), *Marriage in Ireland* (Dublin: College Press), pp 78–98.

---

* Excluding bibliographies and book reviews, but including review articles.

1986

'Popular culture in pre-Famine Ireland' in Cyril J. Byrne and Margaret Harry (eds), *Talamh and Eisc: Canadian and Irish essays* (Halifax, Nova Scotia: Nimbus), pp 12–28.

'The state of eighteenth-century Irish studies', *Irish Review*, 1, 90–2.

1987

'The houghers: agrarian protest in early eighteenth-century Connacht' in C.H.E. Philpin (ed.), *Nationalism and popular protest in Ireland* (Cambridge: Cambridge University Press), pp 139–62.

'Violence and order in the eighteenth century' in Patrick O'Flanagan, Paul Ferguson and Kevin Whelan (eds), *Rural Ireland: modernisation and change, 1600–1900* (Cork: Cork University Press), pp 42–61.

1988

'Albion's fatal twigs: justice and law in the eighteenth century' in Rosalind Mitchison and Peter Roebuck (eds), *Economy and society in Scotland and Ireland, 1500–1939* (Edinburgh: John Donald), pp 117–25.

1989

'Aftermath and adjustment' (pp 1–23), 'The Catholic question, 1801–1812' (pp 24–47), 'Union government, 1812–1823' (pp 48–73), 'Mass politics and sectarian conflict, 1823–1830' (pp 74–107), in W.E. Vaughan (ed.), *A new history of Ireland*, v: *Ireland under the Union*, i: *1801–1870* (Oxford, Clarendon Press).

1990

'The penal laws' in W.A. Maguire (ed.), *Kings in conflict: the revolutionary war in Ireland and its aftermath, 1689–1750* (Belfast: Blackstaff Press), pp 157–72.

1991

'Family, love and marriage: some evidence from the early eighteenth century' in Margaret MacCurtain and Mary O'Dowd (eds), *Women in early modern Ireland* (Edinburgh: Edinburgh University Press), pp 276–90.

Rev. article: J.R.R. Adams, *The printed word and the common man: popular culture in Ulster, 1700–1900* (1987); Thomas E. Hachey, *Perspectives on Irish nationalism* (1989); Cormac Ó Gráda, *Ireland before and after the Famine: explorations in economic history, 1800–1925* (1988); B.M. Walker, *Ulster politics: the formative years, 1868–86* (1989) in *Victorian Studies*, 34, 401–3.

1992

Religion, law and power: the making of Protestant Ireland, 1660–1760 (xi, 346 pp, Oxford: Clarendon Press).

1993

'Patterns of marriage in nineteenth- and twentieth-century Ireland', *Familia: Ulster Genealogical Review*, 2:8 (1992), 87–93.

'Translating history: Brian Friel and the Irish past' in Alan Peacock (ed.), *The achievement of Brian Friel* (Gerrard's Cross: Colin Smythe), pp 149–63.

'The Church of Ireland: a critical bibliography, 1536–1992. Part IV: 1690–1800', *IHS*, 28:112, 362–9.

1994

'Late eighteenth-century Irish politics' (rev. article: James Kelly, *Prelude to Union: Anglo-Irish politics in the 1780s* (1992); Jim Smyth, *The men of no property: Irish radicals and popular politics in the late eighteenth century* (1992)) in *Parliamentary History*, 28, 227–35.

1995

(Ed., with R.A. Houston and R.J. Morris), *Conflict, identity and economic development: Ireland and Scotland, 1600–1939* (x, 275 pp, Preston: Carnegie Publishing).

(With R.A. Houston and R.J. Morris), 'Identity, conflict and economic change: themes and issues' (pp 1–13); 'Popular culture: patterns of change and adaptation' (pp 103–13) in ibid.

'Reformers and highflyers: the post-revolution church' in Alan Ford, James McGuire and Kenneth Milne (eds), *As by law established: the Church of Ireland since the Reformation* (Dublin: Lilliput Press), pp 152–65, 265–7.

'Varieties of Britishness: Ireland, Scotland and Wales in the Hanoverian state' in Alexander Grant and Keith J. Stringer (eds), *Uniting the kingdom? The making of British history* (London: Routledge), pp 193–207.

'The Great Famine and Irish politics' in Cathal Póirtéir (ed.), *The Great Irish Famine* (Cork: Mercier Press), pp 34–49.

1996

'Approaches to the history of Irish popular culture', *Bullán*, 2, 83–100.

'The defence of Protestant Ireland, 1660–1760' in Thomas Bartlett and Keith Jeffery (eds), *A military history of Ireland* (Cambridge: Cambridge University Press), pp 231–46.

'Eighteenth-century Ireland' in D.G. Boyce and Alan O'Day (eds), *The making of modern Irish history: revisionism and the revisionist controversy* (London: Routledge), pp 15–33.

'Revisions revised? New work on the Irish Famine' (rev. article: Donal Kerr, *'A nation of beggars'? Priests, people, and politics in Famine Ireland, 1846–52* (1994); Christine Kinealy, *This great calamity: the Irish Famine, 1845–52* (1994); Cormac Ó Gráda, *Ireland: a new economic history* (1994); Cathal Póirtéir, *The Great Irish Famine* (1995); Alexander Somerville, *Letters from Ireland during the Famine of 1847*, ed. K.D.M. Snell (1994)) in *Victorian Studies*, 39, 205–16.

1997

'Culture, identity and tradition: changing definitions of Irishness' in Brian Graham (ed.), *In search of Ireland: a cultural geography* (London: Routledge), pp 43–63.

'Ulster Presbyterians: religion, culture, and politics, 1660–1850' in H. Tyler Blethen and Curtis W. Wood, jr (eds), *Ulster and North America: transatlantic perspectives on the Scotch-Irish* (Tuscaloosa, AL: University of Alabama Press), pp 24–40.

1998

(Ed. and contributed entries) *The Oxford companion to Irish history* (xviii, 618 pp, Oxford: Oxford University Press).

'"Ag Déanamh *Commanding*": elite responses to popular culture, 1660–1850' in J.S. Donnelly and K.A. Miller (eds), *Irish popular culture, 1650–1850* (Dublin: Irish Academic Press), pp 1–29.

'Swift and Protestant Ireland: images and realities' in Aileen Douglas, Patrick Kelly and Ian Campbell Ross (eds), *Locating Swift: essays from Dublin on the 250th anniversary of the death of Jonathan Swift, 1667–1745* (Dublin: Four Courts Press), pp 28–46.

1999

(Ed.) *Kingdoms united? Great Britain and Ireland since 1500: integration and diversity* (252 pp, Dublin: Four Courts Press).

'Introduction' (pp 9–12), and 'Unnatural death in four nations: contrasts and comparisons' (pp 200–14) in ibid.

2000

(Ed.) *Political ideas in eighteenth-century Ireland* (236 pp, Dublin: Four Courts Press).

'Introduction; varieties of Irish political thought' (pp 11–26), 'The Glorious Revolution in Irish Protestant political thinking' (pp 27–63), and 'Precedent and principle: the patriots and their critics' (pp 130–58) in ibid.

'Reconsidering the Act of Union', *RHS Trans.*, 6:10, 399–408.

'A woman's life in mid-eighteenth-century Ireland: the case of Letitia Bushe', *HJ*, 43, 433–51.

'The Irish rebellion of 1798: an end or a beginning?' in Hans-Dieter Metzger (ed.), *Religious thinking and national identity* (Berlin: Philo), pp 108–22.

2002

(Ed. and contributed entries) *The Oxford companion to Irish history* (2nd ed., xix, 650 pp, Oxford: Oxford University Press).

'Religion in Ireland' in H.T. Dickinson (ed.), *A companion to eighteenth-century Britain* (Oxford: Blackwell), pp 271–80.

'Malcomson's century' (rev. article: A.P.W. Malcomson, *Archbishop Charles Agar: churchmanship and politics in Ireland, 1760–1810* (2002)) in *ECI*, 17, 167–71.

2003

'The Church of Ireland and the royal martyr: regicide and revolution in Anglican political thought, *c*.1660–*c*.1745', *Journal of Ecclesiastical History*, 54, 484–506.

'Jacobites, Whiteboys and republicans: varieties of disaffection in eighteenth-century Ireland', *ECI*, 18, 63–79.

'Tupac Amaru and Captain Right: a comparative perspective on eighteenth-century Ireland' in David Dickson and Cormac Ó Gráda (eds), *Refiguring Ireland: essays in honour of L.M. Cullen* (Dublin: Lilliput Press), pp 94–111.

2004

'The moving statue and the turtle dove: approaches to the history of Irish religion', *IESH*, 31, 1–22.

Contributions to H.C.G. Matthew and Brian Harrison (eds), *The Oxford dictionary of national biography* (60 vols, Oxford: Oxford University Press):

- John Bowes, Baron Bowes of Clonlyon (1691–1767): vi, 935–6
- Dudley Costello (*d*. 1667): xiii, 548–9
- Sir Richard Cox, 1st Bt (1650–1733): xiii, 865–7
- Anthony Dopping (1643–97): xvi, 563–4
- John Hartstonge (1659–1717): xxv, 637–8
- Charles Hickman (1648–1713): xxvii, 19–20
- William King (1650–1729): xxxi, 680–6
- William Moreton (1640/1–1715): xxxix, 92–3 [revision]
- Redmond O'Hanlon (*c*.1640–81): xli, 625–6
- John Scott (1739–98), 1st earl of Clonmell: xlix, 414–17
- John Vesey (1638–1716): lvi, 391–2
- Edward Wetenhall (1636–1713): lviii, 322–4 [revision].

Rev. article: T.C. Barnard, *A new anatomy of Ireland: the Irish Protestants, 1649–1770* (2003); idem, *Making the grand figure: lives and possessions in Ireland, 1641–1770* (2004); idem, *The kingdom of Ireland 1641–1760* (2004), *ECI*, 19, 217–22.

2005

'1690–1800' in Kenneth Milne (ed.), *A Church of Ireland bibliography* (Dublin: Church of Ireland), pp 25–32.

2007

Contested island: Ireland, 1460–1630 (xiv, 426 pp, Oxford History of Early Modern Europe, Oxford: Oxford University Press).

'Religion and nationality in Ireland: an unstable relationship' in Urs Altermatt and Franziska Metzger (eds), *Religion und Nation: Katholizismen im Europa des 19. und 20. Jahrhunderts* (Stuttgart: Kohlhammer), pp 119–34.

2008

Divided kingdom: Ireland, 1630–1800 (xiii, 519 pp, Oxford History of Early Modern Europe, Oxford: Oxford University Press).

'Swift and history' in Hermann Real (ed.), *Reading Swift: papers from the Fifth Münster Symposium on Jonathan Swift* (Munich: Wilhelm Fink), pp 187–202.

2009

'Kingdom, crown and parliament: patriot myth and the origins of the Irish Union' in Andrew Mackillop and Micheál Ó Siochrú (eds), *Forging the state: European state formation and the Anglo-Scottish Union of 1707* (Dundee: Dundee University Press), pp 133–52.

(With Dominic Bryan), 'Identity, social action and public space: defining civic space in Belfast' in Margaret Wetherell (ed.), *Theorizing identities and social action* (Basingstoke: Palgrave Macmillan), pp 220–37.

Contributions to *DIB*:

- Christopher Butler (1673–1757): ii, 101–3
- James Butler (1683–1774): ii, 151
- John Butler (*c*.1731–1800), 12th Baron Dunboyne: ii, 155–6.

2010

'Cardinal Cullen's other capital: Belfast and the "devotional revolution"' in Dáire Keogh and Albert McDonnell (eds), *Cardinal Paul Cullen and his world* (Dublin: Four Courts Press), pp 289–307.

'Old English, New English and ancient Irish: Swift and the Irish past' in Claude Rawson (ed.), *Politics and literature in the age of Swift: English and Irish perspectives* (Cambridge: Cambridge University Press), pp 255–69.

'Society and economy, 1815–70' in Donnchadh Ó Corráin and Tomás O'Riordan (eds), *Ireland, 1815–70: emancipation, famine and religion* (Dublin: Four Courts Press), pp 33–42.

2012

(Ed.), *Belfast 400: people, place and history* (392 pp, Liverpool: Liverpool University Press).

'Improving town, 1750–1820' (pp 161–97), (with Gillian McIntosh), 'Imagining Belfast' (pp 13–61), (with Gillian McIntosh), 'Whose city? Belonging and exclusion in the nineteenth-century urban world' (pp 237–69), in ibid.

'Belfast: the rise and fall of a civic culture?' in Olwen Purdue (ed.), *Belfast: the emerging city, 1850–1914* (Dublin: Irish Academic Press), pp 25–48.

'Like an old cathedral city: Belfast welcomes Queen Victoria, August 1849', *Urban History*, 39, 571–89.

2013

'The limits of democracy: Ireland, 1778–1848' in Joanna Innes and Mark Philp (eds), *Re-imagining democracy in an age of revolutions* (Oxford: Oxford University Press), pp 174–88.

'Religion and Society, 1600–1914' in Liam Kennedy and Philip Ollerenshaw (eds), *Ulster since 1600: politics, economy, and society* (Oxford: Oxford University Press), pp 74–89.

(With A.R. Holmes), 'Popular culture, 1600–1914' in ibid., pp 106–20.

2014

'Patriotism and nationalism' in Alvin Jackson (ed.), *The Oxford handbook of modern Irish history* (Oxford: Oxford University Press), pp 237–44.

Index

Acheson, family, 51, 57
Adams, Dunlop, writing master, 115
Adare (Co. Limerick), 73
An alarm to the unprejudiced and well-minded Protestants (1762), 71–2
Albany (NY), 159
Alexander, Mr, 116
Allen, Joshua, 2nd Viscount Allen, 55
Alliance of the Reformed Churches, 167
Amsterdam, 133
Andrews, Elisha B., 194
Anne, Queen, 26, 28–9, 30, 31, 32, 35, 36–7, 39–41
    as Astraea, 30
    as Deborah, 30, 36
    as Pallas Athene, 28, 36
    compared to Elizabeth I, 28, 30, 32
Annesley, family, 110
Antrim, Co., 208, 209
architecture, 21
Ardstraw (Co. Tyrone), 111
Armagh, 108, 109, 111, 124
    Abp of, 107
    Public Library, 124
    Royal School, 107, 108–9, 124
    other schools at, 109–10, 122, 124
Armitage, David, 128
army, British, 135
Aspinwall, Bernard, 157
Associate Synod of North America, 158, 165
Aston, Sir Richard, 79–80

Bailey, Joanne, 185
—, Pierce, mason and Whiteboy, 80
Baillie, James, schoolteacher, 113
Ballitore (Co. Kildare), 140, 147, 148
    school at, 137–8, 139, 146, 147
Ballycastle (Co. Antrim), charter school at, 112
Ballyferriter (Co. Kerry), 206
Ballymena (Co. Antrim), 165
    school at, 115
Ballynamona (Co. Kilkenny), 210

Ballyporeen (Co. Tipperary), 75
Bangor (Co. Down), 112
banks, 54
Banner of Ulster, 155–6
Barclay, Katie, 170, 177, 181, 182
Barr, Samuel, writing master, 115
Barry, Fr Standish, 80
Battle of the Boyne, commemoration of, 34, 35
Beatty, Norah, brothel-keeper, 97
Beckett, J.C., 51
Belfast, 18–19, 39, 67, 115, 118–19, 123, 124, 169–91 passim, 204
    May Street Presbyterian church, 156
    poor-house, 115
    schools at, 112, 113–14, 121
Belfast Academy, 179, 189
Belfast Ladies' Relief Association, 156
Belfast News-Letter, 115, 172, 193
Beresford, John, 134
Berkeley, George, Church of Ireland bp of Cloyne, 48
    Querist, 60, 72
Bindon, David, 48, 56
Birmingham, 133
Black, John, 105, 121
Blackpool (Co. Cork), 93
Bligh, Lady Anne, 18, 170
Boston (MA), 89
Bower, John, linen weaver, 93
Bourke, family, *see* Burke
Boyd, family, 112
Boyle, Richard, styled Viscount Boyle (later 2nd earl of Shannon), 69, 70
Brackenstown (Co. Dublin), 52
British and Foreign Bible Society, 201
Broad Church party, 202
Brooke, Henry, 106
brothels, brothel riots, 84–103 passim
Brown, S.J., 201
Browne, Darby, Whiteboy, 79–80
— (Sir) John, 52, 53
Bryce, Revd Reuben J., 189, 190

227

Burke, family, 213–14
—, Edmund, 44, 59, 70, 74, 75, 127, 132, 135, 147, 148, 150
—, Peter, 14, 16
—, Richard, 127, 132, 133, 135
Burtchaell, Jack, 211
Busby, —, resident of Dame Street, Dublin, 96
Bushe, Letitia, 18, 138, 169–70
Butler, James, 2nd duke of Ormond, 23, 24, 25–6, 27, 35
——, Mary, duchess of Ormond, 24
——, Somerset Hamilton, 1st earl of Carrick, 69, 70, 71, 73

Caherciveen (Co. Kerry), 215
Caldwell, family, 114
Caldwell, Elizabeth, Lady Caldwell (née Hort), 117
—, Sir James, 4th Bt, 111, 117, 118
Callan, Denis, butcher, 84
Cambridge, University of, 118
Cappoquin (Co. Waterford), 78
Carleton, Deborah, 139, 140, 142
Carlow, 140, 141, 144, 150
Carrick, earl of, *see* Butler
Carrickfergus (Co. Antrim), 39
Carrickmacross (Co. Monaghan), school at, 110
Carteret, John, 2nd Baron Carteret (later 1st Earl Granville), 55, 56, 59
Carthy, Charles, schoolmaster, 107, 108, 114, 121
Casey, *see* O'Casey
Castlewellan (Co. Down), 110
Catholic clergy, 78, 197
Catholic emancipation, 198–9
Catholic relief, 126–36 passim
Catholic troops, 69, 71
Catholic Church, 197
Catholic Committee, 133
Catholic Convention, 133, 135
Cavan, Royal School, 107, 110
Celbridge (Co. Kildare), 64, 65
census (1911), 206
Chalmers, Thomas, 203
charity schools, 111–12
Charleville (Co. Cork), school at, 124
charter schools, 111–12
Chenevix Trench, *see* Trench
Chicago, 167

Christian Examiner and Church of Ireland Magazine, 201, 202
Church of Ireland, 196, 202
 clergy of, 30, 32
 convocation of, 32
 history of, 16
Church of Scotland, 197
 General Assembly, 203
Cincinnati, 159
Cinque Ports, lord warden of, 24
Clanbrassil, earl of, *see* Hamilton
Clapham Sect, 203
Clare, Co. 208
Clark, Gregory, 212
—, J.C.D., 17, 192
Clogheen (Co. Tipperary), 74, 75, 81
Clonfert (Co. Galway), 50
Clonmel (Co. Tipperary), 74, 77, 79
Coagh (Co. Tyrone), 109
coal trade, 50, 57
Cochran, Mary, schoolteacher, 113
Coghill, Marmaduke, 53, 54–5
coinage, 29, 48
Coleraine (Co. Londonderry), 119
 corporation of, 112
 school at, 112, 113
'colonial nationalism', 16–17
Conner, Dennis, 77
Conolly, William, 208
Connolly, family, 207–12
 immigrants into Dublin, 211
 Irish-speaking, 211
 surname, derivation of, 208–9, 212
—, James, 207, 208–9
Conybeare, W.J., 202
Conyngham, Henry, 111
Cooke, Revd Henry, 201, 202, 203–4
Cope, Robert, 50–1, 54
Corballis, John, 146
Cork, city, 39, 68, 74, 76, 79, 80, 91, 93, 95
 mayor, 95
Cork, Co., 67, 69, 78, 80, 208, 209
 sheriff, 81
Cork Evening Post, 72
Cork Journal, 72
cottiers, 75
Cottingham, Revd James, 110
Courtown (Co. Kildare), 65
Cousser, *see* Kusser
Cox, Sir Richard, 36
Crabbe, George, 152

Cranfield Sackville, *see* Sackville
Crawford, Revd William, 123
Crawley, Revd Patrick, 96
crime, 17
Crohan, *see* Ó Cromhthain
Cullen, Louis, 211
—, Cardinal Paul, 205
Cummins, Neil, 212
currency exchange rate, 51
Curry, John, 71, 75

Damrosch, Leo, 43
Davidoff, Leonore, 175, 183, 184
Dawson, Lady Ann, 112
Deacon, John, suspected felon, 92
—, Oliver, executed felon, 92
Dean, Mary, 37
Delany, Patrick, 37
de la Vega, Garcilaso, 42
Denham, Revd John, 167
Dennis, John, mathematics master, 115
Derby, James, writing master, 115
Derry, 121, 124
    diocesan school at, 114
Devonsheir, Abraham, 81
Dickie, William, printer, 108, 124
Dickinson, Mrs, schoolmistress, 113, 122
diocesan schools, 107, *see also* Derry
Dill, Revd Edward M., 158-9, 160, 162
    The mystery solved ... (1852), 162
—, Revd Samuel M., 164, 165
Dobbs, Arthur, 51, 56
Donaldson, Sir James, 194
Donegal, Co., 208
Donnelly, James S., 61
Dorset, duke of: *see* Sackville
Dosker, Henry E., 194
Douglas, William, schoolboy, 114
Doyle, Mrs, 142
Drogheda, earl of, *see* Moore
Drogheda (Co. Louth), school at, 113
Drury, Isaac, JP, 92-3
Dublin, city, 26, 35, 39, 47, 48, 49, 55, 84-103 passim, 117, 139, 140, 141, 145, 146, 211-12, 214-15, 216
    Castle, 22-4, 25, 27, 31, 38, 56, 145
    Christ Church cathedral, 23, 27, 30, 37
    corporation, 31, 33, 34, 35, 36, 55
    Guild of St Luke, 29
    Leinster House, 146
    lord mayor, 38

Newgate prison, 86, 87
Ormond Market, 84, 92
oyer and terminer, commission of, 99
Ringsend, 86, 87
Rotunda, 145
St Anne's parish, 40-1
St Stephen's Green, 26, 31, 47, 92, 97
sheriff, 101
Tholsel, 27, 33, 36, 38, 40
town-major, 101
University, *see* Trinity College
Dublin, Co., 208, 209, 214
    high sheriff, 38
Dublin Society, 59-60
Dumont, —, dancing master, 109-10, 111
Dundalk (Co. Louth), 111
    school at, 108, 110-11
Dundas, Henry (later 1st Viscount Melville), 130-1, 132, 133-6
Dungannon (Co. Tyrone), Royal School, 107, 118
Dunkin, William, 107, 108, 114, 121
Dunkitt (Co. Kilkenny), 210, 211
Dunleer (Co.Louth), 39
Dunton, John, 25

ecclesiology, 196-7
Echlin, John, 37
Edgar, Revd John, 155, 156, 157, 158, 159, 161, 164, 168
Edgeworth, Maria, 106, 149, 150, 189
—, Richard Lovell, 106, 149, 150
Edinburgh, 129-30
Edinburgh Review, 188-9, 202
Edo (Tokyo), 48
Egremont, earl of, *see* Wyndham
Elizabethtown (NJ), 160
Emerson Tennent, *see* Tennent
emigration to north America, 51, 54, 154, 157
enclosure, 64-5, 75
enclosure riots, 65-6
Ennis (Co. Clare), 50
Erastianism, 197, 203, 205
Evangelical Party, 199-200, 202
evangelicalism, 187, 194-5, 199-203

Fabricant, Carole, 43, 44
Famine, Great, 156, 157, 204
Fane, John, 10th earl of Westmorland, 131, 132, 133

Fant, William, attorney, 75
Faulkner, George, 62, 72–3
Faulkner's Dublin Journal, 62, 72
'fearrhaidhes' ('fairies'), 77
Ferguson, Oliver, 43
Fermoy (Co. Cork), 80
Fetherstone, Mrs, brothel-keeper, 100
Finegan, Jack ('Jack Slap'), 96
fireworks, 27, 35, 38
FitzGibbon, John, 1st Visc. FitzGibbon
    (later 1st earl of Clare), 134
Fitzmaurice, Thomas, 21st Baron Kerry
    (later 1st earl of Kerry), 26
Fleming, David, 96
food riots, 67
Fortescue, family, 113
Fossette, Mrs, schoolmistress, 122
Foster, John (later 1st Baron Oriel), 126, 134
Foster, Thomas Campbell, 215
Free Church of Scotland, 157, 203–4
Freeman's Journal, 193
Friends, Society of, *see* Quakers
Fryer, Roland, 212
Fuller, Louise, 192

Gaelic League, 216
Gallicanism, 197, 199, 205
'Galloway Levellers' (1724–5), 65–6
Galway, city, corporation, 38
Galway, Co., 63, 208, 209, 214
Galway, earl of, *see* Ruvigny
Garnham, Neal, 17
Garth, Sir Samuel, 36
George I, 27, 30–1
George III, 69, 134
George, Prince of Denmark, 343
Germany, 194–5
Gibbons, Grinling, 29
Gibson, William, 164
girls' schools, 109–10, 122, *see also*
    Mountmellick, Newry
Glanworth (Co. Cork), 80
Glengariff (Co. Cork), 208
Glengarry Fencibles, 134
Goodwin, Albert, 45, 55
Gordon Riots, 130
Gough, James, schoolmaster, 106
Gray, James, 179
—, Mary, 179–80
graziers, 76
Grenada, 129

Grisar, Hartmann, 194
Grueber, Revd Dr Arthur, 108
Guiheen, Margaret, *see* Sayers
Guild of St Luke, *see* Dublin
guilds, Catholics in, 68

Hagenbach, Karl Rudolf, 194
Halifax, earl of, *see* Montagu-Dunk
Hall, Catherine, 175, 183, 184
—, John, 167
Hamilton, James, 1st earl of Clanbrassil,
    108
—, Sophia, 112
—, William Gerard, 68, 70
Harding, John, 95
harvests, 51, 52
Hawkesworth, John, 118
Hay, George, titular Catholic bishop of
    Daulia and vicar-apostolic in Scotland,
    129–30, 131
Hay Stuart, *see* Stuart
Hays, Mary, *Female biography* ... (1803), 187
Hely-Hutchinson, John, *Commercial
    restraints of Ireland*, 46
Henry, Revd P.S., 169
Herbert, Thomas, 8th earl of Pembroke, 24
Higgins, Ian, 45
High Church party, 200, 202
Hill, Jacqueline, 127, 129
Hillsborough (Co. Down), 115, 202
Hobart, Robert, 133
Hogg, James, 179
    Songs by the Ettrick shepherd (1831), 179
Holland, Joseph, mathematics teacher, 109
Holmes, Andrew, 203
Horetown (Co. Wexford), 211
Hort, Sir John, 1st Bt, 117
'houghers' (1710–12), 17, 63, 64
Hughes, Barbara, 146
Hughes, John, Catholic abp of New York,
    160
Hume, John, 192
Hyland, James, clothier and Whiteboy, 75

Indianapolis, 167
Irish language, 18
Irish poetry, as historical source, 18, 62
Irish surnames, 206–18 passim
Irish Presbyterian, 164
Irish Society ... for Promoting the
    Education of the Native Irish, 201

Index

Irish Society of London, 112
Irish Tenant League, 205
Irish Times, 192, 193
Isle of Man, 133
Ivory, Mrs, schoolmistress, 109–10, 122

'Jack Slap', *see* Finegan
Jackson, Jeremiah, land agent, 73
Jacobitism, 18, 31, 35–6
James II, 21, 196
James, William, police commissioner, 100–1
Japan, 42, 48
Jersey, earl of, *see* Villiers
'Joan Meskel' ('Shevaun'), 77
Jocelyn, Robert, 3rd earl of Roden, 202
Joy, Francis, 172
—, Robert, 172

Kearney (O'Kearney), Daniel, Catholic bp of Limerick, 78
Kenny, Mary, 192
Keogh, John, 133
Kerr, Ld John, regiment of, 91
Kerry, Baron, *see* Fitzmaurice
Kerry, Co., 77
Kilcock (Co. Kildare), 64, 65, 75
Kildare, Co., 212
Kildare Place Society, 151
Kilfinane (Co. Limerick), 75
Kilkenny, Co., 69, 210, 211
Kilkenny Castle, 26
Killough (Co. Down), charter school at, 111–12
Killyleagh (Co. Down), school at, 123
Kilmallock (Co. Limerick), 75
Kilroy, Phil, 138
King, William, Church of Ireland abp of Dublin, 27, 49, 50
King's Co. (Co. Offaly), 40, 208
Kirkcudbrightshire, 66
Kirkpatrick, Revd W.B., 162
'Kirwan', *see* Murray
'Know Nothing' movement, 157
Knox, Robert, 167–8
Kusser (Cousser), John Sigismund, 27, 28, 31–2, 33, 37

Lafayette (IN), 167
Langrishe, Sir Hercules, 1st Bt, 132
Laois, Co., 208
Larkin, Emmet, 205

The late tumults in Ireland considered (1762), 72
Leadbeater, Mary (née Shackleton), 137–53 passim
'Annals of Ballitore', 151–2
Biographical notices of members of the Society of Friends... resident in Ireland (1823), 151
Cottage dialogues (1811), 137, 148, 149–50
Extracts and original anecdotes for improvement of youth (1794), 148
The landlord's friend (1813), 151
Memoirs and letters and Richard and Elizabeth Shackleton ... (1822), 151
The pedlar (1813), 151
Poems (1808), 148–9
—, William, 144, 147
Lefanu, William, 92
Leitrim, Co., 208, 209
'levellers', 77
Levitt, Stephen, 212
Liberty Boys, 84
Lifford (Co. Donegal), 111
Lill, Godfrey, 79
Limerick, city, 74, 79, 165
Limerick, Co., 67, 69, 72, 75, 213
Lisburn (Co. Antrim), 116
school at, 113, 116
Lismore (Co. Waterford), 78, 79
Lloyd, Edward, 35
Locke, John, 106, 107, 108, 111, 120
London, 144
Londonderry, Co., 209
lords justices, 27
Lotz-Heumann, Ute, 195
Loughgall, Co. Armagh, 50–1
Louis XIV, 28
Low Church party, 200, 202
Lowther, Sir James, 4th Bt, 50
luxury, 54
Lystra, Karen, 177–8

Macaulay, Thomas Babington, 189
Mack, Phyllis, 138, 152
Madden, Samuel, *Reflections and resolutions proper for the gentlemen of Ireland* (1738), 57, 60
Magee, William, Church of Ireland abp of Dublin, 200
Mahony, Daniel, 77
Mallow (Co. Cork), 93

Malone, Anthony, 79–80
Manson, David, 106, 119, 121–2, 124
Markethill (Co. Armagh), 51, 57
Marlay, Thomas, 65
Martensen, Hans, 194
Martin, George, 172
Mary II, 26
Massue de Ruvigny, *see* Ruvigny
Mathew, Thomas, 68
Maxwell, Henry, 56
'Mayboys', 80
Maynooth (Co. Kildare), 64
    St Patrick's College, 198, 216
Mayo, Co., 208, 213, 214
McBride, John, 123
McCabe, Thomas, 172
McClure, Gilbert, schoolmaster, 115
McCracken, Ann (née Joy), 172
—, Eliza, sr (née McReynolds), 172, 183, 184
—, Elizabeth, wife of Henry Joy McCracken, jr, 185
—, Francis, 172
—, Henry Joy, jr (brother of Eliza Tennent), 182, 185
—, Henry Joy, sr (*d.* 1798), 172, 183
—, J.L., 58
—, John, jr, 172, 173, 180, 181–2, 183, 184, 186
—, John, sr, 172
—, Mary Ann, 172–3, 183
—, William, 172
McDonnell, Miss, schoolmistress, 113
McKee, Mary, schoolmistress, 113–14
McKewn, Grizel, schoolmistress, 113
McLeod, Hugh, 15
McMinn, Joseph, 43, 53
Meath, Co., 212
medals, 29
Methodism, 200
Miles, Mary, schoolteacher, 113
militia, 72, 79, 80, 126
Milles, Thomas, Church of Ireland bishop of Waterford and Lismore, 40
Mitchelstown (Co. Cork), 75, 77, 80
Mitford, Sir John (later 1st Baron Redesdale), 131
Molesworth, Robert, 1st Viscount Molesworth, *Some considerations for promoting the agriculture of Ireland …* (1723), 52

Molyneux, William, *The case of Ireland …* (1698), 46, 50
Monaghan, Co., 112, 208, 209
Montagu-Dunk, George, 2nd earl of Halifax, 62, 68, 69–70, 71
Montgomery, Alexander, 54, 60
Montreal, 167
Mooncoin (Co. Kilkenny), 210, 211
Moore, Charles, 6th earl of Drogheda, regiment of horse, 74
—, Dudley, 36
—, Pierce, tiler and Whiteboy, 80
—, Sean, 43–4
'moral economy', 63
More, Hannah, 112, 175, 188
    Coelebs in search of a wife (1808), 190
    Essays on various subjects … (1777), 175
    Strictures on the modern system of female education, 187, 189
Morley, Vincent, 61–2
Morphett, James, mathematics master, 114
'Mother McClean', brothel-keeper, 101
Mount Charles (Co. Donegal), 111
Mountmellick (Queen's Co.), 140
    school at, 144
Mountrath (Queen's Co.), 143
Moy (Co. Tyrone), 122
Murray, James, governor of Quebec, 129
—, Nicholas ('Kirwan'), 154, 160–2, 163, 164, 166, 168
—, Revd William, 108
Musgrave, Sir Richard, 1st Bt, *Memoirs of the different rebellions in Ireland …* (1802), 61

Nashville, 159
national debt, Irish, 59
Nativism, 157
Navigation Board, 57
Navy, Royal, 135
Netherlands, Austrian, 22
'New English', 196
New York, 89, 159, 164, 166, 167
    Cooper Institute, 164
New York Observer, 159, 160–1
Newry (Co. Down), 124
    school at, 113, 122
Newry Canal, 57
newspapers, 22, 45, 62
Nivokov, Iakov Aleksandrovitch, 194

Index

O'Beirne, Thomas Lewis, Church of Ireland bp of Meath, 147, 149
—, Jane, 147–8, 149
O'Brien, Anne, Lady O'Brien, 109
—, John, Catholic bp of Cloyne, 78
O'Casey, Sean (Sean Ó Cathasaigh, John Casey), 215–16
O'Connell, Daniel, 199, 204, 215
O'Conor, Charles, 72
Ó Cromhthain, Tomás (Thomas Crohan), 216, 217
O'Dowd, Mary, 170
Offaly, *see* King's Co.
O'Flaherty, Eamon, 127
O'Kearney, *see* Kearney
'Old English', 196
Old School Presbyterians, 158
O'Neill, Kevin, 137
Ormond, duchess of, *see* Butler
—, duke of, *see* Butler
Ormond Boys, 84, 85, 92
The Orthodox Presbyterian, 201
Oxford, University of, 118
oyer and terminer, commission of, *see* Dublin

papacy, 198
parliament, British, 49, 50
   Declaratory Act (1720), 49, 50
   English Catholic Relief Act (1778), 129, 130, 131
   House of Lords, 49
   Patronage Act (1712), 203
   Quebec Act (1774), 129
   Riot Act (1715), 89, 94
   Schism Act (1714), 39
   Scottish Catholic Relief Bill (1778–9), 130
   Scottish Disarming Act, repeal of, 130
—, English
   Woollen Act (1699), 49–50
—, Irish, 37, 47, 56, 57, 59, 60, 70, 132–3
   Act of Union (1800), 198
   Catholic Relief Act (1792), 132–3
   Catholic Relief Act (1793), 126–36 passim
   'Eligit' Bill (1762), 69, 71
   House of Commons, 34, 38, 40, 54, 55
   House of Lords, 23, 33–4, 55, 71
   Navigation Act (1730), 57
   Popery Act (1704), 31
   Popery Act (1709), 31
   Test Act (1774), 129
   Tillage Bill (1727–8), 55
—, United Kingdom
   Irish Church Disestablishment Act (1869), 198
   Old Age Pensions Act (1908), 206
Paton, Mrs, schoolmistress, 113
Payne, William H. 194
Pearson, Jacqueline, 188
Peel, Sir Robert, 2nd Bt, 203
Pembroke, earl of, *see* Herbert
'penal laws', 15–16, 132
Penlez, Bosavern, 87
Perronet, Thomas, 189
Philadelphia, 159, 160, 165, 167
Phipps, Sir Constantine, 35, 36, 37, 38
Plitt, Revd Th., 193
Pigott, Emmanuel, 80
Pimm, Anne, 149
Pitt, William (Pitt the Younger'), 133, 136
Pittsburgh, 159, 167
Pittsburgh Catholic, 159
Popular Party, 200
Portaferry (Co. Down), 117
Portarlington (Queen's Co.), school at, 109
Portora, Royal School, 107, 108
portraiture, 28, 38
Portrush (Co. Antrim), 159
Power, Thomas, 61, 62–3
Presbyterian churches, 154–68 passim
   in Scotland, 157, 197, 200, 203
   in Ulster, 39, 154–68 passim, 171, 196–7, 201, 202, 203
   in United States of America, 158, 160
Presbyterian Church in Ireland, General Assembly of, 154, 155, 158, 159, 162, 164, 203
   Board of Missions, 157
   Home Mission, 155, 156, 159, 160, 163, 166–7, 168
   see also Synod of Ulster
Prime, Samuel Ireneaus, 160
Prior, Thomas, 48, 57
   List of the absentees of Ireland ... (1729), 53, 54, 56, 60
   Observations on coin (1729), 56
privy council, British, 55, 59
—, Irish, 35, 55
prostitutes, 99
'Protestant ascendancy', 132–3, 198

Quakers (Society of Friends), 137–53 passim
quarterage, 68
Quebec, 129
'Queen Sive', 74, 77, 79
Quilca (Co. Cavan), 50

Rabb, Jane, schoolmistress, 121
Rade, Martin, 194
Ravensdale (co. Louth), 113, 131
The Record, 202
Recordite Party, 202, 204
recruitment, military and naval, 69, 134
regium donum, 159, 196, 197
Reilly, James, printer, 124
Reinhard, Wolfgang, 192–3
Remonstrant Synod, 201
revivals, religious, 200
  Revival of 1859, 164
Ridlesdale, Maj. George, 118
riots, *see* brothel riots: enclosure riots, food riots, Gordon Riots
Robinson, Richard, Church of Ireland abp of Armagh, 108
Roden, earl of, *see* Jocelyn
Rodgers, Nini, 137
Rollin, Charles, 105, 106
Roscommon, Co., 63
Ross, Ian Campbell, 43
Rowe, Nicholas, *Tamerlane*, 26
Royal Hospital, Kilmainham, 29, 38
royal schools, 107, 110, *see also* Cavan, Dungannon, Portora
Ruvigny, Henry Massue de, earl of Galway, 25

Sackville, Lionel Cranfield, 1st duke of Dorset, 23–4, 56
St Louis, 167
Sandymount (Co. Dublin), 101
Savage family, 117
Sayers, Peig (Margaret Guiheen), 218
Schilling, Heinz, 192–3
schools, 104–25 passim, *see also* charity schools, charter schools, diocesan schools, girls' schools, royal schools
Scotland, Highlands, 130–1
Scottish Reformation Society, 158
Scully, Denys, 135
sculpture, 29

Searson, John, 113
'second reformation', 201
secularization, 195
Shackleton, Abraham, 139
—, Elizabeth, jr, 152
—, Elizabeth, sr, 137, 144
—, Richard, 137, 139, 144
—, Sally, 143
Shannon, Anne, Quaker, 150, 151
Sharpe, Kevin, 20–1
Sheehy, Fr Nicholas, 62–3, 75, 81
Sheridan, Thomas, 50, 53, 106, 107, 108
'Shevaun', *see* 'Joan Meskel'
Shrewsbury, duke of, *see* Talbot
Sicily, 22
Simpson, Jonathan, 158
Skelton, Revd John, 110
slavery, 158, 203
Sligo, Co., 208
Smith, Erasmus, trust, 108, 121
Smyth, Edward, Church of Ireland bp of Down and Connor, 27
Sorai, Ogyu, 48
Springfield (IL), 167
Stackallan House (Co. Meath), 29
Stackpole, Robert, Whiteboy, 80
Stamer, William, 101
'state days', 25, 33, 34, 35, 38
Stone, Lawrence, 170
Stoughton, Revd William, 33
Strabane (Co. Tyrone), school at, 123
Stuart, Charles Edward (the 'Young Pretender'), 198
—, George Hay, 154, 160, 166
—, James Francis Edward (the 'Old Pretender'), 196, 198
Swan, —, town-major of Dublin, 101
Swift, Jonathan, 18, 24, 40, 42–60 passim
  Drapier's letters (1724–5), 52
  Gulliver's travels (1726), 42
  Intelligencer (1728), 48, 53
  Maxims controlled in Ireland (1729), 46
  A modest proposal ... (1729), 42–60 passim
  A proposal for the universal use of Irish manufactures (1720), 49, 50
  Short view of the state of Ireland (1728), 44, 47–8, 52, 53, 54, 56
Symes, David, 206
Synod of Ulster, 201, 202, 203

Index

Talbot, Charles, 1st duke of Shrewsbury, 23, 24, 37
—, Richard, 1st earl of Tyrconnell, 35
Tallow (Co. Waterford), 77, 78
'Ten Years Conflict', 203
Tennent, Eliza (née McCracken), 169–91 passim
—, Isabella, 175
—, James Emerson, 176
—, John, 119, 173
—, Letitia, 175, 176
—, Robert, 173
—, Robert James, 169, 173, 174, 175–7, 178–82, 186, 190
—, William, 173, 174
Theodor, Jakob, 194
Thomas, Keith, 14
Thomson, John, surveyor and mathematics master, 114
Thompson, E.P., 17
Thynne, Thomas, 1st Visc. Weymouth, 110
tillage, 54
Tilly, Charles, 17, 81–2
Tipperary, Co., 61, 64, 67, 68, 69, 75, 76, 77, 209, 213, 214
tithe, 54, 57, 141
tithe applotment books, 209
Tokyo, see Edo
Tory party in Ireland, 32, 33, 34–5, 37–8, 39, 40
Tralee (Co. Kerry), 26, 163
Trench, Melesina Chenevix, 146, 148, 151, 152
Trinity College, Dublin, 33, 109, 110–11, 145
Troeltsch, Ernst, 194, 195
Trollope, Anthony, *The Kellys and the O'Kellys*, 215
Tullamore (King's Co.), 114
Twomey, Jeremiah, executed felon, 91
Tynan (Co., Armagh), 115
Tyrconnell, earl of, see Talbot
Tyrone, Co., schools in, 163

Ultramontanism, 197, 205
Union, Anglo-Scottish (1707), 31
Union, British-Irish (1800), 136, 198

United Irishmen, Society of, 135, 171, 172, 173
United States of America, 154–68 passim

Vesey, Agmondisham, 56
—, John, Church of Ireland abp of Tuam, 36
viceroyalty, 22–5, 28, 41, 59
  viceregal court, 21–3, 25
Villiers, Edward, 1st earl of Jersey, 25

Wall, Maureen, 16
Wallace, Mrs, schoolmistress, 109
Walsh, Richard, Catholic bp of Cork, 78
Ward, James, 44–5, 54
—, Michael, 111–12
Waring, Samuel, jr, 116–17
—, Samuel, sr, 116–17
Waterford, city, 79
Waterford, Co., 64, 67, 77
Watson, Jane, Quaker, 150
Weber, Max, 195
Wesley, John, 200
Westminster Review, 188–9
Westmorland, earl of, see Fane
Weymouth, Visc., see Thynne
Wharton, Thomas, 5th Lord Wharton (later 1st earl of Wharton), 24, 33
Whig party in Ireland, 32–4, 35, 37–8, 39, 40
Whiteboys, 61–83 passim
Whitehaven (Cumb.), 50
Whitmore, William, 181
Whyte, Samuel, 106
Wicklow, Co., 212
Wilberforce, William, 203
Willes, Edward, 75
William III, 21, 26, 28–30, 31, 32, 33, 35, 36
Williams, Thomas, schoolteacher, 114
Wilson, Christian, schoolteacher, 113–14
—, David, 164, 165–6
Wood's Halfpence, 55, 59
Woodward, Richard, Church of Ireland bp of Cloyne, 198
Wyndham, Charles, 2nd earl of Egremont, 70

Youghal, (Co. Cork), 69
Young, Arthur, 76
Young Irelanders, 204